community

community

BUILDING MODERN AUSTRALIA

Edited by
Hannah Lewi and
David Nichols

A UNSW Press book

Published by
University of New South Wales Press Ltd
University of New South Wales
Sydney NSW 2052
AUSTRALIA
www.unswpress.com.au

First published 2010

10 9 8 7 6 5 4 3 2 1

National Library of Australia
Cataloguing-in-Publication entry
Title: Community: building modern Australia/
edited by Hannah Lewi and David Nichols.
ISBN: 978 174223 042 9 (pbk.)
Subjects: Community development – Australia.
Public buildings – Australia.
Architecture and society – Australia.
Other Authors/Contributors:
Lewi, Hannah.
Nichols, David.
Dewey Number: 307.14
Design Streamer design & communication
Cover image Annerley Library, Qld 1957. Architect: James Birrell.
Photographer unknown. Brisbane City Council.
Printer Everbest in China

This book is printed on paper using fibre supplied from plantation or sustainably managed forests.

CONTENTS

CONTRIBUTORS

KATE DARIAN-SMITH is professor of Australian Studies and History at the University of Melbourne. She has published widely in Australian cultural history, including in the fields of rural studies, memory studies, heritage, childhood and war and society. Her books include *On the Home Front: Melbourne in Wartime 1939–1945* (Melbourne University Press, 2009) and *Stirring Australian Speeches: The Definitive Collection from Botany to Bali* (Melbourne University Press, 2004).

PHILIP GOAD is chair of Architecture and director of the Melbourne School of Design at the University of Melbourne. He is an authority on 20th-century Australian architecture. His recent co-edited books include *Modernism and Australia: Documents on Art, Design and Architecture 1917–1967* (Miegunyah Press, 2006) and *Modern Times: The Untold Story of Modernism in Australia* (Miegunyah Press/Powerhouse Publishing, 2008).

CAROLINE JORDAN is a lecturer in Art History at La Trobe University, Melbourne. She specialises in Australian art of the 19th and 20th centuries. Her book, *Picturesque Pursuits: Colonial Women Artists and the Amateur Tradition*, was published in 2005 (Melbourne University Press). She is currently writing on the influence of the Carnegie Corporation on Australian museums and galleries, with particular focus on Victorian regional art galleries.

HANNAH LEWI is an associate professor in Architecture at the University of Melbourne. Her research interests span modern Australian architecture history, conservation and heritage, and the use of new media technologies for the representation of architecture. She has published widely in international journals and books in these fields. She is the current chair of Docomomo Australia.

DAVID NICHOLS is a lecturer in Urban Planning at the University of Melbourne. His research concentrates on 20th-century planning history, primarily but not exclusively in Australia, often related to issues of community, governance, culture and collective agency. He is co-editor, with Keir Reeves, of *Deeper Leads* (BHS Publishing, 2008).

JULIE WILLIS is an associate professor in Architecture at the University of Melbourne. Her research focuses on Australian architectural history of the 20th century, with particular emphasis on civic, institutional and commercial buildings, as well as the history of architectural education and the profession in Australia. Her books include *Women Architects in Australia* 1900–1950 (Royal Australian Institute of Architects, 2001) and *Australian Modern: The Architecture of Stephenson & Turner* (Melbourne University Publishing, 2004). With Philip Goad, she is editor of the forthcoming *Encyclopaedia of Australian Architecture.*

PREFACE

This book is the result of a cross-disciplinary project conducted at the University of Melbourne between the Faculty of Architecture, Building and Planning (Philip Goad, Hannah Lewi and Julie Willis) and the Australian Centre in the School of Historical Studies (Kate Darian-Smith and John Murphy), awarded an Australian Research Council Discovery Grant between 2006 and 2008. David Nichols joined the project as a research fellow and Caroline Jordan and Helen Stitt have also been instrumentally involved in 2008 and 2009–10, respectively, as researchers.

Impetus for the project extended from Hannah Lewi's research on local swimming pools, which developed into an interest in the ignored mid-20th century buildings of suburban Australia. This had synergies with research conducted by Julie Willis and Philip Goad on modernist architecture for health (hospitals and smaller infant health services), and Kate Darian-Smith's expertise in the social history of Australia. The idea thus germinated into an investigation of the nexus between 'ordinary' public suburban places and the local governments, community groups, planners and architects that created and used them. Modernism in its social and architectural forms was the key ethos here, with issues of planning, building form and social responsibility at the forefront.

Opposite Linocut of Baby Health Centre, East Brunswick, Vic. (c. 1940) by Mia Schoen, 2010

It was agreed early that the buildings to be investigated would be limited to a series of types that could be regarded as 'municipal': baby health centres, kindergartens, community centres, swimming pools, libraries and bowling clubs, together with the public art that was created for such settings. Other nominally 'civic' buildings were excluded largely on the basis of their genesis in state and federal commissioning agencies. Schools and non-municipal sports facilities were the most prominent excluded categories, and warrant their own research projects, by dint of their special uses, value and geneses.

Crossing disciplines between architectural history and Australian social and cultural history is often rewarding and expository. In this case, it has revealed the stories of the civic buildings and landscapes which have enduringly remained at the heart of many of Australia's communities and neighbourhoods; these sites are considered as documents on the assumptions and ambitions of those who made them and those for whom they were made. Indeed, the heritage and history of such places is crucial, leading into the second decade of the 21st century, when a revival of the mid-20th century rhetoric of renewal and community strength appears again prominent, yet the future of many sites is fragile.

The book – along with an attendant database of buildings and numerous journal articles and conference papers – has involved copious research of primary and secondary sources in Australia's national, state and local libraries, local history societies and other archival resources, both private and public.

The authors would like to sincerely thank the University of New South Wales Press, in particular Phillipa McGuinness, Chantal Gibbs and Jean Kingett, for patiently guiding the long progress of bringing the manuscript to fruition. Thank you also to Kate Scott and Bill Nicholson from Streamer Design for the design and layout that has brought alive our vision for the book. This project was generously sponsored by publication grants from the Australian Academy of the Humanities and the University of Melbourne, and supported by the Faculty of Architecture, Building and Planning and the Australian Centre, School of Historical Studies, in the Faculty of Arts. Helen Stitt and Damien Williams have given crucial support in preparing the manuscript. The authors would like to thank many others for their assistance, often above and beyond duty, in our search for images, information and interviews. Further acknowledgments are included in the back pages of the book. Thank you also to Mia Schoen for the preface image that was commissioned for the book.

Finally, thank you to all the families of the authors and researchers for putting up with interruptions to holidays for the last four years, to take 'just one more photo' of 'that' kindergarten, library or bowling club.

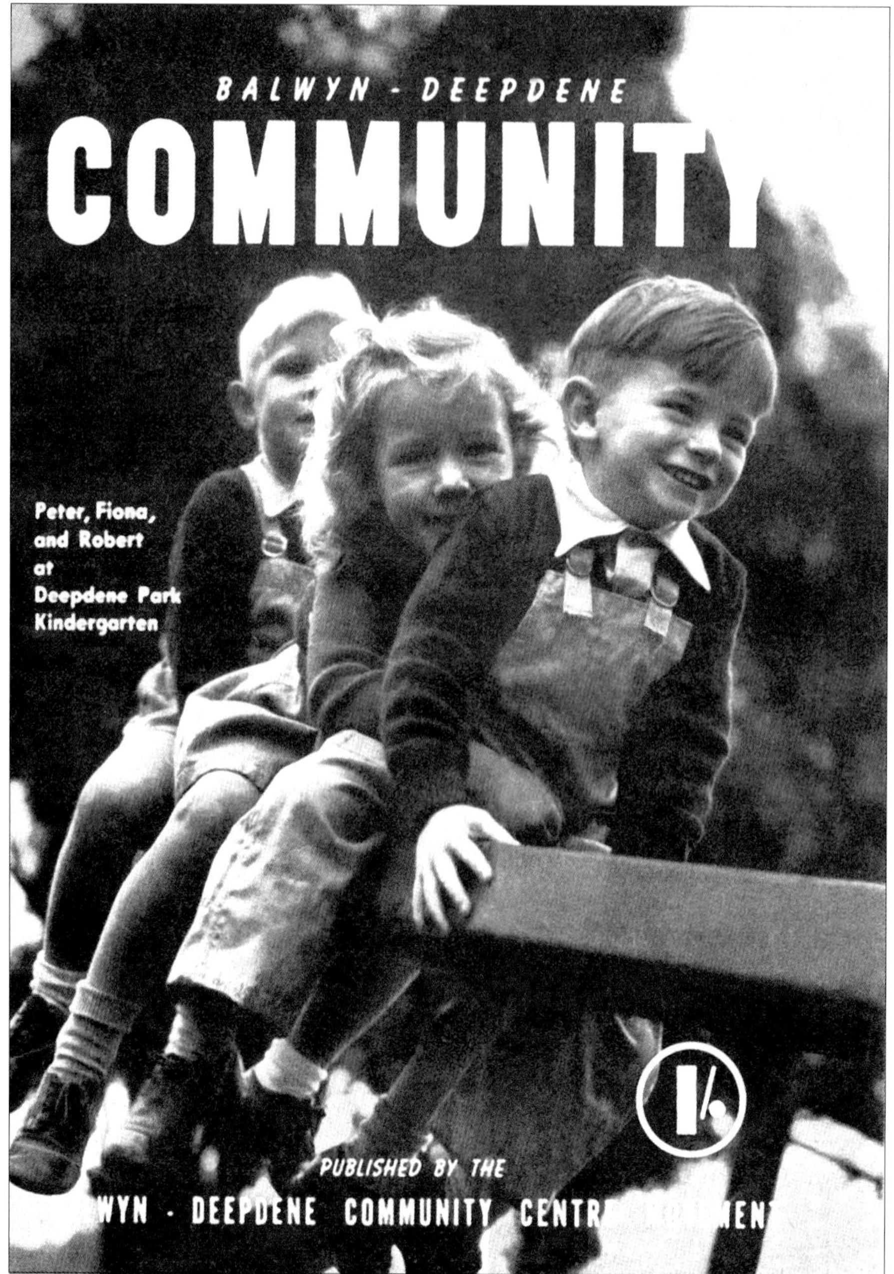

1.1 Cover of community booklet, *Balwyn – Deepdene Community*, Vic.1949

MAKING THE MODERN COMMUNITY

Hannah Lewi, David Nichols, Philip Goad, Julie Willis and Kate Darian-Smith

In 1999, a documentary video was made of Beulah, a small country town in western Victoria's Mallee. Shot by local resident 'Rob' at key moments of social celebration throughout the year, the video was placed in a time capsule for viewing in 2024. In the video, Beulah's civic leaders refer frequently to their guarded, even pessimistic views of the town's future. But they also show a significant pride in, and concern with, a history of community participation and shared experience in the town which has extended before and throughout their own lifetimes.

The presentation begins with a survey of Beulah's community fabric: its railway station, wheat silos, bowling club, football ground, swimming pool and churches. As the video's narrator and cameraman, Rob interviews maintenance officers and supervisors of sporting facilities for tennis, cricket and football; all show a strong understanding of developments and changes over time. While small country towns like Beulah are here assumed to be fading, and the diminishing of services like banks and hospitals seems to be hastening this decline, the mere fact of the video's creation – for viewing primarily by the people featured in it, a quarter of a century later – is in itself a cause for optimism. That Beulah's community life revolves around its communal buildings and facilities is also telling: the town's people clearly see these as Beulah's social focus. Rob's joke that his interviewee from the Southern Mallee Tennis Association is 'the president of probably the most successful tennis club in the modern era' or his more serious observation that the 82-year-old Beulah Bowling Club is 'as you can see here … still prospering', underline the importance of recreation clubs in small communities.[1]

It is probably only residents of small country towns fearing extinction who spend the time taking stock of their surroundings' advantages and value, in a way that suburban Australians would not think to do. Yet in many respects Beulah and hundreds of other Australian communities in cities, suburbs, and rural and remote townships share a strong similarity: they are defined and sustained by their community facilities and amenities, many of which are products of community action and local or state government provision. Sadly, awareness of this often only comes at a time of imminent loss.

Community examines the nexus between community and the built fabric of modern Australia, and the way in which those buildings which house public community services define and perpetuate a sense of belonging and social connection. The use, style, position, size, adaptability, access, ownership and mode of creation are all crucial in definitions of a building's value. Buildings tell their users about themselves and wider society: the buildings retain, too, a record of the culture in which they are moulded. This book draws upon social and spatial histories to explore these links between building and community, particularly through the middle decades of the 20th century when architectural ideas, embodied as modernism, became entwined with ideas of progressive social welfare. Modernism was an architectural approach which sought a universal language that could be applicable to any situation. Inherently ahistorical, and, from its original sources, deeply concerned with social improvement through health, hygiene and housing, modernism became the preferred mode of architectural design across the world after World War II. The designers of the spaces accommodating new social, education and welfare initiatives in Europe, North America and Australia drew on such a language to reinforce and give shape to their community's progressive aims. This book therefore uncovers connections between direct strategies in fostering a healthy, educated citizenry and modern design initiatives.

Buildings tell their users about themselves and wider society: the buildings retain, too, a record of the culture in which they are moulded.

The ideas and places explored herein are a reflection of governmental priorities, delivered largely at state or municipal level, during the 20th century. These initiatives sought to support the health and welfare needs of the whole community, from infants to the aged. They often required new types of public services, many of which had emerged initially as the results of social activism, religious patronage or philanthropy, and then quickly became mainstays of municipal provision. These included baby health centres and kindergartens; libraries; community centres and halls; and recreational facilities such as swimming pools and bowling clubs. Such services and their associated buildings, although often ad hoc and unassuming in their formulation, were quietly instrumental in shaping everyday community life. By the mid-20th century, as such services expanded rapidly, an architectural language of economically lean, functionalist and often aesthetically unpretentious modernism was assumed appropriate to express widely accepted social ideals of community participation and accessible recreation.

Australia and community

Australian society, founded on a strong base of Anglo-liberal thinking, has been portrayed as a social laboratory since the mid-19th century: a place of new beginnings, egalitarian in spirit and a 'paradise for workers'. By the early 20th century, as the new nation began to forge a shared sense of the obligations to, and entitlements of, its citizens there was a growing acceptance by the middle class of an increasingly secular basis to social welfare, aimed at the 'deserving poor'. Services built on activism and religious or lay philanthropy were seen to have universal applicability across the full strata of society without the stigma of charity. New ideas about early infancy and childhood were enshrined in purpose-built facilities, such as the infant health and welfare centre, and the kindergarten. From the 1920s, residents of new and old suburbs or towns would lobby local government for spaces and buildings like bowling clubs and community centres within which they could socialise, using their hard-won hours between work and rest. The national campaign for the local rates-funded 'free' library for the education of young and old grew more slowly but reached a peak in mid-20th century. These facilities, community based and in many cases community run or initiated by local government, are the focus of this book.

World War I was a defining experience for Australia, and heralded a new concern with the suitability of modern city living. The influence of the environment, which had a particular inflection in Australia because of climate – but was also a key element of an emergent modernism in European architecture – was seen to play a determining role in the formation of character. As in Great Britain, Europe and the United States, there were deep concerns about slum housing, poor sanitation and the plight of smoke-choked cities and the possibilities inherent in architecture and planning to ameliorate such conditions in an immediate sense and prevent future degeneration of the society as a whole.

Many Australian planners and commentators came to consider the 19th-century patterns of economic and urban development in the United States as a template for 20th-century Australia. This understanding supported the 'boosterism' of post-war capitalism and reinforced the long-held fears in white Australia over the possibility of invasion from Asian countries to the north. The emphasis on national 'fitness', particularly for the working class, was a prominent force in the strengthening of hygiene, social welfare and education programs across the nation. The Great Depression in the late 1920s and early 1930s resulted in mass unemployment and social despair, breaking apart families and communities and focusing the attention of some social reformers on the importance of the domestic built environment.

During World War II, initiatives for post-war reconstruction responded not only to the degradations of the previous decade's economic hardships but also to optimism for the new society to be created from the ruins of the old. The 1940s saw new conceptions of community and strong federal government support for local participation in community 'rebuilding'. Once again, such understandings of community vitality were often equated with the reconfiguration of built environments – particularly through suburban developments – in both cities and towns, and with the need for central communal spaces such as the civic centre.

The wartime Labor government of John Curtin, and his successor Ben Chifley, laid the basis for Australia's Keynesian economy in the post-war period, with an emphasis on the growth of manufacturing, a large-scale migration scheme, the expansion of social welfare provisions, and rural development. This was all supported by a strong government sector. However, a change of government in 1949, with the election of the conservative prime minister Robert Menzies, was to alter Australian society. Though there remained a strong network of community groups and 'progress associations' within suburban and regional areas which pressed for new local facilities in self-interested altruism, Menzies presided paternalistically over a nation far more individualistic and aspirational than that of his predecessors. Two decades later new kinds of social rupture occurred, with the political consciousness of a new generation raised in protest against policy decisions by Menzies and his successors, and the rise of youth culture and new social movements. In Australia's cities, and particularly the gentrifying inner urban cores, demand for amenities and community consultation was strong. The ascension of the Labor Party to power in late 1972 was a watershed in many ways for Australia. Importantly, Gough Whitlam's policy-makers – self-interested in part, but also engaged with notions of community agency – instituted new medical funding arrangements, urban and regional planning programs, and community art sponsorships. Under Whitlam, community was once again promoted at the fore of Australian society. Here, rather than fulfil a social need for reorganisation and progress, the idea of community was seen to be connected pragmatically both to the counterculture and to new conceptualisations of 'quality of life'. It also, in a related way, joined new imaginings of Australian culture and education to redefine the nation in its own, self-realised, image as a multicultural community – celebrating cultural diversity as a unifying force.

1.2 'Suburbia Forever', Wesley Stacey 1970

Space and community

No all-encompassing volume has yet told the story of Australia's 20th-century urbanisation. But if one did exist, its story would largely be that of continuous *sub*urbanisation, not just of the nation's capital cities since the mid-19th century but also of its federal capital Canberra, its country towns and even its remote mining townships. This phenomenon was also experienced in North America and elsewhere. But what makes the Australian experience distinctive is a vast spatial frontier that encouraged low residential densities and, by the late 1960s, highly built-up urban centres like those of Sydney and Melbourne almost entirely devoid of residential populations. While Caroline Butler-Bowden and Charles Pickett have gone some way to counter this view with their documentation of apartment living close to and occasionally within the Australian city, there is no doubt that the hearts of all Australian cities by 1970 were in essence central business districts, representing the modernist triumph of the wholly functionalised or zoned city.[2] Strangely though, despite most Australians living in suburbia (whether in a city, regional or country town), the architecture, landscapes and urban design of the sprawling suburbs and expanding country towns in the 20th century remain an under-studied and under-valued frontier. There have been detailed discussions on the individual modern house and garden, alongside public housing, as agents of urban and suburban renewal and development but what has been little considered are the public buildings and spaces that have woven together the suburban fabric outside the home.[3] This study is thus a first step in looking at the myriad of unassuming public facilities and landscaped sites that service suburban areas, and what role they played in fostering a sense of modern communal life.

An avoidance of serious architectural analysis of the ordinary suburban public environment may be symptomatic of a previous dismissal of the suburbs as, to use the oft-quoted American term, a 'middle landscape', that is forever caught between the mythologised rural homestead or heroic city.[4] Despite occasional champions such as Hugh Stretton and Patrick Troy, since the mid-20th century 'the suburbs' have been characterised by many Australian commentators as bankrupt of creative merit or stifling of cultural interest.[5] Australia's most renowned architectural critic Robin Boyd famously attacked under-designed, 'bald' suburbs in his biting critique *The Australian Ugliness* (1960).[6] For Boyd, and others, suburbs were ultimately symbolic of dissatisfaction, and were characterised as a mundane, feminised zone. From New York, Lewis Mumford critiqued American and English suburbs as adequate only as 'a nursery for bringing up children ... with little visible daily contact with the realities of the workaday world'. He saw the suburbs as at best a transitional stage like childhood, and at worst as a nightmare more detrimental than the megalopolis.[7] It is notable that for all their wrath both Boyd and Mumford were, for substantial periods of their lives, suburbanites themselves.

Other historians have more positively explored the claim that Australia represents the 'first suburban nation'.[8] Suburban development was uniquely supported in pre-Federation Australia by strong, centralised, colonial governments, and some wealthy municipalities that resourced and coordinated transport and basic infrastructure provision like schools. However, this state support often stopped short and it was typically left to the new communities themselves to provide other facilities for children and recreation, and to attempt to beautify the rawness of the subdivisions through the voluntary work of local progress associations, and women's, sports and church groups.[9] Suburban growth accelerated in the mid-20th century, supported by favourable conditions of accessible land, available materials (despite shortages immediate after World War II), improved wages and an influx of migrants to Australia, including many with a 'do-it-yourself' attitude to building. The community buildings contained within this book are testament to that growth and the unique context of Australia's spatial frontier.

Defining community

'Community' encompasses a group of people bound together by common threads, including geographical location, ethnicity, socioeconomic status, sexuality, or circumstances. It is also a word loved by politicians and lobby groups and used frequently to invoke a brighter future or a nostalgic past. The term is readily used in architectural discourse because it can, as Adrian Forty suggests, be readily explained by 'spatial equivalents'.[10] Politicians, too, often speak of building community through the provision of public infrastructure and services, thus assuming that the creation and management of physical places is a means of fostering community cohesion.

The term 'community' was prominent in public discourse across the period under discussion in this book. But its definitions have been multifarious and elastic. It would also be simplistic to assume that the intensity of discussions around the ideals of community by governments, politicians, professionals and social activists have constituted direct evidence that 'a community' existed in these terms. However, from the vast literature on the topic, there are some enduring concepts that define 'community', and underpin its examination in this book in relation to modern buildings. First, the rise of concerns about community cohesion and identity are historically contingent on the rise of modernisation, industrialisation and urbanisation in the 19th and 20th centuries in the developed world. Here the writings of Durkheim, Marx, Weber and

Tonnies are seminal. Community has come to represent a sense of cohesive 'group-ness' opposed to the perceived tide of individualism, secularisation and isolation brought to bear through modernity. Tonnies famously characterised the so-called disintegration of traditional pre-modern community life as the eclipsing of *Gemeinschaft* (community) by *Gesellschaft* (association). The term 'community' involves 'a lasting and genuine form of living together … through coordinated action for a common good', while the term 'association' implies a rather 'more calculated action on the part of individuals who engage in artificial relations for what they can get from one another'.[11] The notion of community has thereby been typically cast as a natural, organic, stable, traditional and localised way of life that is often under threat. And it is precisely because of these attributes that the ideal of community has been targeted by critics as fundamentally conservative and backward-looking. This sense of loss of traditional community in the face of modernity came to pervade social, cultural and political analysis of the concept for most of the 20th century. In post–World War II Britain, for example, the establishment of sociology and the social professions was in part bound up with perceptions that real communities were being 'torn apart by fundamental shifts of political and economic power'.[12]

Words like 'neighbourhood' and 'community' ... carry with them aspirations that these institutions will assist in the moral and social development of that locality.

Second, not only is the idea of community historically contingent, but it is also intrinsically linked to geographical location. Definitions of locality and proximity are central to the development of ideas surrounding community.[13] Terms like *Gemeinde* and 'neighbourhood' come to approximate 'local community', and thereby allude to a quality of relationships between people in particular places; a sense of group belonging and proximity is implied. Words like 'neighbourhood' and 'community' – when consciously applied to small public buildings – carry with them aspirations that these institutions will assist in the moral and social development of that locality.[14] In the Australian setting, local community institutions were also shaped by their geographical character in sometimes particular ways which set them apart from the context of the modern city. As will be illustrated, these combined geographical and social associations have some fundamental and, at times, unexpected effects on the design of local institutions.

The third enduring concept of community that has shaped the building types presented in this book is one of pragmatism: the practical techniques that have organised social relationships and created buildings and places, typically through direct and indirect government actions and policies.[15] Pragmatic notions of community, as manifest in the 'taken for granted' spaces and places

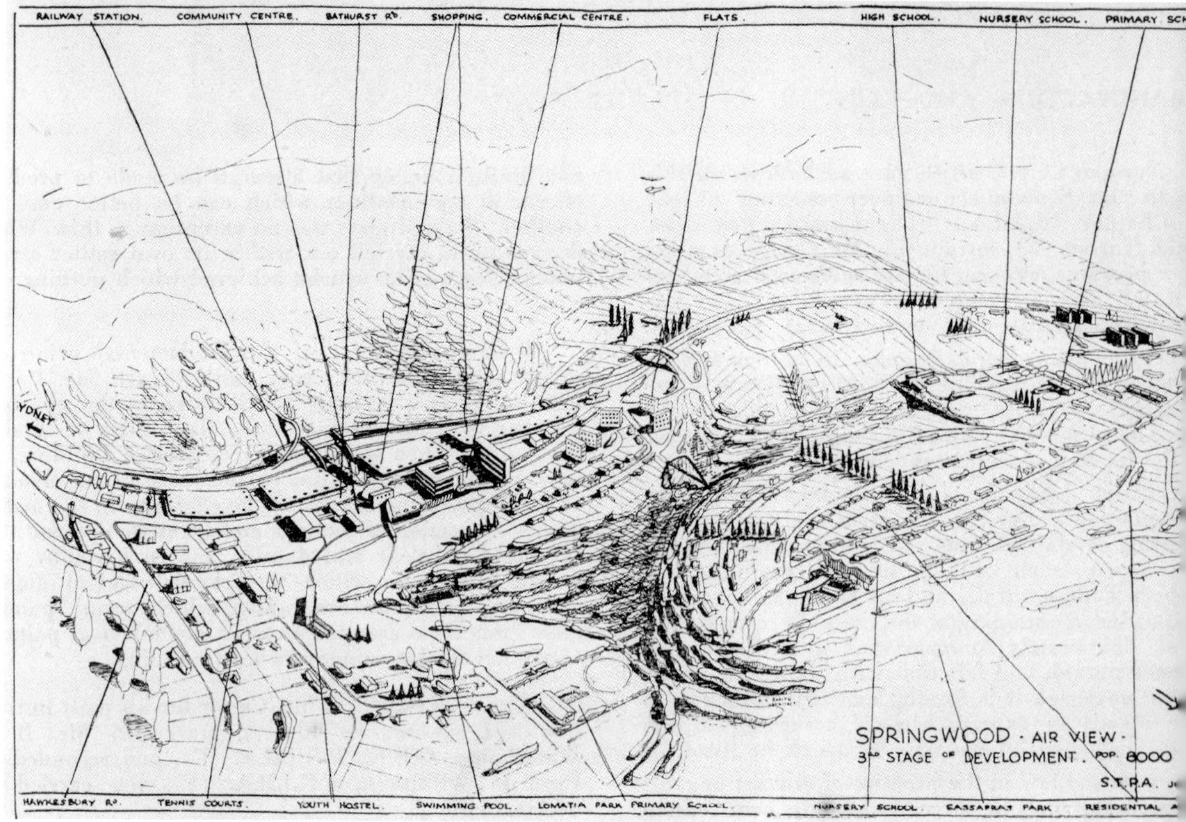

1.3 Springwood Town Plan, Harold H Smith, NSW 1947

of routine living, have been shaped by governments at all levels, through the development of professional knowledges, and through the realities of everyday use. The writings of Nikolas Rose are informative in understanding how, in Britain and Australia, modern governments and professional practice together developed coercive programs that 'shape, guide, channel, direct, control' events and populations in a social form.[16] A key target of this model of coercive government towards community-based ideals has been the sphere of family health and wellbeing, and particularly child-raising, examined in this book through the baby health centre and kindergarten.[17]

From the 1970s, with the privatisation of public infrastructure and amenities, increasing ethnic diversity and changing work-life patterns, writers such as Rose, Manuel Castells and Eric Hobsbawm see defining aspects of community as re-emerging out of an increased emphasis on the personal responsibilities of individuals, families and neighbourhoods to secure the future of their own particular localities.[18] In this way the word 'community' comes to encompass a renewed 'spatialisation of government' that attempts to bring individuals and families into assemblies of 'identities and allegiances' particular to their local place.[19] Community thus resurfaces as a counter-concept to the modern state that is increasingly seen as alienating and remote.

In recent decades, the promotion of community sustainability through the regeneration of buildings, monuments and landscapes has continued through multi-level government involvement that has been often initiated and supported by volunteer groups. The cornerstone of most local planning blueprints has been the expansion of communities for future growth while attempting to maintain distinctive local 'character' and 'liveability'. These plans typically emphasise better integrated infrastructure services, public transport and landscapes, and the need to invest in the reinvigoration of existing small public facilities that have often received little attention since their inception. This firm confidence placed in the construction and reconstruction of bricks-and-mortar facilities to stimulate qualities of liveable and healthy communities thus remains as unchallenged today as it was in earlier decades of the 20th century. If new child-hubs centred at shopping streets and existing schools are built, if modest recreation facilities and pools are maintained, then the nurturing of social communities and localised belonging is assumed to follow.

The values of community participation have also been put under the spotlight of academic and policy review in recent years as the associated terms 'social capital' and 'social fabric' have gained currency. Robert Putnam's widely read and controversial book *Bowling Alone: The Collapse and Revival of American Community* sees an inevitable decline in local community life, while others like David Halpern have concluded that social fabric is under transformation.[20] These general accounts have, however, dealt little with the histories of the community buildings and places of amenity, either as evidence of the maintenance of social networks or as indicators of change. Putnam's observations have been directly taken up by policy-makers, which has in turn fostered government-led design initiatives. To take one example, a research paper initiated by the Productivity Commission under the Howard government in 2003, titled 'Social capital: Reviewing the concept and its policy implications', set out to gauge dimensions of participation including volunteer work, informal social patterns in the local community, and levels of social trust.[21] Recommendations were then made about the design of local areas to address such rates of engagement, which included the provision of more open 'civic spaces' and parks where groups and individuals could meet, the maintenance of community services such as free libraries, galleries and museums, and the retention of sports as 'communal rather than commercial activities'.[22] The report suggested that this could be achieved by the further devolution of government bureaucracies either to local government or non-government neighbourhood and community groups. Such recommendations appear acutely familiar in light of the history charted in this book.

Modernism and community

The shaping of everyday public places and amenities was complicit in the building and disseminating of modern architecture in Australia. It is not the aim of this book to further problematise the already-contested definitions of modernism in relation to architecture, buildings and planning. Modern design is seen in terms of an evolving approach to style, function, planning and provision that occurred most markedly in the decades between 1920 and 1970. As we will demonstrate, during the 20th century modern design shifted greatly in its motivations, practice and character.

International debates and precedents surrounding modernism, which were received and modified to the Australian context, brought together a number of important themes discussed here. Some of these ideas about modern architecture serve as a framework for understanding the particularities of Australian responses in subsequent chapters. Modernism was instrumental in shaping the physical and social health of populations in the 20th century through new approaches to planning for accessible amenities, through the design of new functional types of facilities for health and recreation, and through particular attention to the provision of a modern healthy environment that could productively influence the future of the individual, the child and the family.

Attitudes towards the intimate relationships between space, disease and bodies deeply informed architectural thinking before the 20th century: the city had long been figured as a diseased body that might be healed by both idealistic and practical design and environmental practices of city planning and architecture. However, in the early decades of the 20th century, architecture came to be considered as not just a technique for curing and preventing unhealthy populations, but also as a means for coercively encouraging activities in healthier environments that slowly improved the qualities of everyday life. Indeed, as Christopher Wilk observes: 'The entire Modernist enterprise was permeated by a deep concern for health'.[23] Modern architecture was conceived as an extension of new public medical apparatus that could protect but also enhance the healthy body.[24] Andrew Shanken has noted that modern planning too could be aligned with health, citing Finnish-American Eliel Saarinen's comparison of city form to that of the biological cell; in captions to images in his book *The City: Its Growth, Its Decay, Its Future* (1943): '"healthy cell tissue" became "microscopic 'community planning'" and "disintegrating cell tissue" became "microscopic 'slum growth'"'.[25] Through the ideals of modernism, architecture and planning professions turned their attention to the design of the immediate conditions

'The entire Modernist enterprise was permeated by a deep concern for health.'

1.4 Paddling pool and children in boat at Lady Gowrie Child Centre playground, unknown location 1950s

of individual buildings and subdivisions through provision for greater access to air, sunlight and the outdoors. Attention was also directed to the design of new building types, many of which accommodated social infrastructure encouraging good health, education and recreation.

In Australia, the nascent town planning movement, architects and landscape architects increasingly focused their attention on the need for modern design to serve the interests of the community as a whole. This translated directly into the provision of public infrastructure for shared benefit, which was explicitly promoted in discussion during and immediately after World War II in the context of post-war reconstruction. In 1943, the comments of Frank Costello, Brisbane City Architect and City Planner, reflected the faith in modern planning to provide towns 'in which men, women and children can work and plan and live clean, healthy lives. It will be a potent factor in producing that econ-omic wealth of any national – happy, healthy citizens'.[26] Likewise, in a small, widely available booklet, *Planning the Community*, architect Harold H Smith described in 1945 what he called a framework for Preplanning Reconstruction. Smith identified a Community School Unit as the organic cell on which the town or city planning should be developed. This was similar to Costello's idea of a neighbourhood unit of around 500 families, supporting a kindergarten, a day nursery, a recreational hall, a shopping group, a playing field, a playground and associated recreational areas such as a bowling green and croquet green.[27] The grouping of around five or six such units would support the next tier of amenities such as a municipal library, swimming pool, playing fields, a cinema and health centre.[28] The antecedents and evolution

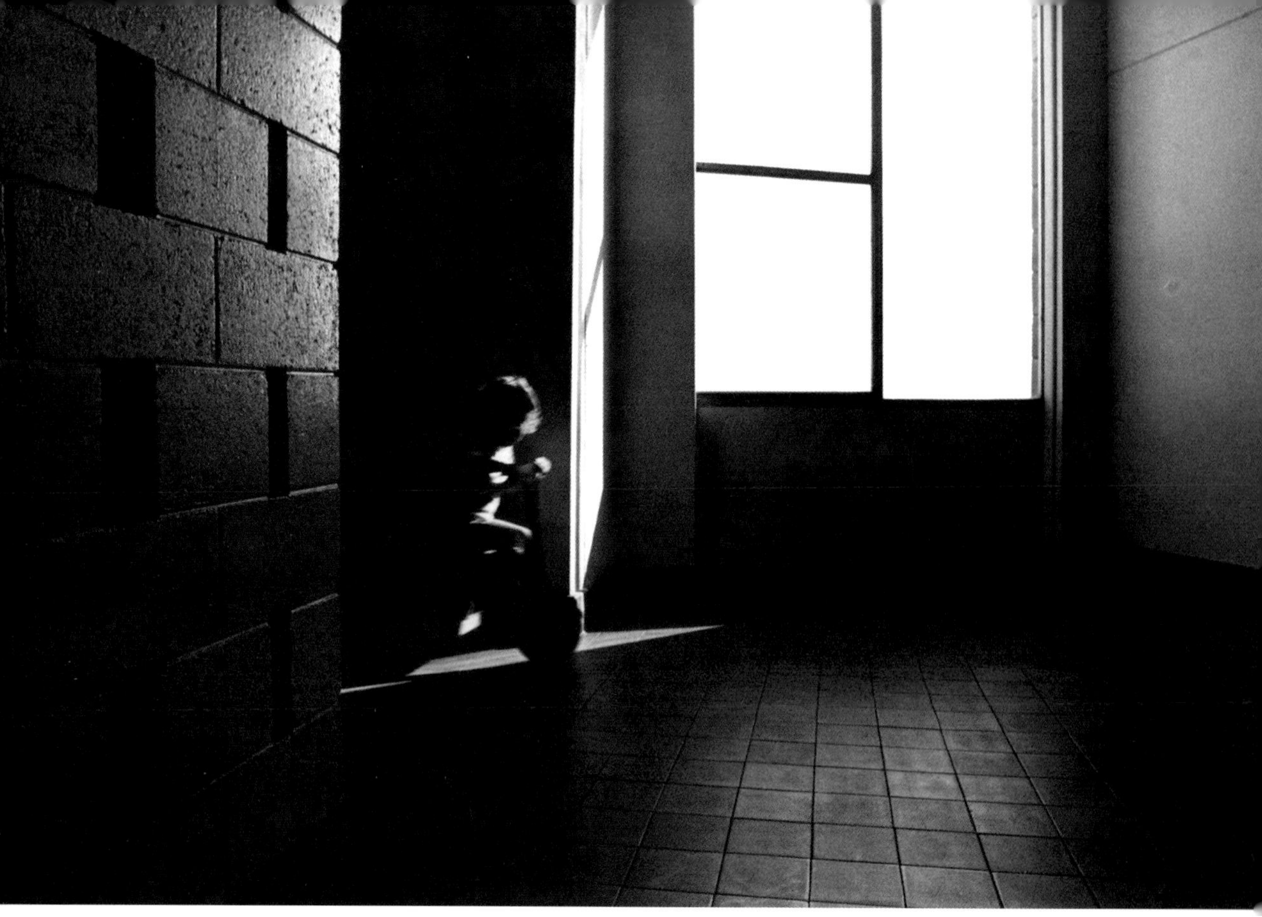

1.5 Child on tricycle at John Byrne Court public housing, Glebe, NSW 1973

of the neighbourhood unit are discussed further in chapter 7. In Costello's plan for Brisbane five gradations of park and recreation areas from the local neighbourhood and community parks containing playgrounds, tennis courts, bowling greens, croquet lawns, football and cricket ovals unrolled a series of appropriate and economically sustainable facilities.

In the face of post–World War II demands for affordable housing in newer suburbs, the built environment professions turned their efforts towards creating infrastructure for communal and democratic neighbourhoods and towns. This focus on community facilities, was not just motivated by economic needs, but also promoted social and governmental strategies that looked outside the confines of the individual home to engage in shared activities and recreation. Charles Whitaker wrote in *Architecture* in 1943: 'It is again part of our great national ambition for recreation and amusement, for a larger measure of social contact, for a greater freedom for individual development'.[29] Such opportunities for individual and shared participation in leisure and recreation would dramatically increase during the 1950s and 1960s, assisted by increased disposable incomes and growing rates of car ownership.

A key facet of modern architecture and planning was its acknowledgment of the centrality of the child and the family to the health and future of national populations. Design and town planning came to be regarded as one important technique in the proper raising of children from the perspectives of health, education and play. Marta Gutman and Ning De Coninck-Smith have reflected 'that spaces and settings made for children are pivotal to the construction of modernity in global society; and that children are social actors in their own right who use and interpret material culture in their own terms'.[30] In 1943, Western Australian architect Harold Boas proposed: 'Children's lives and characters are governed by the houses in which they are born and grow up, and in the surrounding amenities in which those homes are placed'.[31] Town planning, for Boas, was a practical science providing 'recreational facilities, transport, intercommunication, amenity, communal centres, open spaces, disposition of schools and relationship to playgrounds and a great many other considerations essential to the life of the modern community'.[32] Sydney architect Walter Bunning reiterated these calls in his modernist treatise *Homes in the Sun* (1945), arguing for facilities outside the home for children's 'education, leisure, care and health' and that: 'No community in Australia can boast of doing these things adequately'.[33]

Modern architecture was also concerned with the health of the mind through the promotion of life-long learning and engagement in cultural exchange, exemplified by public lending libraries, community centres and halls. Many of these civic places and public buildings in the mid-20th century could be appropriately designed through modern architecture and further enhanced with modern public art. Swiss architectural historian and exponent of modernism Sigfried Giedion was a leading voice in these discussions and promoted the idea that the building of civic centres and the 'designing of community life' held the key to reinstating art and humanity in the modern environment. Civic art, he said, had the potential to 'expand men's narrow private existence' and to invigorate community life beyond job and family.[34]

One way forward for the modern design of such civic and cultural centres was to be forged through a closer and sympathetic collaboration between architects, artists and landscape designers. Civic centres, it was imagined, would be surrounded by greenery and would compose the site for 'democratic community life' and 'collective emotional events', and such aspirations could be represented through modern abstraction and secular symbols. Civic art was often called on to assume some of the burden of the growing dissatisfaction with the deficiencies of modern functionalist architecture to be expressive and welcoming to the person in the street. Such collaborations between artists and architects might assist in creating more human-scaled and accessible civic

1.6 Subiaco Civic Centre and Theatre Complex, WA, built in 1957

centres and community amenities.[35] In this way public civic art developed in conjunction with a new wave of modernism in the 1950s and 1960s that endeavoured to inculcate creative citizenship at the local level, rather than nationalistic unity.

Community and the design professions in Australia

From the early decades of the 20th century in Australia the professions directly engaged in the built environment – architects, landscape architects and planners – and those more indirectly involved yet nevertheless influential professionals in health, education and social welfare increasingly turned their attention to the provision of public amenities and programs for everyday living. Built environment professionals faced conflicting directions and roles as a consequence of modernisation. Amid these uncertainties, which grew particularly after World War II, architects responded to the need for a more socialised approach to their work.[36]

This call to a heightened sense of social and civic responsibility and a duty to engage with public buildings large and small was expressed in architectural publications in Australia as in Britain, Europe and the United States. From the early 1950s, a number of special issues of the professional journal *Architecture in Australia* were themed around particular public building types; for example, two editions in 1951 were devoted to hospitals and public works. In commemorating the 21st anniversary of the incorporation of the Royal Australian Institute of Architects (RAIA) as a professional body, its president Cobden Parkes attempted to define the profession by reaffirming that the institute existed to serve the interests of architecture and not the individual:

> The social responsibilities involved in embracing the profession of architecture cannot be overlooked. We create the physical conditions in which both we, and our fellow men, live. How carefully then must we plan![37]

The contents showed many examples of new public buildings around the country, including a nursing home, a high school and an infant school. Three years later, the 1954 July–September issue also covered public buildings under themes of 'Buildings for Living', 'Buildings for Religion' and 'Buildings for Health'. A particular emphasis pursued in these professional journals was the adoption of a grassroots approach to community-building through the promotion of community participation and consensus. A number of editorials, features and transcripts addressed the problem of galvanising public interest in the planning and making of suburban places. In 1951, for example, Parkes charged members with the duty of bringing architecture 'before the man in the street, because we believe that architecture means so much to the community'.[38] In 1958 WT Haslam, a successor to Parkes as RAIA president, encouraged the professions to engage with the community-at-large, promoting the idea that architects and planners should be profoundly interested in modern life, including the use of leisure time, changes in family habits, and longer life expectancy:

> there is a need for architects to widen their sphere of influence to include all aspects of man's needs ... the social development of the democratic way of life provides him with wider opportunities of fulfilment. This is indicated by the increasing interest of architects in the development of communities. The modern life represents a challenge to architecture which will require a response from architects with ever widening responsibilities.[39]

In the same year Perth architect Mervyn Parry, in an ABC talk titled 'The Living City', deplored 'the absence of neighbourhood development in residential areas, leading to a barrenness in social life and general lack of visual interest' and emphasised the need to galvanise public interest in taking inclusive action for the future of 'children'.[40] Interestingly, this book demonstrates that such calls over the fifty-year period were often answered by municipal agencies or community groups, and then facilitated by a broad cross-section of the design professions. From humble kindergartens designed by society architects like Marcus Martin in Melbourne, F Kenneth Milne in Adelaide and suave design stylists like Sydney's Peter Muller, from a series of suburban libraries in post-war Brisbane designed by James Birrell to even a lawn bowls club by arch-modernist Harry Seidler, a number of these diminutive civic buildings gained considerable design pedigree. But also, there was a significant if often unknown cohort of architects, planners, and shire engineers who devoted their careers to the creation of imaginative and distinctive facilities. This book goes some way to unearthing their contribution.

Realising community

Aside from this developing sense of social responsibility and interest in public and civic institutional building types among the architecture and planning professions, the realisation of local community amenities in Australia has often been made possible only by localised initiatives. Additionally, in some instances the well-meaning actions of one social group on another have also played a strong part: for example, the establishment by middle-class philanthropists of creches and kindergartens within poorer areas during the early decades of the

1.7 Woomera Swimming Pool and Bowling Green, SA

20th century. Support groups and local activism groups were endemic to the broadening and developing suburbs and towns of 20th-century Australia. They were a mix of local chapters of state or nationwide (sometimes even international) organisations, and local progress associations which, while ostensibly unique to their region, were nevertheless of a recognisable genre. It is difficult, perhaps, in the present context of social policy rhetoric invoking ideas of social inclusion and community to envisage the meaning such organisations held for participants in the mid-20th century. In the immediate post-World War II period, and in the 'frontier' stage of suburban development in Australia a strong strand of local participation and activism was key to the origin of specific community-oriented buildings. This was often paired with campaigns for government investment in new amenities.

In Australia the responsibility for the provision of community services, protections and legislation lies in various ways with federal, state and municipal levels of government and often with shared funding arrangements. Since Federation in 1901 this situation has enabled federal and state governments to fund community projects sporadically and in some cases with a cynical eye on the electoral cycle. This has also sometimes meant, particularly if not exclusively during the tenures of conservative governments, a broad lack of attention to the requirements of urban areas.[41]

The responsibilities (prescribed or assumed) of state and local government are not, however, evenly applied across the nation, and requirements or opportunities provided by federal government have also long been a factor in provisions made at a local community level. Duties of local government in terms of service and amenity provision have varied to an extraordinary degree, including in some instances (now largely relinquished) extensive assumption of responsibility for electricity, sewerage, public transport, gas and water systems.[42]

From the 1920s, municipal authorities gradually took on greater provision of social infrastructure – those facilities concerned with fostering health, education and community care within local areas. This is not, and has never been, consistently true across Australia: Margaret Bowman's late 1970s surveys of amenity provision control indicate, for instance, that New South Wales and Queensland are two states where the middle tier of government is less likely to take control of funding and organising such facilities.[43] Generalisations become even more difficult in regional areas, where large industrial companies and particular government responsibilities such as Defence have also at times played a substantial role in funding community facilities.[44] The already complex nature of funding is made more impenetrable when considerations of particular tax exemption arrangements – such as those which prevailed in the creation of post-World War II memorial facilities – are brought into play; and when it is considered that some key facilities – such as primary and secondary schools – were subject to very different funding arrangements to other key local facilities, yet often co-located with them.

Building community

The chapters of *Community: Building Modern Australia* are organised around typological themes that examine a range of facilities and buildings ubiquitous across Australian suburbs and towns. Building type is a perennial ordering device for architectural history. Researching by type, as opposed to historical chronology, authorship, or stylistic themes, is an apt tool for understanding architectural production in the 20th century, when function became a paramount ordering device and new types proliferated.[45] A study governed by building type, and here we mean functional rather than morphological or elemental types, allows fruitful comparisons to be drawn about stylistic and planning variations across place and time. It also appears most appropriate when teasing out the relations between social and bureaucratic programs and architectural design.

The building types selected in this book by no means constitute an exhaustive list, but rather are representative of community amenities that were to support social patterns and stages of everyday life. This study is ordered chronologically around the increasing prominence of such building types at particular historical moments, and the corresponding idea of increased municipal provision for community services for all Australians from cradle to grave. The book opens, therefore, with two chapters on public buildings for child health and education through an analysis of the infant welfare centre in 'A Healthy Start: Buildings for Babies', and the kindergarten in 'Early Learning: The Modern Kindergarten'. Then we examine the rise of municipal libraries in 'Local Learning: The Municipal Library in Post-War Australia'.

There are many contenders for building types that arose to provide facilities for public recreation and leisure at the local community level, from sporting clubs of all codes to playgrounds. 'Making Spaces for Recreation' singles out the public swimming pool as one important exemplar of an amenity that gradually rose from being a novelty in the 1930s to an expected right for all citizens by the late 1950s. Pools are a fascinating index of changing social attitudes to outdoor recreation. 'Lawn Bowls: A Community Game' highlights another recreation type, partly selected because of the particular ubiquity of lawn bowling clubs in the Australian landscape, and partly because bowls is seen as an older person's game with clubs often serving as surrogate centres for senior citizens. The trend for consolidating a number of services and buildings including town halls, recreation centres and civic functions into one larger and multi-purpose community or civic centre in the post–World War II decades is the subject of the next chapter, 'The Community Can do It! Planning for the New Civic Centre'.

Looking across the 1920s to the 1970s, the chapter on 'Commemorating and Enhancing the Everyday' illustrates how approaches to commemoration through architecture, memorials and public art responded to changing times and expectations. The final chapter in the book takes the examination of community buildings forward from the 1970s to the present. It charts the shift in architectural approaches to 'community architecture' in the postmodern decades, and reveals enduring notions of community in current examples of regeneration and growth in towns and suburbs across Australia. The fate of these kinds of ordinary places opens questions about the future of conservation and heritage listing of community buildings.

There are some obvious omissions in this coverage of community buildings and place. For instance, senior citizens centres played and still do play an important role in local communities, as do other buildings such as guide and scout halls, clubs for the Returned and Services League (RSL) and facilities for the Country Women's Association (CWA). Local art galleries and theatres are similarly not examined in any detail. Nor are the myriad of sports buildings like football clubs (Australian Rules and soccer) which are often at the heart of the social life of many Australian country towns as are cricket, tennis and golf clubs.

Finally, it must be stated that while there are very many buildings and places described and illustrated in this book there are also thousands that are not included. The organisation of the book into themes related to building type and function is reinforced by the multiple illustrations presented, particularly the array of images that introduces each chapter and its theme. Here the intention is to capture some of the hundreds of examples collected in the course of our research. In this book on community buildings, the documentation of the ordinary and the recent, rather than just the exceptional and the canonical, is all the more eloquent through the presentation of the many rather than the singular.

BABY HEALTH CENTRE
BABY HEALTH CENTRE

A HEALTHY START: BUILDINGS FOR BABIES

Kate Darian-Smith and Julie Willis

In 1924, the Victorian government launched a distinctly modern innovation in public health education for families in rural communities. Experts on the 'scientific' management of the home and the care of mothers and children joined the orange-coloured Better Farming Train, which travelled to country railway stations throughout the state delivering practical demonstrations and lectures on progressive agricultural methods to farmers. The addition of 'mothercraft lectures' to this program proved enormously

2.1 **a.** Child Welfare Centre, Kensington, Vic. c. 1927 **b.** Baby Health Centre, Oakleigh, Vic. 1928 **c.** Baby Health Centre, Concord, NSW 1943

popular with rural women, especially those in more remote areas such as the Mallee, recently opened up for farming under soldier settlement schemes. The 'Report to the Minister of Public Health on the welfare of women and children' published in 1926 recorded that as:

> the mothercraft lectures were successful beyond all expectations, a car exclusively for Health Centre lectures was granted. In all, fourteen tours have been undertaken, in which ten included the whole train, and four

> the women's section only ... by special request. By this means, visits have been paid to 105 different places, where the lectures and demonstrations have been given. At least 20,000 women have attended ... the women frequently travel 20–30 minutes at great personal inconvenience ... [1]

The mothercraft carriages exhibited instructional films and lantern slide lectures on such topics as 'The Spread of Disease' and 'The Danger of Flies', recognising women's role as the 'leading crusaders' in the battle against germs. Most important, however, was the practical advice on the care of infants and young children, and the distribution of literature from the Victorian Baby Health Centres Association, formed in 1918. It was reported that 'the mothercraft car was packed with mothers who had come to learn',[2] and to receive consultations from trained nursing staff about the development of their babies. Until the Better Farming Train scheme was abandoned during the 1930s Depression, its mothercraft carriages also played a significant role in alerting local municipal councils, and interested residents, to the ongoing benefits of financing a baby health centre – a dedicated building that would offer ongoing support for the health needs of country mothers and children – in their town.

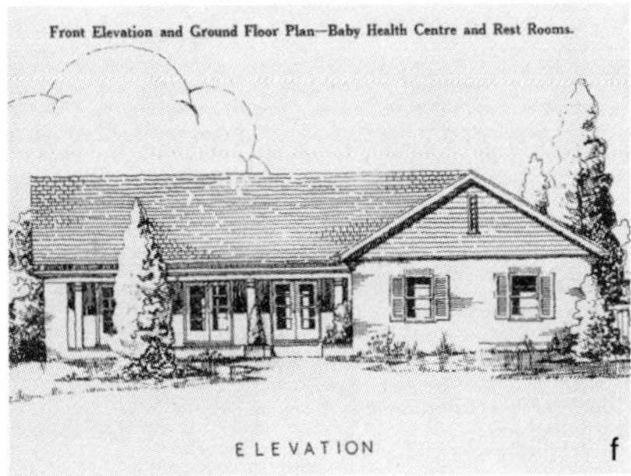

2.1 d. Maternal and Child Health Centre, Black Rock, Vic. 1939 **e.** Baby Health Centre, Lakemba, NSW 1947 **f.** Department of Health pamphlet, Canberra, ACT 1944

By the early 20th century in Australia, municipal governments were taking on increasing responsibility for the provision of what were known as infant welfare or baby health services, a cause seen to be a matter of longstanding local and national interest. From the early colonial period, there were ongoing attempts to encourage the immigration of families and single women to Australia. This was to address the initial imbalance between the sexes within the white population, with a predominance of settler men over women continuing to be a trend, especially on non-metropolitan frontiers, for many decades. The unshakeable belief in the family as the cornerstone of British social formation and respectability was transplanted to Australia, where the growth and physical health of colonial-born children were observed and often favourably compared to those in Britain. In this context, the future of the Australian colonies was seen to lie with the coming generations. The perceived vulnerability of white Australia within the broader Asian region also contributed to a strong racialised strand in policies aimed to increase the birthrate within the white population. Such linking of pro-natalism with the national interest continued into the 20th century, where it was exemplified by population and immigration policies following World War II which called for Australia 'to populate or perish'.

By the late 19th century, as attitudes towards young children and childhood in general grew increasingly sentimental, both the overall birthrate and the infant mortality rate in Australia were in decline. The former stemmed from the influences of industrialisation and urbanisation on family structure, as women sought some measure of control over their fertility. The latter was partly due to some improvements in sanitation and increased medical care for young children, and followed a similar decline in infant mortality in Europe and throughout the English-speaking world. Living conditions, access to medical assistance and climate varied considerably within Australia itself, and as a result infant mortality rates were higher in Queensland, Western Australia and South Australia than in New South Wales, Victoria and Tasmania. Differences between infant mortality in urban and non-metropolitan Australia were particularly stark. Lynette Finch argues that from the 1880s parents in rural Queensland were more likely than their city counterparts to see their children celebrate their first birthday.[3] Nevertheless, it was far more difficult for mothers in such locations to access doctors, with numerous babies dying during arduous journeys in search of medial assistance.[4] In her study of the reactions of rural Queensland parents to infant sickness, Finch found that they did not accept high rates of infant mortality passively, but sought the help of pharmacists and doctors when home remedies failed.[5]

Between 1900 and 1945, Australia saw an extraordinary decrease in infant mortality, as the average number of deaths per 1000 live births fell from ninety-six to thirty-five.

Between 1900 and 1945, Australia saw an extraordinary decrease in infant mortality, as the average number of deaths per 1000 live births fell from ninety-six to thirty-five. This achievement was largely the result of a preventative health strategy that encouraged women to breastfeed and to prepare infant food carefully, so as to avoid contamination which could lead to such illnesses as gastroenteritis. Baby health and infant welfare services, established in all Australian states by the 1920s, became crucial providers of education for mothers about infant care. They spread their message and monitored maternal and infant developments through mobile clinics, such as those aboard the Better Farming Train or specially equipped vehicles, but most importantly operated from modest, purpose-built, community buildings that were intended to be welcoming in their design. The proliferation of these localised services – in combination with the expansion of paediatric and women's hospitals, the availability of immunisation against some common childhood diseases, new town planning schemes that emphasised the necessity for a 'healthy' environment for stable family life, and the growth of kindergarten education – positioned state and municipal-level infrastructure for maternal and child welfare at the centre of the modern Australian community.

International responses to infant mortality

The development of services for mothers and babies in Australia was part of a sweeping international movement during the late 19th century, involving medical professionals, charitable organisations and national and local governments.[6] The high deathrate resulting from modern forms of warfare was, perhaps surprisingly, to prove beneficial in the longer-term to the health of mothers and young children. Defeat in the Franco-Prussian War in 1871 led to alarm in France over the maintenance of its national prestige and power. This prompted investigation into the robustness of the French population, which had the highest infant mortality rate in Europe – a statistic attributed to the high rate of epidemic diarrhoea, especially in the summer months, and more common among bottle-fed infants.[7] French physicians began to establish baby clinics in poorer neighbourhoods, with the express purpose of reducing the mortality rate through the improvement of hygiene and nutrition for both mothers and infants. The clinics, soon known as *Goutte de Lait* ('drop of milk'), offered support to breastfeeding mothers and arranged for supplies of pasteurised cow's milk to be available for bottle-feeding. The results were dramatic, slashing the infant mortality rate in France.[8]

In Britain, national anxieties about the fitness of the British race emerged when large numbers of men enlisting to fight in the Anglo-Boer War in South Africa in 1899 were rejected because of their poor physical condition.[9] In response, there was renewed effort to improve child health, drawing upon existing models of charitable interest in the health education of the poor. For instance, in the mid-19th century the sanitation movement was established in the industrial cities of Manchester and Salford with volunteer or paid 'visitors', the majority of whom were women, travelling door-to-door to dispense health advice. Home visiting was adopted throughout Britain and became highly systematised as its emphasis turned to infant welfare. Again, cleanliness in feeding practices was stressed, and by 1899 the first milk depot for the distribution of hygienic milk for infants was operating. In Britain, the focus on the education of the mother emerged as the most effective and economical solution for infant and child wellbeing. Two conferences on Infantile Mortality held in London in 1906 and 1908 drew attention to the 'the value of maternal education programmes and health visiting systems', and 'maternal instruction' by council officers: it was seen that 'the route to the child was through the mother'.[10]

From 1904, health societies, such as the Westminster Health Society, working with public health authorities and local charities, undertook educational programs and home visiting for mothers and mothers-to-be. In 1905, the St Marylebone Health Society established a centre to which infants could be brought for medical assessment. By 1907, the St Pancras School for Mothers opened, becoming 'the centre round which all agencies revolved for the protection and preservation of the health of both mother and child'.[11]

These British and European developments, and similar schemes addressing infant mortality that were promoted in the United States, were to be influential in Australia. In 1904, Dr WD Armstrong, medical officer of the combined municipal districts of Sydney, began a home visiting service for newborn babies. He had studied the work of Dr Pierre Budin at the Charité Hôpital in Paris and Dr Léon Dufour's *Goutte de Lait* centre at Fécamp and was convinced that home visits would assist in the reduction of infant morality.[12] His visiting program, like the French and British ones, saw impressive results: between 1904 and 1914, some 28,000 newborns were visited, with the mortality rate falling from 116 deaths per 1000 live registered births to 68 per 1000 across the municipalities serviced.[13] In addition, the idea of hygienic milk supplies for mothers unable to breastfeed their infants was also promoted in a number of states, including Victoria, Queensland and New South Wales. However, as elsewhere, this scheme was soon abandoned due to prohibitive costs.[14]

The origins of comprehensive baby health services in Australia, however, took root with the establishment of educational services for mothers. The National Council of Women opened the Alice Rawson School for Mothers in 1908, which serviced the working-class Sydney suburbs of Newtown, Darlinghurst and Alexandria, monitoring the growth of babies and providing advice and classes for mothers. In 1909, another School for Mothers was established in Adelaide by three women, Dr Helen Mayo, Mrs Lucy Morice and Miss Harriet Stirling, who 'shared a common concern for social problems'.[15] Largely inspired by the St Pancras precedent in Britain, it sought to assist mothers in matters of infant nutrition, health and hygiene. Within a few years, the school had gained state government support, with an annual grant of £100 awarded from June 1912.[16]

Concerns about infant mortality also prompted action in Victoria. In what would be the beginning of a long history of volunteerism in the realm of infant welfare and education, the Women's Christian Temperance Union School for Mothers was established in 1914, along with the Marie Kirk Kindergarten in inner-city Richmond. As historian Heather Sheard points out, the Free Kindergarten Movement 'both nurtured, and was nurtured by, the women who began Victoria's baby health centres',[17] indicating a holistic perspective on infant and early childhood health and education services that was to continue throughout the 20th century.

World War I and maternal and child health

By 1914, it was clear that longer term efforts to improve the general health of those living in Australia's cities and towns through the provision of clean water and sewerage services, coupled with a preventative approach to infant health, were showing results. Indeed, infant mortality had fallen, in the space of merely a decade, by around 20 per cent.[18] As in other participating nations, the destruction and loss of life of World War I focused attention on issues of national survival and fitness, and the birthrate. As a consequence, the health of mothers and children – the next generation – was under increasing scrutiny in Australia. A number of state government inquiries into living conditions and children's health were undertaken during wartime, pointing to the need for new and extensive facilities that were freely accessible to women and children. It was during this period that in all Australian states baby health clinics or centres were established through various forms of state government, municipal councils and philanthropic support. These facilities were gradually coordinated and expanded during the 1920s and 1930s. Unlike French and British baby health clinics, however, the medical services offered at Australian centres were advisory only, and the staff were specially trained mothercraft nurses rather than medical practitioners.

In 1914 in New South Wales, concerns about infant health were quickly mobilised by the state government, with the Minister for Public Health, Labor member Fred Flowers, establishing the Baby Clinics, Pre-Maternity and Home Nursing Board which drew together the existing initiatives throughout the state. The Board, which gained statutory authority in 1915, advised Flowers on 'the development of his infant health clinics'.[19] Centres at inner-city Alexandria, Newtown and Bourke Street opened in 1914. By the end of 1915, nine clinics had been established in Sydney and Newcastle in areas with high infant mortality rates; four years later, that number had grown to fifteen, with another planned for Broken Hill.[20]

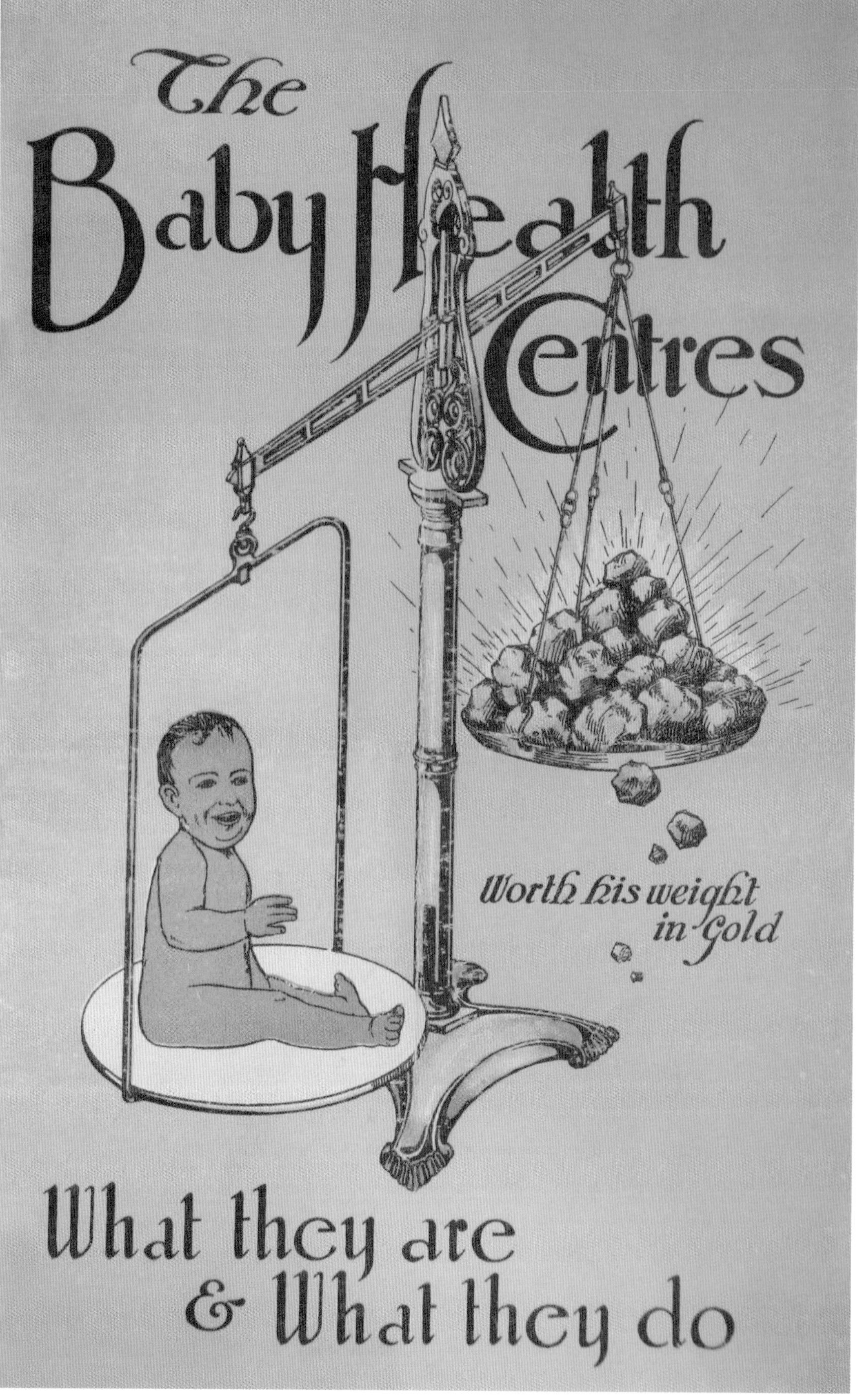
The Baby Health Centres
Worth his weight in Gold
What they are & What they do

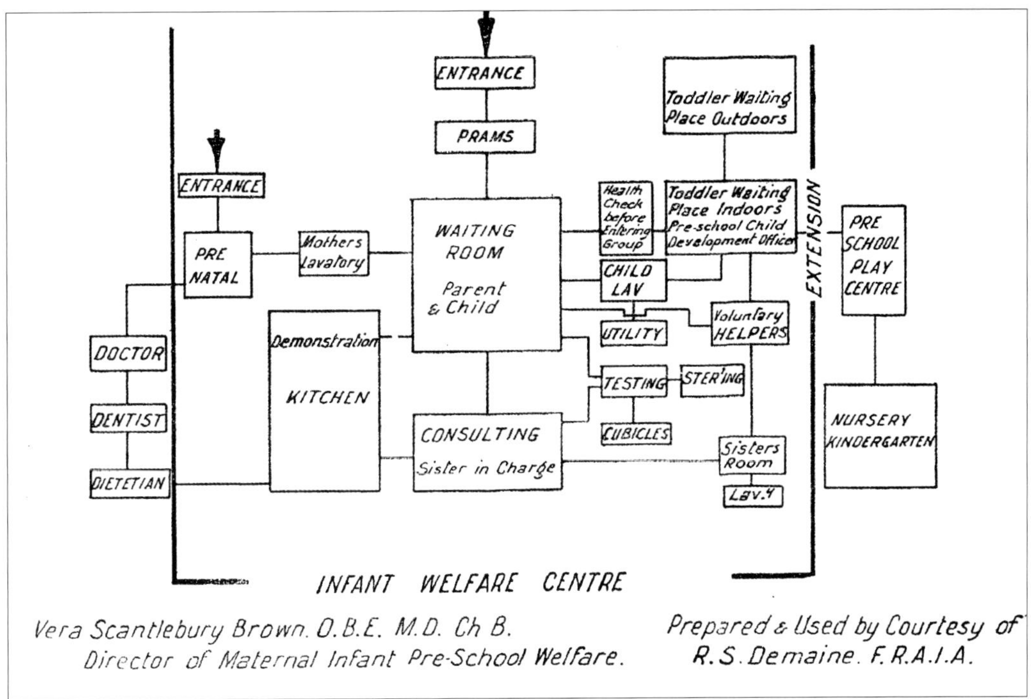

2.3 Analysis of requirements for Infant and Child Welfare Centre, annual report to the Director of the Department of Health, Vic. 1944–45

Melbourne's early baby health clinics were founded in 1917–18 in the crowded industrial suburbs of Richmond, North Melbourne, Carlton, South Melbourne, Port Melbourne, Fitzroy and Collingwood.[21] Like its predecessor, the 'School for Mothers', the first baby health clinic was established in a room at the Boroondara Free Kindergarten, held in St Matthias Church Hall, North Richmond; the model soon extended to include baby health clinics at the Bouverie Street Kindergarten in Carlton, and the City Free Kindergarten.[22] The first regional baby health clinic in Victoria was established in Geelong in 1917.[23] In 1918, the Victorian Baby Health Centres Association was formed, and over the next few years local committees of interested women worked with municipal authorities to set up centres throughout Melbourne's suburbs and in major regional towns.

Queensland, too, quickly established infant welfare services, with the Labor state government opening four clinics in Brisbane, including at Fortitude Valley and Woolloongabba, in 1918.[24] Revenue generated by the Golden Casket lottery was used by the Queensland government to create the Motherhood, Child Welfare and Hospital Fund in 1920; its express purpose was to finance the creation of baby health clinics and maternity hospitals throughout the state.[25] Such a significant line of funding allowed very rapid expansion of both services, so that by 1925, there were fifty-seven maternity hospitals and ten baby clinics in Queensland; by 1938, over 100 baby clinics had been entirely financed by the Motherhood Fund.[26]

2.2 (left) *The Baby Health Centres: What They Are and What They Do* (1929), Division of Maternal and Baby Welfare, Office of the Director-General of Public Health, Sydney

In 1917, the Tasmanian Child Welfare Association was founded. It raised money for clinics, provided clothing and other goods to families in need and instructed mothers on the care of babies and young children.[27] Further impetus for action was encouraged by the visit of child-health advocate Dr Truby King to Tasmania and Victoria in 1919. King, a New Zealand veterinarian who had formulated an uncompromising system of infant feeding and care which gained rapid and enthusiastic support, was hugely influential in New Zealand, Australia and Britain. Societies devoted to the Truby King method were established in Victoria (the Society for the Health of Women and Children of Victoria) and in New South Wales (the Australian Mothercraft Society), and competed with existing infant welfare bodies. The avid support of varying methods or theories of infant welfare by different groups was very apparent during this period, and also included followers of the New Zealand Karitane system of infant feeding. By the 1930s, in New South Wales and Victoria two competing organisations with their own training systems for nursing staff ran infant welfare services, under the umbrella of a government-appointed director of infant services.[28]

By the 1930s, in New South Wales and Victoria two competing organisations with their own training systems for nursing staff ran infant welfare services, under the umbrella of a government-appointed director of infant services.

Western Australia was relatively late in establishing infant welfare services. It was not until 1920 that a school for mothers or infant welfare clinic was established and it was 1922 before an Infant Welfare Association began.[29] But progress was made very quickly thereafter, with five clinics supported by state and municipal funds run by voluntary groups by the mid-1920s and fourteen by 1930.[30] In South Australia, by 1930 there were forty-five infant welfare centres under the auspices of the Mothers' and Babies' Health Association, which received funds from both state and municipal government.[31]

The role of voluntary community and philanthropic organisations in the initial stages of the baby health and infant welfare movement was significant, and such organisations continued to work in tandem with state and municipal authorities; the exception was Queensland, where the state government had directed such facilities from the beginning. The Country Women's Association (CWA) was extremely active in advocating for local maternal and infant welfare centres in regional Australia, playing a leading role in Tasmania and New South Wales, where the organisation had been created by women who had looked on 'helplessly as their children died from minor illnesses'.[32] During the 1920s, the New South Wales government, unable to meet the demand to establish rural maternal and child health services, invited the CWA to assist. The first CWA baby health centre was opened in Moree in 1925.[33] By 1946, 138 of New South Wales' total of 175 baby health centres were established and operated by the CWA, an indication of its spread and influence in regional Australia.[34]

In a rich study of the Aboriginal Burnt Bridge–Greenhill branch of the CWA in the late 1950s to early 1960s, Jennifer Jones notes how its establishment angered members of the white-only Kempsey branch who did not wish to share the town's baby health facilities with Indigenous women.[35] The Burnt Bridge–Greenhill branch, however, thrived with the enthusiastic participation of Aboriginal mothers who, through their successful staging of competitive baby shows, sought to demonstrate their 'constancy, respectability and responsibility' to white CWA members and their right to infant welfare services.[36] The area of baby and maternal health sometimes brought white and Aboriginal women together with a common purpose, and was to contribute to the building of a relationship of trust between women and their wider communities that crossed the everyday racial divide prevalent in rural New South Wales at this time.

Designing for baby health

The infant welfare movement in Australia, as internationally, was driven by real concerns for the health, wellbeing and survival of babies, but it was also closely tied to aspirations for improvement of the fitness of the race. Scientific modern methods of domestic organisation – where the home kitchen was run as a 'laboratory' – and the often rigid expectations of feeding indicated the regulation and standardisation of infant care.[37] Government-sanctioned or government-run, the infant welfare or baby health centre was an instrument by which new forms of state or community intervention into private life were evident.

The infant welfare centre was thus positioned at the interface between domestic and civic life, between the private and public spheres of everyday experience. It was the necessity to speak to both realms that resulted in deliberate architectural effects, which visually signalled such an in-between status. Perhaps more than any other small-scale building type considered in this book, the universalising message of architectural modernism had most effect on the infant welfare centre. In their early incarnations, infant welfare clinics usually began by occupying parts of existing buildings, or colonising corners of church halls or kindergartens. But the importance of the service, particularly in areas of lower and middle socioeconomic standing with proactive and progressive municipal councils, led to purpose-built centres being constructed after the mid-1920s. Some of the earliest buildings drew directly on domestic precedent, adopting the forms of the prevailing housing styles of the day. Yet the buildings still stood out from the ordinary urban fabric around them, as their solid brick construction elevated them above the cheaper construction methods used on most suburban housing of the time, and indicated their civic as well as highly domesticated function.

Dr Truby King had advocated 'home-like' settings for such services, and it is not surprising that the Truby King Rooms (co-located with the City Band) in Coburg, Victoria (1926), used the familiar domestic tropes of pitched terracotta roofs, a shingled porch, and brick-and-stucco walls. The earliest purpose-built centre in Victoria was located in East Kew (1925), and was strikingly similar to a centre built in the nearby suburb of Heidelberg (1928): both were stucco-rendered bungalows with terracotta-tiled pitched roofs, and in common with contemporary house designs had covered porches as part of their entry. The two baby health centres in Melbourne's working-class municipality of Richmond constructed in 1928 (South Richmond) and 1930 (North Richmond) were brick-and-stucco bungalows under a single hipped roof, and featured loggias that wrapped around the edge of the buildings. At first glance, these buildings were strongly reminiscent of domestic houses, as indeed was the architectural intent.

How did mothers experience the buildings and the services that were provided? In her study of Richmond, Janet McCalman found that the women who visited baby health centres were sometimes less enthusiastic about their benefits than the middle-class supporters of such facilities. New mothers without relatives living nearby were often appreciative of the advice offered by the mothercraft nurses, but for many 'there was still resistance to these new notions, especially from grandmothers: "What do you want to go there for? They don't know as much as we do – they've never had babies"', one young mother was told.[38] According to McCalman:

> For too many women the weekly visit to the Health Centre ended in tears. Ironically, it was often the most conscientious new mothers, anxious to be thoroughly modern, who read the medical sympathizers' books and slavishly followed the sisters' instructions, only to find early motherhood a nightmare of guilt and exhaustion.[39]

As Australia's population grew with large-scale immigration after 1949, migrant women – many of whom were not native English-speakers – found the infant and maternal services a source of both bewilderment and illumination. Often, of course, such services were an important bridge for new arrivals in the pursuit of understanding the 'Australian way of life'.

The infant welfare centre, whether in a metropolitan or regional location, had a number of practical considerations that had to be taken into account. The position of this community facility was important, as its clients

– mothers, babies and frequently one or two older children – would generally arrive on foot or sometimes via public transport such as train, tram or bus.[40] The centre also needed to provide sufficient accommodation for mothers and infants to wait for their appointments, and to park their perambulators or prams. Consulting rooms were required for the nursing sisters, and there was also a need for such service areas as a kitchen, toilets, nappy change 'crook' and so on. While the internal arrangements of domestic houses partially echoed these spatial requirements, enabling the adaptation of existing housing stock, the preferred size of waiting, consulting and utility rooms made the design of new facilities a priority.

The designs of the new infant welfare centres needed to reflect not only these internal and external specifications, but to represent the service simultaneously as an authoritative presence and a familiar and welcoming place. Most purpose-built centres actively engaged with the current domestic context – deliberately using the same materials, forms, scale and settings – but included aspects of the civic that distinguished them from an ordinary house. For many older municipalities in Australian cities, the availability of street-fronting land on which to build new facilities was simply non-existent and the new infant welfare centres were frequently sited within parkland.

At the time that these early centres were being built, it was generally accepted that the architectural response to a building with a civic purpose would be distinctly different to that of a domestic dwelling. The divide was so wide that civic and domestic architecture drew on different sources in terms of aesthetics and forms, and the respective function of buildings was easily recognised by the ordinary citizen. Domestic buildings were almost universally placed in a garden setting, back from the street, and had pitched roofs and modest windows and doors. Civic, commercial and institutional buildings, on the other hand, called for design responses that specifically and boldly addressed the street. Larger and more formal elements, such as elaborate entries with multiple doors, were used; larger banks of windows were necessary to light the interiors; facades were given depth to emphasise their gravitas; and steps, porches and arcades were standard devices to mediate behaviour between the open street and the formalised interior spaces. Courthouses or post offices, for example, developed distinctive architectural types, and were instantly recognisable across the nation; the power and authority of their function was thus embedded within the architectural forms they routinely employed.

The infant welfare centre, on the other hand, directly challenged preconceived notions about the type of architectural language and the nature of the formal response that was required. Architects struggled with the civic and domestic natures of their brief, and this was to lead to numerous hybrid designs. For example, the Oakleigh Baby Health Centre, in what is

METH
SPIRIT
ONLY

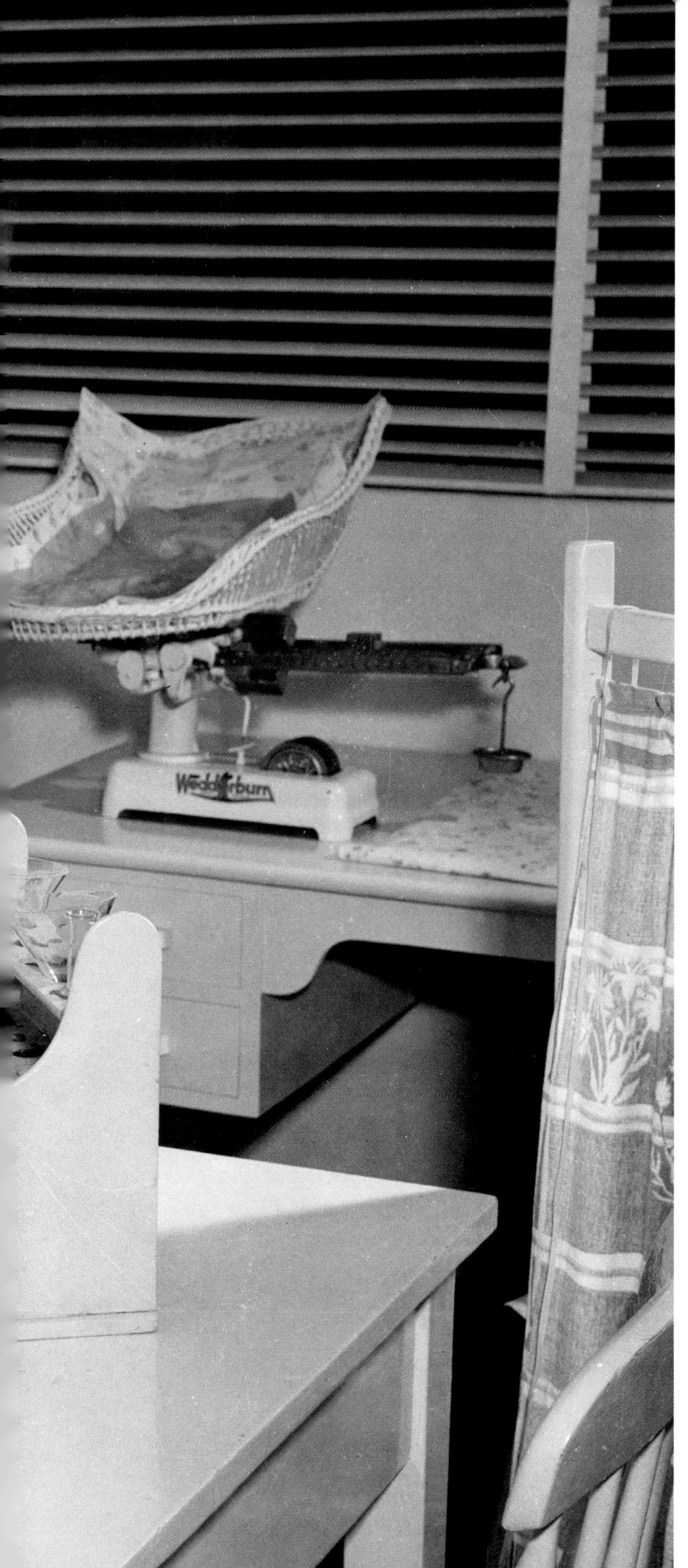

2.4 Baby Health Centre, Campsie, NSW 1956

now middle-ring Melbourne (1928), combined a brick veneer house with a formal entrance porch with doric columns, while the Hamilton Infant Welfare Centre in Newcastle (c. 1950), with heavy brick columns and roughly moulded capitals framing its porch, fronted a simple, domestic-scaled building in a small residential street. The Kensington Baby Health Centre, again in Melbourne (c. 1928), used a more formal approach, with an arcaded Georgian front added to a domestic-scaled, pitched-roof building.

Such buildings embodied a sense of the social improvement that was at the heart of the nation's modernisation. The impetus for much of the development of the modern idiom of architecture during the 1920s was driven by ideas of equality and improving the basic conditions of life for all. Modernist architecture called for a completely new beginning, where the past would be erased in favour of a future that was universal, functional and utilitarian. Modern civic buildings in the 1930s nevertheless brought a sense of street presence to their form that continued to signal a civic character. Various architectural elements, such as vertical fins, slim towers, flat roofs and massing techniques, coupled with modern signage, could indicate this civic identity. The codification of such elements and a consideration of the relationship of the building to the street still allowed, within modernism, differentiation between the civic and the domestic. Although modernism was, in general, slow to find ready acceptance in Australia, there was a greater tendency to apply modern ideas to new building types like the baby health centre.

The adoption of a modernist idiom provided a progressive cast to the infant welfare centre, with the architecture indicating the forward-thinking, scientific nature of the service offered. By the 1940s and 1950s, some designs shook off connections with the domestic, and were confident executions of a modern, small civic building, such as the infant welfare centres in Paddington, Brisbane (c. 1950s), and Lakemba, Sydney (Davey & Brindley, 1958). Others had closer alignment with dwellings, such as the Burnett Gray Baby Health Centre in Elwood, Melbourne (c. 1940s), that at nearby Black Rock (1939) and the East Brunswick centre (c. 1940s) (figure 2.10), where bold moderne fronts were combined with visible pitched roofs behind. The civic connections of these buildings were at times quite explicit: at East Brunswick, a municipal seal was cast as a feature panel above the entrance. They all also announced their function with the use of bold sans-serif lettering emblazoned across their facades – another unequivocally modern 'sign'. Despite this new language, these examples all retained a garden setting and were set back from the street.

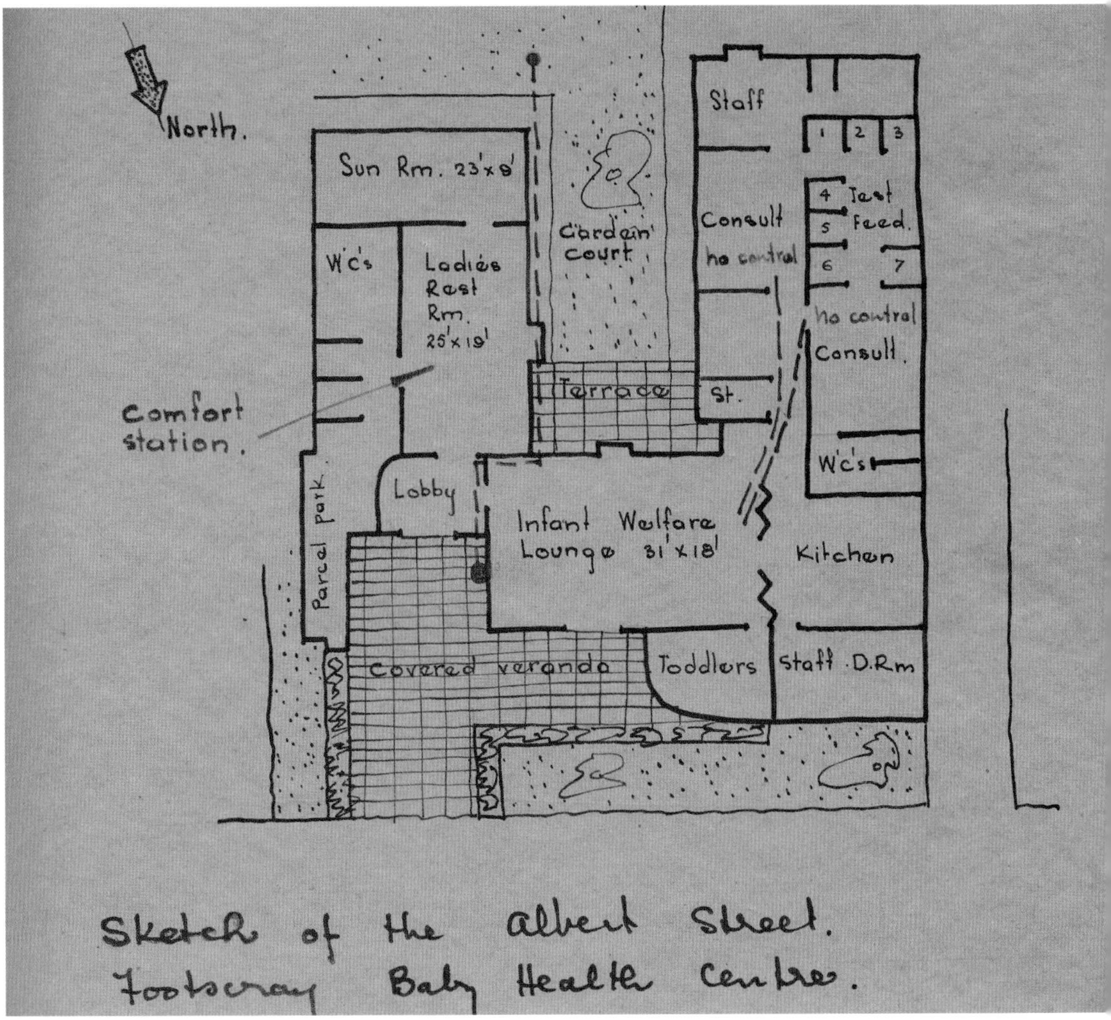

2.5 View and plan of the Baby Health Centre, Footscray, Vic. 1949

2.6 Baby Health Centre, Auburn, NSW c. 1940s

The domestic and the civic

The 1949 design for the Footscray Baby Health Centre in Melbourne's industrial west exemplifies the recurring tension between the civic and the domestic (figure 2.5). The modest, one-storey building signalled its 'in-between' status quite clearly, appearing to weld together a small civic building and a house. Its municipal connections were demonstrated at one end of its front facade, and its close links with the ordinary housing of the day at the other. At first impression, the Footscray centre looked like the home of a well-to-do family: it had a low brick fence, with inset pipe letterbox and simple metal gates, and a front garden. It employed an L-shaped plan fronting the street, typical of much Australian housing from the mid-19th century onwards, with one room projecting forward from the main facade. Over this hung the pitched tiled roof. Coupled with its buff or cream-coloured bricks, it had all the hallmarks of a house. Yet the entrance told a different story. Stretching across the facade was a thin horizontal blade forming an extended veranda: the element was far larger than the modest blades that formed domestic porches. A slim tower replaced the traditional chimney; embellished with three vertical fins it was reminiscent of a town hall

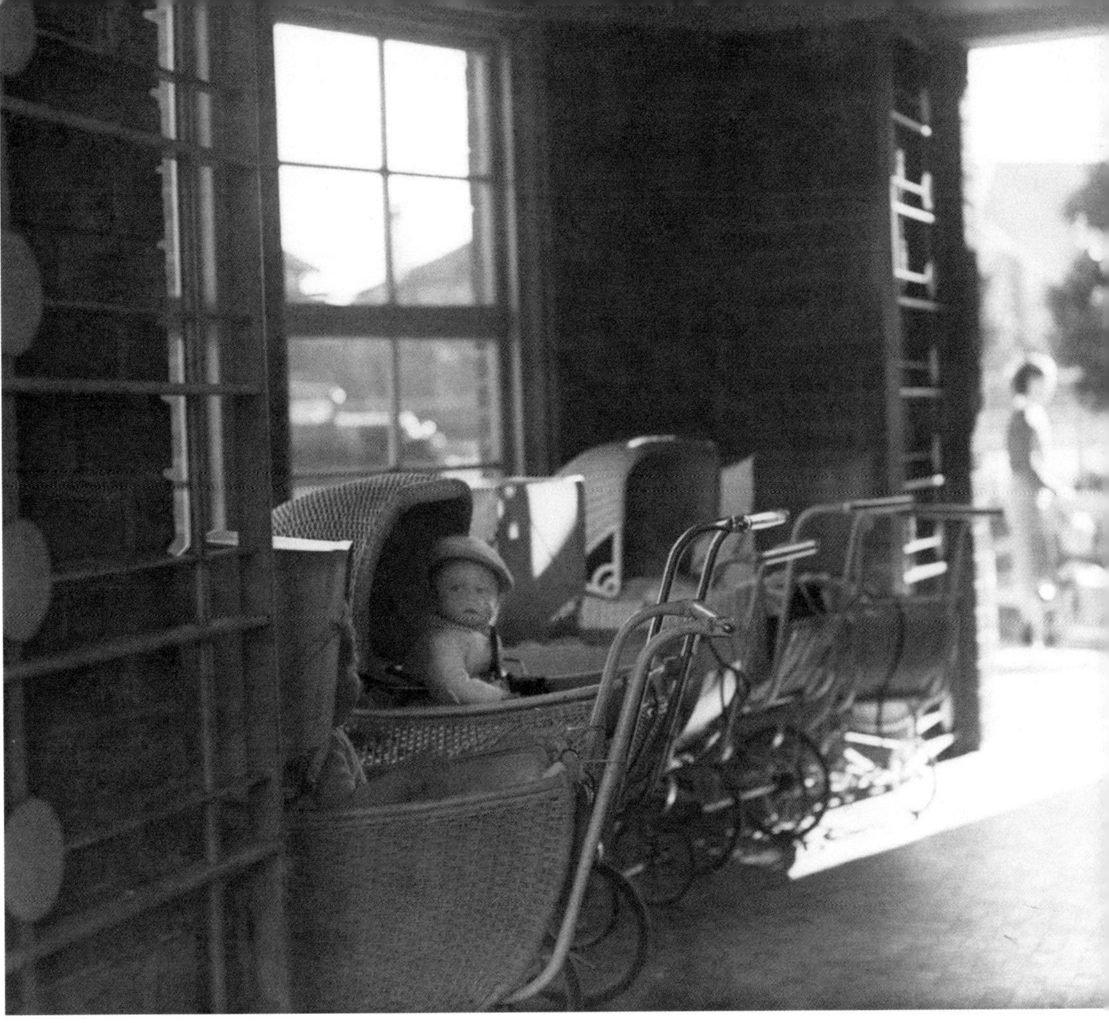

2.7 Prams parked at the Baby Health Centre, Concord, NSW 1943

clock tower. A parapet wall, inscribed with 'City of Footscray', capped the composition, all of which was tied together by the porch blade that gripped both the domestic 'front room' and municipal tower in a tight embrace.

Closer inspection of the Footscray Baby Health Centre indicated large double doors and a spacious inset entrance, clearly intended for a significant amount of foot and pram traffic. The fence, too, signalled the expected number of visitors, with double gates instead of the usual single gate. Architecturally, the building was clearly a hybrid: an attempt to straddle two different agendas, overtly represented in the architectural elements employed in the design. This accorded with the advice given by the federal government in the 1940s that 'designs combining domestic and institutional types of architecture have been found most suitable' for infant welfare centres.[41] The use of a modernist idiom, despite its apparently universal language, had to be mediated to suit the ordinary Australian's vision of domesticity: a sense of home still needed to be communicated within an emergent civic modernism.

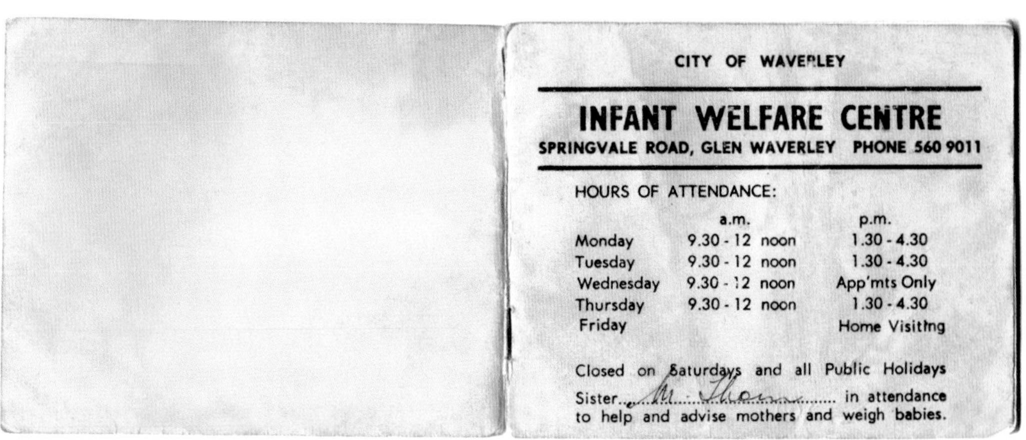

CITY OF WAVERLEY

INFANT WELFARE CENTRE

SPRINGVALE ROAD, GLEN WAVERLEY PHONE 560 9011

HOURS OF ATTENDANCE:

	a.m.	p.m.
Monday	9.30 - 12 noon	1.30 - 4.30
Tuesday	9.30 - 12 noon	1.30 - 4.30
Wednesday	9.30 - 12 noon	App'mts Only
Thursday	9.30 - 12 noon	1.30 - 4.30
Friday		Home Visiting

Closed on Saturdays and all Public Holidays

Sister M. Thom in attendance to help and advise mothers and weigh babies.

BABY'S WEIGHT

Date	Weight	Gain	Date	Weight	Gain	Date	Weight	Gain
20-3-67	10-7½	.	20-6-67	16-13	12½	22-1-68	24-9½	½
29-3-67	11-5½	14	6-7-67	17-12	15	4-3-68	25-11	17½
4-4-67	11-15½	10	18-7-67	18-7½	11½	13-5-68	28-14	51
11-4-67	12-9	9½	3-8-67	19-9	17½	29-5-68	28-12	
20-4-67	13-7½	14½	22-8-67	19-12½	3		L 34⅝	
27-4-67	13-14½	7	4-9-67	20-13	16½	2-9-68	32-2½	
4-5-67	14-3½	5	19-9-67	20-10	-3		L 36	
11-5-67	15-0½	13	3-10-67	21-4	10	24-12-68	32-13	
18-5-67	15-5½	5	2-10-67	21-10½	6½		L 37⅜	
25-5-67	15-11½	6	13-11-67	23-3½	25	3-2-69	33-4	
1-6-67	16-0½	5	18-12-67	24-9			L 38¼	

Baby's Name STITT Helen

Address 10 Charlotte St. G. W.

Weight at Birth 9 lbs 14½ oz

Weight at Discharge 9 lbs 12 oz

Date of Birth 1 - 3 - 67

24-4-67 Phenistix Test Negative

M. Thom Sister

MEASURING BABY

Check your book before each visit and remind Sister if this is due. Baby is fully measured at first visit to Centre and at 3, 6, 9 and 12 months old. Over 1 year, height only measured at periods of 3 months.

2.8 Health chart, Glen Waverley Infant Welfare Centre, Vic. 1967

It is also interesting to note the division in the internal planning of the Footscray centre: the facility included a ladies' comfort station (rest room and toilets) on the civic side of the building. At the time of its opening, it was the 'last word' in baby health centres, featuring an electrically heated floor in the children's playrooms and 'equipped with the most modern facilities for child welfare'.[42] The building's proximity to the local shopping centre meant the comfort station had 'special appeal for mothers as a place to go to rest or feed their babies between shopping'. Its modern kitchen, test feeding room and the presence of 'two trained baby health nurses' made this infant welfare centre 'one of the most up-to-date in Australia'.[43]

The issue of pram parking encouraged the inclusion of extensive undercover spaces in all purpose-built centres. At Footscray, it was an open covered veranda; at Black Rock, it was a glazed semi-circular vestibule; elsewhere attached porches and loggia. At Jeparit, near Dimboola, in the far west of Victoria, such concerns were highlighted with calls for a pram shelter to be built, as 'mothers are having difficulty in keeping prams dry during wet weather'.[44] Evidently those who designed the proposed shelter at Jeparit gave

2.9 Baby Health Centre, Brighton-le-Sands, NSW, built in 1956

insufficient thought as to how it would be used. This attracted the ire of the Director of Maternal, Infant and Pre-School Welfare who wrote to the Shire to point out that while the plan submitted provided 'sufficient space' for prams, it did not link to the centre's entrance so that:

> it would be necessary for the mothers after having put their prams in the shelter to carry their babies out into the open before entering the porch ... have you considered converting the window which will be opening on to the pram park into a door providing a direct entrance from pram park to waiting room.[45]

A series of New South Wales infant welfare centres also incorporated bow- or bay-fronts as part of their entrance sequence, which served as indoor accommodation for prams connected to waiting rooms. Typically built in red brick, the curving fronts were dominated by large windows. At one of the earliest examples of the type, Concord Baby Health Centre in Sydney (1943) (figure 2.7), the windows overlooked a brick-fenced, semi-circular yard that was intended as a toddler waiting area.[46] Similar centres, albeit without the toddler yard, were built in the Sydney suburbs of Glebe (c. 1950), Ramsgate (1952) and Mascot (1946). The capacity to oversee the play area from the building was evidently important, as was the capacity for nursing staff to observe the waiting rooms: for the Jeparit Infant Welfare Centre the regulatory authorities specified 'the provision of an observation window having clear glass area of 12 square feet in the partition between the Sisters' and Waiting Rooms, or glaze the top panel of the door between these rooms with clear glass'.[47] Despite the inclusion of such large expanses of windows, the capacity to see into the interior from outside was cleverly restricted by the arrangement of internal spaces.

One of the recurring themes of baby health centre design was the inclusion of screening devices that sheltered the entrance, behind which mothers could submit themselves to the scrutiny of the nurse but not to the scrutiny of the street-based public. The effect was to reinforce the private or domestic nature of the facility. Some screens were quite perfunctory; others were carefully designed and detailed, such as that by Eric Nicholls for the Willoughby Early Childhood Health Centre (1954); and Brighton-le-Sands Baby Health Centre in Sydney (1956) (figure 2.9), the latter's decorative concrete-block screen flanked by a vivid mosaic-tiled wall. Even though modern design encouraged the use of expanses of glass, allowing space to flow easily from inside to out and welcome the sun into buildings, the infant welfare centre preferred layered sequencing of spaces to reinforce privacy. Indeed it was rare for centres, compared to the other small public buildings of the era such as kindergartens, to include extensive amounts of glazing in their designs.

The success of baby and maternal health centres

By the time Australia was at war again in 1939, the maternal and infant welfare movement was a resounding success throughout the nation. During the 1920s and 1930s centres continued to be built, and the economic hardship of the Depression was to make their role in working-class communities particularly important as a source of advice about infant needs; nursing sisters also offered a source of emotional comfort and support to mothers. The success of this small-scale community facility was such that its presencc in Australian cities and towns was often taken for granted and the services provided were accepted as a right of citizenship.

World War II once again turned national attention to the issue of the birthrate, which had plummeted in Australia during the previous decade. There was considerable discussion about why women were choosing to limit their fertility. Medical experts like Dr Victor Wallace, who was to go on to author the influential text *Women and Children First*, argued that economic constraints were a major cause of family limitation.[48] In 1942 with war now shifted to the south-west Pacific area, and Australian civilians subjected to the most rigid controls over all aspects of their lives under National Security Regulations, the Curtin federal government saw the matter of the Australian birthrate as a priority. The National Health and Medical Research Council (NHMRC) undertook an inquiry on behalf of the government into the declining birthrate and presented a report in 1944, which concluded that the social dislocation of wartime had an adverse affect on fertility.[49] The Department of Post-War Reconstruction responded to the issue with plans for improving the lot of mothers and wives in the post-war world, and hence encouraging reproduction. The expansion of social security benefits to include the unemployed and war widows also provided for maternity allowances, emphasising national support for the role of women as nurturers of family life through the care of infants and children.[50]

Commenting on wartime anxieties about women's increased paid employment, and the effect this might have on post-war family life, Dame Enid Lyons, MP, widow of former prime minister Joseph Lyons and mother of twelve children, was one of many public figures who spoke out against birth control. In a speech on ABC radio, for instance, she emphasised the supremacy of motherhood and argued that 'the vast majority of women will always find their greatest happiness and the readiest outlet for their talents in their traditional occupation as homemakers'.[51] In the copious public discussion about the role of women both in wartime and in peace, and their competing duties as workers and as mothers, there was little mention of the key issue that had occupied such debates in World War I: that of infant mortality. For by the mid-20th century the improved health of babies, and access to antenatal and postnatal care for mothers, were seen as a triumph at national and local levels.

2.10 Baby Health Centre, East Brunswick, Vic., built c. 1940

Throughout the post-war decades baby health centres were built in considerable numbers as they catered for the expanding suburban development taking place in Australian cities and in regional towns. Sheard estimates that, in Victoria alone, between fifteen and thirty baby health centres were established each year during the 1960s.[52] Mobile services continued to operate for isolated women living in remote and rural Australia, with special vehicles and caravans travelling outback roads to provide an essential point of contact for Australian women and their children. Recent theories on child development were integrated into the advice offered. There was a growing emphasis in the 1970s, for instance, on 'the mental health aspects of the mother child relationship' with training of infant welfare sisters now including child psychology, knowledge that was important for assisting both rural and urban families.[53]

By the post-war decades, the practice of placing a civic front on an otherwise domestic building, such as at the West Brunswick Baby Health Centre (1932) or the South Perth Infant Welfare Centre (c. 1950), was well established. The choice of architectural language continued to echo the domestic, albeit with the flatter skillion pitches fashionable in the late 1950s and 1960s. These later buildings did not need to incorporate decidedly civic elements in their designs: the broad adoption of modernism in Australian architecture from the 1950s shifted easily between the domestic, institutional and commercial with only minor distinctions. The many small, functional cream brick structures that were being built in new suburbs and country towns to provide infant welfare services were socially significant, if architecturally undistinguished and 'ordinary'.[54] Every so often an architect would produce a design that moved firmly away from the predominant domestic style and create more interesting

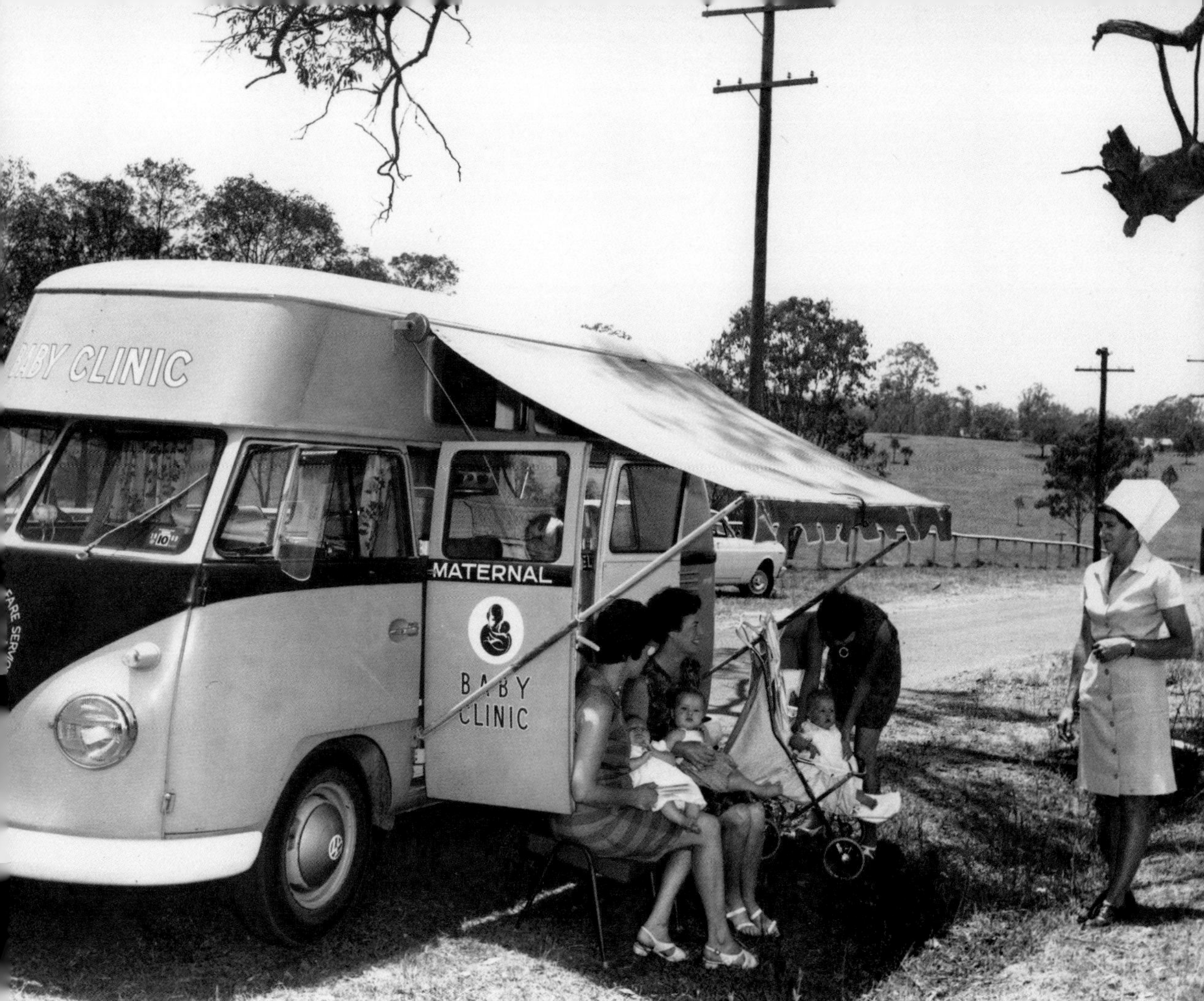

2.11 Mobile baby clinic van, Qld 1968

designs for infant welfare centres. These included the sinuously curved facility at Earlwood, Sydney, attached to the local library, by Davey & Brindley in 1952; the (third) Olive Phillips combined infant welfare centre and preschool at Beaumaris, Victoria, by David Godsell (1975), which was a bush-hammered, concrete, pyramidal-roofed structure with a central sky-lit waiting area; and the spiral-planned infant welfare centre at Bentley, a south-eastern suburb of Perth, by Bill Kierath (c. 1965). This shift away from the overtly domestic indicated that such services no longer needed to insinuate themselves into the community fabric, but could stand in their own right as recognised and valued local institutions.

This slow integration, then benign institutionalisation, of infant welfare services into the Australian urban landscape is perhaps best demonstrated by the facilities created in what is now the municipality of Moreland, encompassing the older municipal councils of Brunswick and Coburg in Melbourne.

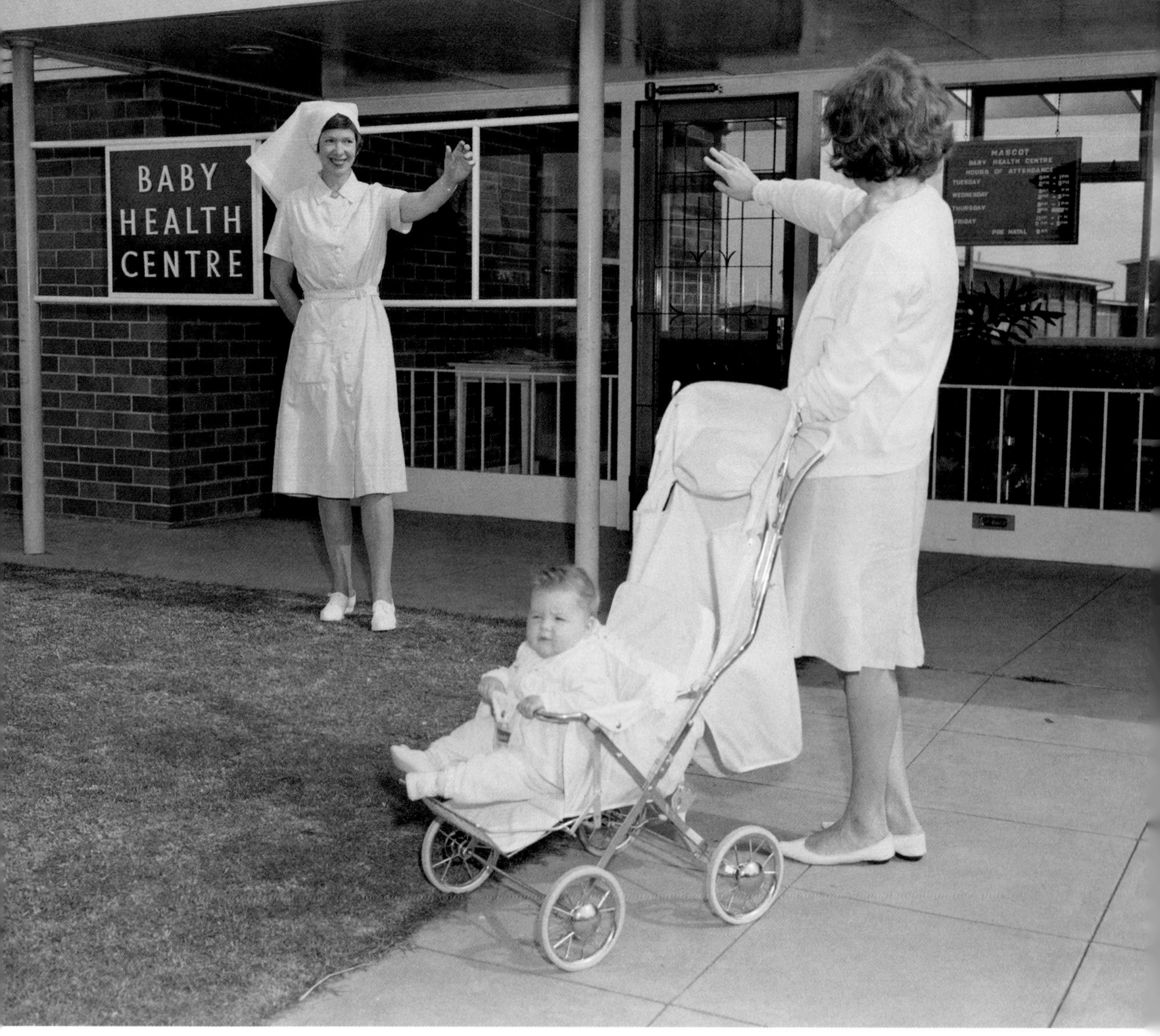

2.12 Jean Coates Memorial Baby Health Centre, Mascot, NSW 1946

Traditionally a working-class area, it had a long history in the municipal provision of services to working mothers with infants and young children, with purpose-built creches and kindergartens having been established in the early decades of the 20th century. Similarly, infant welfare services were an important part of supporting and educating local mothers, with the Truby King Rooms established in Coburg from 1919, and a purpose-built infant welfare centre created in 1926 that deliberately set about creating 'home-like' exterior and interior settings that overtly referenced the vernacular domestic architecture of the period. Its location – on municipal land at the rear of the council offices – was driven more by the availability of land rather than a careful co-location of municipal services (something that would be seen later as eminently desirable in the model community centre).

However, by the early 1940s, the East and West Brunswick infant welfare centres wore their domesticity more awkwardly. Both structures were firmly embedded in the ordinary suburban streetscape, and were consciously placed close to their constituents and thus distant from other municipal services. Their designs combined clearly civic elements, which demonstrated a degree of authority and separation from ordinary housing, yet used domestic garden settings, scale and familiar forms such as tiled pitched roofs. Both, in different ways, used formal design elements to indicate their distinction from their domestic surrounds. At West Brunswick, the infant welfare centre featured a symmetrical front with decorative screen, while the East Brunswick centre (figure 2.10) was distinguished by the prominent use of a council seal, and exaggerated bow front (for pram parking) and the announcement of the building's purpose through modern lettering. By the 1970s, when another Brunswick baby health centre was built in Albion Street, the need for domestic references in architectural design was completely obsolete. The centre was a small, unassuming, dark brown brick structure, with a flat roof: although it included some garden planting, there was no attempt to set the building back from its boundaries. Instead, the Albion Street centre directly addressed the street with minimal transitional space. Its design spoke of a small institutional building, without particular architectural significance, with nothing to prove or proclaim. Such was the success of infant welfare services by this time, that the buildings where they were located had become utterly benign in architectural intent, and the public support they provided for baby, child and maternal care had become an accepted component of the modern Australian community.

EARLY LEARNING: THE MODERN KINDERGARTEN

David Nichols and Philip Goad

The rise of the kindergarten in Australia has many parallels with that of the infant welfare centre, not least because both institutions developed over a similar time period. Additionally, both were initially conceived as a remedial experience for poor and otherwise disadvantaged children, and both were based upon the professionalisation of child-rearing, which included concerted efforts to replace mothers' and extended families' traditional knowledge with scientific method. The kindergarten's evolution

3.1 a. Bowden Free Kindergarten, SA 1928 **b.** Kindergarten, Casterton, Vic. 1954
c. Bendigo Kindergarten, New Creche and Day Minding Centre, Rosalind Park, Vic. 1957

from ad hoc or makeshift to purpose-built premises which served as a marker of a civilised and progressive community, whether suburban or rural-regional, also mirrors the development of the infant welfare centre. By the 1960s, the kindergarten experience was close to becoming as ubiquitous to conventional education in Australia as tertiary education would be in the 1980s and 1990s. As early as the 1930s, modern kindergarten buildings were recognisable in both form and siting as structures exclusively designated for preschool use.

'Foundation stones for the building of a future nation': The early Australian kindergarten[1]

Peter Spearritt writes that the kindergarten movement in Australia developed in the late 19th century as 'part of the growing concern among the middle and upper classes with the inner city slums'.[2] Connections can therefore be drawn between the push for kindergartens and other fields, such as the town planning movement. Women educators and philanthropists of both sexes were especially associated with the idea of kindergarten education as a physical answer to the plight of 'slum children' and 'as a tool for urban social reform'.[3] Fears of children's physical and moral safety were an aspect of this, and Australian educators were impressed by the principles of German educator Friedrich Froebel (1782–1852) emphasising responsibility, and creative and instructional play which did not exert 'undue strain upon the young mind'.[4] 'Kindergarteners' were committed to the concept of children finding natural growth within a stable and idealised learning environment. It was not, however, until 1895 with the formation of the Kindergarten Union of New South Wales in Sydney that the concept of kindergartens in discrete buildings was considered. The first 'free kindergarten' in Australia opened in May 1896 in

3.1 d. Kindergarten, Rose Park, SA 1958 **e.** Kindergarten, Whale Beach, NSW 1958 **f.** Darlington Kindergarten, WA 1969

Woolloomooloo, one of inner Sydney's slums, followed soon after by similar establishments in Newtown and Surry Hills.

By the end of the first decade of the 20th century, kindergartens had been established in all Australian capitals. They were depicted as both social levers and as civilising influences: an anonymous writer to the Adelaide *Advertiser* observed that kindergarten education changed its attendees for the better:

> Children who formerly were greedy, selfish and rough, with little or no self-control, are now sharing all with their fellows, and even sacrificing personal pleasures for the happiness and welfare of the younger and weaker children ... Surely such training is for the good of the nation.[5]

Typically, kindergartens were established in poorer areas by philanthropically or religiously motivated pillars of society. Community need would then be identified in similar areas and a network would form, often in tandem with a training institution for teachers.

Each capital city's kindergarten story is different, though in all capitals kindergartens were popularised and propagated via a Free Kindergartens association or union. Brisbane's case is particularly interesting for its origins as part of a projected suite of facilities. The kindergarten which grew from the Brisbane Institute of Social Service was conceived and facilitated by an American Congregational minister, Loyal Wirt, and his ally Celia Cooper. Operations began in a disused tobacco factory in Fortitude Valley. Beginning with a kindergarten and creche, Wirt envisaged the building's use growing to encompass functions commensurate with a modern community centre, including a reading room, swimming pool, gymnasium and boys' and girls' clubs.[6] Operating from 7 am to 6 pm each weekday, the primary purpose of this kindergarten – and its various branches in other deprived areas of the city – was to assist working mothers by caring for their children during business hours. In line with 'free kindergarten' philosophy, no fees were charged, and notable practitioners within the city gave assistance on a voluntary basis. When Queensland's Creche and Kindergarten Association broke with the Institute in 1910, new branches were opened in a loaned shop front and, more commonly, in school grounds and church halls. In subsequent years the conversion of cottages and houses for use as creches and/or kindergartens (usually co-located) was de rigueur for the Association. In 1915 architects Hall and Dods were engaged to design the first purpose-built of the Assocation's kindergartens at Paddington.[7] Though Robin Dods' 'commitment to the Arts and Crafts', as noted by Harriet Edquist,[8] is evident in this structure, it might also be regarded, superficially at least, as a modified cottage design (figure 3.2).

Kindergarten organisations proceeded apace in all state capitals. Perth's Pier Street Kindergarten serves as a valid example of the everyday trials of an early kindergarten. Pier Street's earliest surviving minute book begins with meeting notes from May 1914: it had opened exactly two years previously and had already expanded its operations to encompass a training centre. We can glean much from discussions, at Pier Street's first meeting, about piano tuning, the need to fix the building's roof, the purchase of a seesaw, and the necessity of regular doctor's visits.[9] The kindergarten was held in an adapted house owned by

3.2 Paddington Kindergarten, Qld 1915

the Railway Department, and its committee was clearly troubled by continual requirements for repairs or renovations such as the installation of skylights. Electric light was installed in April 1919 (including in the passage, the office, kitchen, and an iron construction known as the 'circle room', because one was painted on the floor)[10] and further improvements – such as the gravelling of the backyard and the calcimining of interior walls – were pursued.

Of Pier Street Kindergarten's clientele little is recorded. A 1923 note from the director concerning the need for 'Montessori steps' – presumably 'a low circular staircase' used to teach children to ascend stairs in the 'proper method'[11] – suggests that moral and mental development was her chief concern in the treatment of her small charges. She wrote that it was via these steps that 'the children gain balance and poise … so essential for our new children before we can hope for group discipline'.[12] There is also some indication that cultural assimilation was an issue within the kindergarten. The 'Greek mothers' who assisted in kindergarten field trips would, however, 'not come' to meetings 'because they do not speak English'. Other parents were merely 'very careless &

casual'. Instead, Pier Street looked to formally organised volunteer groups for aid and the Ugly Men's Association, a quirkily named charitable body founded in 1917 in Perth and principally devoted to children's welfare, was valued in this regard. The Association provided both practical help – such as repairs and building work and donations of toys – and advocated on kindergartens' behalf, as it did in 1921:

> The Ugly Men spoke to the Railway people about the back fence with the result that we have a new dividing fence betweenus & Mrs Hard with a gate instead of the broken fence. The worst of the tin has been removed with the old fence so I expect I will have to be content.[13]

The strains of renovating a pre-existing building for use as a kindergarten clearly concerned the staff at Pier Street. The growth of a kindergarten building style at this time was still undeveloped.

Early kindergartens typically demonstrated the validity and importance of their work through the training of their charges' minds and bodies. Advocates, such as the Kindergarten Union of South Australia's director, Lillian de Lissa, were fond of the alliterative dictum of 'head, heart and hand' in regard to kindergarten teaching and as opposed to rote learning and the 'three Rs'. The role of kindergartens in shaping the future of the nation was at the forefront. The simultaneous rise of the 'Little Citizen'in the early 20th century is telling. This notion – its popularity coming perhaps from the title of a 1904 British novel[14] – had its own League (whose members had 'three Ss', promising to grow 'straight, strong and springy')[15] and lent its name to kindergartens in North Adelaide and East Perth.[16] Kindergarteners saw their message as a natural fit with progressive organisations of the early 20th century. The Brisbane Association exhibited a model of a creche and kindergarten at the Second Australian Town Planning Conference and Exhibition, held in Brisbane in 1918. Demonstrations of kindergarten procedure and practice were also prepared for the Royal Brisbane Exhibition and the Children's Welfare Conference.[17] Part of the Pier Street Kindergarten director's concern over the Montessori steps was their projected use in a demonstration in Perth Town Hall.

During the 1920s and 1930s, the number of kindergartens continued to grow. They were increasingly recognised as a valid cause for the involvement of middle and upper class women as organisers, and as an appropriate career choice for women, perhaps in the years before marriage. Significant regional centres, particularly socially progressive primary production areas such as Mildura and Broken Hill, began to run kindergarten sessions and create identified spaces to hold them.

Government interest and intervention

Early kindergarten services largely pertained to children of working-class parents, particularly when mothers worked as well as, or in the absence of, fathers. Health was always an adjunct part of this concern, and disease, poor hygiene and sub-standard housing conditions continued to be of great concern to Australian reformers in the period following World War I. Over time, kindergarten bodies were able to take steps to address these issues. From 1927, the Free Kindergarten Holiday Home and Playroom at what is now known as Forest Hills, near Melbourne, provided holiday accommodation in a bush setting for slum children.[18] In 1936 the Melbourne society architect Marcus Martin provided a new, larger and more modern building for the Home. Fresh air, good food, bucolic surroundings (the 'healthy tang of gum leaves')[19] and a large hip-roofed cottage-styled building of suitably domestic appearance were the ingredients for this experience of a healthy environment.[20]

Apparent symptoms of a declining human species or race were occasionally linked to social and medical theories concerning eugenics and race purity. These concerns were the first sign of a move towards recognition of the kindergarten's value for all classes.

Concern for health had architectural implications, and was often directly associated with the unadorned, hygienic forms of the new architecture connected with the development of the modern hospital, the sanatorium and sun-seeking, stripped-down forms of new urban housing estates. In terms of buildings and children, health and education were combined to provide new and integrated environmental experiences devoted to wellbeing. International inter-war examples include the open-air schools of Johannes Duiker in Holland and Richard Neutra in the United States, the Italian *colonie*, health and education camps like Studio Architetti Belgioioso's *Colonia Elioterapica*, Bianchi Village, Italy (1938)[21] and the kindergarten learning environments created by experimental educators such as American William Curry in association with his architect William Lescaze.[22]

Australia's National Health and Medical Research Council (NHMRC) was created in 1936, and met for the first time early the following year. Here, Minister for Health, former prime minister and honorary 'Ugly Man',[23] WM Hughes, argued for detailed attention to be given to the care of the infant and the growing child of preschool age. The meeting passed a motion directing the attention of the Commonwealth and state governments in Australia to 'serious neglect in adequate supervision of the bodily development of children before and during school age'.[24] It recommended that the whole system of health supervision of children should be immediately reviewed. The NHMRC's second session in June 1937 affirmed this position, but it was at the third session

3.3 JHL Cumpston & CM Heinig's *Pre-School Centres in Australia*, published by the Commonwealth Department of Health 1945

in November 1937, that a memorandum from the medical officer of the Free Kindergarten Union of Victoria, Dr Vera Scantlebury Brown, recommended three fundamental objectives. They were the extension of infant welfare activities to include attention to the preschool child, a model Nursery-Kindergarten Demonstration Centre and research into the child's needs, especially nutrition, for full health development.

The Australian government (led by Joseph Lyons, himself a father of twelve) responded positively and agreed to establish a model demonstration centre for childcare and guidance in each of the nation's state capitals. These would become the incentive and inspiration for kindergarten development for decades to come, and provided a typological basis for the post-war rise in kindergarten construction in new suburbs of all the capital cities and in regional country centres. Each centre was to be completely equipped and furnished and salaries for a full staff and maintenance costs were to be met for five years. The Commonwealth also agreed, for the first time, to fund the position of a Federal Education Officer and, in July 1938, Christine M Heinig was appointed. American-born Heinig was already a key figure in establishing preschool education as a professional discipline in Australia. She had been director of the nursery school at Columbia University between 1928 and 1935, when the Melbourne Kindergarten Training College invited her to become its principal and assist in reshaping its curriculum.[25] During 1937, she had joined with the Commonwealth Department of Health to prepare plans for a preschool parent education program and in doing so visited each of the states, working closely with Dr JHL Cumpston, director-general of the Department of Health.[26]

The Commonwealth required an organisation to establish and operate the six demonstration and research centres. It called upon the recently formed Australian Association for Pre-School Child Development (AAPSCD) to undertake the task. Its president, Ada Mary a'Beckett, was also president of the Free Kindergarten Union of Victoria.[27] In conjunction with the state kindergarten unions (each of which formed a local Child Centre Committee), the AAPSCD supervised the erection of buildings and the equipping and staffing of the child centres. The educational and medical schemes of the centres were the responsibility of Heinig as the Federal Education Officer and the Federal Medical Officer, Dr FW Clements, then director of the Australian Institute of Anatomy.

The Commonwealth government's decision to establish the six demonstration centres gave institutional form to the fundamental shift taking place within contemporary preschool educational philosophy in 1930s Australia.[28] Kindergarten educators would now not only supplement Froebel's rich garden of learning through play with philanthropic goals of moral hygiene and exposure to middle-class values, but also overlay the idea of childhood as something that could be charted, mapped and scientifically studied. As Gahan notes, this shift to child-study arose from a number of sources, from Gesell's work on developmental 'maturation' at the University of Chicago Nursery School, from Susan Isaacs' observational studies of young British children's social and emotional development, from John Dewey's research on project-based learning at his Chicago school and from Sigmund Freud's psychoanalytic work that emphasised the importance of early childhood as critical to an adult's social and emotional future.[29] The physical and emotional states of the young child could be recorded to assist parents and educators to understand the development of their child as a maturing organism. The charting and examination of the physical, social, emotional and intellectual progress of preschool children became orthodox. At the new centres, for example, a complete set of case records was kept for each child and there was a Home School Agreement which parents signed so that each centre could 'study, over a period of time, the normal growth and development of the children enrolled'.[30] Cumpston and Heinig were to say of this project:

> Education and health are both involved; body and mind are, in equal value, the raw material on which we are to work ... The child is ... to receive care and instruction, and its bodily nutrition, growth, and development are to be studied and directed – in short we are not mechanists or psychologists, nor doctors or teachers – but both. The child is not two things, body and mind, but one thing – a growing child.[31]

The Lady Gowrie child centres

Each of the six new centres was named in honour of Lady Gowrie, wife of the Governor-General.[32] During her husband's term as Governor of South Australia (1928–34), she had become actively involved in the kindergarten movement in Adelaide at a time when kindergartens in badly affected industrial suburbs were struggling with resources, poor diet and parlous living conditions. As was usual, the wife of the governor was invited to become patroness of South Australia's Kindergarten Union and in that position Lady Hore-Ruthven (as she was then) was active in political persuasion and raising finance. In 1933 she took a personal interest in the establishment of a kindergarten in Port Adelaide, a particularly economically afflicted district. She was also instrumental in the 1936 conference in Adelaide on the occasion of the Centenary of South Australia which discussed 'Kindergarten matters' and which ultimately led to an interstate Kindergarten Conference in Melbourne in July 1938 and the formation of the AAPSCD.[33] Between 1939 and 1940, Lady Gowrie officially opened each new centre as it was completed.[34]

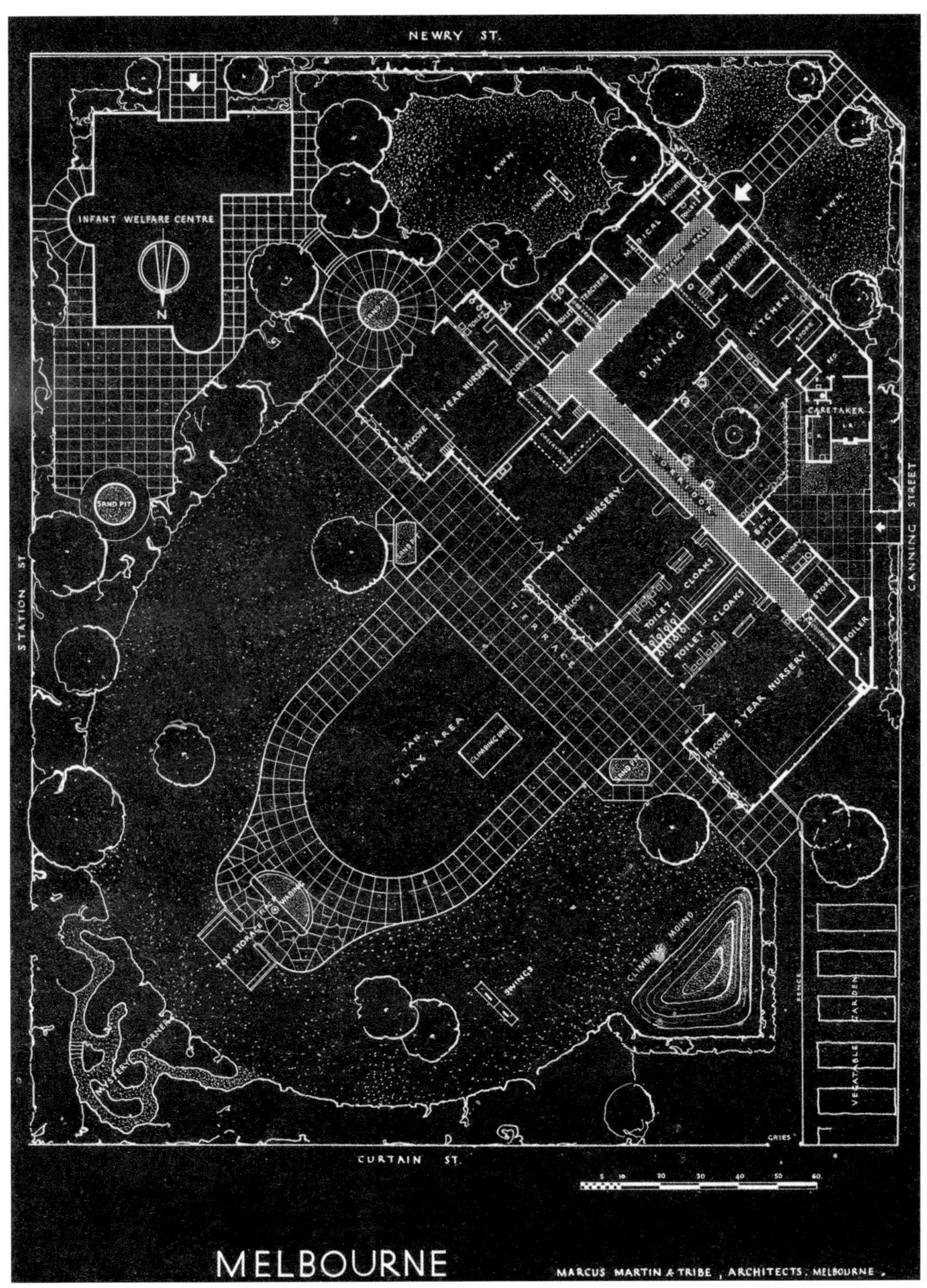

3.4 Plan, Lady Gowrie Child Centre, Carlton, Vic. 1939–40

Their designs were derived from the same basic plan developed by Marcus Martin in association with Heinig and Cumpston, with locally chosen architects in each state adapting Martin's basic model or 'type plan' to local site, climate and construction practices.[35] The choice of architect was almost certainly based on personal connections with each local house committee.[36] Architects outside Melbourne were Fowell, McConnel & Mansfield in Sydney; F Kenneth Milne in association with RV Boehm & LC Dawkins in Adelaide; Hutchison & Walker in Hobart; AE Brooks and AH Job in Brisbane; and Oldham, Boas & Ednie Brown in Perth.[37] Thus it was that six buildings of different character but the same fundamental plan emerged.

The choice of Martin as architect for the prototype centre was a logical one. He had been involved in kindergarten design since 1923 and had an association with the Yooralla Hospital School's Free Kindergarten in Pelham Street, Carlton.[38] From 1930 he undertook work for the Free Kindergarten Society of Victoria (FKSV), assuming the unofficial position as permanent FKSV architect after the death of J Edmund Burke during the completion of his Dame Nellie Melba Free Kindergarten in Richmond. Martin's wife was associated with the Society's wealthy female philanthropists[39] and he also had family connections with Ada Mary a'Beckett. Another notable project was the new Baby Rooms for the Renown Free Kindergarten, Howard Street, Prahran (1937–38), a modest, detached, brick and timber building complementing earlier buildings on the site that consisted of a pantry, lavatories, cloakroom, and two children's rooms with large windows to the north and east, allowing generous sunlight penetration. Joining Martin in practice in 1938 was Horace J Tribe who had returned to Melbourne from the Sydney office of Stephenson & Turner where he had been a senior architect. Under the name Marcus Martin and Tribe, the firm was responsible for the first Lady Gowrie Child Centre in Newry Street, Carlton. In 1941, the firm closed for World War II,[40] re-opened in 1945, and between 1946 and 1949 continued as Martin & Tribe, specialising in kindergarten design.[41] Tribe left the firm to establish and develop his own practice as a kindergarten specialist – he produced numerous buildings for the FKSU in the 1950s – trading on his experience in 'pre-school and preventative health services'. In the 1950s he was one of Victoria's leading kindergarten designers.[42]

Location and siting

A key principle of each Gowrie design was its location in an area with small building allotments and low-rental houses and/or an industrial and working-class inner suburb: generally, areas considered 'slums'. This had been, of course, the norm for kindergarten siting for almost four decades. Such locations were determined by the density of child population in a given area and where the conditions of a kindergarten might, through environmental experience, transform the development of a child's health, education and wellbeing. The next step was to locate each centre 'in the heart ofits community' close to schools paralleling Clarence Perry's neighbourhood unit concept and, 'to save the energy of the mothers', within half a mile of walking distance.

The first Lady Gowrie centre was located in inner-city Carlton – the 'centre of a crowded industrial area, where its services will be appreciated by a large population'[43] – on a clear site surrounded by streets on four sides and on the same site as a new (council-operated) infant welfare centre. Across Canning Street was the parkland of Curtain Square, and the Lee Street Primary School was a block away to the south. The site plan (figure 3.4) shows the building oriented deliberately to the north-east to maximise sun penetration, while the infant welfare centre on the corner of Newry and Station streets conforms in its siting to the orthogonal layout of the surrounding streets.

Each nursery room also had its requisite 'observation post' where parents, students and research workers could watch the children unobserved to see how they reacted to specialised training.

The Melbourne City Council had made the land available on a 25-year lease, and the centre was designed to accommodate 100 children, aged eighteen months to six years, for five full days a week. Its colour scheme was sunshine yellow and dull blue against grey fibro-cement walls and roofing. The construction was simple: timber posts and timber trusses with infill panels of window frames and stud walling bolted to the concrete floor slab.[44] Inside was a dining room and three large nurseries for two-, three- and four-year-olds, the first in a colour scheme of primrose against the warm, biscuit-coloured walls of insulated caneboard (caneite), the second in turquoise blue and the third in 'patina green'. Each nursery had its own cloakroom, quiet corner, shelves for toys, and a low platform for special play. Each nursery room also had its requisite 'observation post' where parents, students and research workers could watch the children unobserved to see how they reacted to specialised training. Each nursery had curtains with painted designs that had been executed by students of the Kindergarten Training College and which depicted fish and sea animals, and Australian flora and fauna. Even the centre's china bore designs of kangaroos and wallabies. The concrete slab floors were sheeted in linoleum. Large accordion doors folded back to give uninterrupted access and at the same level between inside and out (figure 3.5). Other spaces in the centre included bathrooms, staffrooms and offices and a model kitchen, also decorated in 'patina green'.[45]

3.5 Folding doors from the three-year-old nursery open onto outdoor learning and play spaces at the Lady Gowrie Child Centre, Carlton, Vic. 1939–40

The style of the Martin & Tribe building was resolutely understated. In 1947, Robin Boyd was to describe it as a 'significant deviation' in the firm's work, which was more commonly associated with large, expensive houses in Toorak and South Yarra that were styled in Martin's progressive modern Georgian idiom to find favour among Melbourne's wealthy society patrons.[46] Yet Boyd approved wholeheartedly of the Lady Gowrie centre's architecture, describing it as a non-residential example of the 'Victorian Type', his personal term for a regional modernism in post-war Victoria:

> The carefully refined period styling of the big houses disappeared in a simple sweep of gable and glass. The planning was free and wide open. The details were light and without any affectation. The exotic had passed to the exoteric values of the Victorian Type.[47]

In the other capital cities, similar locations were chosen. The Sydney centre was a two-storey building between parkland and a newly built slum clearing housing estate in Sydney's poorest suburb, Erskineville.[48] The ground floor was occupied by the preschool, medical office, dining room and kitchen, with a community hall on the first floor. It was anticipated that this building, more substantial than those in the other states, would become the nucleus of community activities with a playground for older children developed on adjacent parkland. Other major sports facilities including a football ground and bowling club were located nearby.

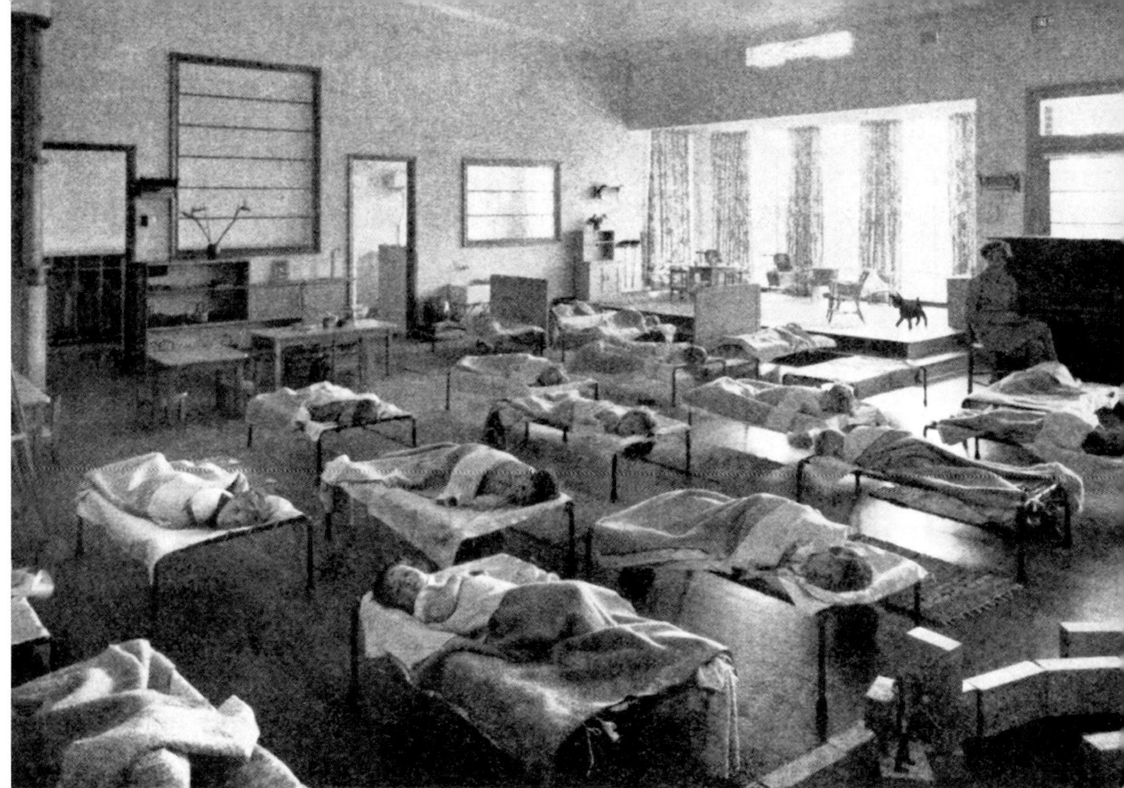

3.6 Children asleep in the three-year-old nursery, Lady Gowrie Child Centre, Thebarton, SA 1940

In Perth, the centre's site in Victoria Park East sat next to a large public reserve on which primary and high school pupils from the adjacent large public school carried out their physical education exercises. In Brisbane, the centre in Fortitude Valley had the Brisbane Public Playground next door and the state's Infant Welfare Headquarters and Training School on the site behind. The Adelaide and Hobart centres in working-class Thebarton and Battery Point were not so fortunate in their situation, having no immediate community functions or close public reserves.

Each centre was designed to accommodate 100 children in a daily program which commonly began at 9 am and continued until 2.30 pm. This five-hour program required a meal to be served so each centre needed a dining room and extensive kitchen facilities. In addition to the classrooms, there was an administration unit that comprised a secretary's office, medical unit, social worker's unit, parents' room and staffrooms. Cumpston and Heinig cited four cardinal features which formed the basis of all centre designs: 1. In the playrooms, 35 square feet (3.25 square metres) was to be allowed for each child;[49] 2. The classrooms had to have northern light; 3. The building had to be designed around the functions of the centre and not be adapted to a preconceived architectural design – in other words, functionalist design principles were to be applied; and 4. The playroom was to open directly onto the playground and be on the same ground level.[50]

3.7 The sunny interior of the Robert Cochrane Kindergarten, Auburn, Vic. 1951

In Australia, a north-east aspect gains optimum sunlight, thus it was a requirement that each centre have its classrooms facing north-east. The only exceptions to this rule were in Sydney where the site did not permit any other orientation as the building had to conform to the general pattern of the adjoining housing scheme and in Hobart where, because of its southerly longitude, an almost true north aspect was better than north-eastern. The classrooms were the largest areas in the bulk of each building, and all had to face north-east and open onto playgrounds (also to the north), the area of which was calculated on a basis of 75 square feet (6.96 square metres) of playground space per child as a minimum. The general shape of each building and its external space was therefore largely predetermined. A typology developed with a linear block of three north-facing classrooms with the entry, administration unit, kitchen and dining room behind to the south. Each classroom was planned to be one open space with a large window area, a glazed partition and door between the classroom and lavatory annexe, an observation booth, and a raised platform alcove (figure 3.6). The lavatory annexe had to be accessible from and close to the classroom and also have direct access to the playground.

A feature which was not replicated in conventional post-war kindergartens following the Lady Gowrie centres was the observation booth. Generally, this was located at the southern edge or corner of the classroom, was to be inconspicuous, sound-proofed and well ventilated, but to command a view of the entire classroom. The booth was to be large enough to contain five people

3.8 Jack and Jill Kindergarten, Beaumaris, Vic. 1958

seated and the floor level was to be raised above that of the classroom to give greater visibility of the classroom. Fine wire gauze was used for the observation booth windows. This permitted vision from within but prevented children from seeing the booth's occupants. Entrance to the booth was from outside the classroom. The raised platforms were ideally located in alcoves to give children opportunities to play somewhat separately from the larger group. In the two-year-old classroom, where the children constantly used larger muscles, the floor levels of the platforms were built 4–5 feet (1.2–1.5 metres) above the classroom floor. Steps and slides led down from these platforms and the space underneath formed storage for stretcher cots. These platforms or balconies could be used for quieter activities of drawing, painting and nature study. In the three- and four-year-old rooms, the platforms were lower, one or two steps above the main floor. They could still be used as a differentiating space within the larger space of the classroom, often becoming a stage, a place for undisturbed play separate from the larger group, or a gallery from which to observe activities in the larger classroom space.

Cumpston and Heinig had advice on all aspects of the building, interior finishes and nursery equipment. They recommended that each centre's internal walls, for example, be sheeted in sound-absorbing material such as caneite which might also extend to the ceilings, though 'perfatile', a sound-absorbent plasterboard, was also recommended. From children's height level to floor, walls were to be painted in semi-gloss washable paint or a dado of waxed natural timber to match the floor. Floors were to be timber or sheeted in linoleum or rubber. Each classroom was to have double doors opening directly onto the playground and at the same level.

When the buildings were being planned in 1939, it was recognised that educational facilities would be obsolete within twenty years and as a consequence brick was not used for the centre buildings unless local council policy demanded it.[51] Wartime conditions also contributed a no-nonsense pragmatism to the visual appearance of each centre. The architectural style of all the Lady Gowrie child centres, like the Melbourne example, was unassuming, even unremarkable, reflecting the development of a relatively new functional type for Australia. As Marcus Martin observed:

> The plan should be essentially functional in character, the conception of which should result in a building with a definite appeal, for the psychological effect on the child mind by immediate surroundings is far reaching. Economy in building will as a rule be essential, therefore a structure that can be quickly erected, and materials that will be adaptable to alteration and addition are desirable.[52]

The architecture of the Lady Gowrie centres was thus not determined necessarily to mimic any specific domestic image, or take on any overt sense of civic form. There was a sense of everydayness about the modesty of these buildings. Indeed, their unpretentious pragmatism speaks more of wartime austerity than the architectural pretensions of their designers. Additionally, none of the designers were necessarily wedded to the progressive abstract forms of European modernism. Society and philanthropic connections to kindergarten activities in each capital city meant that the choice of architects was inevitably connected to the conservative domestic sphere within which those philanthropists moved.

However, the programmatic and planning innovations of the Lady Gowrie child centres were to have national impact. As demonstration centres, the kindergartens received large numbers of visitors. In 1952, for example, the number of annual visitors to the Melbourne centre was 800, in Hobart 250.[53] Visitors ranged from students of education, psychology and medicine to representatives of the Country Women's Association (CWA), and parents from the city, suburbs and country interested in establishing a preschool centre in their own districts. The plan form as developed by Martin was to have national application after World War II, and Cumpston and Heinig's *Pre-School Centres in Australia* was to become a standard handbook for post-war kindergarten design.

Kindergartens for all?

What had begun in the early years of the 20th century as a tool for urban social reform aimed at the working class, through national government initiative became a model admired, envied and desired by the middle class. Whereas the sending of one's children to kindergarten had been a sign of working-class status before World War II, organised and professionally run preschool education came to be seen by many as the standard for all levels of Australian society from mid-century. This was so, notwithstanding the fact that the key components of a kindergarten education varied between institutions[54] and kindergarten remained a non-compulsory option – and, therefore, governments were not obliged to provide the service. Communities, councils and children were brought together via new kindergarten buildings – which often served to signify the value of all three to suburban or regional places.

It is clear that the Lady Gowrie centres had a wide-ranging impact on the design and form of kindergartens. They also signify a change in attitude towards the kindergarten, which began as a remedial or developmental aid for disadvantaged children and became instead an aid to psychological and social growth for all children. Thus, a confluence of influences came into play in the post-war era, in conflict to some extent with the conventional assumption under the Menzies government that women would naturally gravitate towards a domestic, and child-oriented, environment.[55] Many new suburbanites – like their predecessors in the shorter lived inter-war suburban boom – saw themselves as frontier settlers, and were cognisant of their volition in shaping their environments. Progress associations, and other less amorphously directed bodies, were formed in nascent suburbs with a strong leaning towards provision of facilities such as schools, community centres, swimming pools and kindergartens. Thus, in 1951 the Beaumaris Parents'and Citizens' League commissioned local architect Alan Fildes, of Seabrook, Fildes and Hunt, to assist in the design of the Olive Phillips Free Kindergarten in the centre of the burgeoning suburb.[56] In 1958 another kindergarten, the Jack and Jill, opened in the area, credited to an extremely local group: the 'Fourth, Hornby, Hilton and Bolton Streets Progress Association' (figure 3.8). Similarly, in the early to mid-1950s, the *Outer Circle Mirror* reported on the successes of the North Balwyn Free Kindergarten Committee,[57] achieved in 1956 with the construction of a building known as 'The Merrell', named for its honorary secretary.[58] Balwyn was an area within the City of Camberwell, on record by 1954 as subsidising thirteen kindergartens, both church-based and 'free'.[59] This decision was not unproblematic: three years later, councillors disagreed on the best target for its subsidies, and controversially opted instead to fund a local bowling club.[60]

Socially progressive local governments and proactive communities in the mid-20th century led, unsurprisingly, to well-rounded amenity provision. Some communities, however, found local government uncooperative. Ellie V Pullen's memoir of the Ringwood Pre-School Parents Club recounts what might be seen through 21st-century eyes as a concerted battle fought on gender grounds. Ringwood's connection to the city by a regular suburban rail service since the late 19th century made it an early dormitory suburb. In the post-war years, it was a well-established suburban frontier. Pullen relates that the notion of a kindergarten was first formulated in 1944 among young mothers who frequented the tennis club, and was brought into being through discussion with the Infant Welfare Sister. Two local mothers, Rose Storey and Rose Hall, met with Vera Scantlebury Brown 'and others at the Health Department, and observed at the Lady Gowrie Child Centre in Carlton'. Pullen continues:

> A group of warm motherly ladies assisted with the weighing of babies at the Health Centre, then situated in the old Fire Brigade building, back of the Town Hall in Melbourne Street. They were kind and friendly and very helpful to new mothers, and supported the early moves to start the Play-group.[61]

Ringwood Borough Council refused to allow the women access to the town hall's 'small hall' for discussions of a kindergarten:

> There was a great degree of resistance to such a new idea, particularly from councillors and leading people in the town. It was felt that children should be home with their mothers, and not in a Play Centre, and held the mistaken idea, for many years, that such a service allowed too much freedom for the young mothers![62]

The need for a kindergarten being regarded by the group as urgent, a number of suggestions for its housing were floated, including the re-use of Nissen huts, the RSL (Returned Services League) hall, and even a building relocated from the girls' school, Fintona, were discussed.[63] Money was raised through a series of raffles and balls, usually held at Ringwood Town Hall or, for one particularly large event, in the town hall of the neighbouring City of Box Hill.[64] Council having been coerced into providing some space in Greenwood Park, Horace Tribe was engaged to plan what was now considered a fully fledged kindergarten. Pullen recalls that Tribe 'was highly respected for his early design of the first Lady Gowrie child centre in Carlton, and had at that time just completed a re-building programme on the same site after a major fire'. She adds:

3.9 Glass Street Kindergarten, Kew, Vic., built in 1956

> His ideas of laying a floating concrete raft for the floor which would then be level with the playground beyond, was new thinking, and it was questioned at great length as to value and cost. Yet today this manner of laying floors is often the norm. It was early days also, for the open plan design.[65]

The building was opened in 1955. For Ellie Pullen, this was to be the start of a long involvement in preschool advocacy and organisation, as she was first a member of the Victorian Municipal Pre School Association and then its secretary (and by her own estimate, 'driving force') for close to two decades.[66]

Other local councils were less antipathetic to education for young children, preferring to see provision of buildings as displaying both democratic values and progressive modernism. The City of Kew, a leader in the field of local infant welfare centres in the inter-war years, set its long-standing engineer, Roland Chipperfield, to construct kindergartens in its varied precincts. The Glass Street Kindergarten (figure 3.9) was combined with a civic project – the undergrounding of the small tributary, Glass Creek.[67] Chipperfield was to die in harness while working on Glass Street.

Its 'kinder committee' raised close to £2000 towards the construction of a building – by early estimates half the cost, though this would later balloon to £7000.[68] Local councillor Don Chipp was surprised by the amount raised. He felt that this was particularly unusual, in that 'most of the effort is coming from people who can never hope to benefit from the kindergarten, their children being past pre-school age'.[69] But North Kew's residents' interest in a Glass Street kindergarten was a combination of enlightened self-interest (it would add to amenity, and therefore, property values) and genuine community, and national, spirit. When the *Outer Circle Mirror* proudly trumpeted that 'Council supplied the land for this – the sixth kindergarten in the City of Kew'[70] it signified a generation's attitude change: a kindergarten was now a measure of civic and civilised values. The same issue of the *Mirror* announcing the opening of Glass Street also reported on the Windella Avenue Kindergarten Parents' Committee vow to raise £2000 towards a seventh kindergarten for Kew, adjoining Chipperfield's first infant welfare centre for the area.[71]

Chipperfield's kindergarten designs were in the spirit of the times – one or two large playrooms, multi-paned glass frontages in appropriate orientation, often on 'left-over' sites in key Kew areas. Others were ingenious and playful in creating atypical building forms. For instance, John and Phyllis Murphy designed a triangular kindergarten in Emerald, in Melbourne's far-east, in 1955,[72] and Eggleston McDonald & Secomb created a similar building two years later in the regional Victorian city of Bendigo.

The Bendigo Kindergarten, New Creche and Day Minding Centre opened in June 1957 (figure 3.1c). It was part of a civic precinct in the town's centrally located Rosalind Park, adjacent on one side to the 1936 Baby Health Centre and on the other to the post office and lawcourts. The kindergarten had arisen from the efforts of Anne Galvin, Lady Mayoress (1944–45), leading to the establishment of the first creche and day nursery in Bendigo in 1945. Her name is commemorated in the 1957 plaque recording the opening of the new kindergarten.[73] Unusually, the building straddled a creek and its equilateral triangle plan had a triangular garden at its centre, originally open to the sky and later glazed to become a skylight to the main lobby. Another innovation and departure from the normally humble materials and structure palette were the walls which were constructed as steel trusses cantilevering from rigid frames on either side of the creek and a roof supported on exposed lightweight steel trusses.[74] Infill panels were of masonry veneer with sections of floor-to-ceiling glazing with diagonal timber mullions to act not only as bracing but also to hold the glass in place. The intention was that children would enter from one side (the base of the triangle) via a ramp and use another ramp to gain access to an enclosed playground on the other side of the creek, hence the idea of the building as a bridge.

Another triangular plan appeared in architect Charles Duncan's design for the Eltham South Kindergarten (1967) in Melbourne's outer north-east. Beneath a large slate-covered, almost tetrahedral, roof topped by a beaten metal sculpture by Matcham Skipper, the playroom was roughly a hexagon in plan.[75] The contrast to Bendigo's exuberant structural expressionism – kindergarten as bridge – could not have been greater. Duncan's design was earthy, organic and owed much to the local revival of interest in the architecture of Frank Lloyd Wright in the 1960s.[76]

Comprehensive programs for regional kindergarten provision were also instituted. Jim Earle was commissioned to design kindergartens in the regional Victorian centres of Casterton (figure 3.1b) and Camperdown (1956) which also included infant welfare centre facilities. Like Marcus Martin's affiliation with the Free Kindergarten Union, this work came through both church and family connections. Earle told the magazine *Stock and Land* that 'today's pre-school centres are characterized by low lines which have a welcoming look about them. It is important to ensure that the building does not appear dominant and overpowering to a child.'[77] Earle says that both facilities adhered to his design philosophy, which he credits in part to that of his teacher at the University of Melbourne, Roy Grounds, as being to create 'inviting buildings, with some oomph about them, [that] will have a tremendous amount to give'. The Camperdown and Casterton facilities were extensive and geared specifically to regional concerns of distance and accommodation:

> They contained a kindergarten with the rooms, the playroom, the consulting room, and toilets for the children. They provided a waiting space for the mothers whose infants needed care and attention from the district nurse, they were a medical station – wherethe mother could come in and consult ... the Casterton one had a little flat for the kindergarten director, and a car storage space because the nurse often had to go out on tours to surrounding centres.[78]

Another kindergarten that, like Earle's, strove to be child-friendly in scale, was Ken Waldron's Darlington Kindergarten in the Hills area of Perth (figure 3.1f). Once again, the kindergarten was the outcome of lobbying and fundraising by locals for whom 'a kindergarten is a community project' and an opportunity to 'render some service' to the community.[79] With Darlington Kindergarten, which opened in 1969, Waldron created a space with inbuilt play areas catering specifically to a child's sense of adventure. One of Waldron's innovations was an in-ground kitchen area, which allowed any adult within the kitchen to be on the children's 'level', thus potentially supervising and/or monitoring them from something closer to their own height. Like many newly

3.10 (above and right) The polygonal form and plan of Rockingham Park Kindergarten, WA 1969

developing suburban areas of this era – the late 1960s – Darlington sought to retain natural bushland where possible, and to inculcate an appreciation and awareness of the value of the natural landscape, using existing rocks for 'playscaping'. Flora on the site has since grown extensively. Contrasting with buildings located in sculpted 'natural' bush surrounds, other kindergarten buildings in Perth at this time reflect a more European aesthetic: Tony Solarski's courtyard-oriented, Mediterranean-styled, Guildford kindergarten of 1968 is a case in point.

At the same time, in Western Australia's new suburban region of Rockingham, the architect and planner Paul Ritter was commissioned to create a building which responded to the requirements of children and community. With Ralph Hibble and their Planned Environment and Educreation Research (PEER) Institute, Ritter designed the Rockingham Park Kindergarten (1969) (figure 3.10) in the Clarke Gazzard-planned new town of Rockingham.[80] The kindergarten was based on a series of six hexagonal shapes surrounding alarger seventh at the centre, rather like an abstract flower, all unified under one roof composed of three hyperbolic paraboloids pitched upward to the centre and crowned by a 10 metre spire. In the very centre of the kindergarten was the teacher's space – a hexagonal desk. It was, as Ritter described it, 'an appealing central space with almost 360 degree vision of the many activities taking place in the part hexagonal rooms at the periphery, and further into the six verandahs, one outside each room'.[81] Like Earle, Ritter was keen for his kindergarten building to be child-friendly; prior to migrating to Australia in 1959, he had initiated a 'child's eye view' exhibition in Nottingham wherein adults could interact with home environments constructed at 2½ times the usual size, replicating a small child's experience.[82] Similarly, Ritter's choice of the hexagon

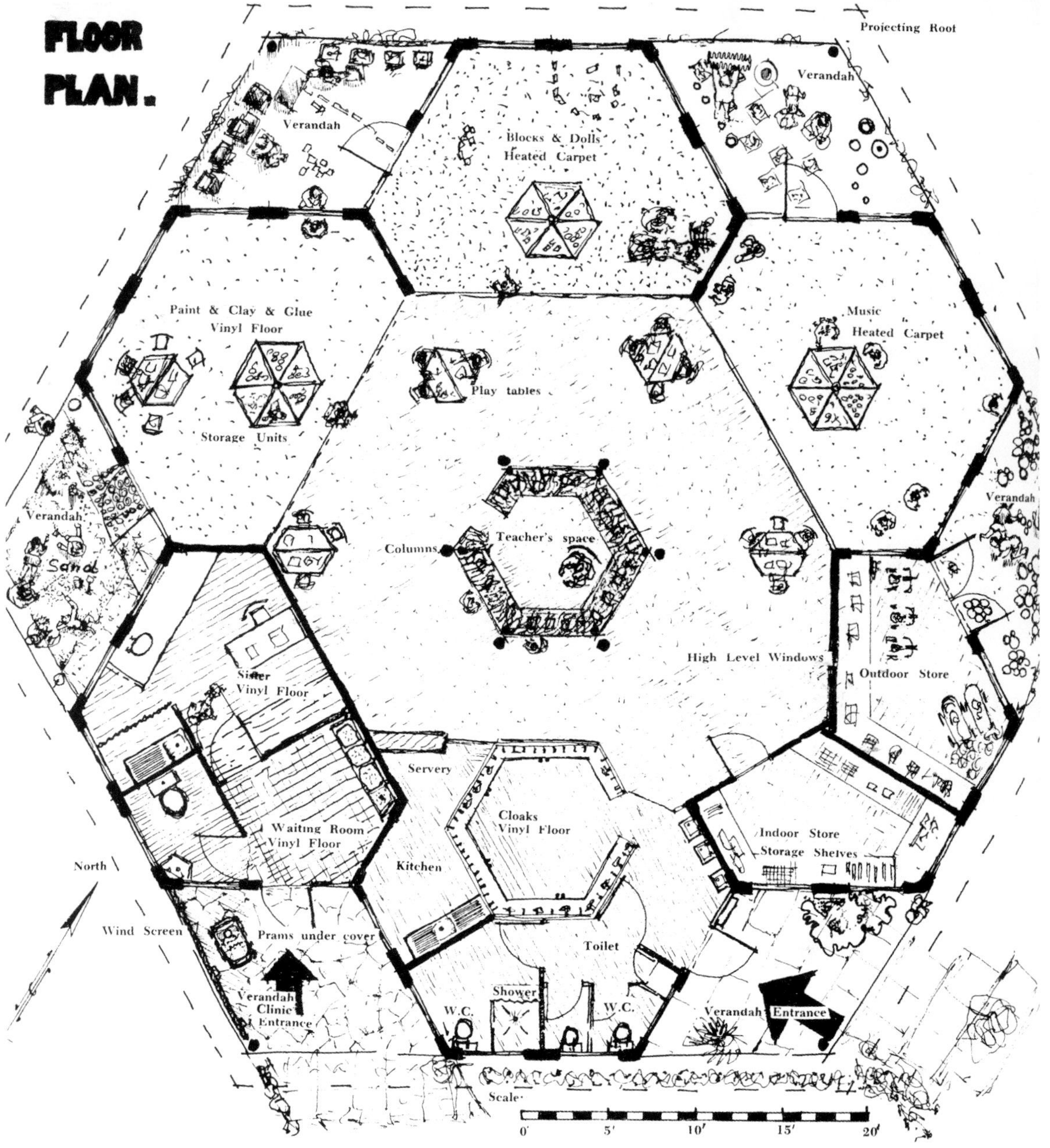

was based on his advocacy of a phenomenological approach to architecture and his deep interest in child-focused conceptions of space.[83]

In Ritter's teacher's space hexagon, Bentham's inspection principle of continued surveillance was hard at work but in service of carefully controlled, sheltering, apparently non-hierarchical enclosures of the polygon plan where walls had been decorated with Ritter and Hibble's patented 'sculpcrete' murals created by the children and where in a room labelled 'Blocks and Dolls' there was 'a great variety of little nooks, niches, shelves, slits, holes and recesses

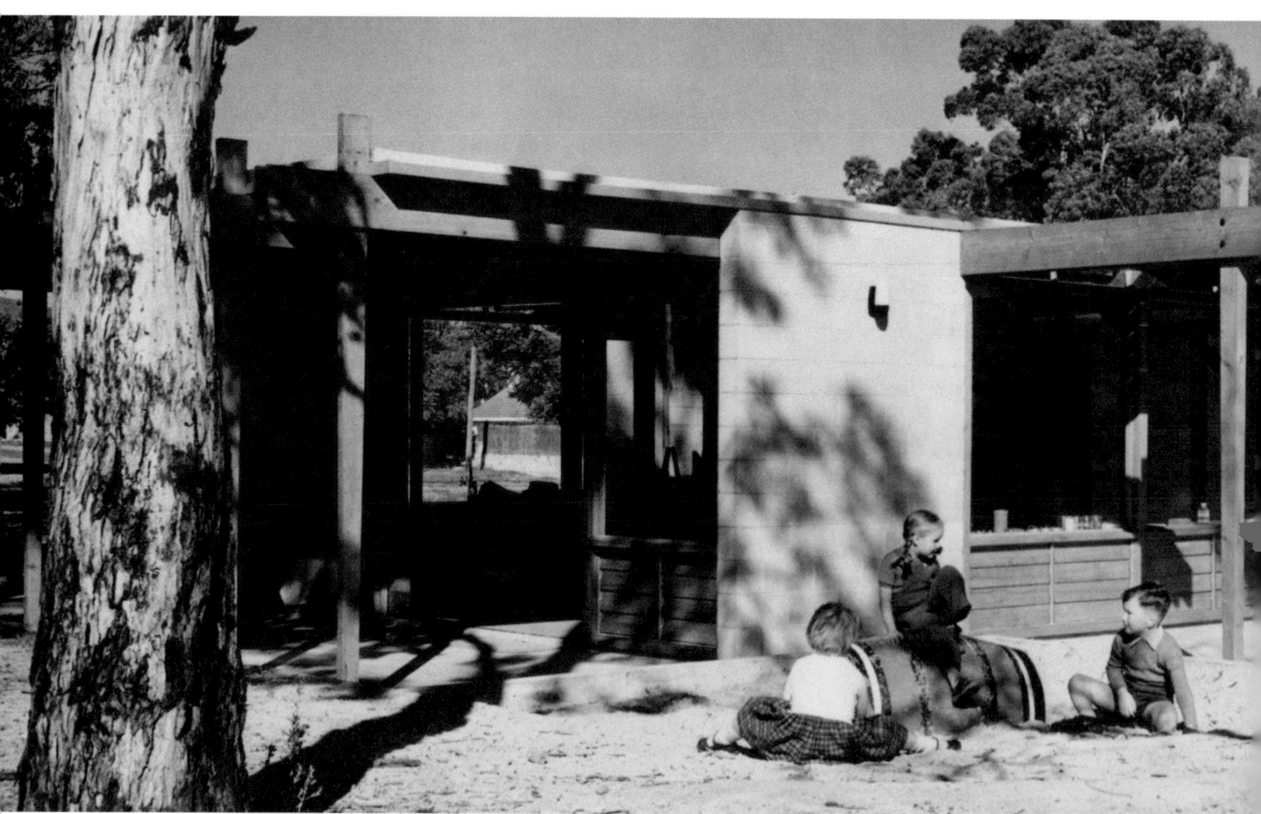

3.11 Located away from the street, the kindergarten and clinic's outdoor play space adjoined council-owned parkland at Erindale, SA 1960

below sill level which invite incorporation into their games by the children as 'aedicules, little houses'.[84] Musical instruments were built into the walls and Ritter and Hibble's friezes were a strong presence.[85] Ritter relates that while the kindergarten itself was, in part, the product of community cooperation, the subsequent relationship with authorities was unhappy, and bureaucracy, as well as unimaginative responses from the kindergarten's teachers, contributed to the decay of the building and its surrounds.[86]

Innovation in kindergarten design, it has to be said, was sporadic from the late 1950s until 1970. In South Australia, sophisticated interpretations of the typology were explored by Hassell & McConnell in a low-key, modernist, flat-roofed kindergarten at Highgate (1954), a disciplined experiment in frame and masonry that was more typical of the firm's national reputation for industrial architecture.[87] This local interest in the module was put to more sensitive use by young architect Brian Claridge (then working in the office of his father, Philip R Claridge), first in the Adelaide suburb of Rose Park where the diminutive kindergarten (1958) (figure 3.1d), located next to a scout hall and a strip of parkland, was framed in a series of steel portals that formed a north-facing veranda opening onto a garden-playground.[88] But it was Claridge's kindergarten design at Erindale (1960) (figure 3.11), within the same municipality as Rose

Park, that suggested a more humane sensibility associated with the discipline of modular design in timber and blockwork.[89] Located at the western edge of a large council reserve that included playing fields and stands of mature eucalypts, the kindergarten shared its covered entry porch with a maternal health clinic, a not uncommon pairing of co-located functions across the nation. Favoured by the generous siting, Claridge was able to orient the main kindergarten room so that it opened onto paved terraces to the north, east and south, entirely shielded from the west and the traffic of Lockwood Road. Unpainted Besser concrete block walls, naturally finished timbers, a lacquered concrete floor and exposed 'Woodtex' panels were part of the earthy materials palette. The highlight of this space was a full-height timber and glass mural (since removed) by Wladyslaw Dutkiewicz, which separated the children's tables from the cloakroom and bathrooms. Claridge had also allowed for ventilation. This main room had timber louvres at ground level and glass louvres under the ceiling between the exposed timber beams.

The more common refinement that architects applied in the 1960s to Martin & Tribe's prosaic formula for kindergarten space design was to treat the kindergarten as a large hip-roofed 'house', but one with architectural rather than vernacular pretensions. Sydney architect Peter Muller, better known

3.12 Set among native eucalypts and designed like a large-scale, contemporary, rural 'home' – St Ives Kindergarten, NSW 1961–62

for his design of extremely large and luxurious private homes, designed a kindergarten at Whale Beach, New South Wales (1958) (figure 3.1e), with a roof clad in diamond-shaped asbestos tiles that was described by *Cross-Section* as having a 'crustacean-like form' despite its form being more akin to common conceptions of what a typical house might look like.[90] Much admired within the architectural profession and included in Robin Boyd's *The New Architecture* (1963) was Collard, Clarke & Jackson's kindergarten at St Ives, New South Wales (1961–62) (figure 3.12), which contained inside 'a warm and sympathetic child environment without recourse to Disneyland exotica'.[91] Designed to accommodate forty children, situated among native eucalypts and subsidised in its construction by the Ku-ring-gai Council, the kindergarten sat beneath a perfectly square pyramid roof, the framing of which was visible from within. The allusion to a traditional rural homestead with a perimeter veranda made this an early progenitor of a design theme that would come to be influential in residential Australian architecture by the mid-1960s. It seems that within the benign setting of the kindergarten, architects permitted themselves to relax hard-line functionalism with thoughtful responses to the creation of centred and contained space, a theme that would reappear in child-centred kindergarten designs by Kevin Borland at the Lady Forster Kindergarten, Port Melbourne (1968), and the rebuilt Boroondara Free Kindergarten, Richmond, Victoria

(1968),[92] and Ian Smith's square-planned and hip-roofed Heathmont East Pre-school centre, Victoria (1970).[93] To these should be added some genuine oddities: the 'Polynesian'-styled Rex-Corrigan Kindergarten, for instance, in the Melbourne suburb of Keysborough which was a sales office for real estate, donated to the community.[94]

A newsreel film made on the Forest Hill holiday home in the 1930s depicted an Aboriginal child who, viewers were told, normally lived with a large family sharing only two small rooms. The implication was that Forest Hills would be an enlightening luxury by contrast. The few purpose-built kindergartens for Aboriginal children in the 1950s aside – such as the Ernest R Carpenter Centre, in Mooroopna[95] – it was not until the 1960s that genuine attempts were made to bring Indigenous Australians into the kindergarten system. Aboriginal education in the 1960s has been typified as confused and inappropriate.[96] Superficially at least, the involvement of Aboriginal children in kindergarten education resonates with the attitude towards non-Indigenous 'slum' children a half-century (or more) previously. It was often compensatory education responding to perceived cultural deprivation.[97] Aboriginal parents in regional towns often requested co-location of children's and women's services,[98] reflecting or perhaps presaging a move to such arrangements in the 1970s and 1980s.

Continued evolution: The kindergarten at the turn of the 21st century

In a survey of kindergarten children's parents in the western Melbourne suburb of Werribee in the early 1990s, the overwhelming reason given for sending children to kindergarten was that it socialised them and boosted their confidence.[99] Kindergartens, it seemed, had taken on a different dimension. As institutions, their reason for being was no longer the bodily health combined with intellectual development that had characterised the establishment of the Lady Gowrie centres across Australia in the late 1930s. Kindergartens had always undertaken this function. Public perception now viewed the kindergarten as a conditioning environment prior to a potentially competitive school – and even life – experience. Children were to be prepared to meet the demands of a socially competitive future.

In architectural terms, however, little had changed since the 1950s. The biggest shift was the complementing of kindergartens with the broader functions and increased size of early learning centres, often run in association with universities focused on early childhood education and privatised childcare facilities where big business was to be had with a workforce where increasingly both partners worked. The modest but fruitful hours of a 'children's garden' were replaced with the extended hours of supervised childcare.

Throughout the decades, the Lady Gowrie centres continued and, in some places, expanded their operations. In 2009, illustrating their continuing influence on child centre projects since the 1930s, Gowrie Victoria opened the rooftop Harbour Family and Children's Centre at Victoria Harbour in Melbourne's Docklands (figure 3.13), an entirely new urban precinct of high-rise residential apartment towers and corporate office headquarters. Using rhetoric similar to Ritter's, architects Hassell planned their centre from a 'child's perspective'. As well as serving its clients in terms of socialisation, it also incorporates a green component. It

> includes a dining room, art spaces and rooms that all open out onto an open air 'living garden' playground on the first floor. The playground includes a sandpit, veggie [*sic*] garden, climbing and digging areas, and plants and trees. The playgrounds are watered from tanks incorporated into the external walls.[100]

The kindergarten's core purpose – specifically, health and scientific care – has altered over time. Environments, placement, shape and value have also changed. Like many of the public buildings surveyed in this book, kindergarten design has reflected the wider world's concerns while often developing unique

3.13 Aerial view of the Harbour Family and Children's Centre, Melbourne Docklands, Vic. 2009

strategies for the facilities' core use. The kindergarten has, however, retained its significance in Australians' lives and continues to be an essential component among community facilities. Its material manifestations over a century can present snapshots not only of attitudes to early childhood development but also understandings of the future shape of Australian society.

LIBRARY
Carla SPORTSWEAR
HEALTH FOODS
CITY BRANCH
LIBRARY
HUNTER STREET EXTERIOR OF CITY BRANCH

LIBRARY

LIBRARY
SHIRE HAL

PUBLIC LIBRARY
GIFTS & TOYS
PUBLIC
LIBRARY

LOCAL LEARNING: THE MUNICIPAL LIBRARY IN POST-WAR AUSTRALIA

Philip Goad and David Nichols

'Librarians know everything', 22-year-old Cec Churm's new father-in-law told him in 1946. This information, intended as an inducement for the recently demobbed British migrant to take the new Library Skills course at the State Library of New South Wales that year, hit its mark. Churm was interviewed for the course by State Librarian John Metcalfe, and enrolled in what seems to have been a somewhat informal yet highly valuable Certificate of Library Training program. The lecturers were members of the State Library's

4.1 **a.** Carnegie Library for Hobart City Council, Tas. 1904–06 **b.** Annerley Library, Qld 1957 **c.** Opening of the Merredin Public Library, WA 1960

staff, and Churm acquired work experience in the Mitchell Library's Australiana collection.

Churm was part of a small intake of local librarians who – with their counterparts in other states – were to assist in adding a new component to the suburban streetscape. The development of local public libraries as discrete spaces funded by the state did not begin in earnest until after World War II. However literate Australia may have been as a nation, the notion of a government responsibility to provide literature on a casual basis for its citizenry was largely ignored until the late 1930s, following the release of the Munn-Pitt report on libraries in Australia, commissioned by the Carnegie Corporation in 1935. Consensus for action existed before World War II, but the coherent development and expansion of municipal libraries across rural and suburban Australia was essentially a post-1945 phenomenon.

The 'free' libraries of the 19th and early 20th centuries were, in almost all cases, operated on a small subscription basis. Mechanics' Institutes (or 'Institutes' in South Australia) and Schools of Arts usually contained libraries; privately run lending libraries were also common, and well frequented. AJ and JJ McIntyre's 1944 survey of Victorian country towns provides a valuable snapshot of the way regional Australians regarded such libraries as existed in the years just prior to the new push for municipal libraries as educational, rather than recreational, facilities in response to the Munn-Pitt findings.

There were notable exceptions of genuine early municipal libraries: Broken Hill in remote New South Wales; Prahran and Hawthorn in Melbourne. Hawthorn Municipal Library is an atypical but instructive case. It began its life in 1860 as the subscription-based Hawthorn Free Public Library, then became a Literary Association in 1861, borrowing books from the Melbourne Public Library. In 1900, the collection was taken over fully by Hawthorn City Council

4.1 d. Library at Community Place, Greenacre, NSW 1961 **e.** Mt Isa Public Library, Qld 1974 **f.** Toorak-South Yarra Library, South Yarra, Vic. 1973

and run successfully as a rates-based library. Located in the town hall, it was moved into a nearby, single-storey, former billiard saloon in 1926. Two shops on the street collected rent that paid the interest on the property.[1]

Plainly, it was not that Australians lacked libraries per se, rather that the quality was uneven and dependent on the waxing and waning of voluntarist energies. With its denser population spread and greater wealth, Victoria in the 1940s probably had more libraries of various descriptions than other parts of the nation, though the standards were as varied as elsewhere. The McIntyres found that 114 towns surveyed in Victoria during the early 1940s had some type of public library, while a further 25 had at least one privately run library,[2] 'that is, a library not run for private profit … run by a publicly appointed committee or trust … financed by shire and government grants and by the subscriptions of members, for although they may be called "free" or "public" this means nothing more than that they have a free newspaper reading room'.[3] Libraries had monthly exchange systems with a private library in the state capital, and parcels of books would be periodically received from the Public Library of Victoria.

Some local libraries in the country towns visited by the McIntyres had a 'club atmosphere … on market days they were usually crowded, not only with people coming in to get books and going again, but with those who had come in to "wait for Mrs. Smith", to "have a bit of a rest", to "have a chat and get warm."'[4] Others were far less convivial and seemingly moribund.[5] Though conducted in the early 1940s, the McIntyres' survey could stand in for any decade between the century's beginning and the onset of post-war reconstruction. A modicum of libraries funded through the Carnegie Corporation's British Empire arm had already appeared in the first decade of the 20th century: Hobart City Council opened one in 1907.[6] In Western Australia, Midland, near Perth, was a recipient of Carnegie benevolence; in Melbourne, Northcote's library was also a Carnegie gift.[7] However, the true forerunner to the municipal public library as it is now known – operating on an educational and an improving, civic impulse – was the children's library; an early example included one opened in the impoverished suburb of Port Adelaide in 1901.[8] In 1924 New South Wales's Children's Library and Crafts Movement opened its first centre in Surry Hills, 'one of the poorer districts of Sydney'. These libraries were rarely given specific, specially designed premises; instead, they adapted themselves to various ad hoc spaces, including, as their 'driving force' as Mary Matheson wrote in 1951, 'service hutments, old schools and halls, plant nursery sheds, disused factories, shop premises, garages, cottages and a rambling mansion house'.[9] The Melbourne industrial suburb of Footscray's Children's Library, which began operations in the following decade, was similarly in improvised quarters.[10] Mosman Children's Library, in the northern suburbs of Sydney, was intended as the first stage of a complex that would also provide for adults,[11] a pattern replicated in the post-war years.

The Munn-Pitt (1935) and McColvin (1947) reports

Ralph Munn and Ernest Pitt were, respectively, director of the Carnegie Library of Pittsburgh and chief librarian of the Public Library of Victoria. The two men inspected more than 100 libraries across Australia, assembled more than 1500 questionnaire results, and prepared a report entitled *Australian Libraries: A Survey of Conditions and Suggestions for Their Improvement.*[12] Published in 1935, advocating government-subsidised and operated public libraries, it was widely reported and adopted in principle by communities around the nation. The report had numerous findings, not the least being that Australian libraries were out of date, the interests of readers had not been maintained, there was inadequate training in librarianship and 'pride in the local institution has been sapped'.[13] In his introduction to the Munn-Pitt report, retired director of Education in Victoria, Frank Tate – who had secured the report's funding – went so far as to quote King George V at the opening of the Manchester Central Reference Library in July 1935. George had observed that 'To our urban population, open libraries are as essential to health of mind as open spaces to health of body'.[14]

The crux of the issue for Munn and Pitt was that (state) government provision of free public libraries was limited almost entirely to a reference library in each state capital: 'The establishment of all other public library service has quite generally been left to groups of volunteers who have banded together to form literary institutes, schools of art, or similar organizations which are open to subscribing members only'.[15] They argued that Australia had been better provided with libraries in 1880, and that in comparison to Great Britain, the United States, Canada and New Zealand, which had established rates-supported libraries, 'Australia had accomplished almost nothing'. The major exceptions were the Sydney and Hobart city councils – which had at least acknowledged this responsibility but had not supported them to minimum overseas standards – and the Institutes Association of South Australia.

Especially scathing in their report, Munn and Pitt also observed that:

> Judged by overseas standards, there is not an acceptable children's lending library in all of Australia, and only a few institutions are even making a credible attempt to provide service to children.[16]

They went on to quote from the English library journal, *Coventry Bookshelf*:

> It would be difficult to over-emphasize the importance of work with children in our public libraries, for it is to be remembered that the child of today is the potential citizen of tomorrow. It is only by stimulating and encouraging in children a real love and understanding of books, that we can develop a true culture in the future generation.[17]

Munn and Pitt were thus amply justified in claiming that Australian children were being denied opportunity. However, their conclusions stopped short of advocating for rates-supported municipal free libraries. While they supported the idea of two distinct libraries, one operated by the state for reference and one by the municipality for lending, they were concerned about duplication of services and the problems of distance and uneven population distribution across the nation.[18] Time, extraordinary rates of post-war suburban growth and an emerging concern of building the nation's future through development of body and mind would, however, prove them wrong, something seen in the extraordinary growth in municipal libraries in the late 1950s and 1960s.

Initially, much of the work of advocating and implementing the report's findings was carried out by the Free Library Movement, which was created in 1935 during a meeting in Chatswood, New South Wales, where education was pronounced a 'lifelong process', to be 'continued through life by daily experiences in one's work and in one's contacts, and … by reading worth-while books'.[19] Library Boards were consequently established in each state between 1939 and 1951.[20]

Librarians Remington and Metcalfe observed of the energetic work of both the Movement and the Boards in 1944:

> It is no longer necessary to argue a case for books; or even to argue a case for free libraries supported from rates and taxes, though there is still inertia and the ratepayer who may campaign against a particular scheme because it touches his pocket. The Library Board has not sought out councils; they have sought out the Board … there is ample evidence of the clearing work already done by the Free Library Movement.[21]

Part of the work of post-war reconstruction included the relocation of populations to regional centres; such places needed, therefore, to be made more attractive to aspirant settlers. New South Wales premier McKell declared in 1946 his 'Government's policy of decentralisation was taking a definite shape and becoming a reality', including public libraries for all 'larger centres of population in inland districts'.[22] The following year saw the Riverina Regional Library Conference make twenty-four resolutions for requests to the NSW premier and his government for establishment of regional library services on both sides of the River Murray.[23] By 1947, forty-nine councils in rural areas of New South Wales operated libraries. The *Canberra Times* reported that 'the councils themselves provided about £54,000, and received a Government subsidy of about £26,000'.[24] The following year the amount expended was expected to increase to £80,000, whereas the subsidy given to Victoria's twenty-two municipal libraries was anticipated to be a comparable £65,000.[25]

In 1947, at the behest of the Commonwealth and state governments and facilitated by the Australian Council for Educational Research (ACER), another report on Australian libraries was produced by Lionel R McColvin, City

Librarian of Westminster, and Honorary Secretary of the Library Association of Great Britain.[26] McColvin's report critiqued Munn and Pitt's earlier findings. Its main emphasis was the strong advocacy of free library services, a nationwide system that did not discriminate on the grounds of geography and a sensible division of responsibility for the provision of library services between state and local authorities. McColvin was deeply critical of the lack of progress in the provision of effective library services in the twelve years that had elapsed since the Munn-Pitt report of 1935. Any progress, he claimed, was due to the good works of a small number of librarians and enlightened individuals.[27] But he was positive about the situation in New South Wales where the Free Library Movement had urged, successfully, the passing of the *Library Act 1939*. Due to the war, the Act did not come into operation until 1944, but by December 1946, sixty municipal and shire councils had adopted its conditions whereby a free library service administered by the local council was entitled to state subsidy. In 1948 it was announced that the New South Wales Free Library Board would be increasing its subsidy of libraries from the previous year's figure of £25,000 to £90,000.[28] The result in New South Wales was a minor boom in the provision of municipal libraries.

Cec Churm and Bankstown: A revolution in post-war suburbia

The year 1946 saw, as Cec Churm recalls, the first suburban libraries in Sydney and a time when new librarians were being trained for what was, correctly, anticipated to be a huge growth in library numbers across the city and state. Thirty-three libraries were established in New South Wales between 1944 and 1947.[29] Churm was one of the first in Australia to launch a career based on the new rollout of municipal libraries. His initial appointment was with the inner-western City of Marrickville. Marrickville's first branch library was at Dulwich Hill where it was located within a former School of Arts building. Churm's memory of the initial confusion this caused among locals illustrates the effect of what was, arguably, a temporary separation of the library as an institution from a centre for community (usually, men's) recreation:

> Many of the Mechanics' Institutes and Schools of Arts were being taken over by the councils. The Mechanics' Institutes were like a meeting place for workers, and this is where libraries took them over – you had to explain to people, when they came to use them, [asking] 'where's the billiard room?', 'where's the bridge playing room?' – this was quite common.[30]

This experience was formative for Churm, who would go on to assist in the initiation of a number of branch libraries in which discussion, education and public meetings were de rigueur. Marrickville Library hosted a music club, and ran a WEA (Workers' Educational Association) program, during which time Churm was obliged to screen 16 mm films every month and then initiate discussion, 'something I had never done and found quite difficult as a young man'.

Churm was to spend decades of his working life as the chief librarian for Bankstown Municipal Library during the time that this suburban area was the largest local government jurisdiction in New South Wales, and growing. Like Mosman's pre-war library mentioned above, the Bankstown Library had begun with a children's collection only. It opened on a momentous day in late 1946 when eager children were not deterred even by the closing of the library's doors: they 'climbed through the windows'.[31]

Bankstown's bookmobile began in 1951; it was not until 1954 that the adult library had its permanent home, designed by Davey & Brindley, for whom such regional amenities were becoming a specialty, and opened by John Metcalfe. This firm had already completed the striking combined civic structure of a local library and baby health centre on a triangular site 'originally intended for the library only' at Earlwood. The site's steepness allowed the health centre to be placed at a lower level where the roof of its waiting room formed an 'open reading terrace to the library'. The architects had hoped for a 'cheerful and informal building which would be in itself an advertisement for the initiative of the local authorities and for the important services it provides'.[32]

The same year that their Bankstown Library was opened, Davey & Brindley created another at East Lindfield (1954). The architects had been presented with the problem of designing a library to include adult and children's sections, a processing area for a future municipal library system and a baby health centre, while retaining the tennis courts that existed on the site.[33] The typology adopted by Davey & Brindley – one that would be adopted by other architects across the nation from the mid-1950s – was very simple: a single, open and well-lit volume that constituted the library proper and which was notionally divided by shelving arrangements into children's and adult sections with separate work and processing rooms. The Lindfield library was prosaically described in the architectural press as a series of bays with freestanding boxed steel stanchions, exposed open web beams and steel decking welded to the beams. However, the treatment of the library's entire western face as a series of floor-to-ceiling fixed timber louvres punctuated only by a flat entry canopy suggested the search for a new contemporary language for civic monumentality, which in this case seems to have been influenced by contemporary Brazilian architecture and local works by Harry Seidler. Just as architects would strive

4.2 Detail from a postcard showing Hawthorn Library, Vic. 1938

for a new imagery for other civic and commercial functions such as banks, art galleries, office buildings and department stores, so it was with the municipal library. With the exception of church design, no other small-scale post-war public building type could make such a claim for architectural pretension in the civic realm.

Indeed, at the national level and at the large scale, it is the rather pompous classicism of the National Library of Australia in Canberra (1968), designed by Bunning and Madden in association with Tom O'Mahony, that was the first major post-war addition to a series of monumental buildings constructed near the centre of the parliamentary triangle in Canberra. Similarly, but earlier and at the local level, the municipal library would often be the first part of a collection of civic buildings of monumental aspiration that would signal notions of citizenship found through community, education and access rather than the vagaries of municipal authority.

Collecting spaces of community

Hawthorn Library, mentioned above, continued to be an important feature of the suburb's life. In 1938–39 (figure 4.2), it was given a facelift and remodelled by architects Marsh and Michaelson, designers of the nearby modernist-styled Glenferrie Grandstand (1938, in association with SP Calder).[34] The entire ground floor was dedicated to library functions, with a 225-person lecture hall on the first floor, and the building was given a new two-storey facade, an exemplar of stripped 'classical moderne' design, complete with a framing device of brick pylons, a central council crest, and the word 'Library' in stucco relief on the top floor. The new building defined a coherent civic precinct of town hall, library and post office.[35]

The co-location of libraries with other features such as baby health centres was a combination of serendipity and – in the case of East Lindfield and others – council ambitions to begin the construction of civic centres with an 'establishing' building.[36] Circumstances, however, varied: in the early 1960s, *Architecture in Australia* noted that regional art galleries 'tended to develop into cultural centres' inviting broader community use 'by including such features as regional libraries, small theatres, meeting rooms and auditoriums'. The subject of this discussion was Douglas Alexandra's Hamilton Art Gallery in western Victoria.[37] In regional Queensland at Millmerran, the library and council chambers (1960) were located under the one broad roof for expediency, while at East Maitland in New South Wales, a municipal building, described as a 'neighbourhood centre' combined library, baby health, electricity and gas offices and a showroom.[38] In the Tasmanian municipality of Clarence, the public library and war memorial hall were combined.[39]

There was also recognition, in some subtle pronouncements of interested parties, of the democratic impulse of the library: in 1954 the chief secretary of the Kew Library, W Galvin, opined: 'The more libraries we open, the greater opportunity we will have to continue living under a democracy, and keep to our own choice of reading'.[40] The 1951 announcement of Bairnsdale's forthcoming 'Modern Library ... to serve [the] whole community'[41] was even more overt in its egalitarian intention.

In Brisbane in 1955, newly installed lord mayor Reg Groom was a purposeful advocate for local libraries. Also relatively new in his job, young Melbourne architect James Birrell – appointed Brisbane City Architect the same year – was requested to design libraries for the suburbs of Annerley, Chermside, Toowong and Stones Corner (this last was not built). Part of Birrell's brief was that the libraries had to be a room where people could meet and congregate.[42] The sites were previously city council depots (Annerley, Toowong) or replaced existing outdated community structures (Chermside).

4.3 Interior, Chermside Library, Qld 1957–58

Annerley was the first to open in August 1957, and was described by Grace Garlick in Brisbane's *Sunday Courier Mail* as 'Brisbane's first new municipal library' (figure 4.1b). Its popularity with local children was such that opening hours had to be extended. SR Jones from the Annerley Junction Traders' Association, which had raised money to contribute to the cost of the building, proudly stated: 'This library is corrective action for children who might otherwise go astray'.[43] The library building was located on a sloping site on the corner of busy Ipswich Road (next to Annerley Police Station and at the end of a shopping strip) and quiet Waldheim Street, the same street as Junction Park State School. Accessed by a ramp that wound its way around what was to become a giant fig tree, the library had solid end walls, one to Ipswich Road rendered with an exposed aggregate of river pebbles, the other brick. The north and south elevations were clad in giant sheets of marine-grade Queensland maple plywood, originally varnished, according to Birrell, to achieve a 'violin finish' with banks of louvre highlight windows to the north.[44]

4.4 Interior, Toowong Library, Qld 1959

Underneath were restrooms which acted as public toilets not just for the library but also for the landscaped site (designed with the involvement of parks superintendent Harry Oakman), which included a playground and sheltered play area to the north. Inside, the library was a simple one-room volume: an information and loans desk separated the children's and adults' library and a collection of 12,000 books that ranged from low- to highbrow: '*Pix* to Poets'.[45] Three rocking stools in the library described as 'international furniture', were designed by the Japanese-American sculptor Isamu Noguchi and represented, according to the *Observer*, the first release in Australia of furniture from the Knoll International, bought from West's in Fortitude Valley.[46] Its proximity to a public shopping street, police station, school and public park, and its public landscape designed for children made Birrell's Annerley Library a modernist civic precinct in miniature.

The library at Chermside (figure 4.3) was opened by Groom in March 1958. Prime minister Robert Menzies sent a telegram of congratulations. Located on the corner of Gympie Road and Hall Street, it was intended as the first stage of a larger scheme to create a civic centre for a suburban community at the end of the train line.[47] Its simple, open design was distinguished by its end walls finished in white marble chips, and its generous glazing screened by a series of canted NACO aluminium louvres. It was located on the shopping street and placed in front of an old timber community hall to act as a buffer to a proposed garden courtyard, children's playground and community hall structure elevated above shared public toilets for the two facilities that would eventually replace the existing timber building.

While the community hall to accompany the library at Chermside was not built, at Toowong the development of a minor civic precinct was carried somewhat further: the library was accompanied by a municipal swimming pool, both to Birrell's design. On the banks of the Brisbane River, the site for the library was a former council depot, while next door the new swimming pool replaced an old grandstand and an existing draw-and-fill pool that was replenished once a week.[48] Birrell's design for the library was unusual, even extraordinary, based on the structural-functional principles of American scientist Buckminster Fuller's Dymaxion House (1927), an engineered polygonal-planned house hung by cables from a central steel mast. Opened in 1959, it housed 35,000 books – making it one of the largest municipal libraries in Brisbane – and had an open twelve-sided polygon plan and a steel roof frame with a ring-beam at its centre (figure 4.4).[49]

Instead of Fuller's perimeter banks of triangular panel glazing, Birrell deployed a series of diagonally placed square panels of cedar-faced plywood and glass set in rose mahogany frames which canted outwards thereby easing visual access to the sloping bookshelves which lined the perimeter wall within. The weight of the books and the outward leaning wall brought the radiating steel beams into tension, hence the need for the central ring-beam and its oculus roofed by an amber acrylic skylight. The internal arrangement was determined not by a central mast but replaced by the panoptic centrality of the sky-lit information and lending desk which had visual control over the front entry. The entire open space of the reading room was divided bilaterally into children's and adults' sections. Behind this desk and concealed from view was a workspace and stairwell to the staffroom at basement level. Sympathetic landscaping of succulents and subtropical plants for the scheme was undertaken by Lionel Steenbom, Oakman's deputy. Next door at the Toowong Swimming Pool (1957–59), Birrell's drum-like entry kiosk, clad in burnt orange bricks, was another textured geometric form, which together with the polygonal library formed a new language for this post-war ensemble of civic form, one for the body, the other for the mind.[50]

A 'beehive of congestion'

In other regions, the library was a distinct component of social engineering experiments. In 1957, longstanding South Australian premier Thomas Playford opened the Elizabeth Public Library and was ceremonially registered as its first borrower. The library was located in the shopping centre of Elizabeth South, one of the new city's first two developed sections.[51] It was the first free public library to be established in South Australia under the new *Libraries (Subsidies) Act 1955*, which had been passed by the Playford government following years of campaigning by the Free Library Movement, Herbert Skipper of the Libraries Board, politicians and community groups.[52] The Act provided subsidies to local councils for the building, establishment and administration of free public libraries. Such was the rush on the first day of opening that the Adelaide Public Library was asked to send two helpers to come out by taxi after 5 pm to assist with customers. The following year the library was issuing almost 400 books a day.

A slight, but temporary, drop in library usage was noted on the introduction of television to Adelaide in 1959; in June 1960 the library's first branch at Salisbury North was opened initially as an adult library with the children's section to follow. It was followed the next month by the Elizabeth North branch; the nature of the development of Elizabeth meant that the branches were established before the construction of a central library. Elizabeth's librarians were unhappy with the limited range of their facilities and premises, and their complaints indicate what was considered best practice in library provision in 1960:

> None of the services which should be incorporated in modern public libraries are available ... Facilities such as a separate children's department, story hour rooms, adult meeting rooms, magazine and newspaper reading stands, map files, study desk and chairs, lounge chairs, cloak and bag space and ample free circulating space are now warranted in the library ... At busy times the branch resembles a beehive of congestion.[53]

On the other side of Adelaide, in the comfortable suburb of Burnside, the story was more positive. In 1957 Philip Claridge raised the idea of a free library at the urging of Burnside's mayor. Claridge was an architect who would be instrumental in encouraging the construction of kindergartens at Rose Park (1958) and Erindale (1960), both in his municipality. Moves had been afoot since 1955 and various costing proposals considered but it was not until April 1961 that the Burnside Public Library was opened with a book stock of 7800, a staff of three, and a children's library. Located next to the 19th-century town hall, in effect consolidating the site as a community locus, the new modern library with its grand, double-height volume and a south-facing wall of glass was designed by architects Bevan Rutt & Roberts. It included a mezzanine floor used as staff workspace, the latest Roksteel adjustable steel shelving and a timber-lined loans desk, all overlooking a new landscaped garden on the Greenhill Road frontage, complete with a donated fountain. Despite concern from councillors and community over cost, proximity to the central city's services and accessibility, the library was an immediate success. By the end of 1962, more than 6500 borrowers were registered and more than 100,000 books borrowed from a stock of 10,000. By 1976, it was reported that 3 million books had been issued since the library's opening.[54]

Going to the library

The way in which the municipal library was incorporated into Australian life during the 1940s and 1950s is extraordinary to contemplate. Branches were a necessity, particularly as Australian suburbia underwent its Menzies-era boom. During his ten years at Bankstown, Cec Churm initiated four branch libraries within that city's boundaries, a considerable expansion commensurate with the extension of the urban area itself. Those branches were located at Chester Hill (1958), Padstow (1959), Greenacre (1961) and Panania (1968).

Churm was an innovator, who had adopted a method of photographing book borrowing records ('photocharging') as early as 1955 to cope with the large volume of traffic experienced at the library, particularly as commuters passed by the library en route to their homes. Bankstown was socially innovative in other ways. Books were repaired by specially trained handicapped workers, and more were trained there for similar work in other libraries.[55] The library also developed a collection for the visually impaired and had a special collection of scientific and technical works for the use of owners and operators of Bankstown's industries. Having become convinced of the importance of film in library education – perhaps from his Marrickville experience – Churm also established the library as a 'centre for issuing documentary films'.[56]

Branch libraries under Churm's aegis were often co-located with other facilities, such as baby health centres, and sited close to transport and retail. The most unusual of these is, perhaps, at Community Place, Greenacre, where a semi-circular library building faces a small park. Greenacre featured, like East Lindfield, ample and generous window space that allowed sunlight to enter the building. Its park placement also echoed another notable library of the same time in Kings Cross. Arthur Collins' design for the Florence Bartley Library (1958) won the Sir John Sulman medal (the building class judged that year being 'public and monumental') in 1959 and was the last of a series of branch

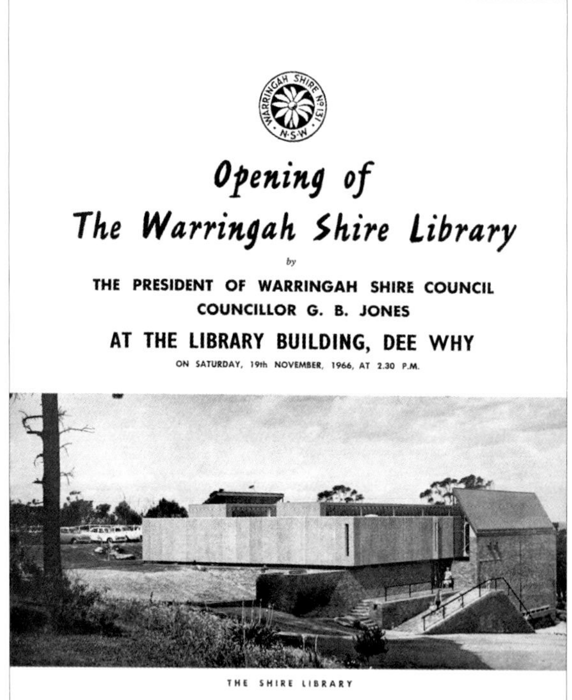

4.5 Program for the opening of Warringah Shire Library, Dee Why, NSW 1966

libraries established by Sydney City Council.[57] Collins was employed at the Architects Branch of Sydney City Council, and the library used the Fitzroy Gardens – 'the only green area in a densely populated district' – as its forecourt. The slender, two-storey building also incorporated an 'aged amenities centre' and an open play area on its ground floor.[58] Upstairs, the library followed the conventional typology with children's and adults' library divided by a 'control desk', both spaces sharing a similar, large, well-glazed linear volume overlooking Fitzroy Gardens. An undeniably prosaic form, the Kings Cross Library at one time included a design for an RSL (Returned and Services League) club upstairs and the library below, clearly as a form of community hub. It may have been awarded the Sulman medal for this reason rather than for its architectural sophistication.

By 1966, 180 local authorities operated libraries in New South Wales (40 did not) and 115 did so in Victoria.[59] In that year, another library won the Sulman award: this was Edwards Madigan Torzillo & Partners' library at Dee Why (1966–67) for Warringah Shire Council. Like so many of its predecessors, the Dee Why Library had been 'designed as an element of a civic centre that may be built on the plateau behind the new building'.[60] However, there was a big difference between this library and its 1950s predecessors. It was larger, architecturally more ambitious, and more pretentious in its structure and material finish, and in terms of a library program, there was a strong focus on borrowed natural daylight and a complex, multi-level interior. A central lending library, housing 45,000 books, the Dee Why Library had as its spatial focus a

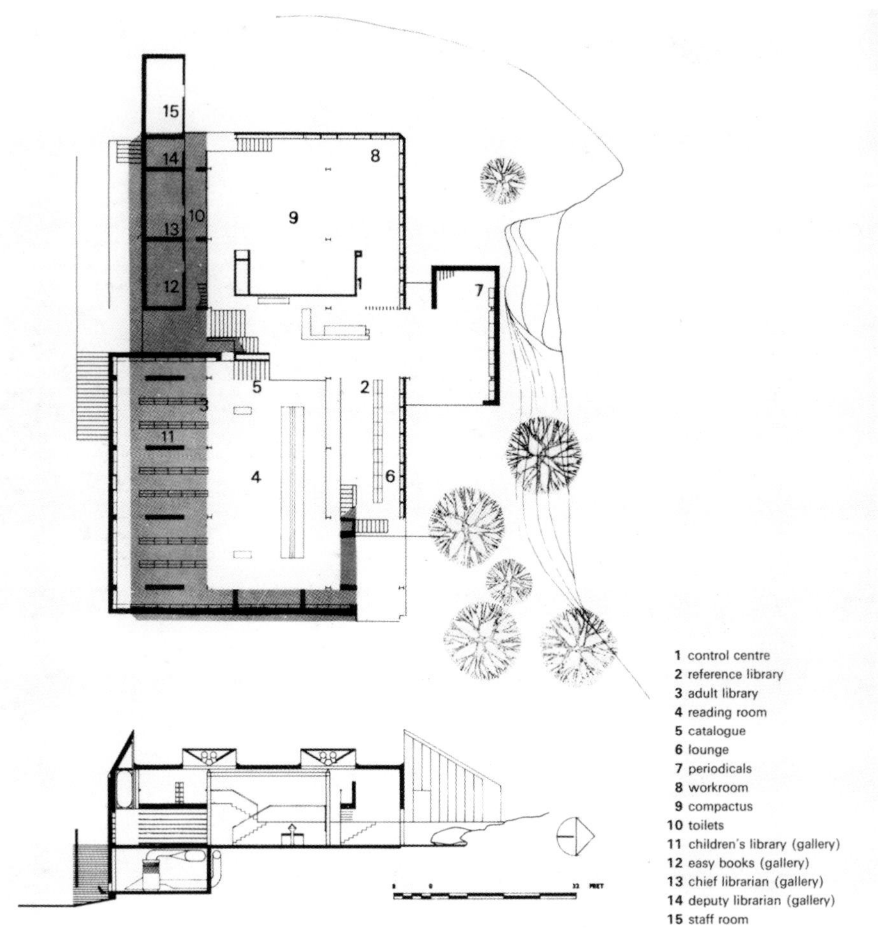

4.6 Plan and section, Warringah Shire Library, Dee Why, NSW 1966

double-height, top-lit reading room surrounded by galleries accessed by ramps and stairs.[61] The articulation of this almost grand space was achieved by a gloss-white painted internal steel frame with intricate detail connections and gloss-white handrails and edge reveals, which as Jennifer Taylor has noted produced a bright, almost 'high-tech', interior.[62] The top gallery had a low ceiling over the children's section, while a centrally located control point on mid-level gave visual control over the entire library. There was a mural by Melbourne artist Tom Sanders, which at £1100 was considered at the time an expensive inclusion. This, along with Scandinavian light fittings and smart Danish 'Reska' shelving, was deemed essential by then shire president Geoff Mill.[63] Architects Colin Madigan and Christopher Kringas had created a light-filled interior landscape, a celebration of reading, collection and contemplation. For Australian architecture, it was one of the most convincing examples in the 1960s of architects seeking, in a non-residential setting, a return to phenomenological principles – of making place and responding directly to the landscape and a program for the creation of a collective public memory – an aim amply demonstrated by Harry

Sowden's evocative photographs of mothers and children wandering between the bookshelves (figure 4.7). Reinforcing the complexity of design intention was the building's earthy wrapping: a massive manganese brick substructure and manganese brick pods with sharply pitched clerestory roofs clad in bronze, containing a suspended 'ring' of exposed aggregate precast concrete panels that delineated the rectilinear outline of the major reading room volume.

In architectural descriptions of the building, much was made of the library's landscape setting and the approach to the building. The site slopes steeply down to Dee Why with a public car park close to busy Pittwater Road and its burgeoning shopping strip. Giant sandstone rocks and native trees and scrub formed the tough setting to this new suburban 'Acropolis' as it was envisaged by Madigan, who had recently completed the nearby Dee Why RSL in 1962 and was then a 'local', living in Narrabeen in a house he had designed in 1956.[64] The Warringah Shire Offices were opposite the Brookvale Oval. Madigan's mission was altruistic:

> If we could make the proposed library at Dee Why as popular as the Brookvale Oval we would be on the way to making the ideal philosopher-athlete for saving our distressed planet.[65]

Money for the new Warringah Shire Library had been set aside from the sale of some industrial land by then shire clerk Jim Morgan. The proposed site for the library on the west side of Pittwater Road comprised a hill, where Madigan envisaged his 'shining place on its green prominence'. Initial ideas for the site were ambitious. Various proposals included a public hall and a gymnasium, a market, an art gallery and museum and a war memorial at the level of Pittwater Road, as well as a library and civic centre. The architects were given a free hand to plan the library and site it as the first element of a civic centre for the rapidly expanding shire. Even while the building was under construction, newly appointed city librarian John Ellis dictated the widening of aisles between bookshelves in view of expected user demand. Like so many similar facilities in mid-20th century Australia, it was an instant success:

> The Library was overstressed from the day it opened, jut as John Ellis had predicted. Membership grew at an extraordinary rate, books disappeared off the shelves by the constant reader, the brick paving wore out with trampling feet and the door furniture could not withstand the continual opening and closing. A library is only as good as the Librarian and John Ellis was in charge of this rush. In short the Library was a long awaited cultural success; here the once deprived reader could assume good value for taxes, but the building was obviously not large enough.[66]

4.7 Interior view, Warringah Shire Library, Dee Why, NSW 1966

With the eventual completion in 1973 of the off-form concrete Warringah Shire Civic Centre situated above and beside the library, Madigan's suburban acropolis was complete, with views to the Pacific Ocean and a landscape still dominated by rocks and native trees. What had resulted was an idealised grouping of community buildings, each carefully planned and modelled and accessed through a series of steps and ramps that was indeed reminiscent of the pedestrian landscape of the Athenian high city and which would shortly find echo in Canberra but on a much larger scale. Madigan even penned a one-act play entitled 'Dee Why Acropolis: A Play – Dreaming' as an ironic demonstration piece years later when council plans mooted the idea of relocating the library and civic centre to alternative sites.

In 1969 Edwards Madigan Torzillo & Partners' Warren Shire Library was built as the first stage of a civic centre 'to serve the cultural needs of the community'. *Architecture in Australia* reported that 'the form of the building was evolved to create the necessary civic scale commensurate with social congregation and relationship with the general life of the community at large'.[67]

Designed again by Madigan and Kringas, the Warren Shire Library, another award-winner, was also completely unlike the modestly scaled 1950s municipal library which tended to be simple, generously day-lit, single volumes. At Warren (figure 4.8), the plan was split into the familiar children's and adult sections, but the focus was on the disposition of blank walls to maximise book storage and minimise the penetration of sun into the building, relying more on reflected light from clerestory windows and an occasional vertical window slot. Using chamfered walls in plan, and chamfered rooflines, the result was an H-plan with a similarly chamfered loans and information desk as the centre of the H, with the junior and adult libraries designed as wings embracing an elevated entry approach of stairs and ramp for pram and disabled access. Raised thus above flood level, the library, like Finnish architect Alvar Aalto's community buildings, was a collection of public spaces, both internal and external; its white forms of steep roofs and chamfered corners of a scale that was contextually appropriate and commensurate with the small scale and pitched roofs of the regional country town. The library was the first of an intended grouping of buildings around a landscaped square facing the town's main street.[68]

For Edwards Madigan Torzillo & Partners, the two library commissions were prophetic.[69] The Dee Why Library with its adjacent Warringah Shire Civic Centre (1973) in particular presaged the firm's most important monumental public commissions in the nation's capital: the High Court of Australia (competition 1972, completed 1980) and the National Gallery of Australia (competition 1968, completed 1982), two buildings which Jennifer Taylor has described as 'the most forthright examples of Australian civic architecture of their decade'.[70]

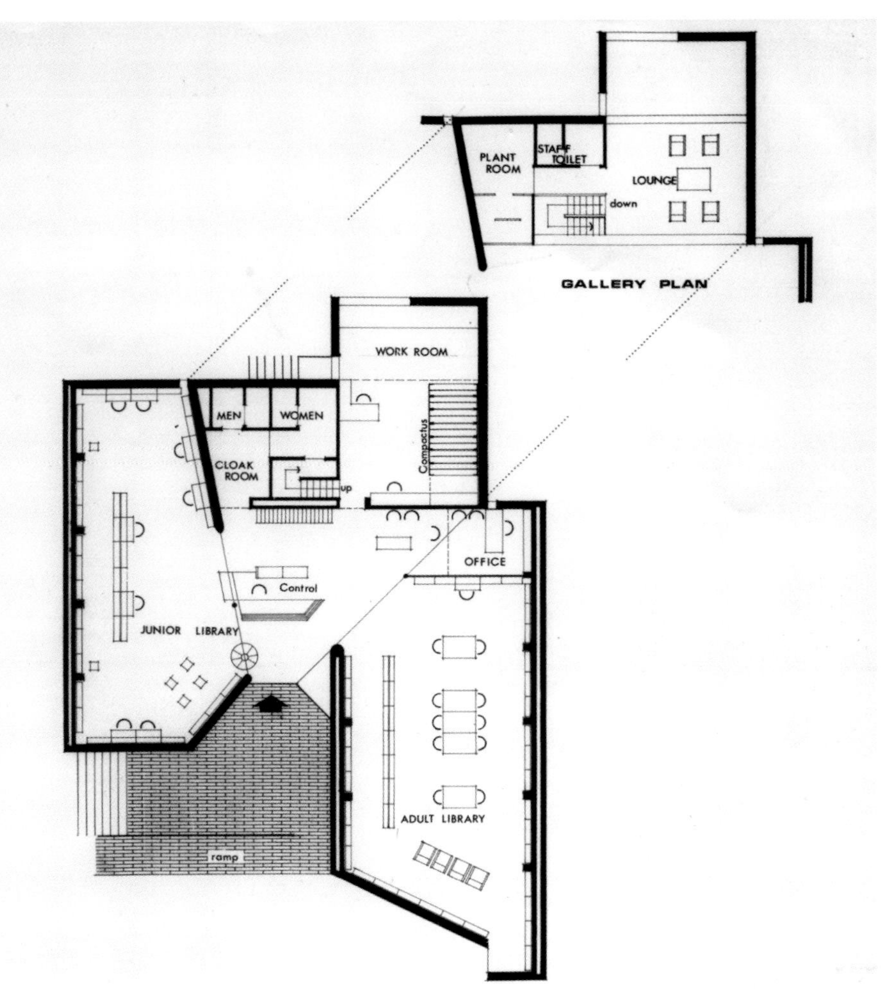

4.8 Plan, Warren Shire Library, Warren, NSW 1966

The post-war municipal library can thus be seen as one of the most powerful testing grounds for questions of the definition of civic form and architectural representation in the 1960s. By 1973 at one end of the spectrum was Iwan Iwanoff's Besser concrete block sculptural tour de force for the two-storey Northam Library, Western Australia (figure 4.9) or the low-key, domestic imagery and friendly spaces of Jackson Walker's Balwyn Municipal Library, Victoria (1978), while at the other was the elegant Miesian neoclassicism of Yuncken Freeman's Toorak-South Yarra Library, Victoria (1973), with its drop-dead chic exterior of glass and black steel and open plan interior with brilliant red carpet (figure 4.10). In regional Queensland, the imagery for the Mount Isa Library (1974) designed by Lund Hutton Newell and Pauson with its dramatic silhouette of copper-clad roof monitors was drawn from the mining structures and heritage of the town. In each case, urban context and considerable municipal pride combined to not only produce invaluable resources for their communities

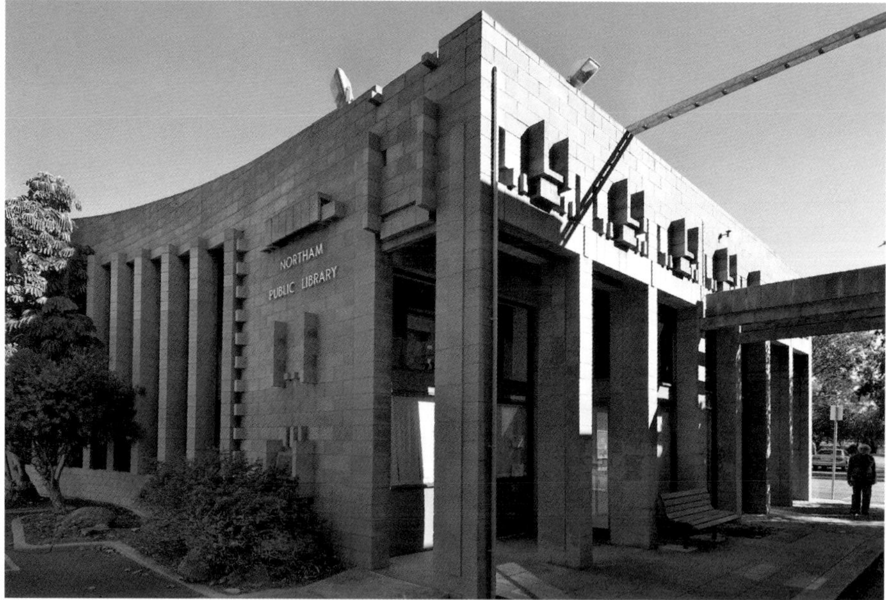

4.9 Northam Town Council Offices and Library, WA 1971–74

but substantial and often not inexpensive markers of permanent commitment on the part of municipal councils to the education of their citizens.

Of all of these libraries built in the 1960s, two stand out: the first because of its sincere attempt to not only cater for reading but also to act as a venue for exhibitions, music and school visits – in effect transforming the local library into a cultural centre; the second because the librarians in St Kilda in suburban Melbourne were so impressed by the program and spaces of the Dickson Library in suburban Canberra that they commissioned the same architect to design their new library in 1969.

In 1967, émigré Italian architect Enrico Taglietti was given his first commission from the National Capital Development Commission: the Dickson Library (1967–69), a district lending library to serve north Canberra and act as a first link in a chain of five children's libraries in the district's outer perimeter.[71] Located on a flat, rectangular site in the Dickson Shopping Centre amid car parks and at the edge of a shopping strip, the library was to accommodate 30,000 volumes, including 10,000 children's books. Taglietti's aim, like Madigan's, was lofty and all-encompassing:

> to achieve a total communion between building and the users and the outside environment; an atmosphere with a complete lack of paternalism and scholarly austerity; the assembly of learning matter within reach of both children and adults without the obstacle of sterilising, formal barriers; the acceptance as far as practicable of everyday (noise and) habits penetrating the building; the successful association of exhibitions with their inherent traffic, music with its distraction characteristic,

> and small children and their natural reactions within the same shell; the creation of a study area which was sufficiently introverted and conducive to concentration.

Remarkably, Taglietti achieved his aim and also remarkably, he did this with off-form concrete, manganese bricks, and boldly expressed horizontal roofs with double-angled moulded asbestos cement fascias, all left in their natural state. Like contemporary European architects such as Italian Carlo Scarpa and Dutchman Aldo van Eyck, Taglietti's architecture spoke to new-found concerns for the ordinary and the everyday – not in the sense of the commercial strip, but, like Madigan's work at Dee Why, in fundamental notions of the provision of space, light and connection to landscape and human engagement with those provisions – ideals captured by photographer Harry Sowden.

Key to Taglietti's design was an encircling concrete wall around the rectangular site which rose at the four corners to form tapered pylons and dipped to contain small gardens and patios, then rose again to form pillars for supports for the over-sailing horizontal flat roofs and their deep fascias, and then dipped again to create space for clerestory windows beneath the eaves. At the entry, Taglietti created a public piazza and set the entry doors deep beneath the roof and flanked them with exhibition cases. Unlike Madigan's introspective reading volume, Taglietti's design combined qualities of openness and introspection. The four corner gardens determined a cruciform plan, which enabled the small children's section, the adult section and the exhibition area to open out to the patios, while in the building's centre was a raised and secluded study area with built-in desks, designed by Taglietti, encircled at its lower level by bookshelves and card catalogues (also designed by Taglietti) that overlooked the rest of the library. This quiet centre was lit by a bank of illuminated light diffusers that gave the impression of a giant skylight, and enabled the rest of the ceiling lined in caneite (low-density fibreboard) to exude a sense of warmth and comfort. In 1995, Taglietti's Dickson Library received a 25-year award for architectural excellence from the ACT Chapter of the Royal Australian Institute of Architects, an honour countered by public comments just three years later that the building was 'really ugly' and 'very grey'. It was also acknowledged as:

> the only 'community service' in the shopping centre core. Library staff are often approached by people wanting to know where a particular business is, bus timetable information or how to find the community services area beyond the swimming pool.[72]

4.10 Interior, Toorak–South Yarra Library, South Yarra, Vic. 1973

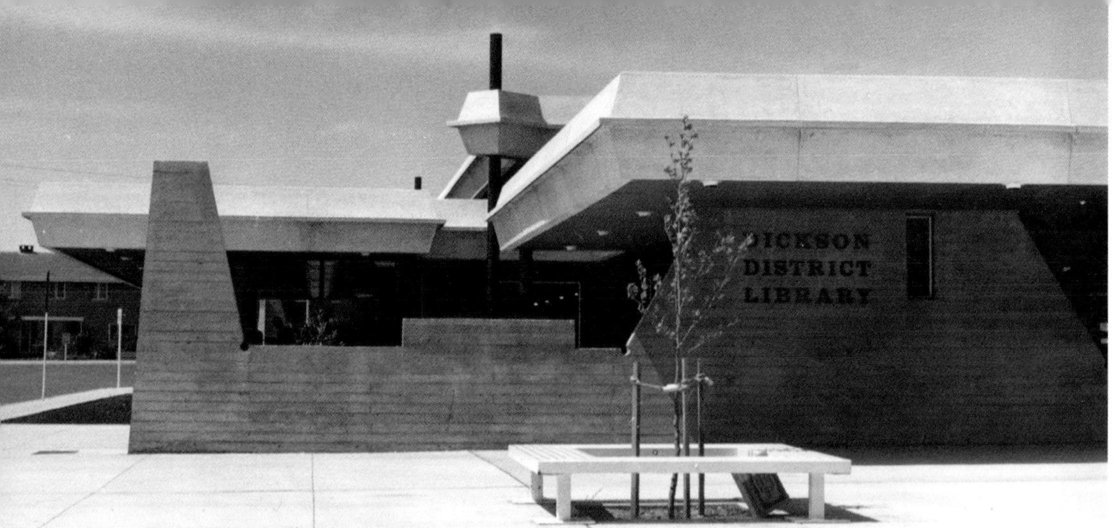

4.11 Dickson District Library, ACT 1969

Dickson Library was influential interstate. Recommended to St Kilda Council when investigating the construction of its new library in Carlisle Street, directly opposite the 19th-century classical pile of St Kilda Town Hall, council and library staff, especially librarian Vida Horn, were convinced by what they saw in Canberra. The result was a much larger and architecturally elaborate library with a similar materials and detail palette, except that grey cement block replaced Dickson's manganese brick and large 1.5 metre square fluorescent light diffusers dotted the ceiling. Taglietti inserted a car park beneath, a large community meeting room off to one side of the entry, garden patios, and a landscaped courtyard entry, complete with a sculptural fountain that housed the building's airconditioning unit. The encircling off-form concrete wall was double-splayed and had a floating concrete seat around its perimeter much like the stone public seats encircling prominent Florentine palazzi (figure 4.12). The low roof of the Dickson Library was now stretched vertically to become a pagoda-like roof, containing a skylight tower over the foyer and information desk. All the furniture, including the desks, in a colour scheme of black, white and red (the colours of the St Kilda football team!) was designed by Taglietti and all still exist, even the exquisite clusters of coloured pendant lights in the children's section.[73]

Opened with great aplomb in May 1973 by the Governor of Victoria, Sir Rohan Delacombe, St Kilda Library is an appropriate conclusion to this chapter. This library, as with a substantial number of those built across suburban and regional Australia in the 1960s and 1970s, remains a vital link in its local community infrastructure. If the buildings themselves have not, they have inevitably been replaced by larger and more substantial facilities on the same site or a nearby site or relocated to 'shop-front' settings in shopping centres. Architects have continued to find the library a rich source for aesthetic expression, program experiment and a situation where conscientious engagement with

4.12 Concept sketch for St Kilda Library, Vic. 1972–73

local library staff, a local community and a local urban precinct is vital. Even the arrival of the digital age has not lessened the role of the library building as a key community meeting point – and may even have enhanced it.

The St Kilda Library has remained on its site and the original structure was altered and extended in 1993 by architects Ashton Raggatt McDougall, who were responsible for an innovative combination of library and cultural centre in Marion, South Australia (2002) and museum and library in Albury, New South Wales (2008). In 2009, the St Kilda Council commissioned architects Garner Davis in association with Lovell Chen, a firm with expertise in heritage, to undertake a master plan to extend and upgrade the St Kilda Library. Garner Davis also had extensive experience in library design, being responsible for libraries in Wagga Wagga, New South Wales (1997–99) and Mornington, Victoria (2003–05). Their project in Romsey in country Victoria (2006–07) combined library, neighbourhood house and childcare centre. At St Kilda, Garner Davis and Lovell Chen decided to hold a workshop with library staff, council and community, and most important of all, with Taglietti himself, then aged eighty-three. Their hope was to discover and recover the original aims of the 1969 design and to understand the qualities of the 1960s building, which today's library staff greatly admire – the warmth, the light, the furniture, even the concrete, but most of all, the positive way in which the original plan worked and continues to function.[74] They heard about Taglietti's original ideas for a cloister entry to the building, about his proposals for a second stage, and perhaps most importantly, his ideas about 'a total communion between building and the users and the outside environment'. It was in effect a restatement of long-held ideals since the 1930s about what a public library might be: a free and openly accessible building where knowledge and interaction might, without prescription, encourage not just learning but the building of a community.

1934
OLYMPIC POOL
CLONCURRY POOL
100
267. HIS EXCELLENCY SPEAKING

MAKING SPACES FOR RECREATION

Hannah Lewi

'Sport to many Australians is life, the rest is a shadow.'[1] **As Donald Horne's ironic observation implies, sport and outdoor recreation loomed large in the formation of Australian identity** and everyday environment in the 20th century. As the academic study of recreation began in earnest in the 1970s, challenges were mounted against the mythologising of Australians' sporting life, with evidence that they have never played, practised, watched or talked about sporting activities to the degree often assumed, and

5.1 a. City of Brisbane Corporation Baths, Spring Hill, Qld c. 1910 **b.** Swimming Pool, Enfield, NSW 1933 **c.** 'People given work during the Depression to build the Parkes Swimming Pool', NSW

certainly to no greater extent than in other countries.[2] Between 1920 and 1970, however, there is no doubt that white Australia fostered the stereotype of a land teeming with healthy, self-grown, natural athletes by combining idealised racial and environmental attributes. This modern image came to stand side-by-side with other formative national themes like the resilience of the worker on the land, and the mateship of war.

The country certainly possessed significant climatic and spatial advantages ensuring that a broad range of seasonal sports could be played. The professionalisation of sports training dates back to the 19th century, and country towns and suburban frontiers were fondly regarded as a nursery for the growing of athletes. But these factors do not fully explain Australia's self-image as a sporting nation forged through grassroots participation. As Elford suggests: 'The vital factor was the active patronage sport received and the rapid acceptance given to it by the community, and this was a product of the belief that sport created better people and hence a better community'.[3]

Since the 19th century, sport and physical education had been promoted as healthy means of shaping social behaviours, moral codes and physical attributes.[4] Participation in sport and recreation can be seen as part of a social and governmental program to ensure a nation of 'civilised' individuals and societies, through coercive programs to make populations healthier, fitter, more productive and contented.[5] The anticipated social and civic benefits of recreation grew in acceptance in Australia from the 1920s, as many sports became 'feminised' through increasing rates of participation and spectatorship among women and families. Popularisation added impetus to provision of small-scale clubs and amenities in areas where families lived. More ambitious buildings and facilities

5.1 d. Dalby Swimming Pool, Qld 1936 **e.** Postcard of Albury Olympic Pool, NSW c. 1957
f. Toowong Swimming Pool, Brisbane, Qld 1959

required the services of professional architects and planners, who increasingly recognised sport and leisure facilities as legitimate and essential public services. The goal of accessible recreation was one concept that underpinned the town planning movement of the 1940s onwards, and endorsement of the importance of the creation of planned open spaces for recreation was evident in many town planning documents and speeches of the period. For instance, the Town Clerk of Brisbane, JC Slaughter, wrote in 1944:

> Recreational areas in unplanned cities are invariably inadequate and mal-distributed, and perhaps this aspect has a much greater significance than has been previously considered. Man has become space conscious and his mind, instinct and intellect are constantly nourished, consciously and subconsciously in an atmosphere of openness.[6]

Professional knowledge in fields of health and fitness, alongside the development of government programs such as the National Fitness movement, and standard codes for sport, were instrumental in this gradual transformation of incidental and recreational locations – the paddock, river or street – into specialised, enclosed and artificial venues.[7] However, as this chapter will describe, the realisation of modern sporting and recreation amenities in local neighbourhoods did not just happen through professional and governmental will but also depended heavily on community support and individual tenacity.

Australian swimming pools in the early 20th century

This chapter examines the public pool as one type of modern recreation facility which, by the mid-20th century, was part of most Australians' expectations of necessary local amenities. Anglo-Australians had bathed and swum in ocean beaches, rivers, lakes and dams since settlement, and each colony supported the building of formal baths and other recreational facilities for bathing and leisure through government programs such as that heralded by the New South Wales *Municipal Act 1860*. Protected swimming pools were defined and modified from, or built into, waterholes, rock pools, river banks and bays around the country. Some more elaborate floating or fully enclosed baths were constructed in Sydney and Melbourne towards the end of the 19th century, such as the heated Grand Natatorium baths in Sydney, opened in 1888. Despite the long-understood health benefits of swimming and bathing, however, less advantage was taken of natural water sites than might have been expected and formalised baths and pools were only slowly introduced.The 1920s saw Australians embrace seaside activities such as lifesaving and a nascent surf culture; rapid changes in social behaviour, attitudes to the body, responsibility of society towards individuals' health and safety, all contributed to the growth of swimming as a sport as well as a leisure pursuit.

The construction of an Olympic-standard artificial pool was a major undertaking for any community to contemplate, finance, construct and manage. They were, in the main, a municipal concern in the period between 1920 and 1970. Their realisation typically depended on collaborative efforts between local community groups, municipal and state governments. Built public pools were regarded with great pride as a local asset that gave a much-needed focus

ADULTS

Yearly Tickets, to date 12 months from date of issue	45/–
Half-yearly Tickets, to date 6 months from date of issue	30/–
Quarterly Tickets, to date 3 months from date of issue	17/6
Monthly Tickets, to date 1 month from date of issue	7/–
Clubs and Parties of not less than 20	4d. each

JUVENILES (under 14)

Yearly Tickets, to date 12 months from date of issue	22/6
Half-yearly Tickets, to date 6 months from date of issue	15/–
Quarterly Tickets, to date 3 months from date of issue	8/–
Monthly Ticket, to date 1 month from date of issue	4/6
Scholars from Schools and Colleges, in parties of not less than 12, accompanied by teacher, with use of lockers	3d. each
Scholars of Primary and Secondary Schools, the boundaries of the City of Richmond or Richmond children attending Schools beyond the boundaries of the City, in parties of not less than 12, accompanied by teacher, for half an hour before 12 o'clock noon	FREE

The above charges will be suspended when the Baths are let for Galas or other Entertainments

Special Carnival Rates for Colleges, Clubs and Associations :

3 Hours—morning	£5/5/–
3 Hours—afternoon	£5/5/–
Saturday Evenings	*By arrangement*

Printed by Geo. Whitehurst, 241 Bridge Road, Richmond *Dec. 1937*

Swim in Safety . . .

Water CHLORINATED FILTERED STERILISED AND HEATED

RICHMOND CITY BATHS

GLEADELL ST.

TRAM TO TOWN HALL BRIDGE ROAD

5.2 Promotional brochure, Richmond City Baths, Vic, printed 1937

for leisure. The 1930s witnessed the first large-scale wave of municipal pool building across Australia. There were a number of factors that contributed to the desire to replace and augment existing swimming sites that had been fashioned out of natural water locations. Where swimming proficiency was once considered only necessary for the armed forces, increasingly it became regarded as a desirable skill for all Australians to master for reasons of health, fitness and safety. By the 1920s 'learn-to-swim' programs had begun with precarious government support, although swimming education for all was not universally adopted as a municipal concern until the 1960s.

Local incidents of tragic drownings in unsafe conditions, and ongoing outbreaks of infectious diseases sparked community concerns about the health and safety of existing swimming sites and fuelled pressure for new, modern facilities. The Coburg Council was, for example, criticised in the *Argus* in 1932 for promoting swimming in the unhygienic Merri Creek. However, the council rejected this criticism with the response that 'bathing in open baths seemed to be the order of the day everywhere, rather than baths in enclosed spaces'.[8] Public health scares coincided with a growing understanding of the side-effects of polluted waterways. In an effort to counter murky visibility, a public health bulletin of 1937 suggested that the addition of gypsum would clarify the muddy waters of swimming pools in dams, lakes and lagoons.[9] As natural waterways became rapidly unacceptable for public bathing, artificial alternatives were increasingly expected.

Many existing swimming sites also no longer provided adequate training venues for national and international swimming competitions that were fast gaining popularity and status. With the formation of standardised international rules for swimming, diving and water polo, and their inclusion in the Paris Olympic Games of 1924, swimming came of age as an international sport. Australia was quick to embrace it, with champion swimmers like Andrew 'Boy' Charlton and Frank Beaurepaire becoming household names. Despite the effects of the Depression, by the early 1930s Australia's reputation in international swimming events continued to grow, which encouraged a view among the general public that it was an acceptable sporting and leisure pastime.

Encouraging participation in swimming was mainly directed towards children, families and young sporting enthusiasts. This increasing emphasis on the modern idea of 'family togetherness' in the 1920s and 1930s further encouraged demand for appropriate safe and healthy bathing and swimming facilities, and assisted in shifting attitudes towards public decorum and the segregation of patrons. Highly codified conventions and modesties were quickly eroded, as mixed bathing became the norm and more women took up swimming. Public pools were subject to tightly governed rules, in contrast to a developing beach and surf culture where behaviours were already becoming less regulated and scrutinised. As one user of the Manuka Pool in Canberra remembers, 'it was all rules', and a good deal of local press coverage was devoted to issues of appropriate behaviour such as opening hours, dress codes, and interaction between the sexes and among children. Rituals of entering the water were driven by practices of hygiene and typically included compulsory footbaths and showers, which changed little over later decades. A number of public pools throughout the country maintained tacit racial segregation policies until the second half of the 20th century.[10]

In the main, however, the pool was projected as a new kind of modern public place: accessible and attractive to a large cross-section of the community. Family swimming was promoted as a popular means of encouraging 'better behaved' communities.[11] The number of pool visitors who were genuinely strong swimmers in these early decades was still low, but many simply came for a fun day out and municipalities had to build or renovate existing facilities to cater for

5.3 Sketch plan for Canberra Swimming Baths, Manuka, ACT 1930

larger numbers of spectators as well as swimmers. Sunbaking platforms, changing boxes and rooms, water slides and diving boards all became common in the best pools. The river pool inscribed in the Swan River's foreshore at Crawley, Perth, is a typical example of a public pool that was gradually modernised with the creation of a separate Olympic-sized pool in 1933, including lighting, extensive changing boxes and a water slide.

Advances in reinforced concrete technologies allowed for more ambitious structures for spectators and divers, and new and more reliable materials ensured better waterproofing. Servicing was also crucial to the development of adequate filtration and chlorination systems from the 1930s onwards. The firm of AH Pierce was just one enterprising Australian pool servicing company, being the first to import calcium hypochlorite from England. A growing number of pool buildings were professionally designed by specialist architects and engineers, with technical and design know-how accumulated through advisory notes and case studies published in national and international journals.

One early and prominent campaign for the building of an up-to-date pool was mounted in the new national capital of Canberra in the 1920s. The question was asked in the fledgling Canberra press in 1927: 'Why not a swimming pool?'

5.4 Lord Forrest Olympic Swimming Pool, Kalgoorlie, WA, opened 1938

The editorial continued: 'A capital city without an open-air swimming bath is as anomalous as a crown un-encrusted with gems'. The ideal pool for Canberra was imagined to include a tearoom shrouded in green plantings and an ample bar, also hidden from view. There was promise of international swimming carnivals, and even swimming breaks for parliamentary sittings; 'children and babies could throw off the constraints of everyday wear and return to a state of Nature and revel in the cooling waters'.[12]

The Federal Capital Commission and Australian Natives' Association (ANA), a mutual society of Australian-born men, took up the cause of building a pool, with long-running delays ensuing over the choice of an appropriate location. Eventually a site near the Hotel Acton and Ainslie School was chosen because it was already established with amenities and shops, and would locate the new pool near to school-age children. Extensive plans were drawn up for a 165 feet (50 metre) long main pool and pools for water polo, paddling and wading, as well as sunbaking stands and dressing sheds. The considerably less ambitious Manuka Pool – a single pool protected on all sides by perimeter pavilions – was opened to great fanfare in 1931 (figure 5.3). The projected swimmers' bar or café enclosed by shrubbery was not built, but there was a modest kiosk in the entry wing, and the pool was set in a gardened park between Telopea Park and Manuka Oval. In 1962 the National Capital Development Commission funded Danish sculptor Otto Stein to model a centrepiece for the children's wading pool. The complex is now heritage-listed on grounds of architectural merit as an example of the early wave of building in the federal capital, and because of its enduring social significance for the local community.[13] One former Canberra swimmer remembers the ordeal of lessons in the pool:

> my mother was just such a dutiful mother ... she took me morning after morning. I never used to get anywhere. We'd have to get up and it would only be half light. And you know the Manuka Pool is not designed to catch the sun – my mother would wait while I did a lesson with a private instructor who also got nowhere with me.[14]

During the 1930s a number of modern artificial pools were constructed in all states. Sydney's Manly Pool, built in 1931–33, was not a municipal concern but received funding from a ferry company. Its lavish facilities raised public expectations for other leisure and recreation pools built in Sydney,[15] which included municipally funded local Olympic pools such as those at Enfield (1933) (figure 5.1b), Bankstown (1933), Granville (1936) and North Sydney (1936). These were all designed by the aptly named architectural firm of Rudder & Grout. The Granville Pool was built on the site of a local duck pond, in a local park setting. The early design had two original pools constructed of reinforced concrete with glazed tiling and a series of pavilion buildings of blond and red brick banding enclosing the perimeter in a similar configuration to the Manuka Pool. The North Sydney Pool would become one of the most iconic in Australia, not only because of its spectacular harbour location next to the Sydney Harbour Bridge and Luna Park, but also as a venue for the Empire Games competitions of 1938 and 1958. The design features polychromatic brickwork with horizontal banding, simple classical archways and arcading, elaborate glazed tiling, and glass and stucco decorations of parrots, frogs, scallop shells and other marine motifs, accompanied by one of the most advanced filtration systems in the world.[16] After 1938 there was a hiatus in pool building in New South Wales, particularly in suburban Sydney and regional areas, as resources were increasingly devoted to the war effort.

In Western Australia the inland mining town of Kalgoorlie led the way with the construction of the Lord Forrest Pool in 1938, the state's first completely artificial Olympic pool.[17] It replaced the former outdoor pool constructed in 1900 that had been filled with salt water from a mineshaft and was converted to freshwater three years later once the Perth-to-Kalgoorlie pipeline began operating.[18] Swimming classes had already been conducted through local

5.5 Drawing of Brunswick City Baths, Vic. image c. 1979

schools since 1906, but the need for a more modern venue for swimming education and school carnivals motivated the completion of the new Olympic pool. The pool was jointly financed by the town council and the Kalgoorlie Chamber of Mines. The initial proposal promised a bold modernist design with an asymmetrical entry, flat roof, contrasting tower element and curved wall. The final design, by WG Bennett, was comparable in style to the Manuka Pool, and more conservative; it featured a symmetrical entry with 'moderne' 'cinema-style' lettering and a hip tiled roof (figure 5.4).[19]

Kalgoorlie's pool was proudly displayed on a corner block set diagonally against the dominant street plan grid, adjacent to parkland. The completed facilities consisted of a swimming and wading pool, change rooms, two grandstands, sunbathing areas, and a striking diving tower that closely resembled the headframes featured across the mining landscape. The latest technology was used for water chlorination and filtration to cope with dust from the goldfields, and a one-way entrance system was designed so that swimmers would pass through a footbath and shower. The main pool conformed to competition standards, and many swimmers trained there in preparation for international and Olympic events, while Kalgoorlie divers dominated the sport in Western Australia.[20] Natural water was a scarce resource, and the pool became the focal point for many community activities, carnivals, water ballet, polo and the 'duck hunt'.[21] Demand was so strong that, although the complex had a capacity for around 700 swimmers, visits at peak times were reportedly limited to one hour. The pool retained its popularity long after its opening; a photograph of the entrance was chosen as the symbol of Kalgoorlie for local celebrations in 1950. Symbolic of a shift in social attitudes towards Aboriginal access to public pools, a snake-like frieze on the entry walls has since been painted in yellow, red and black to acknowledge and welcome Aboriginal visitors and swimmers.[22]

Before the 1930s, five pools were constructed within the contemporary boundaries of the City of Brisbane which included Spring Hill (figure 5.1a), Ithaca, the Valley, Manly and Toowong Baths.[23] The Manly Wading Pool, also known as the Wynnum Wading Pool, is a surviving example of an early tidal pool under the Brisbane City Council's jurisdiction. Located adjacent to the Manly jetty on Moreton Bay, it was constructed in 1932 through the Unemployment Relief Scheme implemented during the Depression. Another early example in Queensland, in the Darling Downs region 200 kilometres from Brisbane, is the Dalby Swimming Pool, built by the local town council in 1936 (figure 5.1d). As the earliest Olympic-standard pool built in the state outside the capital, it was important to the development of competitive swimming in this region. The pool was built on land that had been cleared of the prickly pear cactus pest in the late 1920s and 1930s. With two pools for competition and children's swimming, a separate entrance pavilion and a caretaker's residence, it was a modern, innovative amenity, unusual for a town as small as Dalby. With the latest filtration and chlorinating equipment to treat the artesian water, it provided a model for public pools later built in Brisbane.[24] As well as providing a venue for swimming and lifesaving clubs, the pool also became a focus for many other local community activities, and during World War II it was used to provide sea training for Australian aircrew.

Underwater lights were installed to prolong evening swimming, and spectator benches were installed for formal events and informal people-watching.

Victoria, and particularly Melbourne's suburbs, lagged behind less populous states in the building of new concrete Olympic-pool facilities in the 1930s. One example is the Footscray Pool in the city's inner west that was built in response to pressure for safer swimming conditions than the polluted local river. Work on the pool was carried out by unemployed men during the Depression years under local government programs that generated employment through improvement schemes. Footscray residents were no doubt proud that the sparkling new modern pool became the venue for the Victorian Swimming Association Championships shortly after opening. Behaviours were typically well regulated, with limited opening on Sundays, no alcohol, no dogs and no loitering. No patron stayed more than one hour, there were disinfectant rituals to be followed, and suitable bathers and gowns were to be worn at all times.[25] As popularity increased from the 1930s, underwater lights were installed to prolong evening swimming, and spectator benches were installed for formal events and informal people-watching.

Most local municipalities in inner Melbourne established swimming baths of some description prior to World War II, and the water and health conditions were gradually improved through better filtration systems. Geelong Council, for instance, adopted plans in 1938 to erect a shark-proof swimming enclosure on Eastern Beach as part of a local civic improvement scheme that included a children's paddling pool and a swimming area of Olympic dimensions, a semi-circular promenade and a lower platform for the use of bathers.[26] There are extensive local government and newspaper reports of municipal councillors visiting and inspecting existing pool facilities across the greater Melbourne region in the 1930s, indicating their growing importance as a civic amenity.[27]

With Melbourne's cooler climate, the provision of heating was documented as a matter of particular concern at a number of city venues.

Public pools featured in professional and popular media in Australia soon after World War I. Architecture, construction and engineering journals published local and international articles on public swimming pool construction and management. Existing facilities were widely publicised in a bid to increase awareness of, and engagement with, swimming as a recreational pursuit. When the Brunswick Baths, in Melbourne's working-class inner north, were opened in 1929 they were advertised 'over the wireless and also by the liberal distribution of post cards with photographs of the Baths thereon'. Advertisements for the pool were placed in the local paper, and slides were exhibited at local picture theatres.[28] In Richmond, a brochure was created as part of a concerted advertising campaign for its suburban pool (figure 5.2).[29] Persuasive advertising may also have been needed to counter bad press that the Richmond Pool received; despite being one of the largest fully roofed pools in Australia, it was also described by the *Argus* in 1935 as one of the dirtiest in Melbourne.[30] By 1944, pool inspection results from Brunswick, Box Hill, Richmond, Preston, Camberwell, Malvern, Hawthorn, and the Brighton Beach, Carlton and City Baths were published in a conclusive local government report. Basic, if variable, standards were established at municipal venues of a pool size of 50 metres.[31]

Many municipal Melbourne pools were set in public gardens with their entrances oriented towards the street. Proximity to public transport was essential, and the provision of ample bike racks was seen as important – with some venues even offering valet bike parking for a small fee.[32] Debates about the merits of open seasonal outdoor pools compared to fully enclosed facilities were also raised in the 1944 report – a contentious discussion that remains ongoing in pool management and funding today. Debates also raged over exactly how accessible pools should be to the general public, and whether community pools should be open on Sundays. The Camberwell Progress Association hoped in 1932 to open the local pool to adults on Sundays; as swimming was not yet universally regarded as an 'official' organised sport, this move was resisted as an interruption to the day of rest.[33]

These examples from various Australian states show how pool building grew as a significant concern for municipal governments and local councils in the 1930s. However, it would be misleading to imply that all councils were uniformly in favour of their construction. Many still dismissed the very idea of a public pool as an unaffordable luxury, with the public purse far better invested in roads and substantial community buildings like town halls.[34] Council and local community aspirations, however, would shift dramatically in the 1950s.

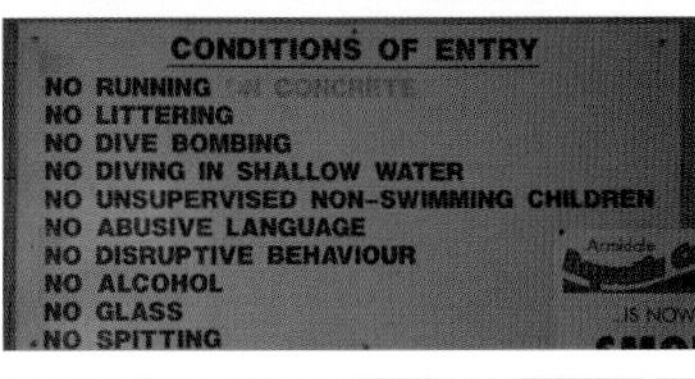

Opened in 1928 Lismore's Memorial Baths produced Australia s and later the Empire Games Lady Diving Champion of 1938, Lurline Hooks.

FITZROY Municipal Baths

ALEXANDRA PARADE,

Close to Brunswick-st., Nicholson-st., & Smith-st. Tram Lines

OPEN DAILY FROM 6 A.M. TO 9.30 P.M.
SUNDAYS, 7 A.M. TO 10 A.M.

MEN'S BASIN - 175ft. x 80ft.

Is the LARGEST IN VICTORIA, and will accommodate 1,000 Bathers.

WOMEN'S BASIN, 70ft. x 30ft.

Admission, 3d. Juniors, 2d. & 1d.

Resident Children, and Children attending schools in Fitzroy, admitted FREE on Fridays, from 3.30 p.m. to 6 p.m., but must bring towels and costume, or hire same at One Penny.

TICKETS.—Per doz., with towel, etc., supplied.
Adults, 2/6; Juniors under 14, 1/9
" " without towel, etc., 2/3
" " Members of Swimming Clubs, without towel, etc., 2/-
Hire of Towel and Bathing Costume, 1d.
Monthly Tickets (Adults only) 5/-

HOT SLIPPER BATHS

READY AT ALL HOURS.

FIRST CLASS	...	Males, 1/-	Females, 9d.
SECOND CLASS	...	Males, 9d.	Females, 6d.

A. DATSON, Town Clerk.

5.6 Swimming pool signage (clockwise from top left):
Conditions of entry sign, Byron Bay War Memorial Swimming Pool, NSW;
Promotional poster, February 1909, for Fitzroy Municipal Baths, Vic.;
'The Great Pool Party' poster, c. 1980, Harold Holt Memorial Swimming Centre, Malvern, Vic.;
Plaque, Lismore Memorial Baths, NSW;
Conditions of entry sign, Monkton Aquatic Centre, Armidale, NSW

Meeting demand for community pools in the post-war decades

After years of lean spending on public infrastructure during the 1940s, new programs for public pool buildings gathered momentum across Australia after World War II. The provision of recreation and leisure amenities was increasingly regarded as a popular symbol of good government, and growing political concern for the creation of social capital through community assets coincided with community need. Through these amenities governments attempted to exert coercive influence over the general health of citizens and foster productive use of leisure time. Widespread outbreaks of polio, alongside associated health scares connected to hygiene concerns in local waterways, fuelled campaigns for artificial pools that had begun in the 1930s, only to be put on hold in the war years. Ongoing demand for universal access to safe swimming lessons also strengthened arguments for artificial pools to replace or augment existing sea, river and lake venues. As a result, between 1950 and 1970 there was a steady increase in dedicated facilities for children and youth, including toddler and diving pools, and on-site childminding centres. As private car ownership increased, a day out to the public pool became a family recreation attraction, and the popularity of competitive swimming as a recognised sport was also given a huge boost through the hosting of the Olympic Games in Melbourne in 1956 and Australia's competitive success in the pool. Thus the below-ground Olympic pool came to slowly take its place as an essential service in the typical modern Australian neighbourhood or country town. Reflecting their acceptance as a place of community life, many commemorative pools were dedicated as 'useful' alternatives to war memorials (see chapter 8).

Swimming pool construction and management remained an expensive undertaking in the post-war decades compared to other recreational building types. They still relied on a messy coalition of state and local government and community groups. The provision of subsidies was much debated in state parliaments in the 1950s. Albert Lind, the Member for East Gippsland in the Victorian Parliament, initiated a discussion in 1954 over funding for country community facilities including town halls, recreation grounds and pools in particular. He argued: 'Swimming pools are an essential amenity in a country town, and they are conducive to the health of the people'.[35] Where pool subsidy schemes were implemented, they remained patchy and somewhat arbitrary in their allocation to country areas dictated by their distance from the coast, which often left inner-city and suburban locations bereft of facilities. For example, the Cain Labor government in Victoria in the mid-1950s recognised public pools as a 'right' for citizens in hot climates, but adhered to the national trend of concentrating state funding in inland districts where children were seen to be most lacking in swimming education.[36] In Western Australia, a similar policy, colloquially known as the 'Ribbon of Blue' scheme, gave some assistance to local authorities to construct pools in towns situated more than 35 miles (56 kilometres) from the coast.[37] Some places such as Richmond, New South Wales, circumvented these constraints by arguing that nearby natural waterways had become unfit for swimming.

Aware of the lack of financial incentives, state governments needed at least to show their willingness to assist with the construction of pools, producing information to help local governments and community groups. For example, the booklet *Standards for Modern Swimming Pools* was distributed to all New South Wales local councils in 1947. Here the Minister for Local Government, JJ Cahill, suggested: 'no form of local government could be considered successful that omitted adequate provision for the cultural and recreational needs of citizens'. Standards and models for pool design were issued as a way of prompting local councils into action. Other states produced similar advice brochures such as Western Australia's *Want a Pool in Your Town?*, which led communities through the daunting process of fundraising. By the end of the 1950s there had been some modest increases in Municipalities Assistance Funding Schemes, however grants were typically capped at 25 per cent of actual construction costs and remained geographically constrained. Increases in government assistance were hard-fought in the Victorian Parliament in 1959 on the grounds of discrimination:

> There are hundreds of thousands of children who are denied the opportunity of learning to swim under the *Herald* learn-to-swim and other campaigns. Every year unfortunately many lives are lost through drowning and most victims are in the metropolitan area. It is time the government turned its back on this ridiculous policy of granting financial assistance for the construction of country swimming pools only.[38]

From 1961, further assistance for pools, halls, playgrounds and parks was increasingly made available through sources like the Municipal Loan Fund scheme.[39] With supplementary community fundraising and volunteer work, by the mid-1960s many country shires and suburban councils had built their own pools. Difficulties in raising capital affected the ambitions of the facilities constructed, ranging from single 25 metre pools to multi-pool complexes with ancillary facilities and buildings. The construction of any public pool, however basic, carried symbolic status of the vitality of local councils which could support new initiatives rather than merely maintain minimal local services. Pool openings gave cause for big occasions, with lofty speeches from the local mayor, members of parliament and community leaders. One example is the Merredin Pool sited in the inland Wheatbelt region of Western Australia, that opened in 1955 as a testament to 'the free democratic spirit which is the essence of local self government'.[40]

While other towns in Western Australia struggled to raise funds, a number of mining and goldfields towns successfully fought to build their own community pools in the 1950s. By the end of the decade a string of pools had been completed: alongside Merredin, already mentioned, were Cunderdin, Northam, Bruce Rock, Goomaling, Bullfinch, Narrogin, Pemberton, Kelmscott, Perenjori, Quairading, Kellerberin, Katanning and Derby and, in the mid-1960s, York.[41] These modest pools were eclipsed by Western Australia's investment in a venue for the Commonwealth and Empire Games of 1962 at Beatty Park in North Perth.[42] The Games were the motivation for state and city investment, and on completion provided a much-needed urban facility for the whole of central Perth that is still in use today.

Between 1950 and 1959 over fifty public pools were built in Victoria, followed by a further seventy in the 1960s.[43] In New South Wales the first wave of pool building of the early 1930s was followed twenty years later with a greater construction boom. These were typically Olympic-sized outdoor pools, as opposed to the earlier sea and tidal pools and baths. The growth of pool buildings in Sydney was clustered in three patterns: as an instrument of inner-urban renewal; following the concentration of post-war suburban population expansion; and in locations where sea pools were inaccessible.[44] For example, concentrations of development occurred south of the Parramatta River and to the west of the city centre, with other developments in inner-city suburbs like Darlington (where a pool was built by the University of Sydney in part to establish its claim to a former residential district), Enmore and Leichhardt, and into the western suburbs where rapid expansion was occurring in areas such as Ryde and Hornsby. Coastal areas followed with the replacement or augmentation of existing sea pools.

In recognition of the importance of a swimming pool to isolated desert communities, the South Australian town of Woomera, established by the Department of Defence, had two Olympic pools in its peak years in the late 1960s. In this state, however, it appears that there was significantly less investment in public pools than in others. By the 1980s only around 40 per cent of local councils surrounding Adelaide owned pools, in comparison to 80 per cent in the wider Melbourne area.

Architects experiment with daring designs

As public expectations for a range of services and amenities intensified, the design of public pools became more specialised and complex. Architects took on commissions for pools and recreation centres, seeing opportunities to

5.7 Canberra Olympic Pool, ACT 1955

experiment with innovative designs that extended one of modern architecture's founding inspirations – the athletic body in space – to new heights of original exploration.[45] With a range of pool complexes being developed from the 1950s onwards, planning and pool shapes also became more experimental, with oval, T- and L-shapes making an appearance. Louis Laybourne-Smith's pool at Nuriootpa in South Australia is shaped in a way that would best be equated to a coffin. Some exemplars found their way into national and international architecture journals, including the *Architectural Review*, that featured complexes in Manchester and Coventry, and often depicted public pools and baths as part of larger reviews on New Town planning. The professional journal *Constructional Review*, in a 1960 article on 'Open air swimming pools', published a thorough guide to the design and construction of municipal pools, including basic considerations such as site selection and ways to estimate numbers of users (working by the rule of thumb that the smaller the community the larger the population percentage using the pool, with peak numbers up to 60 per cent).[46] The concept of a public swimming centre or complex, with a large range of pools and facilities and an associated gymnasium, grew in popularity.

The late 1950s to early 1970s marked an extraordinary period of pool design in Australia. It is true that the majority of suburban and country pools were prosaic and functional, typically providing little more than a single

5.8 Centenary Swimming Pool, Spring Hill, Qld 1957–59

Olympic pool, children's wading pool and perhaps a concrete block changing room, set in a grassy setting. At the other end of the design spectrum, however, notable Australian architects were commissioned to design prominent venues in capital cities where structural invention and playful manipulation of planning were explored, alongside experimentation with materials and colours, and the exploitation of ever-thinner folded concrete slabs and daring structures expressed in ramped entries and diving towers. New servicing and filtering technologies were skilfully integrated and underwater lighting and water jets assisted in competitive diving.

One of the first pools to be profiled in the architectural journals of the 1950s was the Canberra Olympic Pool. It won the prestigious Sulman Award for Architecture in 1955. Designed by the Canberra Department of Works, the new pool was intended to form part of the landscaping concept in central Canberra. Yet the multi-pool complex certainly did not attempt to blend with its natural setting, and featured a light steel geometric frame, up-to-date lettering announcing the entrance, and a bold, multi-coloured scheme for the starting blocks, lanes, planting boxes and umbrellas (figure 5.7). The Auburn Pool in Wyatt Park, Sydney, was featured in the *Constructional Review* and *Australian Architecture Today* journals because of its dramatically thin folded plate concrete roof.[47] The pool included extensive men's and women's pavilions, club rooms, kiosk, manager's flat and spectators' gallery – presenting to the street a striking frontage composed of a concrete screen wall in strong primary colours. Pool users were ushered through the entrance lobby under a cantilevered butterfly roof supported by two large inverted A-frames, and a curved concrete hood rose from the floor to form the cashier's box and turnstile areas. The playful pool was designed by the architect Frank Hines, and constructed under the direction of the local council.[48] A number of architecturally notable modern pools were designed in Melbourne in the 1950s, including the Beaurepaire Centre at the University of Melbourne, designed by Eggleston, Macdonald & Secomb, and the Melbourne Olympic Swimming Pool of 1956 by John and Phyllis Murphy, Kevin Borland and Peter McIntyre and engineer Bill Irwin. Although not strictly public, images of these two pools were widely published and proved influential on later public pool design around the country.

The most inventive design of a civic public pool in the aftermath of the Melbourne Olympics was the Centenary Pool in Brisbane, completed in 1959 (figure 5.8). It became and remained the state's premier training pool until the construction of the Sports Complex at Chandler in 1980. The Centenary Pool was designed by architect James Birrell as the Brisbane City Council's chief contribution to the state's centenary celebrations. The initiative to construct a pool instead of a monument for this occasion confirmed the popularity of public swimming in Australia. Birrell, as Brisbane City Architect from 1955 to

1961, also designed the Toowong Pool in 1959, now demolished (figure 5.1f). Unlike the Olympic Pool complex in Melbourne, the Centenary Pool was always intended to create a new kind of public and social place. As a reflection of the ambitious civic aims of the pool, the opening speech of the Governor Sir Henry Abel Smith was reminiscent of 19th-century statements on public improvements and civility:

> It is only in the immediate past five years that our City has found time and fortune to continue to construct the really civilizing elements of our environment with projects such as the Annerley and Chermside Libraries, the Wynnum Civic Centre, Langlands Park Memorial Swimming Pool and now these Centenary Pools ... The Centenary Pool project is loaded with artistic content, not only of our faith in the future, but to embody and courageously express our first hundred years of development. It could not have been realised without resources of the City's vast administration, and every aspect of this has been crystallised in this complex of building.[49]

If the imperatives of civic improvements were couched in 19th-century terms, the language of the architecture certainly was not. The free-form shapes of the main elements and their organic planning is said to have been inspired by the plastic expressionism of South American modern architect Oscar Niemeyer and European sculptor Hans Arp. The design encouraged, according to the architect, a relaxed and festive air as an alternative to the regimented composition and atmosphere of most modern pools. This daring aesthetic was, for the governor and others, an example of the state's 'faith in our destiny'. Rhetoric aside, the loose composition highlighted that the spaces surrounding the built elements were of prime importance as places of active communal engagement. A sophisticated two-storey restaurant and kiosk occupied a conspicuous place in the design (since altered), which further enhanced opportunities for people-watching. The restaurant and kiosk, also later subject to renovation, created a primary element in the plan. A curvilinear bathhouse on the south-west perimeter of the site added another communal amenity. The palette of materials including off-form and rendered concrete, and brickwork with unraked mortar joints were characteristic of Birrell's work elsewhere at the time. Ceramic tiling is a dominant feature of all modern pools, but here the tiling layouts gave another opportunity for fluid, abstract patterning. While the builders were local, it was mentioned as a point of cosmopolitan pride, that materials were brought in from all over the world – tiles from England, Italy and Japan, diving equipment from England, asbestos from South Africa, and drinking fountains from Sweden.

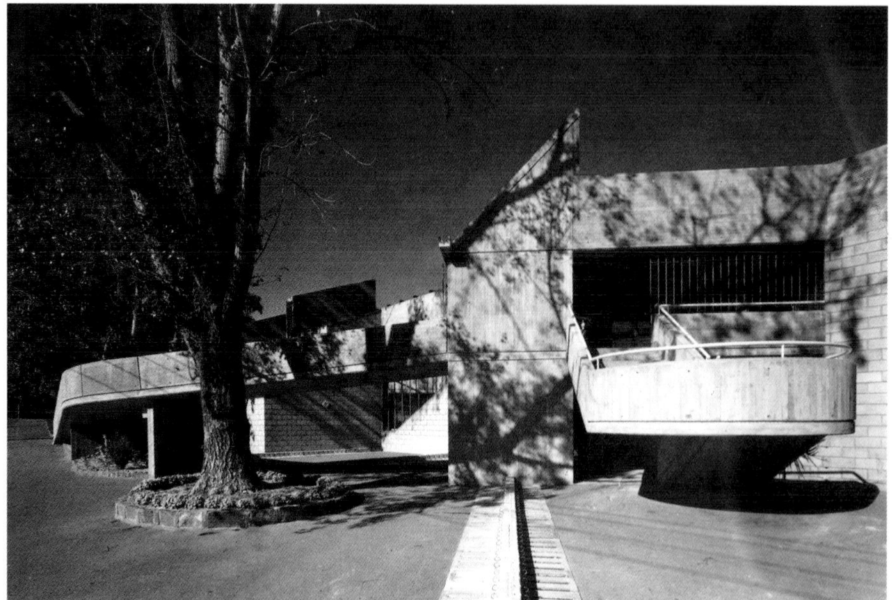

5.9 Harold Holt Memorial Swimming Centre, Malvern, Vic. 1969

The 'modern tropical' landscaping of the Centenary Pool's environs added to the air of playful leisure that existed along Gregory Terrace in Victoria Park. The park and pool together were described as beautifying the approach to Brisbane, with a comparison made to an 18th-century English landscape garden in the tradition of John Nash. Due to the lie of the surrounding land it was hoped that future higher density developments would be obscured, completing the atmosphere of an 'Arcadian glade'. The dynamic ramp entrance to the complex also alluded to the picturesque device of framing shifting views through bodily movement. Until recently the fate of the Centenary Pool was not secure with demolition recommended because of the anticipated costs of renovation to meet contemporary standards of amenity. However, work was completed at the turn of the 21st century and the pool has been retained and heritage-protected.

A decade on from the Centenary Pool, the design of the Harold Holt Pool Swim Centre in Melbourne also explored the dynamism of the entrance ramp (figure 5.9). Built in 1969, this innovative pool replaced the Malvern Swimming Baths that had existed on the same site in the 1920s, which had been the forerunners to open air pools in garden settings. Described as one of Melbourne's first Brutalist buildings, Kevin Borland and Daryl Jackson's design explored an expressiveness rendered in off-form concrete left unpainted. The structure, services and circulation elements, including ramps, mezzanine and walkways, are emphasised as highly expressive elements in the whole composition. The planning schema signalled Borland's interest in trapezoidal geometries and chamfered forms that he explored in a number of other contemporary projects. Parts of the building are highly transparent to deliberately expose the

5.10 L-shaped pool at the Collingwood Swimming Pool, Vic. 1978

activities taking place inside, thus enticing visitors to enter the naturally lit interior. In contrast, the change rooms are private, dark and more cavernous.[50] The expressed pedestrian ramps and stairs further enhance this sense of physical activity. The outdoor pools are enclosed and protected by grassy berms, cypress and date palms, with a dramatic diving tower completing the northern end of the complex, no longer used. The Harold Holt Swim Centre was innovative in its brief and planning through the integration of indoor and outdoor pools for different users, which indicated a conscious move towards community and family-centred recreation.[51] Also new at this time was the accommodation of a modest café and 'dry areas' catering to family spectators.

Daryl Jackson and Kevin Borland's experience with school design was instrumental in their gaining the Holt Pool commission. A key function of community pools was to cater for learn-to-swim education conducted through local schools. Jackson went on to design many other major pools in Australia, including the neighbourhood pool in Collingwood, Melbourne in 1978. Like the Harold Holt, Collingwood Pool was designed to maximise natural light, ventilation and exposure to its setting in Mayors Park in the inner-northern suburbs of Melbourne. In response to the park, the design of the 'wet' glass skin facade was conceived to be opened, thus enhancing the connectivity to the outdoors, much like the Beaurepaire Pool on the University of Melbourne campus. This park setting was resisted by some in the community who saw it as an encroachment on public open space. The interior is enclosed by a distinctive, clear span timber truss structure over an L-shaped pool which accommodates both shallow water use and lap swimming simultaneously (figure 5.10). Another teardrop-shaped pool is exclusively for children – with the space between the two pools allowing constant parental surveillance. Jackson suggests that planning innovations were instigated as much by the architects as by the local government brief. He comments:

> I had to battle pretty hard at Collingwood to get a triangular pool in for toddlers to come with their parents. I built the pool out of the concourse to where it appeared like a super-sized bath, on the basis that a mother could sit next to a little child and lower the child into that in the same way that she lowered it into a bath at home.[52]

Both the Holt and Collingwood pools have been the subject of recent alteration plans which have resulted in public campaigns involving the local community, architects and conservation experts alike. Such efforts to save public assets will be revisited in the final chapter.

The decline of outdoor municipal pools

Until the early 1970s, federal government support for sport and recreation was meagre and local government programs were at the front line of meeting community demands. This did not prevent politicians and local councillors from using the completion or upgrade of a local public pool as an opportunity for posturing. Prime minister John Gorton (1968–71), for instance, was photographed at a number of swimming pools. Under the Whitlam government, federal programs began to play a greater role in fostering local and voluntary initiatives for building amenities. Funds were given to encourage the development of single- and multi-purpose recreation complexes, with a particular focus on indoor facilities.[53] A speech by Whitlam at a 1972 Labor Party meeting in the Blacktown Community Civic Centre encapsulated this new era in governmental thinking on recreation:

> There is no greater social problem facing Australia than the good use of leisure. It is a problem of all modern and wealthy communities. It is, above all, the problem of urban societies and thus, in Australia, the most urbanised nation on earth, a problem of the 1980s; so we must prepare now; prepare the generation of the '80s – the children and youth of the '70s – to be able to enjoy and enrich their growing hours of leisure.[54]

Emphasis was placed on entitlement of access to a richer range of local cultural and recreational amenities, particularly in areas that had few, and to the promotion of opportunities for 'education and self-improvement'. It was envisaged that these opportunities would provide scope for citizens to 'participate in the decisions and actions of the community'.[55] Following Whitlam's election to government in 1972, a federal Ministry of Tourism and Recreation was created which produced a number of key reports into the status, funding and organisation of Australian sport and recreation and served to encourage the states to establish similar dedicated departments.

By the 1990s, in line with community awareness of Australia's ageing population, swimming for all ages had become quite normalised and encouraged through more 'holistic fitness centres'.

From this time on the management of sport and recreation became increasingly 'professionalised', contracted out to private organisations, or devolved into competing areas of responsibility in local government. For swimming pools, following international trends, there was a marked shift towards mixed-use, flexible and larger complexes of combined indoor-outdoor facilities.[56] It was claimed that these were more cost effective than conventional outdoor seasonal pools, and more able to keep pace with growing leisure expectations. 'Alternative Swimming Facilities', as they were described in a 1978 report, were touted as potentially revitalising water recreation.[57] Here recreation was clearly favoured over competitive sport and training, with the claim that 85–93 per cent of Australian and UK pool users came for play and relaxation rather than sport.[58] With new state and federal specialised facilities taking away much of the elite training functions, older community outdoor pools catered less well for unstructured play.

The Department of Youth, Sport and Recreation redirected subsidies away from outdoor single-use pools in the 1970s and 1980s and towards multi-purpose, indoor leisure and fitness complexes. The promotion of diversity of amenities, including heated therapeutic pools, was encouraged as a way of attracting the elderly and the disabled: additions to the Harold Holt Pool in the 1980s included a heated therapy pool.[59] By the 1990s, in line with community awareness of Australia's ageing population, swimming for all ages had become quite normalised and encouraged through more 'holistic fitness centres'.

The fate of the Footscray Pool in Melbourne's inner west encapsulates the much-repeated story of the rise and fall of mid-century municipal outdoor pools across Australia. Demands for a heated pool grew in post-war decades and were ultimately met in 1970, with the building of another pool next door to the existing outdoor facility, alongside a new public library dedicated to the commemoration of war service in World War II.[60] At this time pool management shifted from being a local council concern to that of the City of Footscray Baths Trust – still connected to local government, but with some autonomy. This was symptomatic of the widespread move away from local government managing pool venues, as pools were cast as a burden on resources rather than as a community asset. Another program of upgrades with additional leisure facilities was implemented in the mid-1970s but did not last into the 1980s under pressure from indoor gym, spa, therapy pools, sauna and childminding facilities. The old pools were demolished to make way for a new Swim Centre opened in 1987 within the footprint of the original 1928 pool. However, this complex was also beleaguered; it closed in 2006. This story is symptomatic of many factors affecting municipal pools in the 1970s and beyond. Indoor, climatically controlled venues have largely eclipsed the seasonal outdoor pool, either through totally new centres or major renovations to cover existing pools.

Swimming certainly did not lose its place as a popular recreation activity in Australia in the 1970s.[61] However, studies have charted a significant decline in public pool attendance of up to 65 per cent in selected Australian centres, in part due to an increase in the number of private backyard pools.[62] Further impetus towards indoor pools in the last three decades has been attributed to changing attitudes to sun-exposure in Australia. While Northern European modernism may have been driven by a desire to enhance the body beautiful through maximising exposure to the sun, antipodean postmodern public architecture accommodated quite a different relationship to the elements. Where once the building of a community seasonal pool was applauded as symbolic of municipal and civic progress through investment in safe and healthy outdoor pursuits, by the 1990s many municipal pools were increasingly disparaged as decayed, outmoded, unpopular and unsustainable structures. Many have been closed or significantly remodelled in the last two decades. However, if recent community-led campaigns against their closure are indicative of national trends, the tide may again be turning in favour of the retention of those outdoor pools from the mid-20th century that remain in suburbs and country towns across Australia.

5.11 Berridale Baby Pool, NSW, image 1998

BOWLS CLUB
WAGON WHEEL
WAGON WHEEL

Albert Park Bowling Green St. Vincent Gardens.

THE BOWLING GREEN, BUNDABERG.
W. Blaikie, Bundaberg.

GARDEN BOWLING GREEN

NEW NORFOLK
BOWLS CLUB

ALICE SPRINGS
BOWLING CLUB

LAWN BOWLS: A COMMUNITY GAME

Hannah Lewi

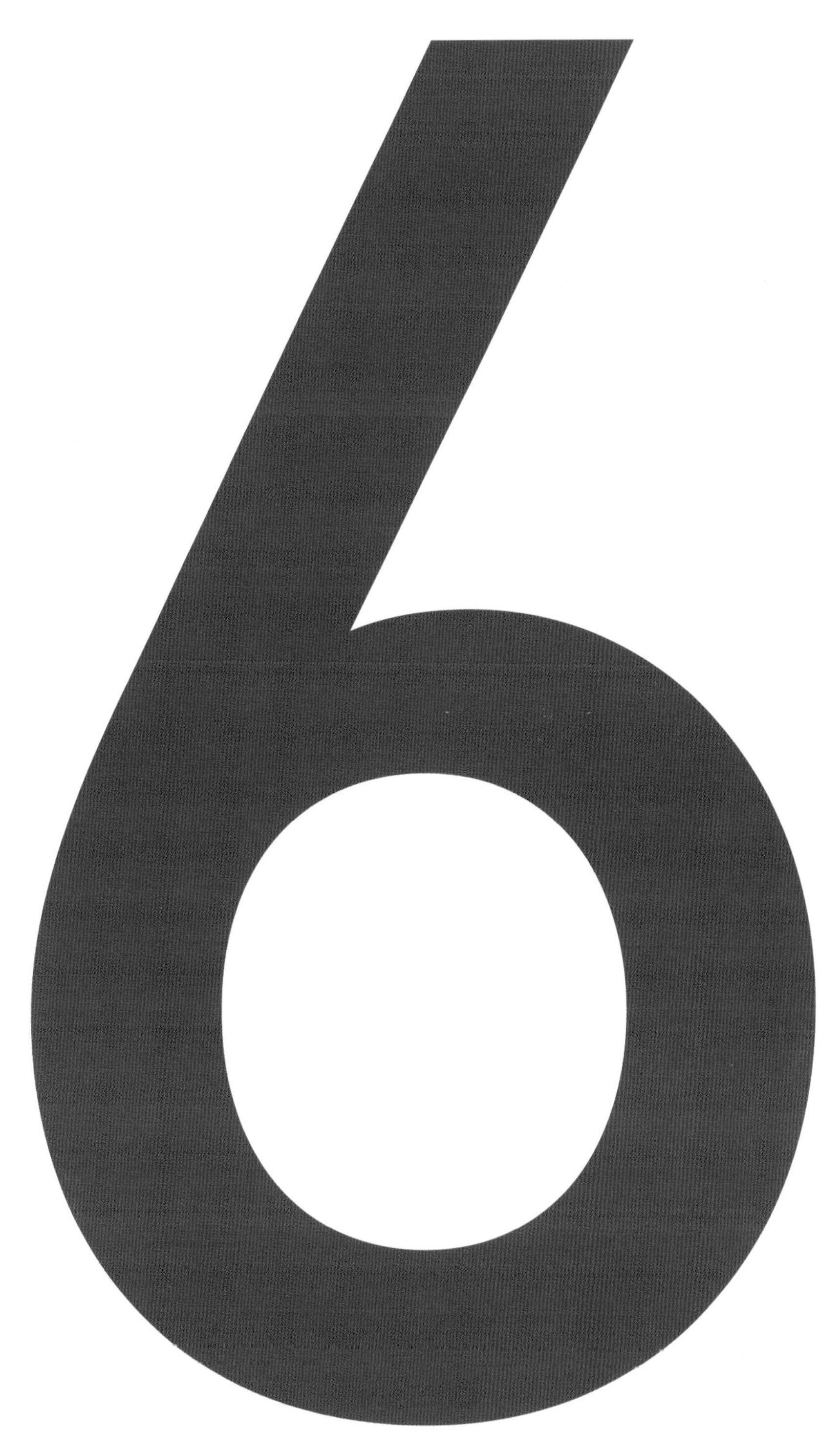

Bowling clubs compose such a mundane sight in Australian suburbs and towns that they have long faded into the realms of invisible familiarity. They may be fairly accused of contributing to what Robin Boyd characterised as the clumsy clutter of suburbia: fences, signs and unremarkable buildings.[1] While images of fastidiously kept greens and serious but convivial play undertaken in uniform whites have been the subject of some fond satire – Mick Molloy's popular 2000 film *Crackerjack* comes to mind – their history has

6.1 a. Adelaide Bowling Club, SA c. 1900 **b.** Hawthorn Bowling Club, Vic. 1938 **c.** Maitland Memorial Park Bowling Club, SA

been little charted beyond the sometimes tedious accounts of individual clubs.

It is partly because of their ubiquity that this chapter sets out to investigate bowling clubs. They form a key exemplar of community recreation amenities that became popular before World War II, and then further rapidly expanded in cities and country towns in the 1950s to 1970s. This is not, however, a building type that attracted much professional architectural attention; rather, it is the realisation of very ordinary and often makeshift local club buildings that forms a focus for this chapter. Bowling also played a significant part in greening and ordering the modern Australian neighbourhood, and its impact on the shaping of suburban landscapes is examined here. Bowling clubs also represent community amenities that provided not only a catalyst for the construction of suburban space, but also for the building of social networks through community fundraising and other activities. More recently many clubs have again become newsworthy because of closures and amalgamations. The chapter concludes by speculating on the effects of their slow disappearance on perceptions of community participation and 'social capital', particularly for older Australians who have typically received more ad hoc government services than the young.

Lawn bowls originated in England and was quickly adopted in the ideal conditions of Australian colonies in the 19th century. It is thought that the first game was played in Australia at a Beach Tavern in Sandy Bay, near Hobart, in 1845; early greens opened in New South Wales in the mid-1840s. Sydney's Balmain Club, founded in the 1880s, remains on its original grounds.[2] In Victoria, the Melbourne Bowling Club opened in Windsor in 1864, soon followed by clubs in Fitzroy, St Kilda and Prahran, and country clubs in Ballarat, Bendigo, Creswick and Kyneton. By 1870 there were Bowls Associations in New South Wales and Victoria with inter-colony competitions underway and clubs in all major colonial centres.[3] By 1910 there were over thirty clubs in

6.1 d. Nambour Bowling Club, Qld, image 1967 **e.** Prahran Bowling Club, Vic. 1961
f. Design for Bowling and Recreation Club, Peakhurst, NSW 1958

New South Wales alone, with numbers growing rapidly as suburbs expanded in the 1920s. In the first two decades of the 20th century, lawn bowls began to make the transition from a 'gentleman's pursuit' towards a more accessible and inclusive sport. Weekend and evening games rapidly became more common for the convenience of working men. Women, however, would not take part in actual play until later decades.[4] Overt documentation about social equity is rare in club histories, although the history of Melbourne's Mentone Bowling Club makes a point of saying that the club gave great satisfaction to local

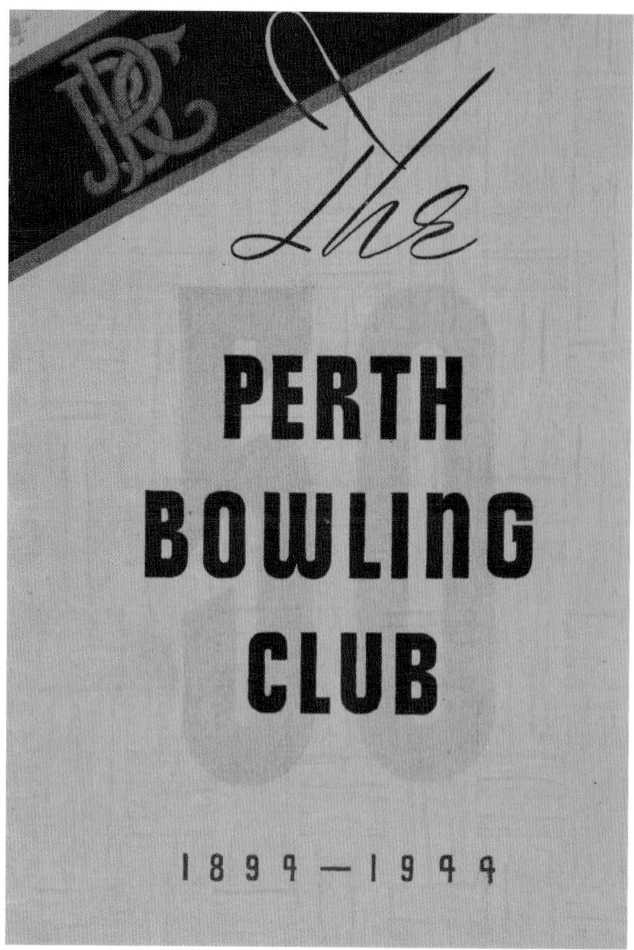

6.2 *The Perth Bowling Club 1894–1944*, cover of the jubilee souvenir history

citizens from every social rank; a well-known local doctor could play 'alongside the local plumber, and people of differing religions talked to one another as friends'.[5] Full membership remained closely scrutinised in many clubs for many years, and women were excluded from membership and play until well after World War II.

Lawn bowls clubs may be an invisible component of suburbia today, but their realisation was hard-fought by local communities and their openings were widely celebrated. Local progress associations and other citizens' groups, with the assistance of local councils and shires, were active in agitating for the establishment of community facilities, including bowling clubs, in all Australian states.[6] When achieved, the opening of a club was typically a big event: like the 'Gala Day at Nambour' with a turnout of over 200, and a deputation from the Queensland Bowling Association and local dignitaries.[7] The fact that Robert Menzies officially opened the Ringwood Bowls Club as the MP for Nunawading in 1931 is testament to the status that bowling had acquired in the community. Even though most local amenities for recreation and leisure were built and maintained largely through community organisations and volunteers, they were championed in retrospect by councils and shires in their own self-promotion and booster publicity, and municipal media often cited bowling clubs and other sporting facilities as evidence of a vibrant, self-sufficient community.

In Australia the game of lawn bowls was profoundly reshaped by modern technological innovations. From the 1930s onwards, modernisation brought night play under lights and a revolution in the shape of a solid plastic ball. Technology would also change the way greens were laid and maintained as better lawnmowers, automated watering, and levelling systems were introduced. In the peak decades of lawn bowls participation in Australia – from the late 1950s to the 1970s – over half a million Australians were recorded as playing either casually or competitively, which went against other falling trends in sporting participation during these decades. It has been estimated that there remain around 250,000 members in 2000 clubs nationwide today.[8] Although it was never prescribed as a game exclusively for the elderly, bowls has been stereotyped as a healthy retirement activity, both on and off the green. Popular perceptions of retirement are shifting dramatically as the population ages, yet it remains true that in recent times an estimated 90 per cent of those involved in bowls are aged forty-five or older.[9]

Laying the greens

In contrast to American indoor bowling, lawn bowls as played in Commonwealth countries is usually an outdoor game played on turf. Its history is thus intertwined with broader landscaping and planning initiatives that sought to cultivate recreation facilities from 'left-over' and reserve sites, and through the development of sporting grounds in existing parks and gardens from the late 19th century onwards. William Guilfoyle's original design for the prominent gardens surrounding Parliament House in Melbourne, for instance, was modified in 1888 to include a bowling green and pavilion alongside tennis courts. While many clubs were set in typical suburban streets, the majority of greens were established within public parks, gardens or reserves and their history can be productively discussed as one agent in the greening of modern Australian suburbia.

By the early 20th century, public parks and gardens were widely recognised as essential to the promotion and maintenance of the health and wellbeing of urban populations: they provided much-needed green 'lungs' in cities and towns across America, Europe and Australia. But where previously sports fields were typically relegated to wastelands and little developed reserves, in the first decades of the 20th century formal provisions for tennis, bowling and cricket, alongside children's playgrounds, began to be drawn into plans for urban park developments and beautification schemes. Most English parks and gardens for instance were now expected to cater for active, organised leisure and recreational pursuits beyond casual walking and picnicking. Fairly tight social restrictions remained in place in the early years of the 20th century and the regulation of behaviour in public parks was bound up with the developing rules and regulations for the sporting pursuits staged within them.[10] Participation in organised and team sports on the weekends became a more common sight in England and Australia from the 1920s.[11] In Australia the effect of war was less directly felt on public parks than in England, and some small-scale developments continued.[12] By the 1940s sport and organised play came to well and truly infiltrate public gardens in all but the most established botanical and commemorative parks in Australian city centres. Sport thus became a key driver in modernising and regularising the community landscape with specialised recreation functions.

Public parks and gardens were widely recognised as essential to the promotion and maintenance of the health and wellbeing of urban populations: they provided much-needed green 'lungs'.

Fulfilment of the ideal for the provision of accessible outdoor recreation was a central aim of modern European urban planning and architecture initiatives under the auspices of the Congrès International d'Architecture Moderne (CIAM), and was expounded by many leading and influential modern architects and planners. These modernist motivations were translated into some nascent town planning recommendations in Australia; however, Australians still turned principally towards Britain for models on the development of accessible open spaces and parklands in a suburban idiom. In particular, the reforming ideas in Ebenezer Howard's seminal text of 1902, *Garden Cities of Tomorrow*, shaped new ways of looking at town and country living that proved ripe for adaptation to Australian suburbia. Howard's diagrams and models on civic layouts and relationships between new towns and existing country were quite explicit in providing not just for gardens to be passively enjoyed, but also active recreation parks dedicated to outdoor pursuits and the playing of organised sports like cricket, bowling and tennis.[13]

'Town-planned' or garden suburb developments, as created and promoted by the likes of John Sulman, Saxil Tuxen, Charles Reade and William Bold, were created in all major Australian cities in the 1910s and 1920s.[14] The town planning movement's influence remained strong in debates surrounding developments before and after World War II which further served to draw attention to the desirability of providing for green zones, local parks and reserves with ample leisure and sporting amenities. The Canberra Croquet and Bowls Club is one example of a bowls and croquet amenity that developed in association with larger landscape and civic plans, in this case for the new federal capital. The club grounds developed around an early hotel for parliamentarians in the mid-1920s, and were included in the plans by Charles Weston and John Smith Murdoch for the Parliamentary Triangle in Yarralumla. Because of its association with the Hotel Canberra, the Canberra Club cannot really be considered a 'community-based' facility. Yet it was embedded in the heart of the Canberra plan, and historical documentation supports the claim that government commitment to develop recreation facilities for early Canberra residents (particularly families) was strong.[15]

Ebenezer Howard's specific advice on the strategies for implementing and managing new garden city and town developments also seemed readily adaptable to Australia. On the subject of park and road ornamentation, Howard suggested that considerable portions of open parkland areas should be reserved 'for cricket-fields, lawn-tennis courts, and other playgrounds, and the clubs using public grounds might perhaps be called upon to contribute to the expense of keeping these in order, as is customary elsewhere'.[16] Adaptation of such strategies to high-density inner-city areas was nigh-impossible, but in the leafy railway suburbs where open space had long been valued, it was a neat fit. Sport indeed became a key motivator in the purchasing of public parklands through the actions of municipal councils, progress associations and sporting clubs.[17]

A well-funded, early 20th century municipal park in Australia thus came to include a patchwork of zones and functions, comprising planting beds, walking paths and memorials, separate children's playgrounds, playing fields and courts, together with various modest buildings and open pavilions. Taking Victoria as one example, Edinburgh Gardens in Melbourne was home to the Fitzroy Football and Cricket clubs from the late 19th century and by the 1880s also housed lawn bowls. A separate ladies bowls club, alongside the Emily Baker Infant Welfare Centre, playgrounds and various pavilions and memorials were all completed by the mid-20th century. Other prominent parks that contain bowling clubs and are now heritage-listed in Victoria include the HV McKay Memorial Gardens in Sunshine, Melbourne; the Flagstaff Gardens in West Melbourne; the Malmsbury Botanic Gardens in the Macedon Ranges; and St Vincent Place in Albert Park that has maintained a bowling green for over a century. In Western Australia, Claremont Park was adopted as the site of the Claremont Bowls Club from 1903, and then was further improved with a monument to World War I service and memorial gardens, a local kindergarten, playground and baby health centre.

The adoption of public parks as settings for private and enclosed sporting clubs has not been free of controversy. Complex and contentious agreements surrounding maintenance and funding have often been fought between municipal councils and private clubs and associations. Keeping in check the

6.3 Fastidiously maintained greens at the East Fremantle Bowling Club, WA

expansionary demands of organised sports over more private pastimes in public gardens also presented challenges, and local disputes often flared. Protest against the encroaching on gardens and parks by sporting amenities resonated with latent fears that sport was contributing to the growing sameness of modern suburban places: natural landscapes were being flattened and regularised to predictable sizes and grassed over for predictable functions.[18] In other situations resistance was met more because of the particular politics of local clubs and their perceived power to enact the sectioning off of public land for semi-private use. This scenario was seen in the formation of the Earlwood Bowling Club, which began through initiatives of the local council members and the progress association at a meeting held in the local scout hall in 1943. Approval was granted by the New South Wales Bowling Association for the construction of four greens and a clubhouse in Earlwood Park, with a request following to the council to annex some of the park reserve. However, the local schools, a neighbouring progress association, and the Earlwood branch of the Communist Society all raised vocal objections. Appeasement of objectors was mounted on the grounds that the proposed area of the park was the least developed to date, and that other landscaping and beautification initiatives would follow. Also mentioned were the potential social advantages of a local bowling club that could run fundraising events for charities and the RSL. Bowling in Earlwood Park

was promoted as an inclusive family affair with the promise of entertainment for members' wives, sons and daughters, thus inspiring not only sportsmanship but also citizenship.[19]

Another club 'dogged by dissension and discord' was the Windsor Bowling Club in Victoria that sparked widespread community resentment in 1930 over its proposal to finance the construction of its greens from public funds, with the Town Improvement Association expressing a desire to lease part of the local park for the club's greens.[20] In a similar dispute in 1951 the *Gippsland Times* reported that the Sale Bowling Club's expansion plans had met with hostile resistance. The reported 'assault' on the Victoria Park grounds to excise more space for the expanding club was described as an attack on local people's rights to retain the use of public lands. Objectors worried that redevelopment would set the precedent for sporting clubs to enclose portions of the parklands and 'leave the real owners outside the fence'. Supporters of the scheme, on the other hand, thought that new facilities would improve and enhance local parks that were seen as 'little more than cow paddocks' in their current state. The local council ultimately rejected the plans. The case of Sale reflects a common situation in much of Australia where open space was still to be found in overabundance, but resources for the beautification and manicuring of these spaces were scarce.

6.4 Hamilton Bowling Club and Park, NSW, image 1930

In the main, development was favoured over resistance. Local councils were mindful of the need to be seen to be balancing the competing uses of municipal parks and reserves, and to assist in improvements. However, early controversies around the intrusion of 'modern' functions into traditional gardens have resurfaced in recent decades as heritage and conservation studies have often concluded that utilitarian, mid-century, sporting buildings, fences and car parks are now 'unsympathetic', and of little significance to overall design integrity. For example, a guide to conserving parks of heritage significance completed by the National Trust of Australia in 1993 cautioned that bowling clubs, sports ovals and swimming pools may leave 'a legacy of visual intrusions, and in many cases physical obstructions that need to be integrated into the remaining parkland'.[21]

Distinctions between public parklands and private clubs cannot, however, always be drawn so clearly. Many sport and recreation clubs – lawn bowls in particular – mobilised community work through volunteer labour to maintain not just their own grounds and greens, but also the public gardens that surrounded them.[22] For instance at the Petersham Bowling Club it was proudly reported:

> All seats, railings etc. have been attended to. A garden plot has been laid out where choice roses and other flowers have been planted. Half-a-dozen ornamental pines in large tubs have been purchased and placed in position on the concrete platform.[23]

This mode of sharing gardening responsibilities evolved in many clubs across the country, including Middle Park in Melbourne, where the club was responsible for the upkeep of hedges and fences surrounding the greens, and the council was responsible for the maintenance of the general park environs. Where older clubs were located in prominent town squares and gardens, there was increased pressure for the clubs to contribute to the upkeep of these public spaces. In the town of Colac in Victoria, the oldest bowling club was situated in the Memorial Square in the town's main thoroughfare, and members assisted in gardening the beds and lawns. This approach of 'do-it-yourself' municipal gardening was not always met with great enthusiasm by landscape design professionals who were beginning to make their presence felt in mid-century. For example, architectural commentator Milo Dunphy highlighted the inadequacy of 'uninformed beautification' around small community buildings such as clubs, schools and baby health centres in his strident lament about the scourge of rockeries and rose gardens published in 1956:

> there is tremendous activity in the landscaping field. Almost every new building is soon complete with its garden. There are numerous parks. Streets are planted with trees every day. Everywhere, from the Municipal Council to the factory management, the urge to beautify, is strongly felt.[24]

Club buildings: From makeshift huts to modern pavilions

Bowling was an all-consuming and serious passion for many. At the Camden Bowling Club it was said: 'Men dream, and from these dreams develop ideas that must be discussed and carefully considered before action is taken'.[25] Although many and varied, local club histories tend to fall into a typical narrative that describes similar formative stages in the life of clubs. Land was usually selected in consultation with the Royal Bowling Associations in each state, and then either donated through church or RSL sponsorship, or more likely leased from local councils through share or debenture schemes. Preparation for the laying out of the greens followed, with the provision for adequate drainage, and the levelling of land was always a major cost. The laying out of turf and its upkeep was paramount, with the all-important task of grounds-keeping key to a club's success: 'The standard of a bowling club is only as good as its greens'.[26] Until the 1950s, clubs typically made do with very minimal tin sheds or weatherboard huts to house meagre facilities. There are, however, many notable exceptions of older clubs in capital cities that achieved ambitious clubrooms. For instance, the St Kilda Bowling Club, established in 1865, was added to in many stages with the original weatherboard pavilion designed by architect Sydney Smith in 1876, followed by a new bungalow pavilion added in 1926 featuring half-timbered gables overlooking the greens. The St George Club in

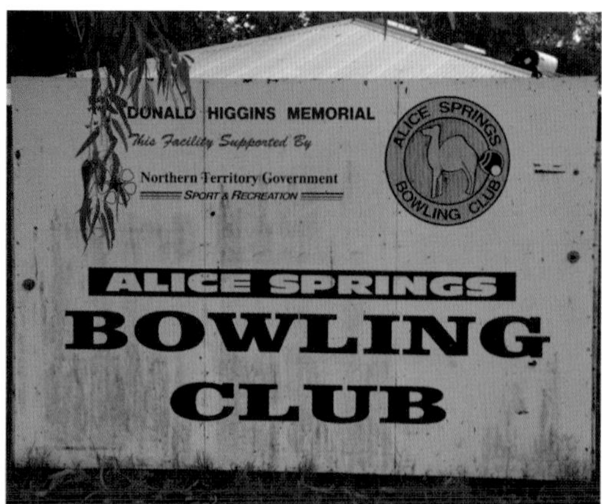

6.5 Bowling club signage (clockwise from top left):
South Coogee Bowling Club, NSW; Alice Springs Bowling Club, NT;
Belfield Bowling & Recreational Club, NSW; Alice Springs Bowling Club, NT;
Hurlstone Park Bowling Club, NSW; Maroubra Bowling Club, NSW

6.6 Bowling club interiors (clockwise from top left):
Hawthorn Bowling Club, Vic. 1938; Alphington Bowling Club, Vic.;
Clovelly Bowling Club, NSW 1951; Earlwood Bowling Club, NSW, image May 1957;
Mildura Bowling Club dining room, Vic., image c. 1950

Rockdale, New South Wales, built in 1919, is a significant brick building, and the Mosman Bowling Club, Sydney, of 1927 is a fairly elaborate example of an arts and crafts style design with a gabled entry and seven-bay veranda. Some older clubs also took advantage of state government grants for the relief of unemployment in the 1930s, as in the case of the construction of the Gosford City Bowling Club, that was allocated funding by the New South Wales government in 1937 for the building of a green and clubhouse, tennis courts and grandstand in the local park.

As bowling rapidly swelled in popularity in the 1950s through to the 1970s, a new wave of clubhouses was built to replace or extend and upgrade existing amenities. These more elaborate facilities were constructed to meet new liquor licensing laws that often required site power, public kitchens and toilets. In Western Australia the Peppermint Grove Club (1927) added a new clubhouse in 1962; the Mount Lawley Club (1921) took over the neighbouring tennis clubhouse in 1958; the South Perth Club (1916) added new premises in 1958; and many others such as North Perth and the Manning Memorial Club were founded in the late 1950s.[27] The building of licensed and rentable amenities was seen as the solution to many clubs' revenue worries. The Hawthorn Bowling Club with its new pavilion and bar, for instance, was able to host card get-togethers, their own orchestra nights and fortnightly dances, and electric light tournaments from the 1930s onwards when night games under lights became possible.[28] Fitzroy Bowling Club was rejuvenated in the late 1960s with the obtaining of a liquor licence and new premises completed in the early 1970s. With more elaborate bar and poker-machine licences installed in clubs that would accept them, prominent sponsorship by breweries like Carlton, Emu and Courage soon followed.

Another important factor in the need for building expansion plans was the gradual acceptance of women into every aspect of club activities. Ladies' Auxiliary Associations began in select larger clubs from the mid-1940s onwards (with earlier exceptions), and some totally separate women's clubs were formed. These 'courageous' advances in equality brought women out of the shadows of the club kitchens and onto the greens. Betty Stewart, for instance, dressed in uniform each Saturday and waited expectantly to join play at the Ararat Club, Victoria. She waited for two years until 1954![29] The partial segregation of play and social events was, however, still the norm, and so the acceptance of women often meant the building of separate clubrooms, or additions to the existing in the form of another wing – often to form an L-shaped plan enclosing the greens.[30] In Earlwood, New South Wales, a separate women-only club took over the old clubhouse when the men moved into a new wing. However, access to the central bar remained off-limits to women 'except on special occasions' when they were allowed to 'borrow' one of the men's poker machines as long

6.7 Yandina Ladies Bowling Club opening, Qld May 1956

as it was reinstalled in the main bar by 4 pm each day.[31] The role of tea ladies remained an important one for women players and non-players alike:

> Traditionally, a game of bowls has been regarded as incomplete without afternoon tea and so it has been at the Nambour Club. Mrs Dixon set a high standard of service in the area and the Club has been graced with a small but excellent team of 'tea ladies' over its sixty years.[32]

With so many new buildings and major extensions built during the late 1950s and 1960s, similar styles prevailed across clubs. Like their predecessors, these amenities were functional and domestic in scale and idiom, with simple rectangular pavilions and low-slung hip or skillion roofs, oriented towards the rectilinear greens. Materials were dependent on vernacular building traditions across different regions and ranged from timber weatherboard and tin in older premises and country towns, to brick or blockwork, tile or corrugated iron, depending on the materials to hand. Car parking became a dominant consideration as the potentials for additional revenue were realised. With few resources, distinctive elements were often reserved for the 'trimmings' of buildings: the entrance gates, boundary fences and screens, veranda posts and

6.8 Bowling club entrance gates (clockwise from top left):
Alphington Bowling Club, Vic.; Campsie South Bowling Club, NSW – Plaque at entrance reads: 'This entrance was officially opened 11th April 1954'; Henley Bowling Club, Adelaide, SA; Murrayville Memorial Bowling Club, Vic.; Ardrossan Bowling Club, SA 1962; Hampton Bowling Club, Vic.

scoreboards, or the prominent signage facing the road and car park. Wealthier clubs could afford to make their individual mark with a gate, rock wall or colourful entrance doors – all features which Robin Boyd denounced in his critique *The Australian Ugliness* as examples of 'featurism' that subordinated whole design to the accentuation of separate decorative elements.[33] The Alphington Bowls Club in Melbourne, for instance, features the club initials 'ABC' in white wrought iron gates around the greens. Similarly the Mount Lawley Club in Perth highlighted its club name in iron; the Nambour Club in Queensland, opened in 1956, honoured its founder with elaborate iron and brick 'Day' memorial gates, and the East Launceston Bowling Club's memorial gate commemorates both the club's first twenty-five years (1916–41) and its benefactor. If clubs were inaugurated through memorial funds, it was the gates that were often inscribed with a memorial signature. The Dungog Memorial Bowling Club in New South Wales, for example, erected by the Women's Bowling Club in 1947 in honour of those who served in both world wars, features grand entrance gates.

In the spirit of 'making do' with the bricks and mortar of community buildings there are interesting cases of existing buildings being re-used as clubrooms, including surplus military huts and wireless stations,[34] a fish hatchery in Bright, and a former exhibition building from the 1899 Western Australian Mining and Industrial Exhibition which was recycled as the Coolgardie Bowling Pavilion from 1907 to the late 1970s.[35] In some cases this trend was reversed when a purpose-built bowling club building was re-used for other purposes, such as the art deco style Yamba River Club House built in 1930, which was moved to the golf club in 1960, and then taken over as the local museum premises in the 1970s. In Victoria the Maffra Bowling Club, built with volunteer labour in 1926, was sold to the council in the 1950s to be used as a facility for disabled children.

On rare occasions unique designs for new clubrooms were provided by architects – often club members – and building works were also sometimes organised and subsidised through donated materials and labour also from members.[36] The Bareena Bowling Club, for instance, was designed by Geelong architects Laird and Buchan in 1915, and the Prahran Bowling Club, designed by Leslie M Perrott and Partners, was published in *Architecture in Australia* in 1962 (figure 6.1e).[37] The upgrade of the Orange City Bowling Club in New South Wales, designed by the firm Christian and Gerrett, included very elaborate facilities with a ballroom-size auditorium, separate bars and poker-machine areas. Other more propositional and daring designs, never realised, included Loder & Dunphy's space-age scheme for a bowling and recreational club at Peakhurst (figure 6.1f), and Ian McKay's design for Croydon Park, New South Wales, inspired by Frank Lloyd Wright's American domestic architecture.[38]

6.9 (above and right) View and plan of Canberra South Bowling Club, ACT 1959

The most widely recognised Australian modern architect to be engaged by a bowling club to design their premises was Harry Seidler who, in collaboration with Colin Griffiths, designed the elaborate clubrooms for the Canberra South Bowling Club, sited in grassed parklands in Griffith (figure 6.9). Constructed in 1959, the building featured in an issue of *Architecture and Arts*, alongside other community and sporting facilities that were topical building types in Australian professional magazines of the late 1950s. The planning was far more considered than many clubrooms, and included a main hall as the focal point for gatherings and social functions with free-span and flexible rooms overlooking the paved terrace and greens. The simple square plan emphasised the axial relationship between the entrance shaded by a curved canopy, and the curved 'selector's stage' room that overlooked all play areas. Pale red-brown face brick and suspended concrete slabs were simply expressed along with exposed grey steel columns and timber for the entrance canopy, bar surfaces and parquetry flooring. Other clubhouses, like Nambour, although not necessarily designed by well-known architects, had increasingly complex design programs to cater for new expectations in entertainment amenities (figure 6.1d).

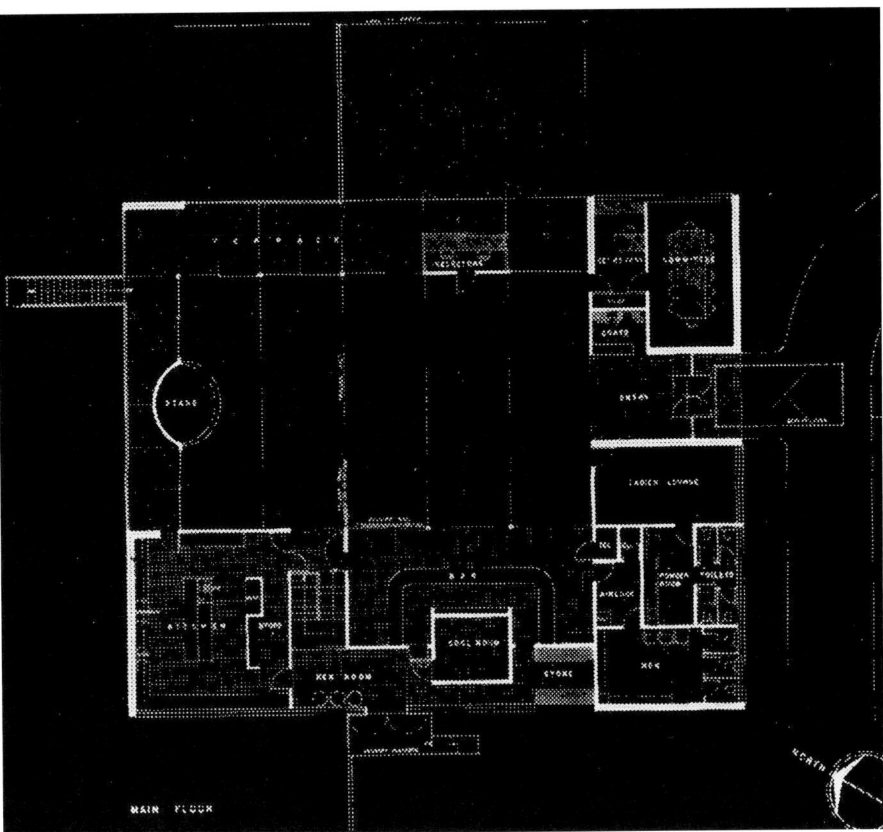

Building community networks through bowling

Although bricks and mortar were necessary, in fact most local bowling club histories make little or no mention of the design and building of their clubhouses. It is the story of the players and the club organisation that takes centre stage. Bowling clubs were an important venue for creating social networks and community cohesion in city centres and country towns alike – at least for a limited sector of the population. The ongoing necessity for fundraising to bolster meagre municipal and other financial assistance brought players and clubs together in communal social activities. There are countless accounts of ingenious ways members achieved their goals in starting clubs, building new premises and maintaining grounds. The Marong Bowls Club in Victoria, for instance, organised fundraising to build a new club in the district through cake stalls, casserole luncheons, bingo and the selling of cut wood and straw. Early club amenities were often makeshift, such as the Canterbury District Diggers Bowling Club where members gathered to make plans for new premises around 'barrels brought from a cool room and a poker machine in the back of someone's car'.[39] Fundraising work was by no means limited to self-interested causes, and clubs took pride in being instrumental in broader community events. For

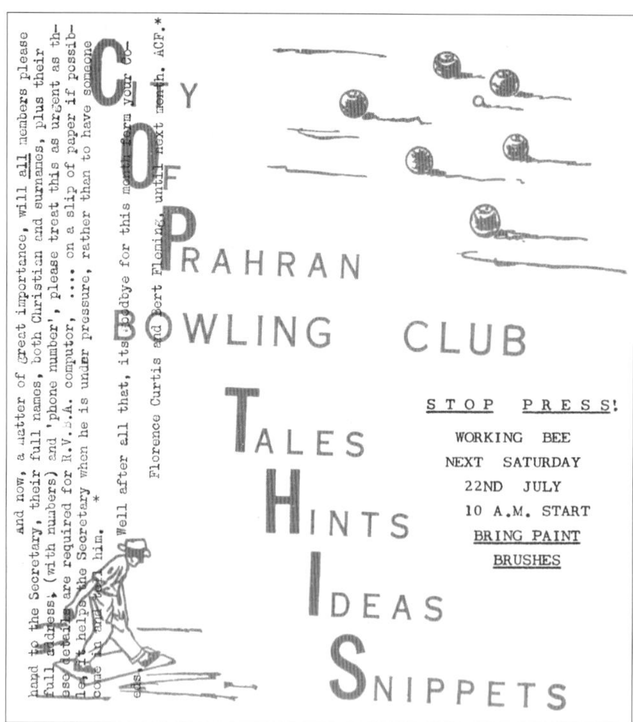

6.10 City of Prahran Bowling Club newsletter, *Cop This*, Vic. 1967

example, the Lakemba Women's Bowling Club in New South Wales raised generous donations for 'the disabled and the distressed' in the community.[40]

Bowling competitions were suspended formally from 1942 to 1945 in many areas, and informal play also dramatically decreased, but clubs used their social networks to raise funds for the war effort and to provide food and comfort parcels for prisoners of war. During the war years at the Canterbury Women's Bowling Club, lady members concentrated on a 'sewing circle' where 'hundreds of pillowslips, underwear, socks and scarves were made for Comfort funds'.[41] Play resumed in the late 1940s and home-grown hospitality and entertainment again flowed with the resumption of pennants competitions.[42] Similarly at the Rochester Club, in evidence of its role in fostering community spirit, during the war years money was actively raised for donations to comfort funds, the Red Cross, Food for Britain, and Welcome Home funds.[43] Tournaments for ex-servicemen were organised around the country following World War II, which included carnivals for the Limbless Soldiers Association and blinded bowlers.

The building of community spirit through recreation was all the more needed in isolated and small country centres where clubs often thrived. One of Western Australia's oldest clubs was founded in the mining town of Kalgoorlie in 1906. Many new clubs followed in the Wheatbelt and towns in the far north, including Karratha, Port Hedland and Newman. As testament to the dedication of players, pennant days in the town of Dampier included matches between Karratha and Port Hedland. Players could make a round trip by car of

6.11 New Lambton Bowling Club, NSW

200 kilometres on any one Saturday![44] The provision of sports and recreation facilities in company and mining towns had always been targeted as a means of fostering some attachment to the local place for a largely itinerant population. Clubs were again typically founded through combined assistance from local government and industry engaged in the townsites. The Adaminaby Bowling Club first met in 1959 in a building donated by the Snowy Mountains Hydro-Electric Authority and was funded through loans from the Snowy River Shire. In the town of Woomera in central South Australia, established by the Department of Defence for the testing of missiles in the 1950s, the Entertainment and Recreation Committee was deeply involved in the organisation of social leisure for residents through sports and hobby clubs. In 1968, at the town's peak, there were more than eighty-two active clubs, including what has been described as an excellent bowling green with a clubhouse that 'made a democratic alternative to the messes'.[45] Other companies and government organisations also sponsored country clubs; these included the Victorian Railways Institute which, after World War II, used its state-wide facilities in many small towns and larger rural centres to promote social and sporting activities, such as lawn bowls, for railway workers and their families.[46]

6.12 70th anniversary celebration, Southport Ladies' Bowls Club, Qld 1999

Throughout the literature and local histories of clubs around Australia there is little mention of the predominant age or ethnicity of members. The stereotypical image of lawn bowls, as held by the baby-boomer generation, is of an old persons' game for predominantly Anglo-Australian retirees. Although this has not always been so, it is fair to say that memberships in early clubs in the main comprised men coming near to and in retirement, and then from the 1950s onwards increasingly included older women in all aspects of the game. The social networking and community involvement some members gained through their local bowls club thus provided an important social facility to senior citizens who otherwise received little in the way of structured and targeted government schemes for the promotion of sociality and leisure.

The local Senior Citizens and RSL clubs were another obvious focus for both the formal and informal delivery of programs for retirees and senior citizens, who often had close involvement in bowling clubs. In one rare discussion from the 1950s on the issues of an ageing population, the growing prevalence of loneliness in the community was noted. A 76-year-old interviewee plainly stated: 'I was lonely until I joined the bowling club'.[47] This

study suggested that increased participation in local community clubs for the elderly and other leisure pursuits like bowling was inversely correlated with complaints of loneliness and isolation. More frequent club visits fulfilled needs for social contact through events and shared activities, the serving of meals and drinks, games nights and so on. However, this study also concluded that the actual rates of membership for a range of community clubs, including bowling clubs, was seen as low in the early 1950s, attributed in part to the lack of premises available at that time that had proper clubrooms, kitchens and so on. This concurs with the many histories of local bowling clubs that indeed greatly expanded their amenities and memberships from the late 1950s through to the 1970s.

By the 1970s, shifting social times were registered by a number of clubs. For instance the history of the Fitzroy Bowling Club in Melbourne recognised that the local community was undergoing great change. The impact of the building of the Housing Commission flats in Fitzroy was discussed in terms of the issues faced in bringing 'new' and 'old' Australians together. Yet the club, it was felt, was 'something of an oasis' for locals whatever their origin:

> People come along and look through the railings. They are always invited to come in to the surrounds and watch the play and sometimes into the clubhouse for a cup of tea. The detriments of unbroken asphalt and paving and closely built streets may, in fact, really prove to be an asset.[48]

This view of the way the Fitzroy Club might engage with social change was overly optimistic. From the mid-1980s onwards the playing of lawn bowls as a non-professional recreation underwent a sharp decline, as did new and existing club memberships. One local club history described its loss of living club memory in nostalgic terms: 'All of those who participated in the discussions pertaining to the new Gosford Bowling Club, the unofficial and official openings of the green and clubhouse have now passed on to where the green is always perfect and the atmosphere is always convivial'.[49]

In New South Wales alone over forty bowls clubs and over sixty RSL clubs closed between the early 1990s and mid-2000s, including city and country clubs like Newcastle City, Kirribilli Ex-Service Bowling Club, Granville, Lakemba Workers' Bowling Club and countless others. The Narwee Women's

6.13 The green at Clovelly Bowling Club, NSW, built in 1951

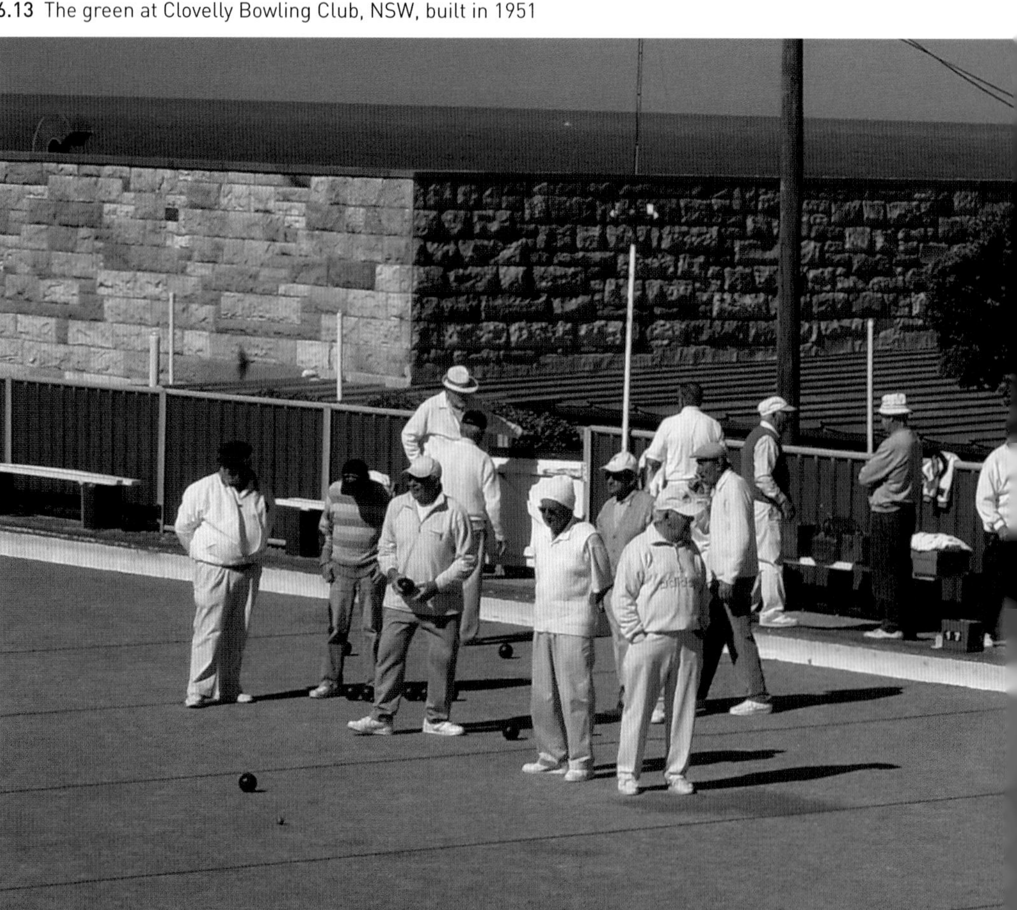

Bowling Club closed in 1994 due to unpaid council rent while it still had an active membership of sixty-six and was one of only two women's clubs remaining in Sydney.[50] Countless other closures and amalgamations of clubs have been enacted around Australia due to declining active memberships and changing leisure patterns, increased financial demands and changing economic expectations in local government that markedly affected the way assets were managed.[51] If bowling clubs did not yield to the pressures of poker machines and liquor sponsorship they came to face tough competition from other venues that provided far more elaborate bar and restaurant facilities and gambling options, including many RSL clubs. As one woman bowler declared in 1986: 'Bowls seems to have lost some of its flavour for people who would prefer to go to bingo or have one of the cheap meals at the RSL'.[52]

With an ageing population, one might think that this decline would not have occurred so sharply in Australia. The complex web of factors that has led to shifts in social and recreation patterns in local communities has been the subject of much analysis and debate in recent years. Robert Putnam's controversial thesis on the collapse and revival of American community in *Bowling Alone*

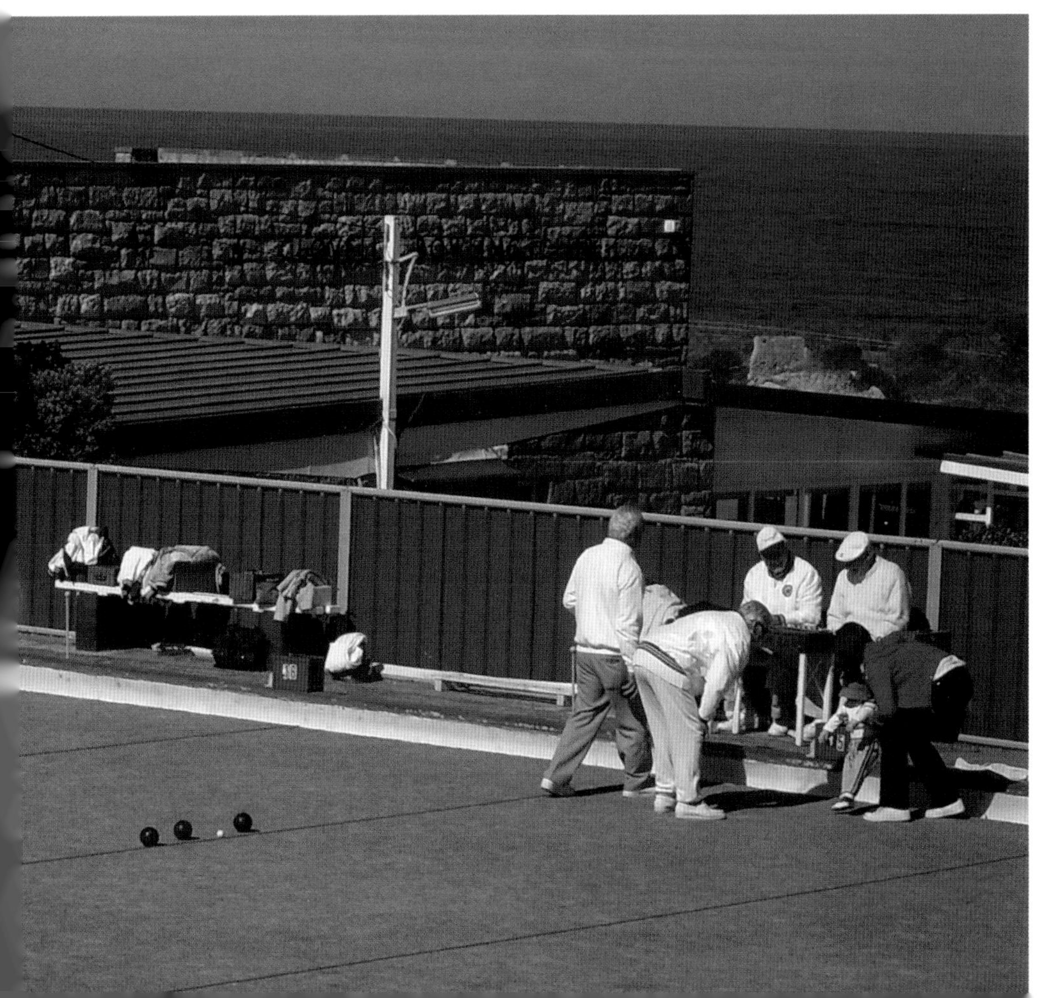

uses bowling participation as an index to support his arguments.[53] While Putnam is discussing ten pin bowling – a very different phenomenon to lawn bowls – the example could extend to any community-based sporting activity. Putman asserts that, unlike all other organisations of sports and leisure activities, indoor bowling has come close to sustaining its participation rates over the last few decades – with, for example, 91 million Americans bowling at some point during 1996. He reports that more young people are taking up bowling than ever before, and all ages and classes participate on a casual basis. However, what has sharply declined by some 40 per cent since 1980 is organised league bowling. Putnam extrapolates this finding by attributing a generalised decline in civic engagement through organised clubs, community projects and activities to a cocktail of causes including changes in working patterns, family compositions, social networks, urban sprawl, increased digital media and television watching, and shifting racial distributions across urban centres.

The American situation is different in many ways to Australia and Putnam's study has been highly contested. Yet there is no doubt that the research rings true for many policy-makers, and it is evident that many lawn bowls clubs in Australia have experienced steady decline in the last two decades. As there are far fewer opportunities to participate in lawn bowls outside an organised match, the reported decline in competitions and regular pennant competition has had a marked effect on the survival of many urban and rural clubs. Informal reports also demonstrate a growing lack of interest in formal competition: 'The trouble is that generally about 70 per cent of bowlers are not interested in competition bowls … If it's hot, cold or wet they won't play.'[54] Another current study of women's participation in lawn bowls in Western Australia has also remarked on the changing attitudes of younger members who do not want to participate in off-the-green duties such as volunteering in the kitchen.[55] The assumption that members would contribute voluntary labour, particularly when they become physically unable to play but do not want to retire, has always underpinned the running of clubs.[56]

Club closures have certainly been perceived as having an impact on community life and the maintenance of social networks.[57] For instance, the president of the Narwee Women's Bowling Club remarked that the club's potential closure would 'spell the death of friendships, social outings and bowling for the majority of members … There are so many elderly ladies here it's their only means of getting out and about … More than 50 per cent would never go into a men's club. They'd never play bowls again.'[58] Linda Heuser's perceptive analysis of women bowlers, conducted in 2002, has concluded that participation in bowling has created a particular kind of 'women's time and space' and has thereby built rich and meaningful social connections and a sense of community.[59]

Active participation in the bowling club has been seen in these personal accounts as a healthy physical and social activity that has helped relieve the potential isolation and loneliness of old age. As one participant says:

> I mean if I wasn't playing bowls, I'd be sitting at home doing the housework. Doing things like exercise even though it's not strenuous exercise, it still keeps you going … Otherwise I'd probably be fiddling around, wasting my life away.[60]

In light of recent policies addressing the perceived declining participation rates in community recreation and civic engagement, state and federal government programs have backed local initiatives such as the current 'Get on the Green' campaign by Bowls Australia which is taking place in 250 clubs nationwide.[61] The campaign aims to 'reposition the game of bowls to the Australian public' by promoting younger players to join more relaxed and flexible clubs.

In recognition that local recreation is 'vital to the social fabric, strength and wellbeing of communities young and old', direct government assistance schemes have also been instrumental in giving much-needed drought assistance to affected clubs in recent years.[62] In urban and rural areas alike, where once the sight of well-watered expanses of grassed ovals and greens was the norm, it has in recent years become an increasing rarity in many parts of the country.[63] The president of central Victoria's Landsborough Bowls Club said in a recent interview:

> We seem to get by. The green's not as good as it could be, because of water shortage at critical times, but it's still playable. They're hard enough to maintain in good conditions and plenty of water. But if you've got to work the green around lack of water, it makes things three times, four times as difficult.[64]

These schemes are bound up with broader indirect government strategies to promote more grassroots participation in healthy recreation for young and old, and to assist country towns suffering decline. However, in the main, as this chapter has illustrated, it remains beholden to local organisations to build and maintain the everyday environs of Australian communities.

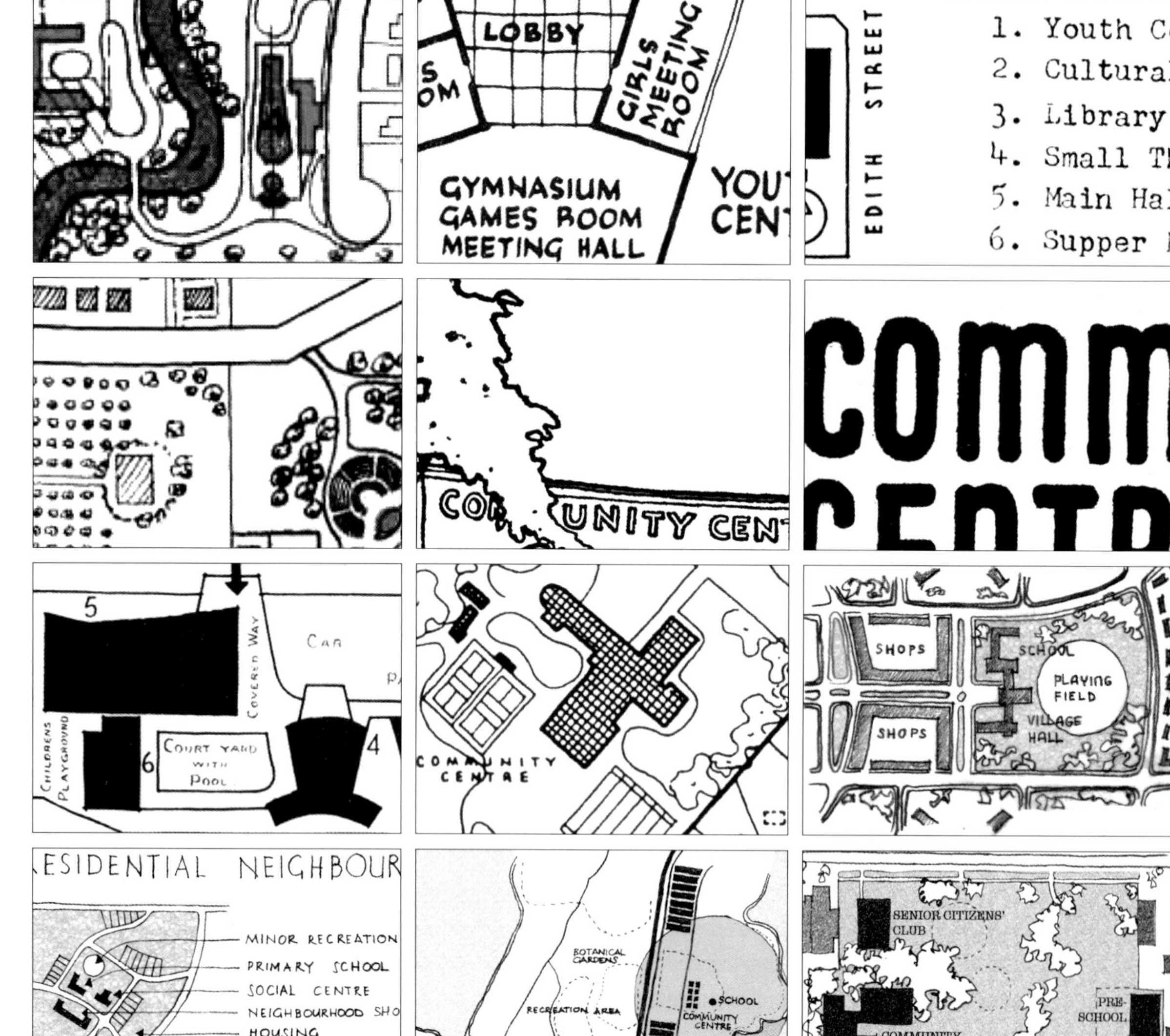
LOBBY
GIRLS MEETING ROOM
GYMNASIUM
GAMES ROOM
MEETING HALL
YOUT
CENT
EDITH STREET
1. Youth Ce
2. Cultural
3. Library
4. Small Th
5. Main Hal
6. Supper F
UNITY CEN
COMM
5
COVERED WAY
CAR
CHILDRENS PLAYGROUND
COURT YARD WITH POOL
6
4
COMMUNITY CENTRE
SHOPS
SCHOOL
PLAYING FIELD
SHOPS
VILLAGE HALL
ESIDENTIAL NEIGHBOUR
MINOR RECREATION
PRIMARY SCHOOL
SOCIAL CENTRE
NEIGHBOURHOOD SHO
HOUSING
BOTANICAL GARDENS
RECREATION AREA
SCHOOL
COMMUNITY CENTRE
SENIOR CITIZENS' CLUB
PRE-SCHOOL
COMMUNITY THEATRE + ROOMS
MUNITY HALL
ITORIUM
NASIUM
BROOMS
-SCHOOL
POOL
FUTURE CITY
NEIGHBOURHOO
COMMUNI
KINDERGARTEN MEETING ROOMS LIBRARY
CLUB ROOM YOUTH REFRESHMENT
OCIAL HALL AUDITORIUM THEATRE AR
YOUTH RECREATION INFANT WELFARE CENTR
PROPOSED

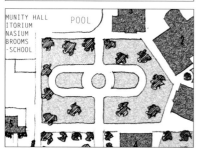

THE COMMUNITY CAN DO IT! PLANNING FOR THE NEW CIVIC CENTRE

Kate Darian-Smith, David Nichols and Julie Willis

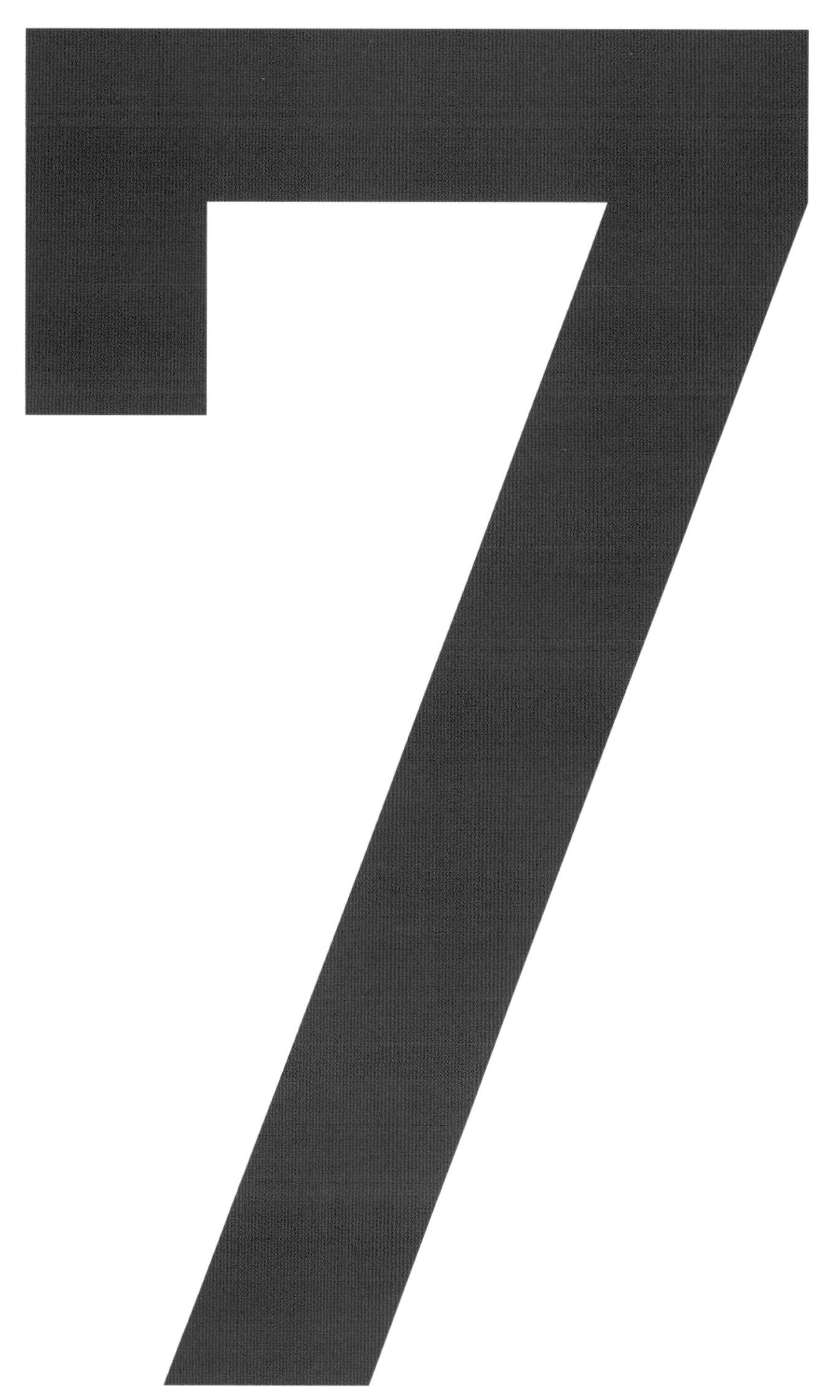

There's a new spirit abroad – the spirit of community. Maybe it's a revival of an organisation that goes far back into the history of our people – the gathering of British men and women around the village.[1]

When the ABC broadcast these words – part of a lecture series entitled 'The Community Can Do It' which was later published as a pamphlet – it was reflecting on a social pattern familiar to many Australians. From the time of colonial settlement, Australian cities, towns and suburbs were commonly structured around a centrally located and, if funds permitted, imposing town hall in an arrangement reminiscent of a European village square. During the 19th century, these buildings were almost universally built in ornate classical

7.1 a. and b. Social infrastructure was considered central to the modern community. *Shepparton: Today and Tomorrow*, Shepparton Borough Council & *Shepparton Advertiser*, Vic. 1946

styles that emphasised the grandeur of their function as the site of municipal government, remote from the centre of Empire but yet an implacable part of it. However, by the mid-20th century, democratic impulses of modernist design were well underway in transforming community buildings into more accessible facilities. The social disruption arising from the 1930s Depression and World War II, coupled with intense planning for the post-war 'reconstruction' of the nation, was to provide an impetus for the reconceptualisation of social organisation and community and the rights and responsibilities of the Australian people. As a consequence, the extraordinary flurry of architectural plans and proposals for public community buildings and precincts that circulated during and after World War II consciously encapsulated a radical new spirit of Australian community in their design:

In 1941, for example, urban planner and architect Frank Heath was commissioned by the newly formed Borough of Swan Hill, a regional Victorian town on the Murray River, to design its future development. Heath was dismissive of Swan Hill's existing town hall, completed only five years earlier, because it abutted the street and had limited amenities for residents. Instead, he proposed a civic centre situated in open park space providing facilities for a range of cultural, educational and recreational services for all ages as the 'focal point of administration and social life of the town'.[2] Heath's vision reflected a shift prevalent among planning professionals away from imposing, street-focused, civic architecture – a stentorian town hall – towards a multi-purpose centre or cluster of buildings in a 'welcoming' open setting. In mid-20th century Australia, advocacy from architects and planners for this new form of modern public building design converged with widespread social debates about the meanings of community, and the influences of the natural and built environments on the practices of responsible, participatory citizenship.[3]

A Pattern For Living

b

A modern call to community

Late in 1942, HC 'Nugget' Coombs, economist, policy-maker and soon-to-be appointed director-general of the federal Department of Post-War Reconstruction, gave a rousing speech on ABC radio that outlined a radical vision of post-war Australian life. World War II had stimulated rapid industrial expansion after the economic downturn of the Depression, leading to full (male) employment where 'every willing pair of hands has found worthwhile work'. In looking to the future, Coombs advocated a comprehensive scheme of town and urban development that extended beyond capital cities to regional centres. Post-war homes, nurturing individual family stability, would be 'the nucleus of social organisation' and thus should be properly grouped in relation to facilities and each other. Coombs dismissed the notion that the individual would be subsumed in a society based on community, insisting instead that:

> Proper grouping of homes in 'communities'... make possible common playgrounds, nurseries and schools ... The grouping of homes in communities suggests, too, another change in our environment. Many people fear the individual will be lost in the group. This fear is false. It is only in a community that the individual can develop ... I believe that the community in this sense will give us the characteristic buildings and institutions of the post-war world ... Libraries, theatres, social and political clubs, halls, health centres, sporting facilities. These are, so to speak, the capital equipment of human relationships; it is in them that our friends, our lovers, our comrades, our rivals and our enemies are met and where the essential business of life is carried out.[4]

Coombs' comments came at a time when the strains of war were most telling. The entry of Japan into the conflict in December 1941 meant Australia was the base for Allied operations in the Asia-Pacific military theatre. Between 1942 and 1945, more than 1 million United States service personnel passed through Australia. This influx of American troops into Australian cities such as Melbourne, Sydney and Brisbane – in combination with thousands of Australian service personnel and war workers – revealed the pressures on housing stock and public infrastructure.[5] Coombs' words illustrate how the impact of war on all aspects of daily experience in Australia – from employment, consumerism, travel, manufacturing and agriculture, communications, and social relations – was to underpin a broad ideological platform for post-war planning and the consequent rebuilding of domestic and public life. By 1945, after years of deprivation during the Depression and the war, there was a shortage of at least 350,000 homes in Australia.[6] Moreover, the standard of household amenities, such as the provision of labour-saving devices like washing machines, and even simple conveniences like hot water in kitchens, was grossly inadequate in a considerable percentage of Australian homes. The daily drudgery of the housewife was seen by government authorities and social commentators as discouraging women from embracing motherhood: and the low birthrate in Australia, a trend that predated the war, was a matter of national concern. Once again, attention turned to the notion of the suburbanised environment as an appropriate environment for an ordered, stable and supportive social life.

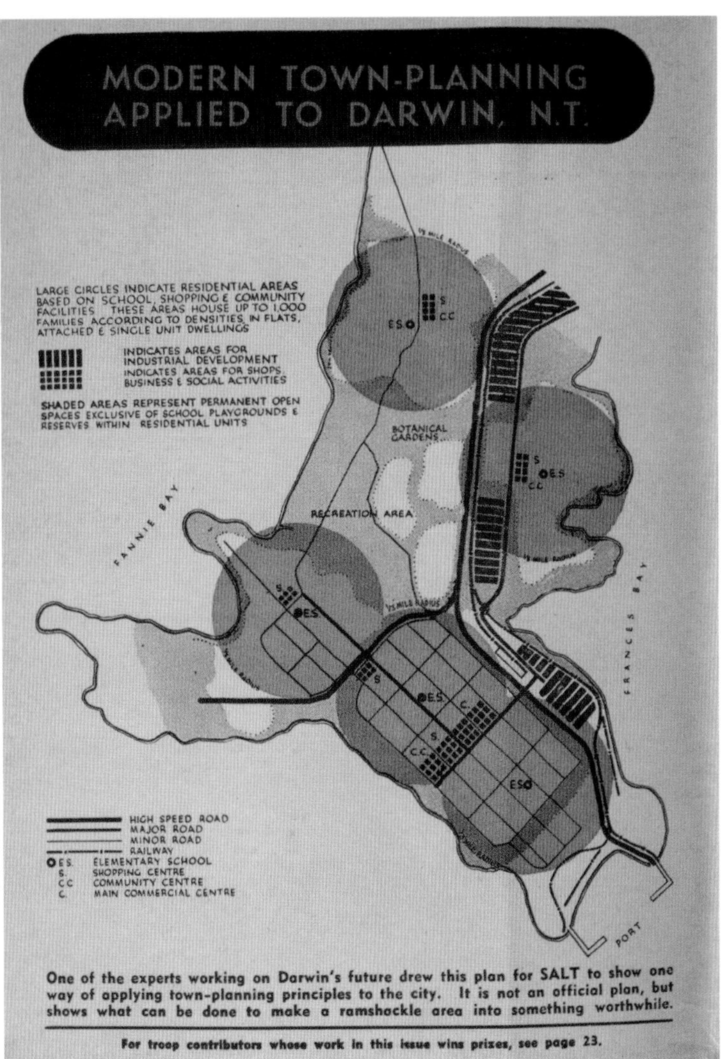

7.2 'Modern town-planning applied to Darwin', 1945

While Coombs was not explicitly describing the 'neighbourhood unit' concept in his vision of post-war community, he was surely cognisant of its influence on modern town planning. The concept, first proposed by Clarence Perry in the early 1920s and applied in a 1929 regional plan for New York City, powerfully conceptualised community needs at different scales. It could be argued that the notion derived from private practice (exemplified by JC Nichols' neighbourhood-oriented Country Club estates in Kansas City, Missouri) or from earlier town planning forays such as Raymond Unwin's Hampstead Garden Suburb in London.

These ideas would have been familiar to Frank Heath: he could also have seen nascent Australian examples in action, too, at sites like the surveyor, planner and planning advocate Saxil Tuxen's Merrilands estate in Melbourne's northern suburb of Reservoir, or in the Sydney suburb of Daceyville.

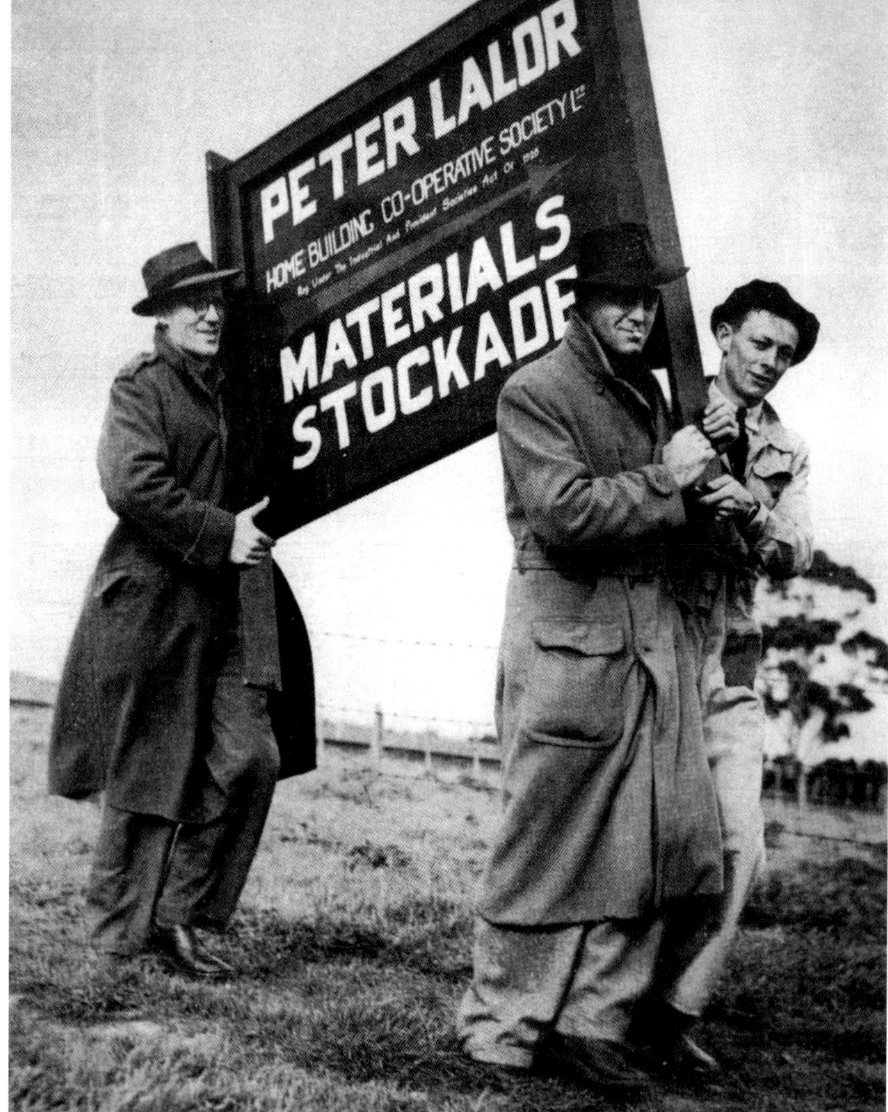

7.3 The Peter Lalor Home Building Co-operative Society 'Materials Stockade'

Heath's plan for Swan Hill drew on Perry's idea, dividing the expanded town into five self-contained residential districts, each with its 'central community centre park' where communal facilities were sited.[7] The neighbourhood unit ideal was reflected in numerous town planning schemes in Australia at this time. For instance, Ronald McInnis' ambitious 1944 plan for the rebuilding of the northern town of Darwin, after it was bombed by the Japanese in 1942, featured a series of residential areas that each included a commercial and cultural hub with a shopping centre, kindergarten, schools and playgrounds. These localised neighbourhood facilities, based upon contemporary town planning developments in the United States and South America, were supported by a central civic square with a town hall and government buildings, and a community centre with a cinema, swimming pool and meeting and clubrooms.[8]

For the purposes of maintaining wartime morale, federal and state post-war reconstruction schemes emphasised improved domestic accommodation as necessary for economic and population growth and stability. This view was fuelled by a popular 'strong desire for a better and more gracious way of life',[9] a credo enthusiastically adopted by the new group of professionals, including town planners and architects, as well as social and health workers, now influential within official planning bureaucracies.

These expert beliefs reflected and reinforced a discernable change in the attitudes of the Australian population. In the mid-1940s Australians flocked in their thousands to displays of housing and town planning: in one week in October 1944 over 20,000 people visited a Melbourne exhibition entitled 'American housing: Past, present and future'. A national competition for suggestions for 'Victory Homes' launched by the *Australian Women's Weekly* – which played an active role in advocating the need for government support for young couples and their families – resulted in hundreds of entries.[10] By the mid-1940s, the responsibility of government to provide access to affordable housing *and* related community facilities for recreational, health and educational needs was widely accepted as a right of citizenship for all Australians, regardless of income and status.

In response to the housing shortage, a key feature of post-war urban development was the expansion of public housing estates and the rapid growth of fringe suburbs on the edges of cities and regional towns. In some instances, cooperative housing societies offered alternative ways to finance and build new homes. The Peter Lalor Home Building Co-operative Society, which secured land on the northern outskirts of Melbourne, was led by a group of ex-servicemen who were inspired by the political ideology of the labour movement (and named their society after the leader of the 1854 Eureka Rebellion). By 1947, they had built a 'Materials Stockade', where construction materials and tools were stored (figure 7.3); by 1948 more than 300 people were participating in working bees erecting homes. This strong sense of community solidarity was echoed in the original plan (one of the last such schemes by Tuxen) of this garden suburb for workers. Not only would there be provision for a primary school and shops, but also for a large community building situated in a park and a separate 'Theatre & Palais'. This indicated the significance accorded to communal places, situated close to both home and the local railway station, for recreation, socialising and sport.[11]

7.4 Robert Arthur Gardner (1945) *Community Centres*, Opportunity Club for Boys and Girls, Melbourne

7.5 'Township of Seymour, Civic Centre Aerial View', Vic. 1947

Town halls, civic centres, community centres

From the 19th century, the architectural language of government in Australia was almost universally classicism. By the 1930s a greater diversity of architectural styles emerged in municipal buildings, including the Spanish baroque of Joseph Plottel's design for the Footscray Town Hall in inner-western Melbourne (1936), or the refined art deco or streamlined 'moderne' styles such as DB Gardiner's Rockdale Town Hall in south-western Sydney (1938–39) and Eales, Cohen and Fitzhardinge's Guildford Town Hall in Perth's north-east (1937). Like their predecessors, these buildings nonetheless consciously evoked a seriousness of purpose and grandeur. Design elements common in imposing municipal buildings included a formal entrance, with an elevated porch with wide steps, a colonnade or arcade providing a sheltered exterior vestibule, while clock towers were more often planned than executed.

Municipal town halls were historically intended to provide space for local governance and structured social events, rather than operating as sites for 'hands-on' community participation. The experiences of World War II, including an unprecedented high rate of voluntary work undertaken by civilians in an 'All-In' war effort, created a heightened expectation about community needs and the capacity of ordinary people to transform their own society. This required new public spaces. Prior to 1940, most Australians would not have been familiar with the newly revised definition of the term 'community centre'.[12] The idea of the purpose-built, multi-use community centre had gained popularity in Britain from the 1920s, particularly through the work of the National Council of Social Service and later the Department of Education.[13] The British model quickly became influential in Australia, assisted by the Department of Post-War Reconstruction which reproduced key British documents on community centres for Australian readers.[14] Philanthropic and voluntary organisations were enthusiastic about such networks as a public facility that would actively assist in the task of the rebuilding of community connections in peacetime.

The buildings designed (if not built) for such community centres were distinctly different to most existing public buildings in Australia. The community centre was described as democratic and classless in its reach, functional and modern in its design, and secular in its intent. Its facilities catered for all generations of Australians, from small children and adolescents through to the increasingly larger group of older and retired citizens. It sought to bring together the formal and large civic spaces found in existing town halls, with smaller, more intimate, spaces that were reminiscent of church or club meeting rooms. Through this combination of dedicated and flexible spaces, the community centre could accommodate large-scale community events as well as more specialised community-led groups. In pamphlets and plans which promoted the community centre ideal, a strong socially focused rhetoric was explicitly linked to modern buildings that rejected an architectural language of authority in favour of one that emphasised utilitarianism and informality.

The idea that maternal health centres, kindergartens and libraries should be arranged in proximity to one another was increasingly promoted, alongside discussions about multi-function community or civic centres.

As the definition of the modern community centre was evolving in the early 1940s, the term 'civic centre' – already in common use in the early 20th century – was also being applied to buildings serving some similar purposes. While the terminology was often interchangeable, there was usually a greater formality associated with the civic centre. The municipal council of the

Victorian town of Seymour, for instance, when commenting on a 1946 town plan by Frank Heath (figure 7.5) noted that its civic centre was 'the outward expression of the aesthetic standard of the community where progress and civic pride are manifest'.[15] In any case, space was needed to situate new community buildings, most often found in parklands and sometimes in the reclamation of spaces through urban renewal schemes. During the post-war era, the idea that maternal health centres, kindergartens and libraries should be arranged in proximity to one another was increasingly promoted, alongside discussions about multi-function community or civic centres.

Community functions: Mechanics' institutes and schools of art

While the civic or community centre was heralded during World War II as an innovation due to its democratic inclusivity and multi-purpose nature, the notion of a building or institution for adult or informal learning was not new in Australia. Indeed, from the colonial period, the mechanics' institutes (Victoria, Tasmania and Western Australia), institutes (South Australia) and schools of arts (New South Wales and Queensland) were widely distributed in Australian suburbs and towns.[16] These institutions, which drew upon British precedents of self-help associations, were envisaged as venues where the educational and technical skills of working-class men would be improved through classes and demonstrations, and where respectable forms of social behaviour were encouraged.[17] Local councils were often involved in their foundation: for instance, the meeting for the creation of the Adelaide suburb of Norwood's institute was staffed by prominent citizens and presided over by the mayor.[18] Usually subscription-based, mechanics' institutes and schools of arts served as, or included, a library. The Hotham (later North Melbourne) Mechanics' Institute is one example. Here, from the mid-1880s, adjoining the town hall, was a purpose-built institute and library for men, women and children, with which were associated a literary and debating society, a choral society, a gymnastic class and a billiards room, all of which operated until the late 1940s.[19]

While municipal councils were usually reluctant to assume sole financial responsibility for mechanics' institutes and schools of art, there was certainly a perception that a fine building housing such an organisation was a boon to civic pride. It was no accident that mechanics' institutes were often sited prominently on a hill or in a main street. In some cases, and with reference to their strong associations with a working-class male clientele, these buildings were reconfigured and renamed to add reference to World War I. In South Australia, for instance, reading rooms and institutes at Ardrossan, Bute and Snowtown all reopened in expanded form as soldiers' memorial halls in the early 1920s.

By the 1940s, mechanics' institutes and schools of art were in decline, in part due to the relocation of some of their more popular and, indeed, lucrative functions in other, purpose-built structures.[20] Throughout the early 20th century, local organisations such as progress and special interest (including religious) groups continued to develop, and often constructed their own hall or meeting place. In one such metropolitan example, the East Kew Progress Association in Melbourne's east purchased a block of land in 1927 for the construction of a hall where they might hold 'concerts, dances or meetings of any importance', thus stimulating growth within the suburb.[21]

Perhaps more importantly, the building and renovation of town halls during the suburban expansion and brief prosperity of the 1920s, and the continued refurbishment of many suburban town halls in the 1930s, saw many municipal councils discovering means to profit. Such profits could come in the form of both financial and cultural capital, from the council's control of a central, accessible, reputable and (often) well-maintained public space.

In regional areas, many town halls were remodelled in the 1920s and 1930s specifically to serve as venues in the lucrative travelling cinema circuit. Architect Chris Smith is an unusual example of a practitioner whose most prominent work incorporates both purpose-built cinemas and town halls, often in the same building (for instance, at Clare, Hindmarsh, Brighton, Minlaton and Port Adelaide – all in South Australia).[22] In Sydney's southern suburbs, Rockdale Town Hall was rebuilt in the late 1930s to an expanded floorplan, becoming 'one of the most popular venues in Sydney for musical productions and dance competitions and was widely used for political and public gatherings'.[23] In the same year, the Horsham Town Hall in Victoria's western region was erected, with 'provision … for public function of all kinds', including an auditorium with movable seating which, when in place, would accommodate 1000; it hosted art, ballet and Council of Adult Education events.[24]

As we saw in chapter 4, the assumption of responsibility at local government level for public libraries also saw this aspect of mechanics' institute activities taken into purpose-built environments. When in 1944 the Community Centre Committee in Footscray mooted the cooption of the local mechanics' institute library into a foundation collection for a new public library, it was participating in an emerging trend. Libraries of the 1950s increasingly took on the wider educative role of the mechanics' institutes and schools of art. The Maitland Institute, on South Australia's Yorke Peninsula, wound up operations in 1940 to sell its capacious and well-liked building to the Maitland Town Council, whence it became the town hall, retaining many of the same functions – including that of library – for many years.[25] This use and re-use of public buildings in many urban and rural municipalities across Australia illustrated the changing priorities, and costs, associated with community infrastructure across the 20th century.

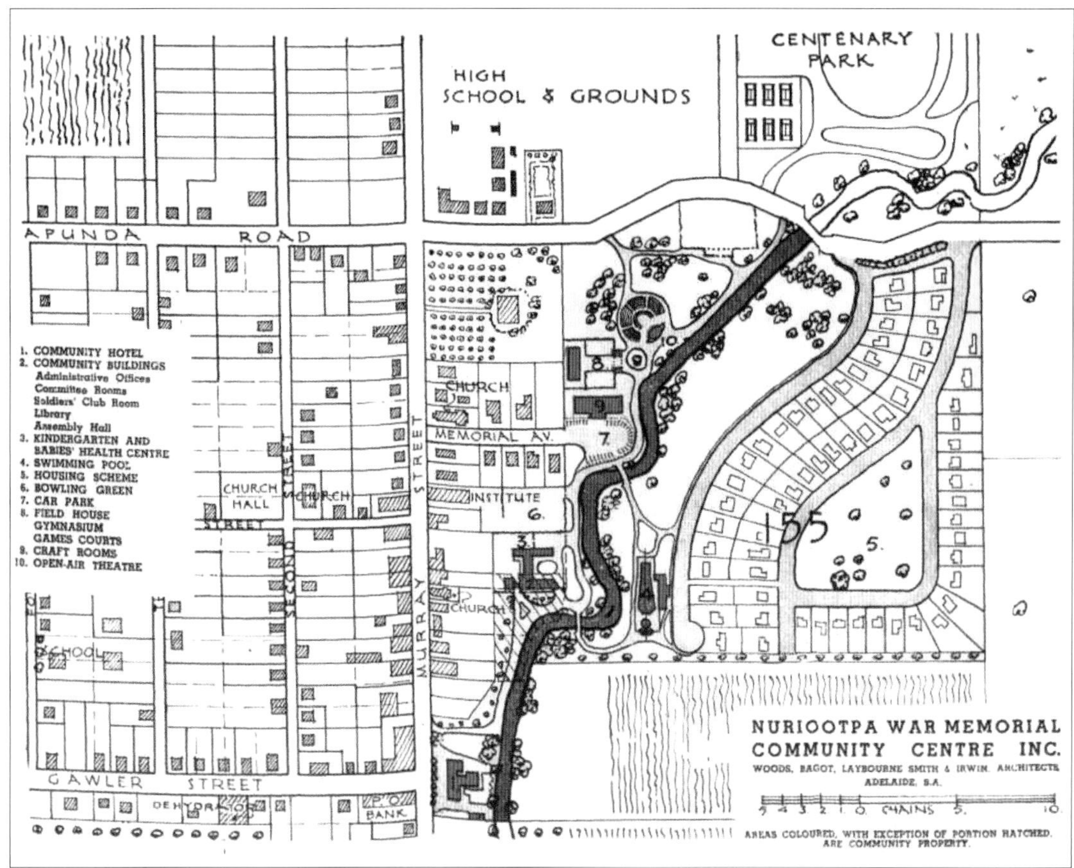

7.6 Plan for Nuriootpa, SA c. 1940s

'Community centre grounds', precincts, and multi-use buildings

The most important element of change in the new community centre was the recasting of public venues as overtly inclusive and family-oriented spaces. This contrasted with the primarily adult male domain of mechanics' institutes and schools of art and many sporting clubs, and signalled a new awareness of the physical and social needs of children, adolescents and women. However, there remained a lack of clarity or agreement on whether the best community centre was a large, multifaceted building, or an array of co-located services.

The most prominent community centre activist movement was Common Cause, a short-lived but influential group which formed in Adelaide in 1943 and did much to promote community in the Barossa Valley in South Australia, specifically in the town of Nuriootpa.[26] Louis Laybourne-Smith was engaged to create the Community Centre area for Nuriootpa on land donated for the purpose (figure 7.6). He laid out three streets adjacent to the development which contained 155 detached houses, the sale of which was to pay for the public works. Laybourne-Smith evoked rhetoric from the garden suburb movement to describe his vision, wherein the town would be 'extended on orderly and beautiful lines, with provision for playgrounds, crèches, a community swimming pool, and kindergarten, as well as dwellings'.[27] The finished plan included a beer garden, soldiers' clubroom, library, war memorial assembly hall seating 400 and equipped with stage and dressing rooms, and 'a bio-screen and lantern room'.[28] A kindergarten and baby health centre (with a pram park and doctors' rooms) were connected to the assembly hall via a covered way. In addition to the money made from the new houses – their mere existence representing great optimism for Nuriootpa's future growth – funding for the communal facilities came from the town's community hotel ('acquired and rebuilt'[29] by citizens in 1937 to a pattern familiar in eastern South Australia) and cooperative stores. Today, this community area is well used and attractive, and comprises most of the facilities originally envisaged. A similar scheme for another community hotel-funded 'community centre grounds' space was undertaken, but only partially implemented, for the lake shores of Barmera to Nuriootpa's east.[30]

The progressive plans put forward by the borough council of the regional Victorian town of Shepparton at mid-century reveal a further instance of some contemporary conceptions of community. In 1946 Shepparton published a small booklet outlining its development plan, and the assistance of architect-planners Stephenson & Turner ensured the publication was amply illustrated with architectural proposals. Though Shepparton's population was 8000 in the immediate post-war years, the proposal plan looked, via a series of five-year intermediate steps, towards a projected population of 30,000 inhabitants.

Shepparton's plan 'was a clear recognition that the precious legacy of the past, which is the present day Shepparton, must be guided wisely to a brilliant and happy future'.[31] The chair of Shepparton's public works committee quoted Aristotle: 'A city is a place where people live together a common life for a noble purpose'[32] and under such subheadings as 'Our future progress' and 'A vision of the future', the plan foresaw tree-lined parks and streets, modern housing and spacious surroundings, as well as:

> noble public buildings; happy and healthy children on their way to fine conveniently located schools; a modern hospital … to care for the sick; kindergartens and community centres to cater for the young … In short – a city of which everyone can be justly proud.[33]

The Shepparton Plan sought to examine all aspects of planning, including transport, zoned industrial areas, housing, and health and educational facilities. Of particular interest was the detailed consideration of recreation, especially for younger residents. The civic centre (figure 7.7) was conceived as a collection of facilities for the community, with the majority of space reserved for cultural and educational activities:

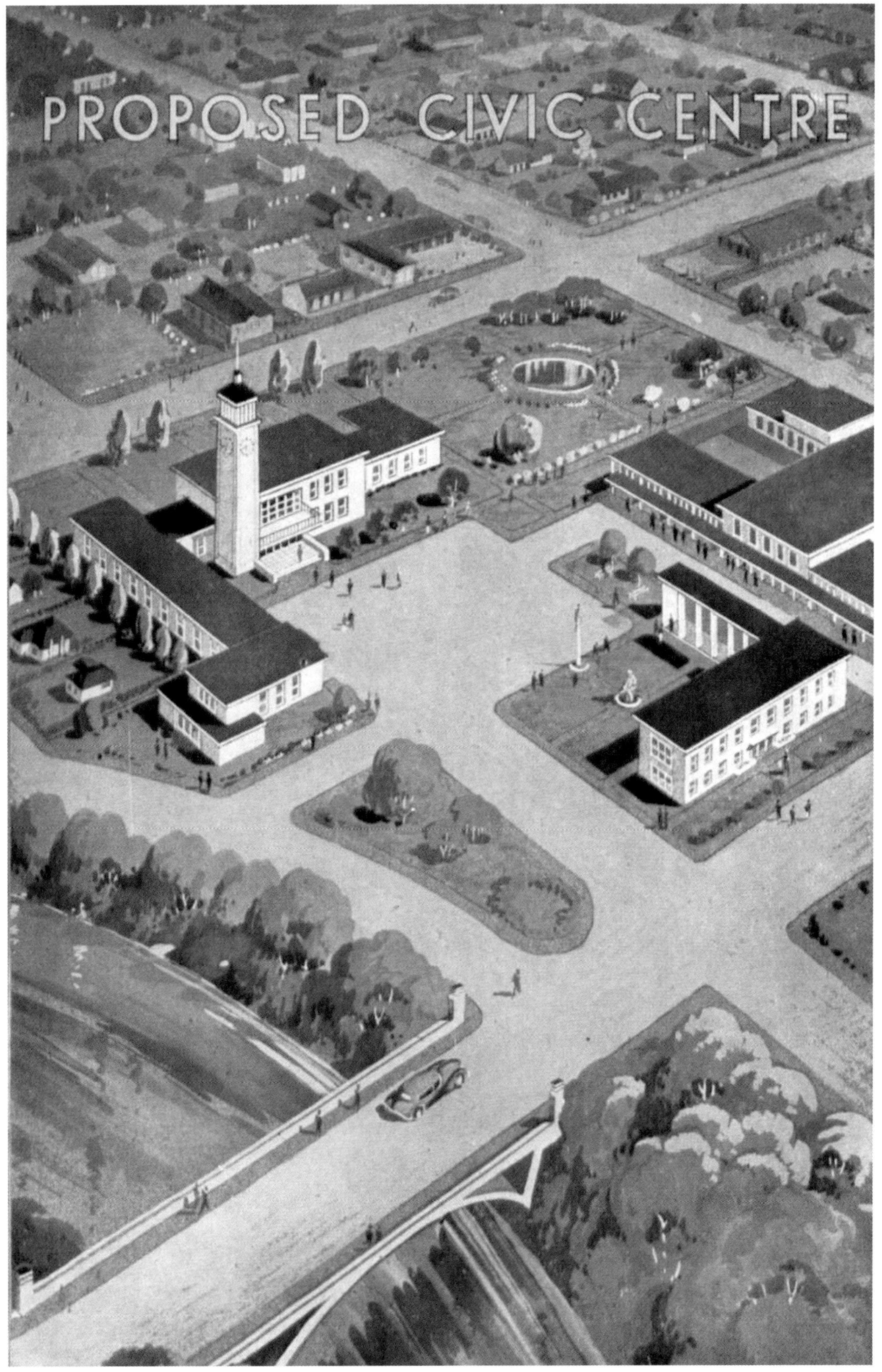

7.7 'Proposed Civic Centre', *Shepparton: Today and Tomorrow*, Shepparton Borough Council & *Shepparton Advertiser*, Vic. 1946

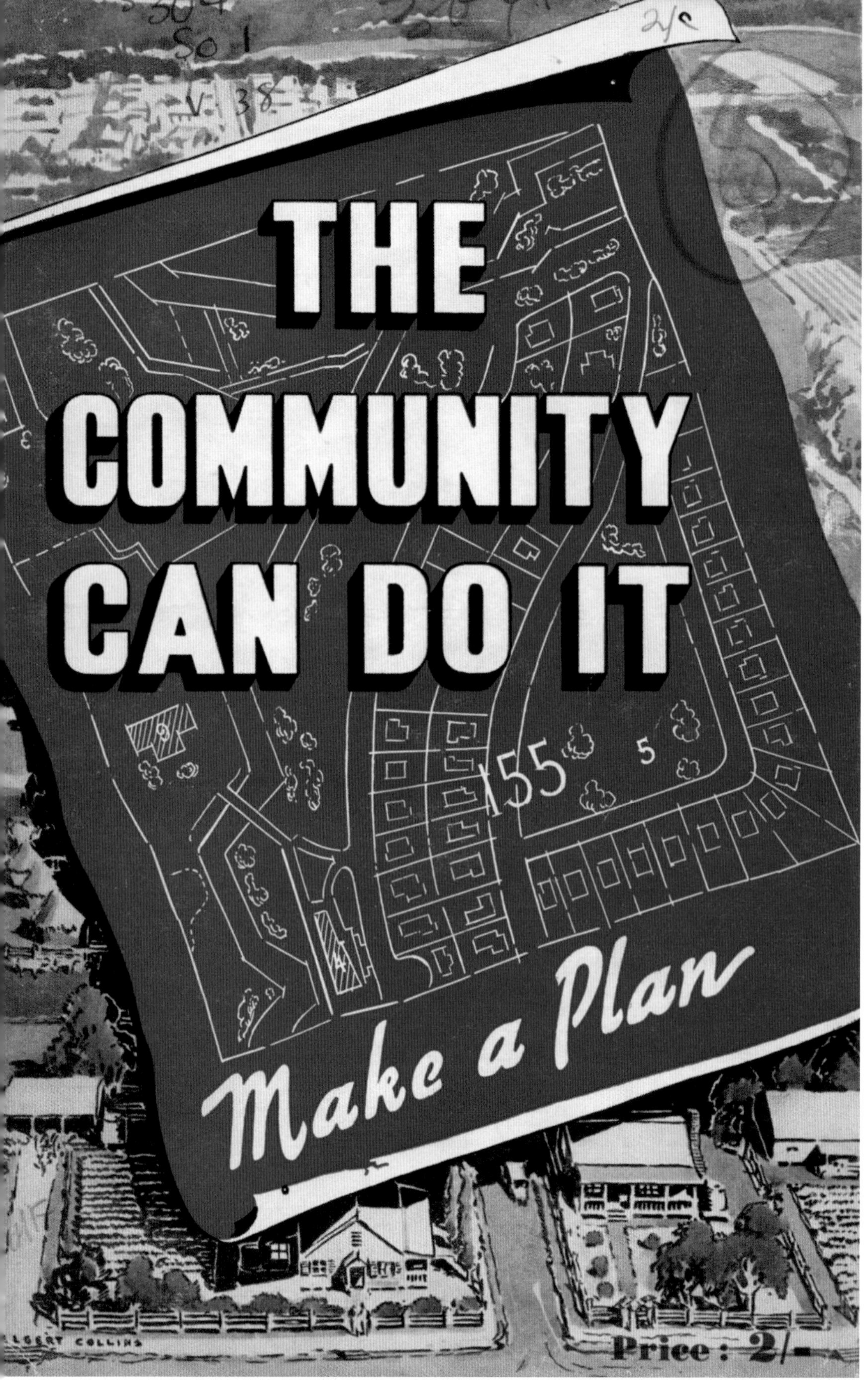
THE
COMMUNITY
CAN DO IT
Make a Plan
Price: 2/-

public buildings should be grouped and modernised to permit of public business being carried out quickly, efficiently and at the least cost to the taxpayer.

But public buildings differ from commercial premises in an important respect. They are the seat of local government, civic entertainment and ceremonial, and the visible expression of the resident's pride in his town.[34]

These buildings had necessarily, then, to exhibit efficiency and beauty requiring cultivated open space both for ornamental flora and space for community gatherings on 'national occasions'. Facilities were to be grouped about, or adjacent to, a civic square and included a large (capacity 1500), a medium (500) and a small (250) hall for meetings, lectures, performances and dances; an art gallery; a public library; a museum; a youth centre; a returned services club and war memorial; and council facilities (including council chambers and administrative offices). These functions signalled the transition of Shepparton from a town of business transactions to one of community activity.

With its illustrations, some brilliantly coloured, of proposed buildings, places and settings, the plan was a literal translation of the modern Australian conception of community. Its emphasis on the requirements of the young, cultural pursuits, social gathering, fitness and recreation was representative of a changing society, where the investment in communities and particularly children would reap rewards for the town, region and nation as a whole. The architectural renderings of an imagined and socially integrated town depicted modern buildings both functional and utilitarian, with clean lines, expanses of glass and bold forms. The undecorated surfaces of the new buildings meant that the future(s) of Shepparton could be projected onto these places without recourse to past ideas of decorum or propriety. In this regional town of the future, community facilities would be accessible to all, with development planned and overseen by ratepayers and local government.

Shepparton had hoped to attract a significant increase in population with its plans. Other towns and suburbs simply bundled existing and new features into a rebranded array, and many community centres were, in 21st-century parlance, virtual: in South Australia, Edwardstown's 'Greater Community Centre' appears to have been, at its beginning in 1942, a multiplicity of centres spread throughout ad hoc accommodations. Its secretary, the Reverend HA Parrott, claimed 'We are not a building'.[35] The Community Centres Planning Committee of New South Wales used the same words, insisting that a community centre:

7.8 (left) Australian Broadcasting Commission (1945) *The Community Can Do It. Make a Plan*, (incorporating plan of Nuriootpa) The Commission, Sydney

> is not a building, but an organisation by which a community endeavours to provide itself – in its leisure – with healthy mental and physical recreation, leisure-time education, and perhaps certain facilities of public health.

If buildings were grouped,

> much greater facilities, more general use of those facilities, and a corporate impulse and guidance, as well as mutual help by the community, are possible.[36]

The Community Can Do It – a highly influential booklet published by the Australian Broadcasting Commission in 1945 (figure 7.8) to accompany radio broadcasts – strongly favoured community-based decisions on the appropriate form and style of a centre. Yet the process was never straightforward. In 1947 architect Harold H Smith diligently recorded the frustrations of the 'energetic people' of Springwood, in Sydney's Blue Mountains, who in April 1944 had resolved that 'a plan be prepared in a democratic fashion "as far as possible" without political or sectarian bias'.[37] After concentrated discussion and research, the group presented a scheme (see figure 1.3 in chapter 1) including safety replanning around the railway line; road improvement; helicopter landing fields; and, most importantly, amenities that included an 'up-to-date standard-size swimming pool', a 'new public library and lecture hall … in the town reserve', as well as 'a gymnasium' and 'youth hostel' and many health facilities.[38] However, as Smith reported to the readers of *Architecture*, the local council lacked 'a desire to meet any of the wishes of the people … or even indirectly assist in the implementation of the scheme'.[39]

It was easier to promote a building rather than a precinct, at least as a first step. In 1943 Kathleen M Gordon, an officer for the National Fitness Council, presented a diagrammatic 'Minimum accommodation for a community centre in a small country town' in an influential pamphlet. The largest component of Gordon's building was a community hall, to which were attached a library, kitchen, and rest and meeting rooms, set in an environment of recreational grounds. Diagrams for comparable facilities in large country towns, industrial suburbs and new housing estates also featured buildings for gymnastics, preschool children's care, a 'games room', a workshop, hobby and clubrooms.

Seeking 'a co-operative spirit working for the common good', Gordon declared:

> We hope that they will be the first rung in the ladder – in the revitalising of languishing democracy – which life in modern cities with its industrial living conditions, shifting population, decaying family life and scramble for existence, has caused to fall sick. By comparison, the old rural communities, with their regular gatherings, farmers' associations, &c., had all the characteristics of true community centres.[40]

Location, wrote Gordon, was to be 'related to the flow of community life' – near a shopping centre, 'the civic centre', or a school. Of the building(s) required, she was non-committal, and deliberately so: 'Communities will develop changes in tastes and activities, so that a building needs to be flexible enough to meet those changes'.[41]

The 'democratic' angle of community centres alluded to by Gordon was less defined. In 1945 barrister Richard Windeyer suggested to the Darlinghurst branch of the Labor Party in inner Sydney that 'what is required' in a community centre was encouragement of 'mutual sympathy':

> When people are so drawn together for recreational interests it seems that it soon follows that views are exchanged as to the more serious problems of life, to which so few people, living as they do for the most part in comparative isolation, pay sufficient attention. From their recreational activities there develops a cultural interest, and community centres bring about activity and discussion … This might largely extend if in all community centres there were debating rooms and debating organisations.[42]

The twin concepts of community and democracy were also reflected upon by journalist Loree Hancox, writing in 1946 in the Melbourne *Argus* on a project envisaged by her family's architectural firm of Buchan Laird & Buchan. In her article 'Why not community centres as war memorials?', Hancox discussed a proposal for the Housing Commission of Victoria's East Geelong project in which a community centre (featuring facilities for youth, 'physical training instruction and hobby rooms' and providing a 'meeting place for all members of a family') would be paid for by public subscription. As a '"living" war memorial', this would provide returned servicemen and women with 'a memorial which will give them and their families some happiness'. It would be 'controlled and operated by a democratic body' rather than by a government arm.[43] The idea that utilitarian amenities such as parks, swimming pools and particularly halls were preferable over static decorative icons such as war memorials gained considerable popularity after World War II.[44] The 'living memorial' of an integrated community centre was mooted regularly in

Main Entrance to War Memorial Town Hall

7.9 (above and right) From *Cottesloe War Memorial Town Hall and Civic Centre*, WA 1950

the immediate post-war years, including in the initial designs for Launceston's Windmill Hill community precinct (figure 7.10).[45] The town hall and civic centre in Perth's suburb of Cottesloe occupied an existing building, illustrating the trend towards creating civic centres as war memorials, and by the 1950s even as tourist attractions.

Kathleen Gordon's paper quickly gained currency. Melbourne's Footscray had long held the status of a polluted, dense, working-class area but nevertheless enjoyed a progressive – if economically straitened – local government. It convened a Community Centre Committee which began operations in earnest in early 1944 and which quoted Gordon's estimate of the concept as 'an extension of the family unit to a larger group' in its October 1944 *Report of a Proposed Community Centre*.[46] The committee saw the creation of a community centre as combining older tropes (civic pride and advancement, the core concern of many municipalities – as seen in the Seymour example) with new themes ('the Centre may be required to become the home of a greater variety of activities than any other building in the modern scene').[47] With this latter idea in mind, it explored a holistic approach to recreation ('intellectual and physical' recreation)[48] and advocated life-long learning.[49] Architect John Scarborough (also a prominent member of the Victorian Town Planning Association and

Another view of the crazy-pavement court. This is fast becoming the rendez-vous of the majority of interstate and overseas visitors to Western Australia.

chairman of the Architects' Panel of the Housing Commission of Victoria) prepared sketch plans for several buildings on a site he considered ideal. Scarborough's lot was selected for its size, proximity to public transport and its potential for conformity with a (by this time, fifteen-year-old) proposal by the Metropolitan Town Planning Commission for what might now be termed 'a green wedge'. Here, Scarborough placed four buildings – a 'Small theatre' seating 300; a 'Physical Culture Centre' in which men's and women's gymnasia were, notably, the same size; a 'Swimming Pool'; and a 'Stack Building/Cultural Centre', in essence, a well-stocked library of 25,000 books – in informal park space. Like so many of these impressive, multi-function civic statements of the post-war era, the centre was not built.

In the remote semi-desert of South Australia, Woomera Village emerged as the nation's first designed and constructed post-war planned town. Founded in 1947 as the residential and administrative centre for the Joint UK–Australia Long Range Weapons Project, plans for this isolated defence settlement embodied modernist principles of the British New Town movement. The emphasis was on functional architecture that encouraged the integration of family, work and recreational life and collective goals. Community facilities such as the town hall, community meeting rooms and health and educational services were conveniently and spaciously situated in the town centre. Entertainment was seen as a priority; when the original wooden theatre burned down, it was replaced in 1963 by a 700-seat landmark public building.[50] Elsewhere in Australia, in response to the resources boom, other special-purpose model towns were built in remote areas along similar lines during the 1950s; these included the mining towns of Batchelor and Mary Kathleen in the Northern Territory.

Community centres in the 1950s and 1960s

By the 1950s, the community centres movement could expect far less federal government encouragement than it had in previous years. This was not merely a result of the Liberal government under the leadership of Robert Menzies attaining power in 1949. Menzies' emphasis on state enterprise and economic security, family stability and home ownership continued to embrace the idea of community, albeit in a different timbre to that of the Labor Party. But during the 1950s, a decade of considerable social and economic upheaval as well as social conservatism, the fervour for community centres expressed so ardently by residents groups at the end of World War II gradually abated. At the same time, many municipal councils were quickly swept up with localised economic and political concerns. In a typical example, twenty-one years after Shepparton proposed its idealised proposal for a community centre, a much smaller, limited, civic centre was erected in the town. At the opening ceremony, the mayor somewhat apologetically explained that in the immediate post-war period the conception of the Shepparton Plan 'appeared to be visionary, rather than capable of attainment in the foreseeable future'. Funding, it seemed, had been the major constraint for the council, particularly for the acquisition of suitable land.[51] The new civic centre included many features intended in the earlier plan, but at reduced capacity: an art gallery, a theatrette seating 200, an auditorium seating 1000, a stage, small hall and supper room, a 'smoke lounge' and municipal offices and council chambers.[52]

Community centres might still be required to address perceived social ills. In the early 1950s Labor politician and journalist James Fraser,[53] in his capacity as a member of the Australian Capital Territory Advisory Council, advocated two community centres for Canberra to address what he saw as 'the complete absence of community spirit' in the capital. [54] These would include:

> A large hall with a dance floor and stage, and provision to amplify either recorded music or artists; Milk bar and cafeteria; Reading room; A well-stocked popular library; A billiards room; A table tennis room and badminton court; Wide, glassed-in verandahs with tables and chairs; A Band rotunda, and a promenade with lawns.[55]

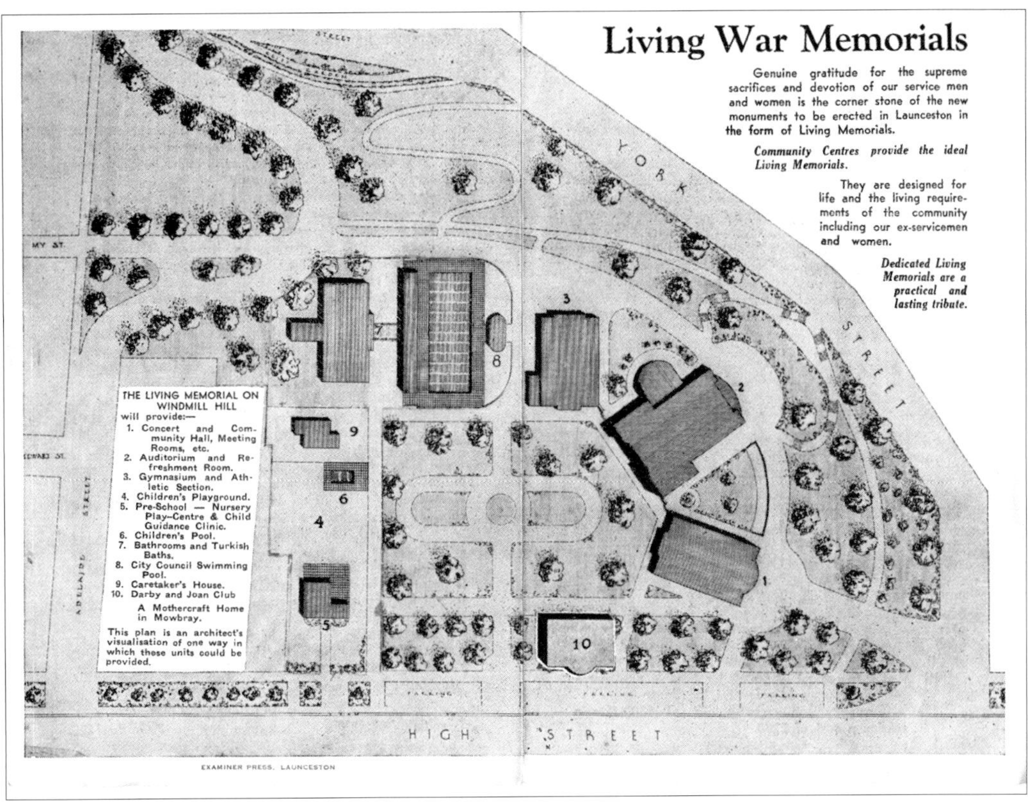

Living War Memorials
Genuine gratitude for the supreme sacrifices and devotion of our service men and women is the corner stone of the new monuments to be erected in Launceston in the form of Living Memorials.
Community Centres provide the ideal Living Memorials.
They are designed for life and the living requirements of the community including our ex-servicemen and women.
Dedicated Living Memorials are a practical and lasting tribute.
THE LIVING MEMORIAL ON WINDMILL HILL will provide:—
1. Concert and Community Hall, Meeting Rooms, etc.
2. Auditorium and Refreshment Room.
3. Gymnasium and Athletic Section.
4. Children's Playground.
5. Pre-School — Nursery Play-Centre & Child Guidance Clinic.
6. Children's Pool.
7. Bathrooms and Turkish Baths.
8. City Council Swimming Pool.
9. Caretaker's House.
10. Darby and Joan Club
A Mothercraft Home in Mowbray.
This plan is an architect's visualisation of one way in which these units could be provided.
YORK STREET
HIGH STREET
EXAMINER PRESS, LAUNCESTON

7.10 'Living War Memorials', *Examiner Press*, Launceston, Tas.

Fraser's wish-list leant towards the values and interests of young people, and it was the scarcity of entertainment that led him to describe the social environment as 'deadening'. There were, as it happened, already plans for four such centres underway in the city; a few months prior, the progress and welfare association of the Canberra suburb of Narrabundah had planned a deputation to the Department of the Interior to discuss the size and scope of its new community centre, intended to include primary and preschools, a mothercraft centre, community hall, music lawns, and sports facilities.[56] This ideal was envisaged to cater comprehensively to all sectors of a local community – not merely for local recreation and health requirements but also for the fostering of a very local sense of belonging to place and an engagement across generations and genders.

More broadly, co-location by design and intent demonstrated those facilities that were seen to form the foundation of community life and drew together civic necessity (municipal offices) with meeting halls, auditoria, recreation facilities, libraries and children's services. Municipal requirements were necessary projects, but the far greater emphasis in the plans lay upon the various gathering spaces that encouraged physical exercise, social events or education. The proposal for Launceston's Windmill Hill – initiated as one of Australia's first post-war community centre plans, but only partially built by the late 1950s – saw a cluster of community buildings surrounded by parkland

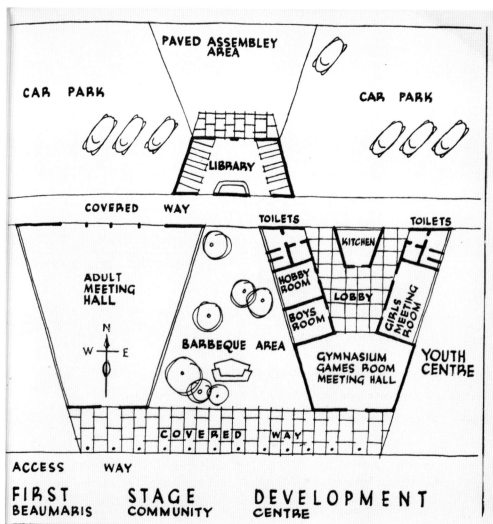

PAVED ASSEMBLEY AREA
CAR PARK
CAR PARK
LIBRARY
COVERED WAY
TOILETS
TOILETS
KITCHEN
ADULT MEETING HALL
HOBBY ROOM
LOBBY
BOYS ROOM
GIRLS MEETING ROOM
N
W
E
BARBEQUE AREA
GYMNASIUM GAMES ROOM MEETING HALL
YOUTH CENTRE
COVERED WAY
ACCESS WAY

FIRST STAGE DEVELOPMENT
BEAUMARIS COMMUNITY CENTRE

ARCHITECT'S DRAWING ABOVE shows proposed youth centre, adult meeting hall (cultural centre shell), and library. Tentative estimate £20,000.

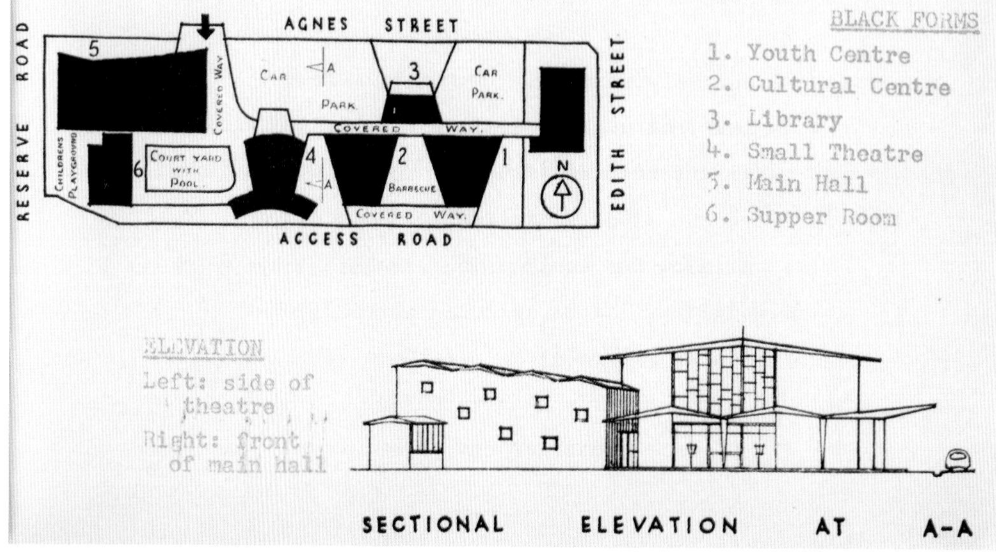

BLACK FORMS
1. Youth Centre
2. Cultural Centre
3. Library
4. Small Theatre
5. Main Hall
6. Supper Room

ELEVATION
Left: side of theatre
Right: front of main hall

and featuring a swimming pool, Turkish bath, nursery and 'Children's Guidance Clinic', concert hall and auditorium (figure 7.10). A similar approach was seen at Beaumaris, a newly developing southern suburb of Melbourne, where two community centres were developed as a result of strong local advocacy. They included co-located facilities that again placed emphasis on the cultural, social and educational. The initial Beaumaris plans called for a youth centre, cultural centre, library, small theatre, main hall and a supper room (figure 7.11).[57] A substantial library and hall were built adjacent to the Beaumaris shopping strip, behind which a series of smaller buildings dedicated to community uses, such as an art club, were added over time. Two kilometres east, another smaller group of community buildings was constructed, also in a park setting, including a kindergarten, senior citizens centre, scout hall and a theatre for the local amateur players, still operating successfully half a century later. In a pattern reproduced around Australia, the Beaumaris scheme was for some a push for recognition as a neighbourhood, and perhaps the first step towards self-government.

By the end of the 1950s, the idealism of the one-stop shop approach to community building promoted through colour pamphlets and pithy statements had generally fallen from favour. It was replaced by what might be seen as a paternalistic model combining community facilities with administrative offices, either within the one structure or in a sub-facility – usually, a community hall – within a particular civic centre concept. The complacency and parochialism which enabled such a conception of Australian life is exemplified by a message from the mayor of the Melbourne middle-class, beachside suburb of Brighton, R Ward, to his constituency on the occasion of the opening of a new civic centre (figure 7.12) – the design of which was distinctly modern and international, directly referencing Frank Lloyd Wright's Guggenheim Museum in New York (1956–59). 'Yes, let's face it, Brightonians are conservative people', Ward wrote:

> That's because we all have something worth conserving. And if we don't take enough interest in what happens far beyond our front gates, it's probably because we take so much pleasure in our homes and gardens. Yet, as a community, we are still small enough to feel that we belong to each other ...[58]

Ward assured his readership there was no intention to return to the 'spacious but unhygienic' conditions of the previous century, but rather to marshall 20th-century technology towards the 'interests of a full and happy life'.

By the late 1960s, when, for instance, Gerd and Renate Block prepared their plan for the Nunawading Civic Centre in Melbourne's eastern suburban ring, their vision of the form had consolidated into a rational single building for both public access and use, and municipal administration.[59] The centre enjoyed

7.11 (left) Plans and section, 'First Stage Development Beaumaris Community Centre'. From Parents' and Citizens' Association of Beaumaris, *Development in Beaumaris*, Vic. 1959

7.12 Civic Centre, Brighton, Vic. 1960–62

a park setting and elements of monumentality. Twelve kilometres to its west, in the affluent suburb of Camberwell, a civic centre was produced in competition with neighbouring Kew, as well as for its potential to generate revenue through the hiring of facilities. Sited in park space beside the old town hall (retained to serve as a library), the civic centre had a theatre 'of European standard' suitable for orchestral and chamber music performances. This was intended to satisfy locals who would otherwise travel to central Melbourne for concerts, suggesting that the facility contributed to social improvement through the provision of 'high' culture. By the 1980s, however, it was reported that the theatre was running at a loss, facing competition in particular from the Victorian Arts Centre, located in the centre of Melbourne, as a professional classical music venue.[60]

Indeed, it was competition from other recreational venues and entertainment buildings, as well as generational change, that influenced how the post-war community centre ideal was realised in subsequent decades. By the 1960s, many municipal councils in Australia were planning to open, or had already opened, new multi-purpose civic centres. Simultaneously the political and social upheavals that reverberated through Australia during the 1960s and early 1970s reflected a reformist agenda that encompassed equality for women; increased access to welfare and education; civil and human rights, including for Indigenous peoples; and a growing interest in environmental issues. Community, at a municipal level, was no longer understood as a single entity made up of different age groups; instead the diverse, multiple communities within the municipal boundaries were acknowledged. In this climate, many forms of authority were brought into question and change was advocated through collective action. At the local level, many self-help and grassroots groups were formed with the aim of promoting their immediate locales as places restoring a sense of neighbourhood, fostering demographic diversity in community and encouraging new demonstrations of social connection.

These localised groups were responding to broader concerns about the disintegration of community bonds, attributed to such factors as the fragmentation of the extended family, separation between home and workplace and the dominant role of technologies such as the car and television. Certainly, the post-war expansion of housing developments on the outskirts of Australian cities and regional towns was seldom quickly matched with the provision of public transport, shopping strips and adequate municipal infrastructure ranging from libraries to kindergartens. Commentators – eager to critique – increasingly portrayed new suburbs as places of acute social and cultural isolation, particularly for women, teenagers and the elderly who had limited access to leisure, training and employment opportunities outside their immediate locality.[61] But a growing sense of social alienation was not restricted to the recent suburbs. By the 1960s, inner, traditionally working-class areas of all cities – from Battery Point in Hobart to Leederville in Perth, but perhaps most significantly in Sydney and Melbourne – were undergoing significant demographic and socioeconomic change as a result of the large-scale influx of migrants, the implementation of 'slum clearance' programs and the beginnings of urban gentrification.

Neighbourhood houses

The neighbourhood house movement arose in this context, drawing upon a renewed impetus for localised opportunities for informal or 'drop-in' social interactions, as well as a need for a venue where meetings and educational classes could be held at a low cost. The movement drew upon earlier ideologies advocating community participation as a significant force in the improvement of society, although by the 1970s community action was to be underpinned by a strong belief in the importance of empowerment of both individual and community.[62] Yet it also harked back to the fullest expression of the community centres movement of the post–World War II era and its very local – albeit purpose-built, rather than adapted – neighbourhood centres. By the early 1970s, there was a growing number of small-scale and distinctively 'home-like' community buildings being established in most Australian states.[63] These were supported by a variety of funding for community development available at all

7.13 Marion Cultural Centre, SA 2001

levels of government – although it has been municipal government that has continued to be the most involved in many of these organisations. The short-lived Assistance Plan of the Whitlam government provided an early policy framework for locally initiated social planning with the integration of community services decision-making that underpinned many of the aims of this movement.[64] Indeed, by the mid-1980s, hundreds of small neighbourhood or community centres in Australia had organised themselves into political networks, with representative lobby bodies. Their activities continued to be state or federally funded, and were often linked to philanthropic bodies; in some states, the educational services offered at neighbourhood houses were also accredited and supported through state systems of technical and further education (TAFE).

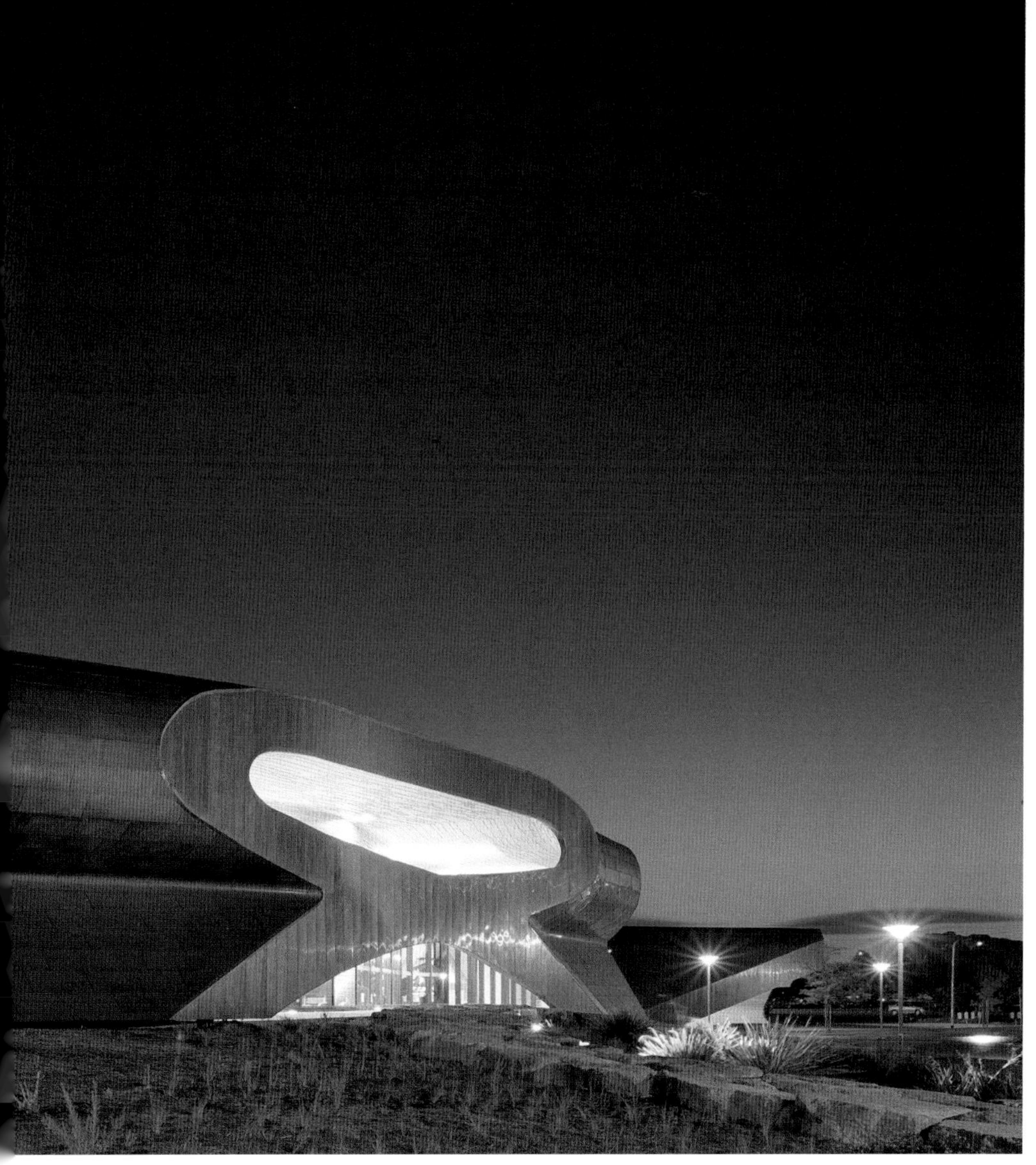

Neighbourhood houses were also known as community houses or learning houses – names that reflected their activities, although in Victoria, where the movement was strongest, these were more diverse in scope.[65] Their services generally included the provision of adult learning opportunities, especially for women and non–English speaking migrants; filling a 'gap' in the provision of municipal facilities such as childcare; and providing a venue for special interest and self-help groups to gather.[66] Neighbourhood houses explicitly fostered community values and social networks where local people could meet their own needs. They were often first mooted at public meetings.[67] Women, in particular, took on key roles of organisation and advocacy across this movement.

The stress on informal community networks was reflected in the buildings that were converted into neighbourhood houses. Overwhelmingly, these were existing houses and sometimes shops, and were unobtrusive in appearance. Such 'ordinary' buildings indicated the facilities on offer were for immediate community use, but also were a low-cost and flexible option for local government authorities. Melissa Permezel's study of neighbourhood houses in Melbourne highlights how local activist groups, predominantly comprising women, were instrumental in the creation of 'a place where they could meet and pursue recreational activities'.[68] In some Melbourne suburbs, such as Hawthorn and Fitzroy where the town halls were ponderous 19th-century edifices associated with council bureaucracy, or in inner-city Carlton where there was no town hall at all, the rationale for alternate community spaces lay in practical and perceived demands for community accessibility to municipal-funded space. In others, such as the south-eastern suburb of Springvale, where the local council commissioned a purpose-built structure, using local materials of mud brick and the labour of local residents,[69] unique, but still informal, spaces were created.

'A developing common purpose'

Today, seventy years after the fervour of the post-war call for community centres, the municipal public buildings dedicated to a suite of community facilities are most likely to be divided into two groups. There is the neighbourhood or community house, a very local and informal meeting space embedded deeply into the ordinary suburban fabric of its municipality. Then there is the civic or cultural centre, which caters to the higher aspirations of the local community. There has additionally been a renewed focus on a 'statement' venue that can showcase art and culture and become easily identified with a suburb or town. The award-winning design of the Marion Cultural Centre (2001) in suburban Adelaide by Phillips Pilkington and Ashton Raggatt McDougall (Architects in Association) (figure 7.13) mixes multiple iconographic references of both the local (letters spelling out the suburb's name are an integral part of the facade), the artistic (the artwork of Adelaide-born Jeffrey Smart) and the architectural (such as Adelaide's original David Jones store in Adelaide, designed by Hassell). As Sean Pickersgill has commented, the building combines 'the text of language with the text of iconic fragments from the culture of art and architecture. Importantly these references all occur within the context of Australian culture, further locating the building in a discourse particular to our community and respectful of the uniqueness of the Australian experience.'[70] This imposing and grand structure returns the civic centre to the position of the figurehead building, upon which the aspirations of the municipality are writ large. Nonetheless, the Marion

Cultural Centre has not abandoned community usage, incorporating a theatre, library, gallery, cafe and meeting rooms.

In many ways, the combination of service to the local, the familial, and the encapsulation of the aspirations of the municipality are today, as earlier in the century, constantly in tension. The post-war desire to combine community buildings and needs into consolidated precincts was rarely achieved, despite the grand and numerous plans circulated in the 1940s and 1950s. The slow pace of building such precincts inevitably meant that the priorities of community needs and appropriate municipal provision of spaces – and therefore plans – changed over time. Yet, more recently, with state and federal government attention devoted to the promotion of the concepts of community 'vitality' and sustainability, there has been a re-emphasis on the unification of municipal services into a central location in the form of 'community hubs'.

Such hubs are, in so many ways, a contemporary rendition of the 1940s community centre or precinct ideal – although now the emphasis is on accessibility to co-located facilities by car, rather than by public transport or walking. Indeed, despite communications technology and the greater personal mobility that characterises the 21st-century 'way of life', many new housing developments proudly proclaim their 'village' atmosphere through the grouping of community facilities at a central 'heart'. In other suburban developments, the absence of small-scale municipal community infrastructure has prompted forms of neighbourhood action that again draws upon historical precedents in its rhetoric and demands. One example will suffice: in early 2010 in the burgeoning northern Melbourne suburb of Craigieburn, residents were increasingly frustrated at the lack of shops and other infrastructure. A group called the Craigieburn Town Watchers sought to hold the private developer and the City of Hume to often-repeated promises to provide a 'town centre' with communal facilities.[71] In Craigieburn's case, whether the community 'could do it' – and a private developer is of course a different administrative authority than local government, though both were held responsible in this case – remains to be seen. But this community action perhaps demonstrates a core truth expressed in the influential text – *The Community Can Do It* – of 1945:

> Original ideas develop, new ideas spring from daily contact with one another, and so the community is held together by a developing common purpose.[72]

WAR MEMORIAL LITERARY INSTITUTE

HERAGHTY PARK
OLYMPIC POOL

REDCLIFFE WAR MEMORIAL
SWIMMING POOL

THIS MEMORIAL POOL
HAS BEEN ERECTED BY THE CITIZENS
OF GUNNEDAH AND DISTRICT AND
IS DEDICATED TO ALL THOSE WHO
SERVED AUSTRALIA AT WAR
LEST WE FORGET

COMMEMORATING AND ENHANCING THE EVERYDAY

Hannah Lewi and Caroline Jordan

Commemorating and enhancing the everyday

However ordinary and prosaic they seem on the surface, the functional public buildings and open spaces of Australian country towns, suburban centres and urban neighbourhoods are often imbued with humanist gestures of commemoration. They commonly memorialise historical events, important figures who served the community, and local lives lost in war and other tragedies. They can also express shared meaning through public artworks.

8.1 **a.** Interior of the new Memorial Hall, Sea Lake, Vic. 1924 **b.** Soldiers Memorial School of Arts, Wyalong, NSW 1928 **c.** 'Proposed Services Memorial – Club Rooms and Shrine', Shepparton, Vic. 1946

This chapter addresses the important role of commemoration in community-building in two parts. First, we examine the creation of 'useful' municipal amenities erected between 1919 and the late 1960s as alternative war monuments. These proliferated through the fundraising efforts of the Returned and Services League (RSL) and other community groups. Second, we look at new varieties of public art that began to emerge from the 1950s onwards. As war memorials came to be considered less relevant and desirable, communities turned to other forms of commemoration in civic places through public art.

Artists and architects debated in professional journals of the day the need for new expressive forms of monumentality and humanism to compensate for the technocratic drive of modern functionalism. Sculptors and painters also responded to the yearning for a new sense of monumentality in the modern environment by creating mainly figurative but also abstract artworks located in community settings. The Australian sculptor Tom Bass for instance wrote in 1955:

> The role of the sculptor in the community from its most primitive times has been to provide society with the emblems it needs to make it conscious of itself as a society, to keep it reminded of its objectives and make its members aware of their obligations.[1]

While many of these mid-century public artworks aspired to the representation of lofty and universal truths, others called on the community to engage in individualistic, interactive and expressive ways through public art. Play was an important concept in modern architecture, seen in various experiments with amenities for public play in sports and recreational facilities, and in parks, where fountains and water features became popular from the 1960s. It was

8.1 d. Memorial Baths, Lismore, NSW 1928 **e.** Memorial Pool, Gunnedah, NSW 1959
f. War Memorial and memorial gates in front of Alphington Bowling Club, Vic. c. 1950s

also increasingly recognised that attempts to bring imagination, humanity and creativity into civic places should not necessarily be the exclusive preserve of professional artists and architects. The idea of direct community participation was powerful in the politically radical 1970s, which saw the beginnings of the community art movement. Murals in particular in this decade were reinvigorated as a people's artform commemorating significant places, events and personalities in and on community buildings, with the active participation of local communities.

8.2 Memorial Hall, Healesville, Vic., Armistice Day, 1939

Useful memorials for Australian communities

After World War I, the popular desire to create permanent memorials to honour the service and supreme sacrifice of Australian soldiers led to the erection of hundreds of stand-alone statues, cenotaphs, avenues of honour and plaques in small rural communities, cities and suburbs. Unsurprisingly, this flood of memorials prompted some dissident voices. While Australians' 'open-heartedness' and eager work in erecting monuments was praised, concerns were also expressed that too many were 'inartistic'. In 1919 a deputation of architects appealed to the federal Minister for Local Government on the need for state legislation and an advisory council with the charter of exercising more aesthetic design control over the building of local war memorials. Others disagreed with traditional monuments altogether and felt that meagre resources should instead be more productively used to erect community facilities. While both types of memorials were commonly built in Australia, the purely monumental sites have been much more thoroughly documented by the RSL and Australian historians than other forms of commemorative buildings, core services and public spaces that were built in the name of remembering war.[2]

Decisions surrounding the type and utility of monumental structures escalated as a matter of public concern in the 1920s.[3] Even the construction of Australia's most significant state war memorial in Melbourne was highly contested, with a concerted campaign for the alternative of a memorial hospital gaining strong support. 'Useful' soldiers' memorials, such as hospitals and halls, were proposed, with the hope that the sometimes 'sinister' connotations of war memorials might be replaced by a more 'tangible, practical and indestructible form', that was of active benefit to the community.[4] The concept of commemorative buildings and services to be used by the living represented for their advocates a more modern, egalitarian and enlightened option.[5] It was reported that Americans were already in favour of utility, but the idea had not yet been taken up with much enthusiasm in the United Kingdom or Europe, where the provision of core services like hospitals, schools and roads was seen to be the responsibility of good government rather than public philanthropy. Some saw utilitarian structures and services as less durable and in danger of being outmoded more quickly than stand-alone monuments. Others felt that traditional monumental statues would lose their relevance to future generations and therefore be more likely to fall into disrepair. In general the Australian RSL favoured the gravitas of the traditional

The popular desire to create permanent memorials to honour the service and supreme sacrifice of Australian soldiers led to the erection of hundreds of stand-alone statues, cenotaphs, avenues of honour.

monument, while some citizen groups and government bodies began shifting their support towards utility.[6] Around 60 per cent of all Australian dedications to those who fought in World War I took the form of traditional monuments, with memorial halls and schools following as the next most common. These were seen as promoting community comradeship for returned soldiers and civilians, and representing renewal through education.

Memorial halls were built in country towns and districts in every state in the 1920s, ranging from modest weatherboard buildings to grand brick structures. Openings were proud local occasions. The Soldiers' Memorial Hall in Healesville (figure 8.2) was opened in 1924 by the Governor-General and the local population, visitors, school children and scouts gathered in festive ceremony to mark what was reported as the 'greatest day' in Healesville's history. Hall buildings of this size were a major undertaking, and this one dominated the social life of Healesville in the early 1920s. Creative fundraising events included the 'mile of pennies' and a three-day picture show carnival. The honour board in the new hall commemorated the names of 185 local citizen soldiers, 37 of whom had lost their lives in World War I.[7] At Swan Hill, Victoria, some 900 men volunteered to serve in World War I and 150 died. Those who returned home to form the local RSL branch held the ambition of building their clubrooms as a memorial hall. Financed by local subscriptions, the substantial Swan Hill Memorial Hall was opened in 1924 by the Minister for Railways. The building was rented out as a picture theatre and dance hall, raising considerable income for the RSL.[8] This serving of multiple functions for the community over time was typical. Soldiers' Memorial Halls newly built in other states included Moree and Guyra in New South Wales and Dilston and Triabunna in Tasmania. Others expanded on existing structures, such as Snowtown's 1881 Institute in South Australia, which with the addition of a new hall – supported by the RSL – became the Snowtown Soldiers' Memorial in 1924; similar changes took place around the state as mentioned in chapter 7. The Tamworth Memorial Town Hall in northern New South Wales was designed by Peddle, Thorp and Walker in 1927, but most were not the work of architects. Many were plain and frugal, with just a simple place name above the entrance, such as the Sea Lake Memorial Hall in Victoria (figure 8.1a).

After World War II the focus turned away from explicit political or nationalistic sentiments and towards conscious renewal and community-building.[9] A gallup poll conducted in 1944 revealed a definite swing in favour of utility and growing dissent in many Australian suburbs and towns over the need for any additional monuments to war service.[10] This groundswell in community enthusiasm for the building of amenities useful to local communities, such as schools, hospitals, roads, parks and recreation facilities, reflected a general shift in society towards secularism and away from unquestioning faith in older spiritual and political tropes, such as Christianity and the British Empire, bolstered by the aesthetic and philosophical trends in architecture and planning underpinning modern functionalism. Changes of heart also indicated more relaxed social attitudes on the question of what constituted appropriate public behaviour and propriety. By this time it was common, and seen as perfectly appropriate, to enjoy family recreation in a memorial pool, or to play bowls at the local club where honour boards and gates marked the memory of those who had given their lives. To do so was to confirm an interpretation of soldiers' sacrifice as made in defence of a 'way of life'.

New thinking in inter-war planning had encouraged civic centres that included a hall or municipal chambers and a library or cultural centre, sited around public gardens with statues and fountains. This could easily be converted to become an integrated civic memorial precinct. Ambitious and expensive, such schemes often proceeded fitfully over decades and arrived only after many changes in direction and much compromise. In many places, memorial precincts failed to eventuate in their entirety – or at all. Sometimes only one or two buildings from civic schemes or gardens were completed. In Lismore, New South Wales, the council hoped for a memorial hall, council chambers, school of arts and soldiers' club but delays in the framing of an architectural design competition for the £18,000 project saw enthusiasm dwindle. By 1926 requests were downgraded to the construction of swimming baths as a fitting memorial to the Great War, on a site which could also house the soldiers' club. Eventually in 1927 the public pool went ahead without the club building.[11] Nonetheless, substantial memorial precincts of varying grandeur can be found in many country towns, such as Geelong, Bendigo, Harcourt, Ballarat, Mildura and Wangaratta in Victoria.

Some memorial civic schemes were overtly proposed as mechanisms of renewal, as in Launceston, Tasmania, where, as mentioned in chapter 7, a 'grand conception of a living War Memorial' was proposed in 1944 on the prominent Windmill Hill. This plan was offered as a means to renew an otherwise 'unsavoury wilderness' close to town where immoral acts were known to take place. Despite a successful public appeal for funds, building proceeded slowly; the Community Centre hall (figure 8.3) was joined by the Launceston City Baths but this public pool was not opened until 1957.[12]

The townspeople of Nuriootpa, east of Adelaide, and of Sale in Victoria also worked hard to raise funds for the building of their architect-designed memorial centres. In Nuriootpa, Louis Laybourne-Smith was engaged to design a scheme with facilities including a soldiers' clubroom, library, and memorial assembly hall. Funding came in part from the profits of the local community hotel that was acquired and rebuilt by the town's citizens in 1937. Sale's included council chambers, a large public hall to accommodate 1000,

WAR MEMORIAL
COMMUNITY CENTRE
1953
The War Memorial Hall
NOW UNDER CONSTRUCTION—TO BE OPENED ON
THE DAY OF THE ROYAL VISIT, FEB. 23, 1954

8.3 'The War Memorial Community Centre, Launceston, Tasmania' 1953

another smaller hall, a library, and various community meeting rooms for organisations such as the RSL and the Country Women's Association (CWA). The community backed a modern, 'up-to-date' design with 'sweeping lines' and an enclosed ceremonial forecourt by the Geelong-based architects Buchan Laird & Buchan. The war memorial itself, commemorating Sale's significant role in the recruitment and training of Australian service men and women, was relocated from the Princes Highway into the forecourt of the new library, with the project being completed in 1963.[13]

One of the larger and more ambitious memorial precincts in Australia was built in the 1950s and 1960s in the city of Newcastle in New South Wales. Newcastle is notable not just for its complex of civic, cultural and educational buildings, but also for its contemporary public art and design, discussed later in this chapter. Begun in the early 1950s, the plan had been conceived in the 1930s and put on hold until after the war. In general, the community was not in favour of public investment of funds at a time of housing shortages, but finances were raised and the development constructed in stages beginning with the laying of the foundation stone in 1949 to those who sacrificed their lives in 1939–1945, followed by a public library, conservatorium, and art gallery.[14] The buildings were set around a park precinct, including a reflection pond designed by Wilson and Suters, and a cenotaph war memorial that became the focus of civic ceremonies and performances.[15] The commemorative fountain located in the park and defining the axis between the City Hall and library was designed by artist Margel Hinder, following her success in a national competition, and completed in 1965–66.[16] The commissioning of a well-recognised Australian artist for memorial structures was symptomatic of the gradual move away from traditionally styled monuments towards more individual, expressive designs for fountains and sculptures. The line between the purely monumental and the useful was blurring as well, with arguments sustained that commemorative gardens adorned with drinking fountains, gates, bell towers, or lookouts were places of pleasure as well as utility. In a few cases, earlier monuments were modified to take on added functions in the post-war era. This occurred at the Kangaroo Ground War Memorial in Victoria where a substantial stone tower built to the design of Stephenson and Meldrum's Percy Meldrum in 1926 was modified twenty years later to become a fire-spotting tower.

As discussed in chapter 5, public swimming pools were another popular choice for commemorative buildings in the 1950s when towns and suburbs struggled to raise sufficient funds for local pools. Support from the RSL and municipal councils for the designation of a memorial pool often assisted the painfully slow task of raising money, finding labour to bolster construction programs, and alleviating tax. The story of Rockhampton's memorial pool shows how the typically dilatory support for public pools could be given a significant boost by the involvement of military associations. An Olympic pool had been planned before World War II but failed to gain the support of ratepayers; in 1952 mayor Reginald Pilbeam renewed the cause through voluntary public appeals for funds for a memorial pool. At a vocal public meeting the scheme was finally accepted and was completed through city council and state government funding; Rotary built the diving tower. To signal the site's memorial status the ship's bell from the HMAS *Rockhampton* was installed alongside the pool, two German howitzers reconditioned by the local RSL were set on concrete blocks at the entrance, and the Airforce Association donated an electric wall clock.[17] The pool was finally opened in 1960 with premier Frank Nicklin and swimming champions Dawn Fraser and Ilsa Konrads adding to the fanfare.

The memorial pool in Warracknabeal, Victoria, was also a long time coming with suggestions first being put forward in 1946 for a substantial civic soldiers' memorial including a community centre, hall and swimming pool to be built in Anzac Park. The pool was the only one of these facilities eventually realised, and this some eleven years later co-located with the Memorial Kindergarten.[18] There are many examples of memorial pools across all Australian states from the 1920s onwards, with varying expressions of monumentality from a simple name above the entrance, to separate monuments sited adjacent to the building. Inverell Olympic Pool in New South Wales and Wagin Olympic Pool in Western Australia both have a cenotaph memorial adjoining the pool entrance; Mount Isa Mines Memorial Swimming Pool features a stone war memorial at the entrance to the pool, and the Lismore Memorial Pool, dedicated in 1927, has developed over time into an elaborate memorial precinct which includes a relocated Boer War statue and marble monuments commemorating World War II and the Vietnam War.[19]

The line between the purely monumental and the useful was blurring ... commemorative gardens ... were places of pleasure as well as utility.

A number of other public pools today owe their survival in substantial part to their status as memorials. A Queensland icon, the Tobruk Memorial Baths in Townsville, is listed on the State Heritage Register as one of the country's most substantial public memorials to the 1941 siege of Tobruk.[20] The ocean setting on The Strand had been associated with public swimming and bathing since the 1870s; the city council was responsible for funding, designing and carrying out the work on the new pool which commenced in 1941, despite concerted public appeals to halt construction during wartime. The building program did, indeed, stall when Townsville found itself at the epicentre of the Pacific War efforts in 1942, but the Olympic and toddlers' pools, cafe, grandstands, dressing rooms, courtyard and grassed areas were completed by 1950. Like many other memorial structures, the pool and accompanying clock tower are located in a public site that was redesignated as 'Anzac Memorial Park'. The modern lettering announcing the name of the pool at the entrance, alongside depictions of swimming in the glazed entry doors, brings together the somewhat unlikely associations of aquatic recreation and remembrance.

As lawn bowls swelled in popularity after World War II, bowls clubs also came to be seen as opportune venues for commemorations to war service. Support and involvement from the RSL was common, with many leagues providing competitions and fundraising events for returned soldiers, as outlined in chapter 6. Most clubs marked their commemorative status in name only, while others constructed elaborate, decorative, memorial gates at their entrance or in adjacent park settings, like the gates at the Dungog Memorial Bowling Club, New South Wales, erected in 1947 by the Women's Bowling Club. Countless other clubrooms displayed rolls of honour dedicated to the memory of members and friends. The Rathmines Memorial Club held a particularly close association with war service as it was housed in the former officers' mess at the Rathmines RAAF base, with a memorial wall dedicated to all those who served with the seaplane and flying boat units. The Fitzroy Bowling Club added memorial gates and a fountain to the arbour already constructed by the various sporting clubs that used Edinburgh Gardens in Melbourne after World War I.[21] Clubs created other monuments, too, as well as war memorials that commemorated longstanding involvement and general service to the local community, such as the Edna Browne memorial stone and fountain at the Lane Cove Women's Bowling and Recreation Club in Sydney.

Bowling clubs and public pools were often planned as part of larger renewal schemes that were oriented around either an existing park, or a renovated and renamed public reserve. Anzac Parks can be found all over the country from Toowong and Townsville in Queensland to North Sydney, Orange and Gwabegar in New South Wales, to Bunbury in Western Australia, while Gallipoli Park in Marysville was the site of tragedy in the Victorian bushfires of 2009. Although better known for his association with the Australian War Memorial, war historian CEW Bean was a key figure in the Parks and Playgrounds Movement in New South Wales and a keen supporter of the view that local memorials should be of purpose and benefit to communities. Bean's involvement in parks and playgrounds extended this pursuit of utility through outdoor recreation, which resonated with his ideals of 'bringing the country as close as possible to the town'.[22] The RSL was actively involved in many local initiatives to create memorial parks and playgrounds. In the New South Wales town of Picton, for instance, the local RSL helped to build and dedicate a war memorial playground in 1951. Other memorial facilities focusing on maternal health and 'rest areas' for women were built in parks and country towns such as the Angaston Memorial Women's Rest Room, South Australia, in 1956.

Places and services associated with the health, education and welfare of children and families were also often dedicated to the fallen after World War II, a commemorative act that gestured towards the future and youth.

Places and services associated with the health, education and welfare of children and families were also often dedicated to the fallen after World War II, a commemorative act that gestured towards the future and youth.

Hospitals were popular memorials, in particular medical centres for children.[23] Memorial kindergartens and baby health centres were also common. Although there was widespread agreement, led by the state Kindergarten Unions, from the 1940s onwards that each child should have access to a kindergarten in every neighbourhood, there were shortages of materials and public money to build centres.[24] Governments had begun to assume responsibility for funding and training in early childhood services, although funding still fell short and local communities were forced to find additional resources. These efforts were sometimes strengthened by the attribution of memorial status, hence the proliferation of memorial kindergartens, baby health centres and playgrounds. The building of the Mt Evelyn Memorial Kindergarten in Victoria was, for example, driven by a local community group who believed that the area did not need another commemorative avenue of trees but *did* need a kindergarten.[25] Similarly the Eltham Progress Society resolved in 1945 that the community war memorial should take the form of a baby health centre with creche and children's library.[26] Other examples include the Lambton Memorial Baby Health Centre built in the late 1940s in Newcastle; the War Memorial Kindergarten in the Melbourne suburb of Ivanhoe, constructed in 1960; and the Memorial Baby Health Centre in Blayney, New South Wales, built next to the war memorial and hall. As mentioned above, War Memorial Kindergarten in Warracknabeal, Victoria, was built in the town's Anzac Park in 1955, yet in recognition of fierce competition for scarce resources the council decreed that the kindergarten was not to be designated as '*the* town war memorial while fund-raising was still ongoing for their memorial pool centre'.[27] Other kindergartens and baby health centres acquired commemorative status, but were dedicated to pioneers of the childhood education sector rather than the remembrance of war. Sale, for instance, had the Annie Pain Memorial Kindergarten built in 1922 in the name of the president of the Sale Ladies Benevolent Society which served the poor and marginalised, and the Sister Muriel Peck Infant Welfare Centre, named for her leadership in infant health in Victoria.

Art in public places: A new monumentality

After World War II, public opinion polls revealed a steadily growing dissatisfaction with the continued erection of war memorials in Australia, whether traditional or useful, favouring instead modest additions to existing rolls of honour, or doing nothing further at all. Objections towards the monumentalisation of war were motivated on a number of grounds from political to feminist and aesthetic. An opinion article in a 1944 edition of the Australian journal *Architecture* predicted 'the unhappy prospect of yet another crop of unworthy "War Memorials"'.[28] The thorny issue of the appropriate

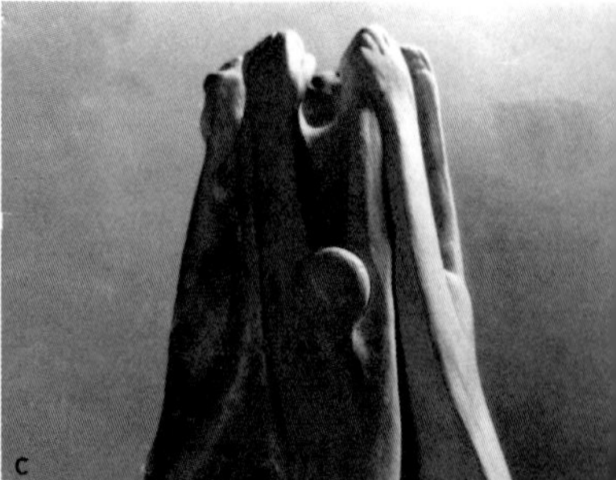

8.4 **a.** Bas reliefs of Aboriginal life, bronze doors, eastern entrance of the Public Library of New South Wales, Sydney, 1940–42 **b.** *Two Piece Reclining Figure No. 9*, outside the Australian National Library, ACT 1969 **c.** Maquette for sculpture at public gardens in flats, Melbourne, Vic. c. 1950s

design of all types of modern monuments was re-opened, and calls for a dedicated federal Ministry of Fine Arts were rekindled to allow more influence to be exerted over the design and aesthetics of monuments in the public environment.[29] If traditional war memorials were increasingly no longer seen as an appropriate way to invest public spaces and buildings with a sense of shared memory, public spirit and civic importance, how could architecture and public art play other roles in the monumentalising and humanising of towns and suburbs? What new kinds of monuments could take their place in community settings? How could public art offer alternative expressions of the individual's role in creating new modes of citizenship?[30] Here Australia was influenced by international debates raised in the wake of World War II, when nations were preoccupied with the problems of how best to remember, yet simultaneously heal and look forward. These discussions surrounding the creative possibilities of achieving a 'new monumentality' were played out through international meetings, books and professional journals like the highly influential British *Architectural Review*.[31]

New forms of civic art absorbed some of the burden of the growing dissatisfaction with the deficiencies of modern functionalism and the desire for public monumental places to become more expressive and welcoming to the person in the street. For the urban historian Lewis Mumford, monuments and modernism were fundamentally incompatible.[32] Other critics and practitioners, however, saw the modernising of the monumental as pivotal to the popularising of modern design.[33] Margaret Garlake suggests: 'In replacing slums with decent housing, the new cities had also swept away the complex, informal networks that bind a society into something more than a number of households. One of the functions of post-war public art was to create the visual, symbolic reinstatement of a sense of community.'[34]

8.4 d. Baby Health Centre, NSW c. 1960s **e.** James Cook Memorial Fountain, Civic Park, Newcastle, NSW 1961–66 **f.** Mural on Broadmeadows Neighbourhood House, Vic. 1985

The work of English sculptor Henry Moore offered one possible solution for a new kind of modern monument that 'was neither overtly celebratory nor a memorial, yet retained a symbolic content'.[35] Moore was a close friend of key European modern architects, and was well aware of the discussions in *Architectural Review* led by JM Richards surrounding the 'new monumentality'. Moore was to recast his own work into a more monumental depiction of the human figure, typically through the tropes of the family group, the reclining figure and the mother and child.[36] This pursuit of the figurative coincided with a firming of Moore's own communitarian and social concerns: the status of sculpture above all as a 'community art'.[37] This aligned with the interests of some planners in the 'democratisation of monumentality', and Moore began to work closely with a number of English local authorities in the 1950s. He created the *Family Group* for Barclay School, Stevenage (designed by FRS Yorke, 1948–49), under the direction of the Hertfordshire Education Authority, and worked in the Harlow New Town (1954–55) on another figural piece set in the town's environs. Through these situations Moore's work became, according to Garlake, 'embedded in the day to day fabric of society, the values proclaimed by the two groups (family) are those which cement communities together'.[38] This increased 'visibility' of the family held much currency in the era of Britain's welfare state and was productively translated into Australia's social policy contexts.

Moore's sphere of influence in modern sculpture was far-reaching. Many important Australian sculptors trained and worked in England both before and after the war, including Inge King, Leonard Shillam and Gerald Lewers, and a direct flow of ideas between European and Australian practitioners was further supported through the migration or return of a number of artists and architects to Australia. Lenton Parr trained as a sculptor in Melbourne and worked in Britain as an assistant to Henry Moore in 1955–56, before returning to become head of sculpture at Royal Melbourne Institute of Technology from 1966. He and other antipodean sculptors like Alan Ingham – who worked for Moore on key commissions in the 1950s – strengthened appreciation for Moore's work and ideas on the purpose of sculpture in the public field. Moore's public figurative work for the English New Towns and the UNESCO building in Paris of 1957 were widely published in Australian publications. Local commentators cited Moore alongside other sculptors, like Naum Gabo and Barbara Hepworth, as models for the emboldened way forward collaboration with modern architecture. Tom Heath, for instance, wrote in *Architecture in Australia* in 1959:

> The time of the little dab of sculpture scrawled in the bottom left hand corner of a façade like a rude word on the behind of a plaster cast and the mural struggling hopelessly to compete with the gridiron joints of the 1 × 1 mosaic tiles in which it is embalmed, should be past. We should begin to take art seriously. To succeed a painter or sculptor can do only two things with a building: he can lick it, or join it ... to lick it – it must be big enough and a masterpiece … the second option is to become subordinate to the architect … to join the work.[39]

Many architects, however, remained wary of tempering the scientific rigour of functional modernism through wilful public art that might open the door to the whims of fashion or the 'intuitive processes of the artist's mind'.[40]

Modern buildings were considered self-sufficient, sculptural objects in their own right, and attempts to integrate either art or monuments amounted at best to superfluous decoration and at worst to an unsightly excrescence. Parr quipped: 'In 1955 I heard one of Melbourne's best architects address a group of sculptors and, in most vehement terms, express his conviction that a building itself must be conceived as a sculptural expression and that sculpture, architectural sculpture at least, was an anachronism'.[41]

Artists, too, questioned the possibility of a comfortable relationship between sculpture and architecture given the unprecedented scale of modern high-rise buildings.[42] The journal *Architecture and Arts* served to temper antagonism and encourage productive collaborations that could assist in creating more human-centred civic and community amenities.[43] By the late 1950s it was also somewhat hopefully suggested that modern architecture's 'austere and purely functional phase' had passed and that art should again be seen as integral. The work of Melbourne artist Ann Marie Graham was cited as one example of fruitful collaboration. Graham, better known through her painting, was at this time working in mixed media, including sculpture: a maquette of two gossiping women for an apartment block (figure 8.4c) and a bronze figure relief above an entrance to a sports pavilion.

Leading Australian artists, including Clement Meadmore, wrote instructive and provocative articles for the architecture press about how best to plan for the careful integration of sculptural works and murals at the outset of any commission.[44] Artist Douglas Annand gave an address to the New South Wales Chapter of Architects in 1949 in which he offered slightly tongue-in-cheek praise to modern architecture for creating such plain and beautifully proportioned surfaces for artists to add suitable decoration: 'Your logic can be humanised,' remarked Annand.[45] Parr spoke to the planning profession on sculpture in the urban environment, setting out three ways in which it could be used for public purposes: first, as monuments and memorials; second, as an integrated element in architectural design; and third, as open garden or plaza sculpture.[46]

In reality, it was some time after World War II before Australian architects were in a position to entertain the inclusion of the sculptural into what were typically cash-strapped, primarily functional, public buildings. Parr – and others – saw glimmerings of a more welcoming, if still superficial, organic relationship.[47] He attributed this change of heart to the role architects were beginning to play in promoting sculpture to their clients, both public and commercial, and to Australian sculptors finding 'a voice' through groups such as the Society of Sculptors and Associates. Some states were more proactive than others in facilitating public art, with Melbourne leading both in modern architecture and sculpture at the time, and productive opportunities for exchange developing.[48]

Sculptor Peter Gelenscer was far less positive about the situation of public art in Perth in the late 1960s. Gelenscer, who was born in Hungary and studied in Europe, completed works in Europe and the USA before migrating to Western Australia where he gained few public commissions. Gelencser again cited Moore's *Reclining Figure* at the UNESCO building in Paris as a fine exemplar, not because the sculpture and building were in harmony, but rather because the figural work offered some kind of supernatural possibilities as a disconnected 'meteorite' in the face of modern internationalism.[49] He saw attempts at collaboration in Australia as less than ideal, however, feeling that sculpture, where present, was used merely to fill an empty space or a vacant wall of a public building project.

Government and public bodies were promoted as new patrons to foster Australian artists' careers by creating opportunities hitherto provided by individuals or family businesses.[50] Support, however, was slow in coming and, when it did come, was slight. Various proposals for public art schemes had been aired in the late 1940s, including the idea of a percentage-based budget of important public commissions being reserved for murals, sculpture or mosaics. Australians were told that similar schemes had already been successfully implemented in Sweden, America and other 'civilised countries'. The plan received government backing, and was favoured by architects and artists as a way of breathing new life into the largely conservative Australian art scene; however, funding did not eventuate until decades later. A government body with the charter of exercising more quality control in public art commissions, along similar line to the Arts Council of Britain, was also mooted. [51] The degree to which artistic freedom should be permitted in public works was hotly contested. For instance the first chairman of the Arts Council in Britain, economist Maynard Keynes, saw his role as providing government patronage, but at the same time allowing artists to remain courageously free and 'unregimented' in their practice. 'He cannot be told his direction,' Keynes said of the artist. 'He does not know it himself.'[52] Despite some support in Australia, and the recognition that public art could provide a strategy for mobilising government objectives surrounding 'participatory citizenship', and 'responsible leisure and consumption',[53] the federal Australia Council for the Arts was not established until 1968. Its aim was to integrate the arts into the mainstream of cultural and leisure pursuits. With state and federal government policy and patronage remaining piecemeal for all but the most prominent commissions, fundraising was typically left to municipal and local leadership.

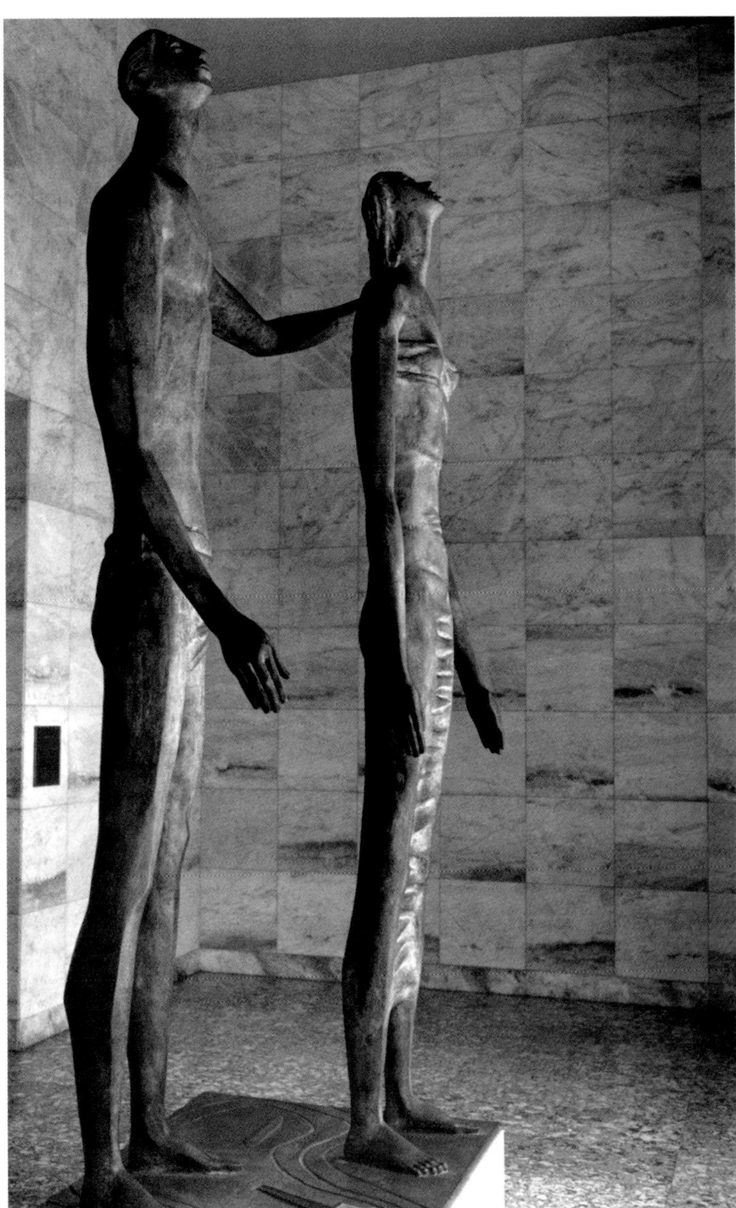

8.5 *Figure Group*, Newcastle War Memorial Cultural Centre, NSW 1957

Figurative art in community settings

The recasting of the human figure offered a way for public art to satisfy the desire to humanise modern settings, yet also to work in harmony with modern architecture's reconfiguring of the modern modular body. But the numerous examples of figurative work in post-war public settings in Australia – both public and private commissions – were not completed without controversy and insecurity. In fact, the moment of figurative public art was brief, and it has gone on to receive little attention in Australian art history, perhaps because of its seemingly retrograde symbolism and uneasy truce with modern architecture.

Lyndon Dadswell's war memorial sculpture in Newcastle is a major mid-century figurative public art commission. Few examples of successful competitions to commission public works for municipal council plans and buildings in the 1950s and 1960s can be found, with Newcastle a prominent exception. A competition was held for a sculpture to be located in the foyer of the new memorial cultural centre building that would commemorate war service outside the traditional monument. Dadswell won, with a sculpture of male and female figures symbolising humans emerging from great suffering with their heads held high (figure 8.5). His design pushed public expectations of a war memorial and it was labelled a 'monstrosity', 'bodgie art' and 'something to frighten naughty boys'.[54] The work, however, was installed and later acquired the fonder nicknames of 'Him and Her' and 'Dave and Mabel', after Steele Rudd's popular *On Our Selection* stories. Dadswell continued to pursue similar figurative themes in commercial commissions, such as his *The Community and the Family* (1954) work for the Commonwealth Bank in Hobart, as did other contemporary sculptors.

The post-war development of Canberra provided a significant platform from which to make universal representations of civic humanist ideals. The National Capital Development Commission (NCDC) funded what have over time become iconic public artworks. Australian sculptor Tom Bass was a dominant force in this niche situation of public commissions, sustained by a powerful personal philosophy that 'sculpture is the most social of all arts'. As he explains:

> [Sculpture] is something in the open air; it is associated with the great buildings that have a kind of symbolic significance for communities, or with religion … so that all the time it was the sculptor making a significant symbol, or totem for the community. The sculptor has always been the seer or spokesperson for the community. I decided that was the kind of sculptor I would become.[55]

Bass created perhaps the most overt expression of community in 1950s Australian sculpture with the work *Ethos* of 1959 (figure 8.6). It was sited in the new civic square precinct, designed by Yuncken Freeman, which also featured a public library, government offices and, later, a theatre. It was the first artwork commissioned by the NCDC for a public place and funds were raised by the selling of miniature versions of the sculpture. *Ethos* is a young winged female figure of cast copper, her robes embossed with symbols and figures representing many facets of community life from working the land to civic organisations and sites of learning.[56] She holds aloft a flaming sun symbolising the enlightenment of Canberra. The figure is set in a hexagonal, dish-shaped base that is inscribed

8.6 (left) *Ethos*, Civic Square, Canberra, ACT 1959–61

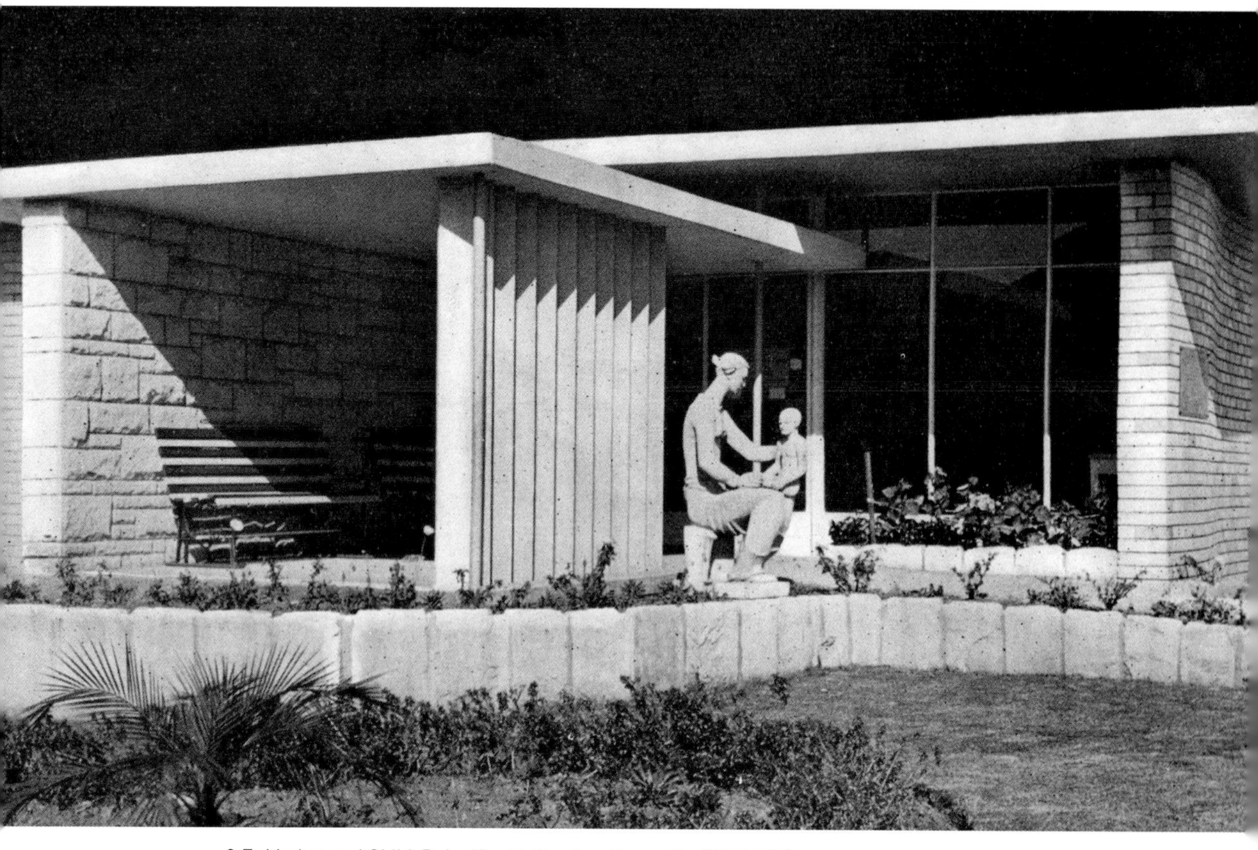

8.7 *Mother and Child*, Baby Health Centre, Campsie, NSW 1956

with the Griffins' Canberra Plan, beauty thus arising from the planned city. For Bass, *Ethos* offered 'a great opportunity to create a totem' for a synthetic city, placing at its heart 'the model, the type, the perfect immobile symbol, which for a moment cools the incessant fever of man'.[57] Australia's first internationally successful pop group, the Seekers, gave the piece their imprimatur when they performed in front of *Ethos* in a 1967 television special.

Another figurative work commissioned for Bankstown Civic Centre and chapel was created by Alan Ingham in 1964. Titled *The Spirit of Botany* as a tribute to Joseph Banks, the female figure sits in a sandstone pond, with arms stretched upwards, holding a botanical specimen, symbolising the quest for scientific knowledge.[58] As an assistant to Moore on works including the *Reclining Figure* for the Festival of Britain in 1951, Ingham met the likes of art critic Herbert Read, and modernist architects Le Corbusier and Walter Gropius. Moore assisted Ingham in mastering the casting of large pieces.[59] This sculpture has recently experienced a renaissance, with the city taking its image as the driving theme for its Public Art Framework program.

Public libraries have long been seen as appropriate civic institutions for the installation of public artworks. Australian state and municipal libraries in the mid-century often commissioned artists to create either stand-alone works or elements integral to the architecture that reinforced the ideals of seeking wisdom and self-betterment. The bronze entry doors to the Mitchell Library in Sydney of 1940 – modelled on the Renaissance artist Ghiberti's doors for the baptistery in Florence – feature Australian explorers, while the inner doors depict a series of Aboriginal figures by artist Daphne Mayo (figure 8.4a). The Newcastle Library, 1957, has two stone reliefs by Paul Beadle depicting works of 'Music, Literature and Art'. Tom Bass and Len Shillam, who with his wife Kath was active in public art in Queensland, used such commissions to create universal symbols for social agendas such as public learning. Shillam's aluminium sculpture *Enlightenment* (1959) for the extension to the Public Library of Queensland comprises three figures reaching up towards the sun. Bass's major commission for a sculptural relief over the lintel above the entrance doors to the National Library, Canberra, in 1967–68 is titled *Knowledge*. The huge copper work again represents the theme of enlightenment, with the National Library symbolising an ark-like repository.[60] A cast of Moore's own sculpture, *Reclining Figure No. 9* (figure 8.4b), was installed outside the National Library in 1970, thus reinforcing the orthodoxy both of Moore and monumental figurative works in Canberra.

Baby health centres provided a more modest setting for the inclusion of latter-day mother and child sculptures, on the rare occasion when funds stretched to incorporate non-essentials.

Baby health centres provided a more modest setting for the inclusion of latter-day mother and child sculptures, on the rare occasion when funds stretched to incorporate non-essentials. A theme could easily be found in the targeting of the family as a site of public and governmental concern in the 1950s, as well as serving to signpost these otherwise often anonymous buildings. Erwin Guth's work at the Longreach Community Health Centre in Queensland, and the Campsie Baby Health Centre work in New South Wales by an unknown sculptor (figure 8.7) with seated mother and child figures at the entrance, published in *Architecture in Australia* in 1956, are two examples. Other efforts were more bizarre, such as the memorial baby health centre in western Sydney that featured toddlers climbing up the sheer brick walls as if making their great escape.[61]

In a few instances figurative works depicting the family or mother and child were commissioned for public parks instead of more traditional memorials. A fine example is Margaret Priest's memorial to the pioneer women of Australia, constructed in Kings Park, Western Australia, in 1968 (figure 8.8).

The 'uncompromising' bronze figure of a mother holding her infant in her arms and stepping forth to 'meet her destiny', forms the centrepiece of a water fountain and pond designed by architect Geoffrey Summerhayes.[62] The CWA was instrumental in campaigning for a public work that symbolised the vital part that women played in building the state and its local communities. The resulting work forms a stark contrast to other, earlier, monuments and war memorials scattered throughout the park.[63] Priest also designed a bronze family group sheltering under an abstracted bird's wing for the State Housing Commission in East Perth in 1978.

Despite some instances of public and creative successes, by the late 1960s figurative monumental art with a social agenda seemed passé. Throughout that decade Bass had been prolific in creating totemic representations for modern Australia that attempted to articulate communal meanings and inculcate public values of good citizenship. In this endeavour he directly acknowledged the influence of Moore, whose pursuit of archetypes was described by the art critic Herbert Read as symbolising 'the universal in the particular'.[64] However, Bass's confidence was not to withstand changing times and he recounts a personal collapse in his ideals over sculpture's future role in society. His dominance as an 'official' artist and his success in commercial commissions resulted in him being ostracised by the art establishment, with offers of sculpture commissions for national and state collections declining. The figurative public work of Bass, and others like him, fell victim to the paradox of 'new monumentality' which, while predicated on modernity and social renewal, was in form and content often derivative and traditional. Literalistic interpretations of universal and community aspirations could turn swiftly from lofty idealism to retrograde populism. Robert Hughes, for instance, dismissed Bass's contribution to Australian art in acerbic rhetoric as the modern equivalent of 'pious' 19th-century public sculptors who turned out countless 'bronze-bellied aldermen on pedestals'.[65] Despite a growing and often productive dialogue between artists and architects, figurative and organic pieces arguably sat less easily against the backdrop of modern architecture than more abstract and applied works. Through the influence of events like the 'Recent British Sculpture' exhibition shown in Australia in 1963, a new generation of British sculptors who were exploring other ideas aside from Moore's dominant pursuit of the organic and the monumental, was finding critical acclaim.[66]

Public art and public play

Modern architecture experimented with other ways to complement the dictates of efficiency, functionalism and minimalism aside from memorials and artworks with overt social meaning. Art could also be exotic, playful and emotional. Even

8.8 (left) Pioneer Women's Memorial Fountain, Kings Park, Perth, WA 1968

8.9 Bathing pavilion, Lower Sandy Bay, Tas. 1962

Moore's figurative works sometimes brought a surreal element into their modern, mechanist settings.[67] Clement Meadmore likened sculpture to 'a foreign body' that could inject an occasional burst of sexual or supernatural passion into an otherwise understated, 'honest' or spiritually bankrupt, everyday environment.[68] Moore's own views on sculpture were also influential in attempting to challenge the prevailing generalised oppositions between 'rational' architecture and 'decorative' art. Sculpture could be 'functional' in arousing sensory awareness of space and modifying the landscape.[69] Sculpture in the field could transform an otherwise empty landscape from 'one encountered to one participated in'. Many modern architects – including Harry Seidler – were advocates of this productive role that art played in providing haptic and emotional effects.[70]

Twentieth-century artists and architects also shared a longstanding fascination with play through the fostering of abstract imagination and the 'playful spirit'. Play in a 'non-goal directed manner' was considered a vital form of freedom of expression by Johann Huizinga, who had introduced the concept of *homo ludens*, 'playing man', to modern architecture in 1938.[71] In Australia, the aspiration of freedom to play found sympathetic political reception in the 1960s and 1970s, as governments more readily turned their attention to providing for accessible play through sport and recreation. Prime minister Gough Whitlam spoke directly on this theme at a national seminar on leisure in 1974:

> No government's responsibility terminates with bread and butter issues, with matters of finance, employment and defence – though material prosperity and national security are essential for the good life. To an increasing degree governments are expected to improve the intellectual, artistic, recreational and sporting opportunities of their people. There is more to life than work, no matter how creative or absorbing that work may be ... But man does not live by work alone; *homo sapiens* is also *homo ludens*. The capacity for leisure, the enjoyment of games, arts and conversation for their own sake, is one of the defining qualities of our species.[72]

The Whitlam government was pioneering in developing a host of new national recreation and cultural programs to support these aims, but firmly put responsibility for planning and realisation on local communities. New community buildings provided new amenities for public play, and created innovative settings for individualistic expression and interaction with works of public art.

A potent example of the application of *homo ludens* in a recreational building is the Sandy Bay Bathing Pavilion at Long Beach in Hobart, designed by Dirk Bolt of Hartley, Wilson & Bolt, in 1962 (figure 8.9). The pavilion features striking pre-cast decorative concrete panels by artist Ronald Sinclair, a collaborator in Bolt's work throughout the state. Bolt describes the direct casting of the panels on the beach sand using sand moulds coated in hairspray. Passers-by thought they were designing sand castles, which Bolt felt nicely reflected the spirit of *homo ludens* in the project design and artwork. Huizinga defined this as the conceptual space in which play could occur, and stressed its importance to the generation of culture. A contemporary photograph of the pool in its setting captures this concept as bathers and children playing in the sand in front of the bathing pavilion.[73]

Swimming pools in the northern hemisphere had a long tradition of incorporating sculptures, murals and decorative mosaics, like the Bath House in Trelleborg (1939), Sweden, by Erik Fehling, where the interior was enlivened by statues and mosaic panels of bodies in movement.[74] A prime example in Australia of the coming together of modern art and recreation can be seen in the Beaurepaire olympic pool and gymnasium at the University of Melbourne (1954–57), designed by Eggleston, MacDonald & Secomb. Critics singled out for praise the striking integration of a tiled frieze on the entrance facade (figure 8.10) and an abstract interior painted mural in the hall by Leonard French.[75] The seamlessness of the Beaurepaire collaboration contrasts with Melbourne's Olympic Pool, built for the 1956 Games. This featured a large ceramic piece by Arthur Boyd and other Australian artists' work, but the art remained quite separate from the building itself. Different again, and still a

8.10 Glass mosaic frieze, Beaurepaire Swimming Pool, University of Melbourne, Parkville, Vic. c. 1957

popular form in sporting contexts, was the add-on of distinctively Australian folk sculpture. Sculptor Daphne Mayo completed a commemorative statue of a 'swaggie' to commemorate Banjo Patterson's *Waltzing Matilda* in Winton, Queensland, for the local public swimming pool in 1959, and another of a miner with shovel for Gympie's swimming pool in 1960. The commissioning of public art to 'trim' bald, functional architecture for sporting venues was not, however, universally admired.[76]

Playful fountains and water features in new, striking and abstract designs – whether organic or constructivist in derivation – broke away from the more traditional memorial fountains that had been erected in the early 20th century and became a common feature in parks and civic precincts in the 1960s. While the more abstract and avant-garde designs were applauded by critics in-the-know, the general public was often less receptive or enthusiastic. Many preferred designs like Gerard Haveke's sculpture and fountain for Hyde Park, discounted in the architecture press as clichéd 'coffee-bar whimsy'.[77] Woodward and Taranto's El Alamein Memorial Fountain (1959–61) in Kings Cross, Sydney, managed to achieve broad appeal while exploring an abstract design derived from an interest in organic architecture and the principles of cellular and biological structures.[78] Margel Hinder's Captain Cook Memorial Fountain for the Newcastle memorial civic precinct (1965–66) was not so fortunate. It was subjected to a barrage of public criticism when opened, being likened to 'a bird, or beast ... or outsized bootlast'.[79] Inspired by the Russian constructivist sculptor Naum Gabo's work, Hinder created a non-representational monument that was neither bird nor beast, but rather aimed to create and occupy space through the movement of water in playful arcs of spray. Hinder later completed an abstract puzzle-like piece in aluminium for the Woden Town Centre plaza in Canberra.[80] A number of other female Australian artists designed notable fountains for public settings of this period. Norma Redpath was interested in exploring the monumental, but her work pursued abstract themes outside the directly figurative, through strong fragmented and textured bronze sculptures including the major commission for the Treasury Fountain in Canberra (1968); Inge King created a fountain for the civic centre in Wodonga, Victoria (1971).

Places for children's care, play and learning were also deemed fitting settings for sculptural work, in support of the ethos that public art could nurture and promote creativity and participation. A piece by Mitzi Cunliffe titled *Saddle Slide* was prominently published, for instance, in the English *Architectural Review* of 1955, and was described as both a sculpture and a play structure:

> Besides being part of the plastic education of the child, a play-sculpture must also give maximum support to the infant imagination. Topologically there must be no dead surfaces, and no dead spaces, inaccessible to the child – from both the didactic and the re-creative points of view every part of it should be accessible.[81]

Again Moore's figures were seen as inspiration for the making of holes in the cast concrete organic form, thus maximising opportunities for imaginative exploration and occupation. The Australian architectural press also featured some discussion on play sculptures and playgrounds, in the main to make the point that Australia lagged behind in innovative structures for outdoor play in nursery schools and kindergartens.[82]

The community art movement

Community engagement with public art could occur in many ways, from sober remembrance to playful interaction. But in all these forms, the collaboration that produced public art was between artists or designers, architects and commissioning bodies. The community's role was essentially that of consumer. In the 1970s a radical shift occurred from this 'top down' model of public art to a 'bottom up' one that directly involved local communities in the creative input and actual making of public artworks, in varying degrees of collaboration with professional artists and architects.

A common and visible form of this participatory art in community settings from the 1970s into the 1990s was the painted outdoor mural. Twentieth-century Australians were familiar with murals in various media on public and private buildings by artists such as Napier Waller, Arthur Murch, Douglas Annand, Leonard French and Harold Freedman. Some were popularist, and others were realist, as befitted the mural's common role of commemorating and narrating the history of place or identity. The 1950s and 1960s also produced some notable abstract murals such as Lindsay Edwards' glass mosaic mural on the William Street extension to the State Library of Queensland of 1958–59. The 1970s community mural was distinct from these, first in the devolution of the mural's location to humbler community buildings such as neighbourhood kindergartens and swimming pools, and anonymous urban 'waste sites' such as car parks, underpasses, water towers, disused industrial buildings and walls abutting small park reserves, and second in its conscientiously consultative approach to production. With goals of regenerating neglected public spaces and amenities and of fostering local identity and pride through direct participation, a mural project could have a potentially transformative impact.[83]

The community arts movement evolved out of the broad social and political struggles of the 1960s and 1970s: anti-Vietnam war activism, feminism and Aboriginal land rights. In the art world, it was associated with a crisis within the modernist avant-garde, criticised as having abandoned its earlier revolutionary potential to become elitist and commodified. These radical stances encouraged the flourishing of non-mainstream art practices in the 1970s, from esoteric performance and conceptual art to populist 'community art' in which self-styled 'artworkers' (as opposed to bourgeois artists) sought ways to involve working people in the arts by taking it to the streets.[84] The federal government's establishment of the Australia Council for the Arts in 1968 provided official support. With various programs springing up at state and local government levels, a range of what had been 'alternative' arts practices in the 1970s rapidly migrated from the fringe to the mainstream in the 1980s, to the concern of some who saw the ideal of community organisation compromised by being made subject to the regulation and funding of government bureaucracies.[85]

Among the notable pioneers of 1970s community murals were Geoff Hogg in Melbourne, Rodney Monk and David Humphries in Sydney, and Anne Newmarch in Adelaide. These artists were part of an international community mural movement that swept the United States, Britain and Europe in the late 1960s, the revolutionary early 20th century Mexican muralist Diego Rivera being a common hero.[86] Hogg studied in Mexico and worked on the Notting Hill mural project in London and in the public art workshops on the south side of Chicago in 1974, while Humphries worked on murals in New York's Lower East Side in 1976.[87] He returned to direct a massive outdoor community mural on the perimeter wall of the old Gasworks in Orange, New South Wales, for its 1977 Festival of Arts with funding from the Community Arts Board. Hogg, commencing on a smaller scale in Melbourne, helped found the left-wing Community Arts Workers' (CAW) group in 1975. CAW produced a number of inner-city murals in 1975–76, locally sponsored by arts and student groups and councils such as the City of Collingwood, including ones commemorating International Women's Year, student activism at Swinburne Institute of Technology and the new community radio station 3CR.[88] Hogg went on to direct many large-scale mural projects in Melbourne in the 1980s, although these were still typically on shoestring budgets, with scaffolding and paint donated by companies or local businesses. These included the Builders' Labourers Federation mural (1977), the Royal Melbourne Institute of Technology mural (1979) and the Turana Youth Training Centre mural in Brunswick (1979–81). Realist and humanist, and dedicated to themes such as equality, democracy, community and the dignity of manual labour, Hogg's complex figurative compositions often derived from composites of photographs drawn from and relating to a particular community.

In the 1970s a radical shift occurred ... one that directly involved local communities in the creative input and actual making of public artworks.

While Hogg jokes about 'St Petersburg vs Tinseltown' in observing the difference between Melbourne and Sydney styles of community murals in the 1970s and 1980s – one ostensibly more didactic and political, the other more whimsical and hedonistic – the working process of research, community consultation and participation was equally seriously respected. Hogg's Turana mural had the working title of *Brunswick Images* (figure 8.11) and concerned the history of a proudly working-class suburb rather than just the history of the correctional institution

8.11 Turana Youth Training Centre mural, Brunswick, Vic. 1979–81

for boys, thus reflecting the goal of integration of the facility into the wider local community. Hogg and his team found rich resources within community groups, local government, the library and local historians Les and Bernie Barnes. Through these connections, the community collaborated by bringing in photos and materials for the artwork that took as its central theme the story of leisure pastimes in Depression-era Brunswick. The Turana boys contributed, working in collaborative groups helping to paint and manage the site.[89]

Humphries recounts a similar process for the 1980 mural on the courtyard walls of the Bondi Pavilion at the iconic beach. The immediate constituency consulted for the mural was neighbourhood activity groups who used the building as a community-based arts centre, and sun worshippers from the Bondi beachfront. A team of artists refined concepts for the mural through talks and workshops at local schools, surf clubs and the library. The theme arrived at was *Bondi the Beautiful* (figure 8.12), using tourist imagery of lifesavers and bathers from the 1920s and 1930s – the era of the building's construction. During production, kids in bathers and towels wandered in off the beach to assist in the painting. The process of democratic participation was taken even further with a mural by directed by Humphries and Monk at Casuarina Swimming Pool, Darwin, titled *Children of the Billabong* (1984) (figure 8.13). This was funded as a six-week residency for an unemployment training program in which the Sydney artists trained three young locals as community muralists. After the usual round of consultations, three or four designs were developed. At a well-attended evening public meeting and barbecue, the designs were projected onto the huge wall and the community voted for their favourite, which was duly painted.

8.12 (top) *Bondi the Beautiful*, community mural, courtyard of Bondi Pavilion, NSW 1980

8.13 (above) *Children of the Billabong*, community muralist training project, Casuarina Swimming Pool, Darwin, NT 1984

Although good 'process' was deemed essential, egalitarianism was not enough to ensure a mural of high standard: it was the artists' job to structure community input, coordinate the overall design and maintain quality control. But as community murals became more prevalent in the 1980s so did the number of poorly planned and executed examples, while once-excellent murals declined through non-existent maintenance. This has encouraged reflexive criticism by architects and the public alike of 'community art' as 'bad art' that detracts from the built environment. As a counter to this perception, Humphries cites the temporary 1983 mural for the tenth anniversary of the Sydney Opera House. Thematically workshopped in exemplary community fashion in high schools around the city and executed by busloads of schoolchildren, the mural was enthusiastically endorsed by the Opera House's original architect, Jørn Utzon, and provides a rare example of the happy union of modern architecture and community-led embellishment.

Australian communities have always used buildings to consolidate their own identities and express a sense of belonging to a place and a shared history. In the decades between 1920 and 1970, dominated by two world wars, communities hard-hit by their human losses saw a double value in channelling a desire for commemoration into utilitarian buildings and precincts of tangible and lasting value. Memorial halls, swimming pools, baby health centres, sporting clubs and parks all became part of the rich, but often taken-for-granted, commemorative fabric of the everyday Australian built landscape. Public art as monument was initially tightly enmeshed in this commemorative fabric, but gradually from the 1950s was detached from its formal memorial role and began to engage in a more independent and internationalist dialogue with modernist architecture. Both figurative and abstract art symbolising enlightenment ideals that was integrated into civic spaces and buildings had their moments in the ensuing decades of the 1950s and 1960s. When successful, art and architecture together commemorated and also humanised the potentially alienating functionalism of the typical modernist environment, while also expanding a local notion of community to the universal 'family of man'. In the 1960s public art sometimes became more confidently monumental, as seen in the fountains that were the new centrepieces of parks and squares, and at other times more playful and experiential, inviting physical and emotional responses rather than an apprehension of a 'message' by its users. By the late 1970s there was a return in public art to the grassroots community level, where communities gathered to fundraise and argue about the right sort of memorial for their locality, as they had done in the war years. Radical artists began to produce murals collaboratively, enlisting members of the communities themselves as consultants and artists rather than commissioning recognised artists. The shifting values and expressions of community and commemoration were intertwined throughout the 20th century and have remained so into the present, where public art continues to flourish as a solution to the drawing out of identities of place and people.

8.14 (clockwise from top) Mural, *Koor Koorliny Bilya*, John Williamson 2000 on wall of Moora Council Chambers and Library building, WA; Andor Mészáros' c. 1959 statue of William Shakespeare outside the 1955 Ballarat Civic Hall; mural en route to the Bombala pool from Monaro Highway; statuettes of Australian and American cartoon characters at Bombala and District War Memorial Swimming Pool (1968)

9.1 *Undulant*, installed at the Logan Community Health Centre, Qld 2005

REGENERATING COMMUNITIES: THE 1970s AND BEYOND

Hannah Lewi, David Nichols, Philip Goad,
Kate Darian-Smith and

Julie Willis

9

On Christmas Eve in 1974, a tropical cyclone of a force never experienced in recorded Australian history devastated the northern frontier city of Darwin. During Cyclone Tracy's onslaught, school buildings provided places of refuge for residents; the city's twelve health centres were badly damaged and the majority of houses were completely destroyed. Most of Darwin's 46,700 residents were evacuated, and almost half would never return.[1] The cyclone brought massive loss but also presented a unique opportunity to improve community facilities, including cultural and recreational buildings and open spaces that had been below the standards of much of southern Australia. Prime minister Gough Whitlam moved quickly, establishing the Darwin Reconstruction Commission to oversee the rebuilding effort. This familiar language of reconstruction spoke of the symbolic importance invested in the built environment to foster community spirit at the local to national level.[2] In practice, however, the re-envisaging of the city on a grand scale through sweeping urban plans was in large part not enacted.[3] Government-driven planning interventions and tough new building regulations also led to a perceived feeling of 'loss of control' over people's lives, and as a consequence 'resident action groups sprang up all over the place'.[4] Many isolated examples of new community facilities for health and recreation were, however, completed by the late 1970s, with neighbourhood buildings designated as public shelters.[5] The city's civic centre of 1969, which was only superficially damaged, was also retained for both symbolic and pragmatic reasons.

Cyclone Tracy provides a dramatic snapshot of the central themes of this book. Most obvious is the interdependence between community and built infrastructure. More interestingly, the reconstruction efforts reveal how community-building is shaped through an interaction between government policy and grassroots implementation and initiatives. Further, this tension between policy and implementation is exposed through dramatic moments of rupture. As this book has shown, such ruptures, whether in the form of natural disaster, war, or economic depression, create catalytic moments in the progressive development of an everyday modernism for community buildings in Australia.

Cyclone Tracy occurred at the end of the fifty-year span from 1920 to 1970 that has been investigated in this book. This last chapter briefly surveys the ensuing forty years. In this period, creeping and complex cultural, demographic and architectural shifts have resulted in some radical reassessments of the provision and form of public community facilities. By the 1970s Australian cities had been completely transformed from those of the 1920s. Largely as a result of massive post-war migration schemes, which assisted the arrival of migrants from Britain, Europe and, more recently, from the Middle East and South-East Asia, the national population more than doubled from around 5.5 million in 1921 to over 13 million in 1971. By the 1970s this growth was clearly manifest within the ever-expanding suburban hinterlands of major capital cities, which had all increased in population by over 50 per cent in just twenty-five years. In response to what was characterised by vocal social commentators as the sharply rising feelings of alienation and banality within these suburbs, governments at all levels in the 1970s began to re-invest in new and varied ways to build bricks-and-mortar amenities for health, leisure and education.[6]

The election of the Labor federal government in 1972 introduced a rhetoric around community that emphasised its link with state provision and modern citizenship – which was to be determined not by individual income but, as Whitlam put it, 'by the availability and accessibility of the services which the community alone can provide and ensure'.[7] Since the 1970s, government policy and rhetoric across the political spectrum have continued to appeal to a notion of community values by attempting to claim some middle way via communitarianism. The conservative government of John Howard (1996–2007), for instance, harked back with nostalgia to what it saw as the more cohesive community values of an earlier period.

In 2007, the government of Kevin Rudd came to power with an agenda to facilitate community development via more direct communication between federal and local levels through its 'Community Cabinet Meetings' initiative. This government gave great prominence to major funding schemes for community infrastructure redevelopment through economic stimulus to counter the 'global financial crisis' of 2008–09. Local councils, schools and community organisations, recreation and sporting clubs across the country gained grants, small or substantial, to be rapidly spent on the building of new amenities and the long-term renewal of outmoded ones, with the aim of creating more sustainable services and landscapes that would respond to shifts in demographics and public expectations. The last decade has also seen the establishment of various departments of 'Communities' by all state governments except Tasmania, and organisational structures that generally combine social services with equity, planning and recreational portfolios with the aim of maintaining 'strong', 'vibrant' and 'sustainable' communities.

This chapter traces some of the factors – both home-grown and internationally determined – that have led to more diverse approaches in the engagement of community through architecture and planning, in response both to the demise of modernism and the rise of new modes of public–private patronage. It concludes with reflections on one of the heartfelt motivations of the research that has shaped this book: the imperatives of historical documentation and conservation of small, public places before they are lost or irrevocably altered.

Modernism in crisis and the rise of 'community architecture'

By the time of Darwin's reconstruction, architectural and planning professionals around the world were seriously questioning the belief that well-designed buildings could neatly symbolise community aspirations, let alone house large populations comfortably and economically. Such a crisis in the dominance of architectural modernism as an environmental solution for social dislocation had been brewing for over a decade. There was growing international recognition that *tabula rasa* solutions that had been prevalent in new housing and urban precincts of post–World War II reconstruction were not always effective in creating any sense of social space and cohesion. In the Netherlands, for example, attempts were undertaken to 'democratise' planning through shifts towards smaller and more fragmented public housing and urban planning schemes that responded to new modes of welfare delivery that were less reliant on wholesale urban erasure and more interested in working within older neighbourhoods using experimental functional programs.[8]

In parallel with social and academic reassessments of the conceptual meanings and governmental definitions of 'community' during the 1960s, a movement labelled 'community architecture' grew out of radicalised social movements in the UK and northern Europe that would prove influential in Australia. Change was driven from bottom-up activism, with localised protests intensifying against proposed new infrastructure such as freeways threatening to carve through inner-urban neighbourhoods or destroy river ecosystems, and against public housing schemes imposed by 'faceless' government authorities. Alternative planning and design solutions were sought that safeguarded the remaining physical environs of urban and rural communities, and pursued experimental, lower energy and smaller scale architectural solutions. Change was also driven from top-down patronage and professional agitation for change in powerful government planning departments and local councils who were looking for an alternative way of governance that allowed community input.[9]

aa
architecture in australia, student edition, april 1975, registered for posting as a periodical - category b
RIPOFF INSURANCE
OFFICE BLOCK
soft architecture

9.2
Cover of 'Soft Architecture', a special student-edited issue of *Architecture Australia*, April 1975

In England these moves were lent legitimacy by Prince Charles' controversial architectural assaults in the 1980s that further fuelled popular distrust of modernist solutions. 'Community architecture' became an umbrella term embracing these new democratic ambitions in planning and design. Prince Charles became the patron of the community architecture movement, and in addition a series of internationally influential 'Building Communities Conferences' disseminated new modes of practice.[10] It was a movement characterised more by these alternative processes of practice and less by stylistic outcomes, with an emphasis on community consultation, participation and responsibility in the determination of site planning and functional briefs, and sometimes even the modes of construction.

But the tide was also turning in relation to issues of architectural style and attitudes to history. In 1965, well-known Australian architect Robin Boyd published *The Puzzle of Architecture*, in which he suggested that all was not well with architectural modernism's claim to a correct way of defining the language of the built environment. By the mid-1970s, professional engagement in design took an increasingly more focused account of local geographies and historical and cultural contexts. This coincided with the postmodern turn in architecture internationally, encouraged by books produced by architects and commentators like Robert Venturi's *Complexity and Contradiction in Architecture* (1966) and Charles Jencks' *The Language of Post-Modern Architecture* (1977), that endeavoured to topple previous decades of fundamental dismissal of local identities and history. Strong influences took effect in Australia from European and American investigations into popular culture such as the American architects Venturi and Denise Scott Brown's advice to architects to ignore the singularity and purity of modernist doctrines in favour of bringing a more 'ad hoc' approach to planning and architecture. The view that the 'ugly and the ordinary' might be not only tolerated but also productive was to assume particular potency in suburban contexts.[11]

The postmodern turn in architecture ... endeavoured to topple previous decades of fundamental dismissal of local identities and history.

In Australia, response to this crisis of architectural modernism as expressed in Europe and America was genuine and simultaneous, instigated mainly by students and younger members of the architecture profession. International architects leading radical splinter groups away from modernist orthodoxy were invited to student and professional conferences in the 1960s. Australians joined voice in these forums; Paul Ritter, city planner and architect for Perth and author of the internationally important *Planning for Man and Motor* (1964), and *Educreation: Education for Creation, Growth and Change* (1964), spoke at a Perth student convention in 1966. He would later be an instigator in the hands-on involvement of children in the design of wall panels for the Rockingham Kindergarten in Western Australia.

Ten years later, it was students again who compiled a special issue of *Architecture Australia* devoted to 'Soft Architecture' (figure 9.2) reinforcing the strong interest of young architects in alternative modes of practice such as cooperatives and the conservation and adaptive re-use of existing buildings for public purposes.[12] Exemplar projects based on the tenets of consultative community architecture included the Aboriginal Community Housing Project in the inner-city Sydney suburb of Redfern, claimed as a model for developing distinctive communities within cities. Other key projects were those developed to cater to new forms of household and institutional organisation, such as the cooperative housing development in Carlton, Melbourne, by Earle Shaw & Partners, and the architectural co-op established in Hobart by architects, students and academics as a forum for experimentation with new ways to build with 'a commitment to the community and environment of the city'.[13] In 1970, Sydney architect Richard Johnson wrote about the challenges of creating a sense of community but also privacy in suburbia, a resounding echo of Berkeley-based academics and architects Christopher Alexander and Serge Chermayeff's *Community and Privacy: Towards a New Architecture of Humanism* (1963), that was widely admired by other Australian architects such as Kevin Borland, Daryl Jackson and Evan Walker.[14]

If these publications were evidence of changing approaches to practice, they also pursued a common theme in rethinking architecture's ability to express ideas of local community in more humanly engaged ways. Vestiges of faith in the original agendas of modernism certainly did remain, with the goal of social betterment through the provision of responsible buildings, environments and landscapes for community still holding currency, but without the unwavering belief in architectural determinism. The very gradual recognition and acceptance of the suburbs as a key locus of everyday life would add strength to this architectural resolve in Australia in the 1970s and beyond. This was seen in many works combining popular 'low' culture and architecture, perhaps none more expressively than the gritty, suburban-scaled buildings of the Melbourne firm of Edmond & Corrigan. The Belconnen Community Centre, Canberra (1985–88), for instance, brought an ad hoc, messy urbanism using vernacular forms and materials to the federal capital. The assembled fragments that recalled the density of an agglomeration of older buildings typical of inner-city Melbourne or Sydney accommodate a childcare centre, performance space and civic facilities that compose a stark contrast to the planned uniformity of the setting.[15]

Engaging community through design diversity

The shift in architecture culture in Australia as a response to the crisis of modernism paralleled grassroots activism in environmental awareness, heritage and community participation. If there was one area where government at a national level complemented municipal, private and community-run facilities it was in buildings for children. The intensification of interest in the education and care of children in the 1970s coincided with broader social shifts, including an increased participation of mothers in the paid workforce and a renewed emphasis by the Whitlam federal government on the importance of early childhood education and the provision of amenities for children outside the home. As a result the childcare sector expanded dramatically in the last decades of the 20th century, with a substantial increase in the number of private, municipal and community-run childcare centres and creches that in many cases also ran kindergarten programs.

Planning and funding programs that aimed to build designated 'community centres' for childcare and recreation began to be more common and were typically managed through cooperatives and neighbourhood bodies. For instance, following the passage of the *Child Care Act 1972*, capital funding schemes introduced by the Whitlam government were responsible for distributing funds to smaller community and municipal groups. This resulted in some 200 local childcare centres and multi-purpose developments being constructed around Australia by 1980.

Although most buildings were fairly standard and minimal in their design aspirations, there were occasions when architects rose above the demands of tight budgets and the insistence on low maintenance to create innovative buildings. As evidence of this new professional engagement in buildings for children, *Architecture Australia* published a special issue in 1977 on the impact of federal programs for childcare and education started under the Whitlam government.[16] New architect-designed centres and kindergartens that were published showed the diversity already apparent. The Athol Park Child Care Centre in South Australia, by Birchby and Associates, was civic in outlook, the first stage in the planned development of a community hub with childcare amenities at its heart. Two childcare centres built in the eastern bush suburb of Eltham in Melbourne, by Whitford and Peck, reflected the contemporary interest in timber construction and organic forms. The Birralee Child Care Centre in Brisbane, by Nutter & Stevenson, returned to the notion of creating the centre as a 'home away from home' through a low-slung domestic idiom in brick and tile. By contrast, the Brompton Parent-Child Centre by the Public Buildings Department of South Australia, located in West Adelaide – an area with a high population of new migrants and working mothers – was consciously not domestic in style but experimental in its use of exposed steel and concrete structures and mezzanines, stimulating colours and super-graphics.[17]

Small and large private architectural practices, alongside government offices, designed innovative amenities for children in keeping with the contemporary architectural concerns. For instance, Melbourne architect Greg Burgess worked with existing houses in Carlton to create the Wimble Street Child Care Cooperative (1974), and the Italo-Australian Education Foundation Child Care and Community Health Service, to make spaces of adventure, interest and colour through largely interior-focused design moves.[18] In 1976 the large commercial firm of Bates Smart McCutcheon, in collaboration with architect Peter Elliott, designed the Fitzroy Community Child Care Co-op as a robust work for a dense inner-city setting. In Sydney other architects were experimenting with projects generated by community groups. Desney and Korzeniewski's neatly named childcare buildings 'Kidsville' (1977) innovatively adapted an existing church hall and storage shed to display

9.3 Community Health Centre, Brunswick, Vic. 1985–90

the careful integration of new and old. Their Ana Kindergarten (1981) for Sydney's Turkish-Australian community was a substantial remodelling of a house to create a series of interconnected brick-and-timber pavilion rooms and courtyards, with the lyrical spatial design integral to the child's learning and stimulation. Inspired by American architect Louis Kahn, Korzeniewski's design reflects a renewed interest in classical forms and the materiality of brick in the 1970s and 1980s.[19] The work of Morrice Shaw, also in Sydney, exemplified the community architecture movement through his practice and teaching involvement with local, low-cost constructions for children's environments. Shaw had been exposed to community architecture while working in New York, and brought this experience back to the University of Sydney where he actively encouraged students in the processes of design and building participation. Shaw and his students worked on projects to create parks and playgrounds through engagement between local councils, community organisations and workers, alongside students and children.

From the 1980s, all state governments, with the exception of New South Wales, gradually closed their public works offices. This meant that private architectural practices took on work that would previously have been the domain of government architects. As a result, schools, community childcare centres, civic and health facilities, as well as dedicated health and recreation services for senior citizens, were the beneficiaries of this new approach to design process and plurality of style. As well, there was the development of new types of community buildings. For example, Lawrence Nield's design for the Ultimo Community Centre (1996) consolidated a number of services provided by the Sydney City Council and deliberately broke down their institutional coherence to create a more approachable casual or planned awkwardness through a series of infill elements. In Melbourne, architecture firm Ashton Raggatt McDougall (ARM) was an early pioneer in the community healthcare centre. Both the Kensington Community Health Centre (1984) and Brunswick Community Health Centre (1985–90) (figure 9.3) explored the suburban vernacular through a conglomeration of institutional, civic and domestic features that responded to older, working-class suburban settings which had undergone substantial changes through immigration and gentrification. Nearly twenty years later, ARM's Ian McDougall's published answer to 'Why architecture matters' reads like a restatement of ideals consistent with the aims of 1920s and 1930s architects and social reformers, but without the hubris of modernism's architectural ambition:

> Schools, colleges, libraries, community centres – these are the basic elements in which communities profess their cultural presence … Whether they are in the bush or in the city, they should be full of foibles and frailty, but also of strength and resolve. Architecture matters when it works for its community with integrity, passion and humour.[20]

Development drivers in renewal: City, suburb and remote settings

If there was in the late 20th century a shift in the aesthetic aspirations of architecture to serve community needs, there have also been substantial shifts in recent decades in those who would be patrons of community architecture. From the 1920s through to the 1970s, patronage was largely implemented through municipal means – a local council – often supported by state or federal funds, or both, depending on the nature of the building's function or by partial funding through the local community itself. In some cases, community facilities were retroactively placed within suburbs developed under private aegis which had lacked services for decades. In the last thirty years, private finance has come to play an increasing role in the provision of community facilities through both inner-city regeneration and suburban growth.

With economic upswings in the 1980s and 1990s, and recognition of the value of investment in urban renewal as a route to prosperity, numerous large-scale inner-city suburbs across Australia have flourished. With the widespread encouragement of both families and 'empty-nesters' to move back into the city, a broad range of public amenities and services have needed upgrading or renewal through new urban models. Governments at all levels have participated in planning projections that engage the regeneration of public infrastructure. The redevelopment of the inner-urban area of East Perth by the East Perth Redevelopment Authority (EPRA) has been a leading case of public–private partnership in the 1990s, with new infill mixed housing replacing a largely industrial urban fringe, and the provision of public areas of landscaping that integrate private and public recreation amenities. Reflecting increasingly blurred lines of separation between government and the market, within the planning, design and management of East Perth it appears that public and private realms have been combined into a new model that is part gated resort and part accessible public park.

In another example of the reclamation of an older, industrial, inner-city area through a blend of public and private investment, old and new have similarly been merged in Beacon Cove, a brownfields development in Port Melbourne derided by neighbouring locals in its early years as 'Legoland', which relies heavily on nearby existing community facilities.[21] Here, the Swallow Street Residents Association was formed by residents of one street, alarmed at the development activities in the area. In recognition of a fait accompli, this association has now become the Beacon Cove Neighbourhood Association, which meets regularly at the Sandridge Senior Citizens and Trugo Club in the adjoining Garden City, created in the 1930s by the Housing Commission of Victoria.

In the nearby Melbourne Docklands redevelopment zone, evidence that a new and varied demographic has made the inner city its home can be found in demands for community services that have resulted in the building of new children's facilities and a school. The innovative Harbour Family and Children's Centre, designed by Hassell Architects in 2009 for the City of Melbourne, VicUrban, Bovis LendLease, and Gowrie Victoria as combined clients, is located on the rooftop of the largest supermarket in the Melbourne Docklands. With capacity for 150 children and an emphasis on outdoor rooftop play areas and sustainable gardens, the centre is showcasing one future for early childhood education and care appropriate for the inner city.[22]

In the face of this expansion ... major new private players began to rethink community aspirations.

Despite these examples of successful renewal in inner-urban contexts, the major impact of privately driven community development has occurred in the outer suburbs of urban centres as the demand for typically low-cost dormitory suburbs has grown dramatically. In the face of this expansion, and suburbia's resultant generalised image as a place of social and planning deficiencies, major new private players began to rethink community aspirations. Lyn Richards' study *Nobody's Home* surveys a 'shiny-clean new', privately developed suburb

9.4 Tom Price Community Centre under construction, WA 1966

'Green Views', 21 kilometres from Melbourne, initiated in 1981.[23] Here, the extent to which developers were eager to provide civic amenities can be gleaned from the fact that Richards found real estate agents in surrounding areas who regarded Green Views residents as 'spoon-fed'.[24] The residents of Green Views themselves appreciated the extant developer-built sporting facilities and infant welfare centre, but still hoped for more. Those responsible had gone so far and no further, and Richards' interviews revealed the discrimination against housewives and teenagers apparent in the 'lack of any community centre'.[25]

The private–public partnership movement in suburban development was in full swing by the 1990s when Mawson Lakes – a 'lakeside town centre' and surrounding 'residential villages' with its genesis in the ill-fated Australian-Japanese Multifunction Polis of the late 1980s – was launched by Delfin and the South Australian government. Here, a 'Fully Planned Community' including a 'Library and Resource Centre' and childcare and medical facilities were planned to 'open in the early stages of the development'.[26] As mentioned in chapter 7, Delfin's development at Craigieburn, in Melbourne's north, was augmented in 2008 with plans for a 65 hectare site for 'retail, commercial, residential and community facilities'.[27] Delfin's success in marketing and building new suburbs has come with the recognition of the essential nature of some 'traditional' community elements: the firm, for instance, advertised co-located preschool and maternal and child health facilities at their Caroline Springs' Brookside Centre to the west of Melbourne. The Caroline Springs library and civic centre by Suters Prior Cheney was opened in 2008.[28] In their marketing material, developers like Delfin and EPRA have also spoken directly about their role as creators of community facilitated through commercial town centres, and through contemporary mechanisms like the provision of private health and leisure centres, cafes and the internet.[29]

As Hamish Lyon of NH Architecture has recently remarked in an essay on 'DIY community', such services and lifestyle or 'activity' centres promoted as the heart of new community life in developer-built suburban estates have, in many cases, replaced earlier kinds of small public institutional types. Despite some creative drive being drawn from suburbia over the last forty years, architects have, however, been somewhat reluctant to take the context of these new private developments into serious consideration: Lyon suggests that it is high time they received more adequate design attention by the architecture, landscape and planning professions in order to creatively address the profound social and sustainability challenges of the urban periphery.[30]

A different sort of pressure for the provision of community facilities in remote towns has also arisen in the last two decades from the huge national economic growth stimulated by mining exports. North-western Australia has been targeted by state and national governments for significant regeneration of public infrastructure and amenities in key regional town centres including Karratha, Port Hedland and Newman. With over 3000 children under the age of ten currently living in the Shire of Roebourne alone, child health, education and sport have been identified as key factors in community redevelopment. In response to local and state government policy studies like the *Newman Tomorrow* document drafted in 2008 by the Shire of East Pilbara under the banner of 'Creating Communities', town plans have been generated and new public buildings, parks and artworks have been commissioned with the aim of improving 'community health and wellbeing'.[31] The Shire of East Pilbara has expressed its direct commitment to assuming responsibility for the growth of towns like Newman which is the second largest inland town in Western Australia, to 'normalise them as vital towns rather than company dormitories or encampment that left a legacy of lack of community development'.[32]

With a perceived decline in quality of life associated with the erosion of permanent residents and the prevalence of 'fly-in, fly-out' employees, better services for infants, youth and the aged, alongside allied health services, are being demanded in the hope of stimulating more permanent and demographically 'balanced' communities.[33] The building of tangible services has, as always, been recognised as holding the capacity for increasing local engagement and social capital, with volunteer work on the rise when such community facilities are realised.

Taking the town of Karratha as an example, a 2008 planning document has addressed growth and climatic concerns, while architectural briefs for one-stop recreation facilities and community centres are seen as the foundation for upgrading local sporting amenities. The brief defines an aspiration that such a centre will 'create an architectural statement from which the community can draw some pride'.[34] As a result, two new community buildings in Karratha are

9.5 (above and right) Bulgarra Community Centre Design Proposal, CODA Architects, WA 2010

currently under design by the Western Australian architectural practice CODA for Bulgarra and Baynton West that co-locate sporting clubs, community hall and childcare spaces (figure 9.5). In CODA's opinion the brief is less about the deliberate statement of a landmark, and more about creating new centres through buildings that connect to and are used by locals in their daily lives. Design strategies employed to localise the buildings in their tough settings include attention to expansive sheltering roof structures, an internal courtyard, and industrial materials combined with playful colour and pattern to further communicate the centres as approachable.[35]

As in Karratha, a desire to use architecture to instil some sense of monumentality and permanence in the north-west town of Newman is being voiced, alongside serious acknowledgment of the need to engage the local Aboriginal Nyiyapardi and Martu people in any successful building and governance of community and cultural centres in the region.[36] Finn Pedersen, of Iredale Pedersen Hook Architects, suggests that a building cannot resolve issues faced by Indigenous communities but it can provide a piece of infrastructure that can be more than functional, and which might facilitate connections between users and its architecture.[37] This Western Australian practice has also designed projects for communities in the state's north-

west, including a community centre for the small population of Djugerari in the Great Sandy Desert, south of Fitzroy Crossing (figure 9.6). Located in Walmajarri country, a series of pragmatic structures offering enclosed and open-air shaded pavilions provides flexible meeting and teaching spaces, a painting workshop and a potential 'ethno-tourism' venue. Its key role, however, is as a place where local Indigenous people, particularly Indigenous youth, can learn about their own culture.

The complex aspirations for making a permanent sense of community in the towns of the north and central-west of Australia reflect concerns that lie at the heart of this book, and that have long been associated with the creation of local amenity and cohesion through public buildings. While policy rhetoric and architectural language may be modified by awareness in cross-cultural dialogue, environmental awareness, and the desirability of community activism, there exists the enduring imperative to create aesthetically memorable yet also functional and approachable facilities that will be appropriated by locals.

9.6 Walmajarri Community Centre, Djugerari Community, Great Sandy Desert, WA 2006

Memory, loss and community

The loss of community facilities, and indeed whole communities through the ravages of natural disasters, forms a recurring story in Australia's history. Cyclones and flooding continue to bring damage to towns in Australia's north, and bushfires have wrought destruction across the country. As Tom Griffiths has suggested, the language used to describe the impact of major fire disasters in Australia has mirrored that of the ravages of war, and its aftermath demands similar responses through physical and emotional rebuilding.[38] Such a language of crisis was applied to the Black Saturday fires that swept through Victoria in February 2009 and destroyed lives and whole towns. The town of Marysville was wiped out with shocking loss of life and infrastructure, including the local primary school, kindergarten and baby health centre, museum and countless other community buildings, as well as the commercial and residential core of the town. A year later work commenced on the $7 million first stage of rebuilding the town, with consultation invited from residents on a draft plan by NH Architecture (figure 9.8). The designated community and recreation hub – which includes the co-location of a new primary school, early learning centre, recreation facilities and child health services – is to be sited in their predecessors' position adjacent to Gallipoli Park. It is testament to the importance of rebuilding better local public services to facilitate recovery, and echoes current state and federal government commitment to create multi-purpose hubs for children and recreation services. That the new building is a 'hub' indicates a rebranding that can be seen as an appropriation of British terminology often used in regard to inclusive communities. In recent decades the Australian-British relationship is closer to a discussion than a transmission from London's brightest; British social inclusion policy, for instance, is one manifestation of a back-and-forth development particularly common to British and Australian left-wing policy-makers.

Loss of public facilities has also occurred slowly, silently and in a piecemeal way across the country. The kinds of shared buildings and places that have been examined in this book have, by their very nature, become so much a part of the local environment that it is not until they are threatened or gone that their value to communities is recognised. As Kathy Burrows comments in 2008 on the possible loss of the Mayfield swimming pool in Newcastle: 'You never appreciate what you have until there is the chance you may lose it'.[39] From the 1990s, changing demographic, recreational and planning needs have led to the closure of hundreds, if not thousands, of local bowling and sporting clubs, swimming pools, kindergartens and other community facilities including memorial halls. In some instances there has been media coverage, the strength of interest usually being dependent on the coordinated campaigning of local residents and interest groups. With the redefining of local government management structures, centralising of services, and outsourcing of facilities, the importance of maintaining and renewing physical assets with the aim of building social engagement in local communities has at times been lost.

The closure of public swimming pools has perhaps incited more media and political attention than any other community amenity type in recent decades, as seasonal outdoor pools have become largely superseded by indoor and mixed-use recreational developments. Campaigns to prevent closure, privatisation or relocation have garnered vigorous and diverse support. Despite some claims of a decline in numbers of active public pool users, swimming pools seem to have sustained their potency as rallying points for community action like no other amenity in local neighbourhoods. As one report in Melbourne's *Age* summarised it: 'Community swimming pools are, indeed, just that: the social interchange they provide, between those of all ages and backgrounds is like no other. But they are also an invaluable resource for exercise as well as pleasure'.[40] Scepticism over local government arguments and statistics regarding financial and water losses of existing facilities has also grown, and a general sense of outrage against the all-too-easy relinquishing of public assets that were typically built through hard-fought community effort and volunteer labour in the post-war decades. A deep sense of nostalgia for the outdoor Australian pool in summer time, with all its discomforts, permeates these campaigns with countless reminiscences of days at the pool as a rite of passage: 'Icy poles drip through sticky fingers on to hot concrete. Old people shuffle by on stick legs in the shallows, while zinc-striped kids play and pee in the water.'[41]

Pool closures do not seem dependent on geographical location: in the last decade in Canberra the Dickson, Civic, Tuggeranong, Erindale and Deakin pools were all threatened with temporary or permanent closure, as were public pools in Darwin. Nor have country towns been exempt, with rural and mining towns alike unable to sustain the upkeep of their pools in declining centres like South Australia's Woomera and Coober Pedy, where both towns' pools have been closed. In the 1990s the viability of a number of public pools in Brisbane was questioned in the 'Pools2000' commissioned report with a recommendation that the Centenary Pool designed by James Birrell, described in chapter 5, be demolished because its popularity was seen to be in decline and the costs of restoration unwarranted. The pool was subsequently renovated in the late 1990s without losing too much of the character of the original design. Other pools by Birrell, however, like the Toowong Pool, were destroyed. In Melbourne, in the same decade, there were at least six major campaigns to prevent closures of outdoor public pools and

9.7 Marysville sports pavilion, Gallipoli Oval, Vic. 2007, which did not survive the fires of 2009

many more closures,[42] and a similar story can be told about the fate of public pools in Sydney.[43]

There has also been the occasional success story. The coordinated efforts to re-open and maintain the Coburg outdoor pool drew on the long and rich history of the pool and its site to bolster support.[44] In recent years swimming numbers declined as nearby indoor pools were opened and threats to close the 1965 pool building surfaced. In 2006 it was abruptly closed for repairs and reportedly because of the impact of water restrictions and the need to rationalise the suburb's existing facilities. In response, the 'Friends of the Coburg Olympic Pool' group was formed, mainly by concerned local families and mothers. Vigorous and coordinated campaigning was conducted through online channels and community networking, as well as persuasive appeals to local politicians and council members resulting in the re-opening of the pool for the 2008–09 summer season. But the building's future remains uncertain.[45]

Conserving the everyday

Australians today live with the built legacies of previous centuries, and those legacies' implicit conceptions of community. These buildings and sites for recreation, health and learning continue to shape everyday routines of life, despite continual efforts to re-inscribe new governmental structures on the

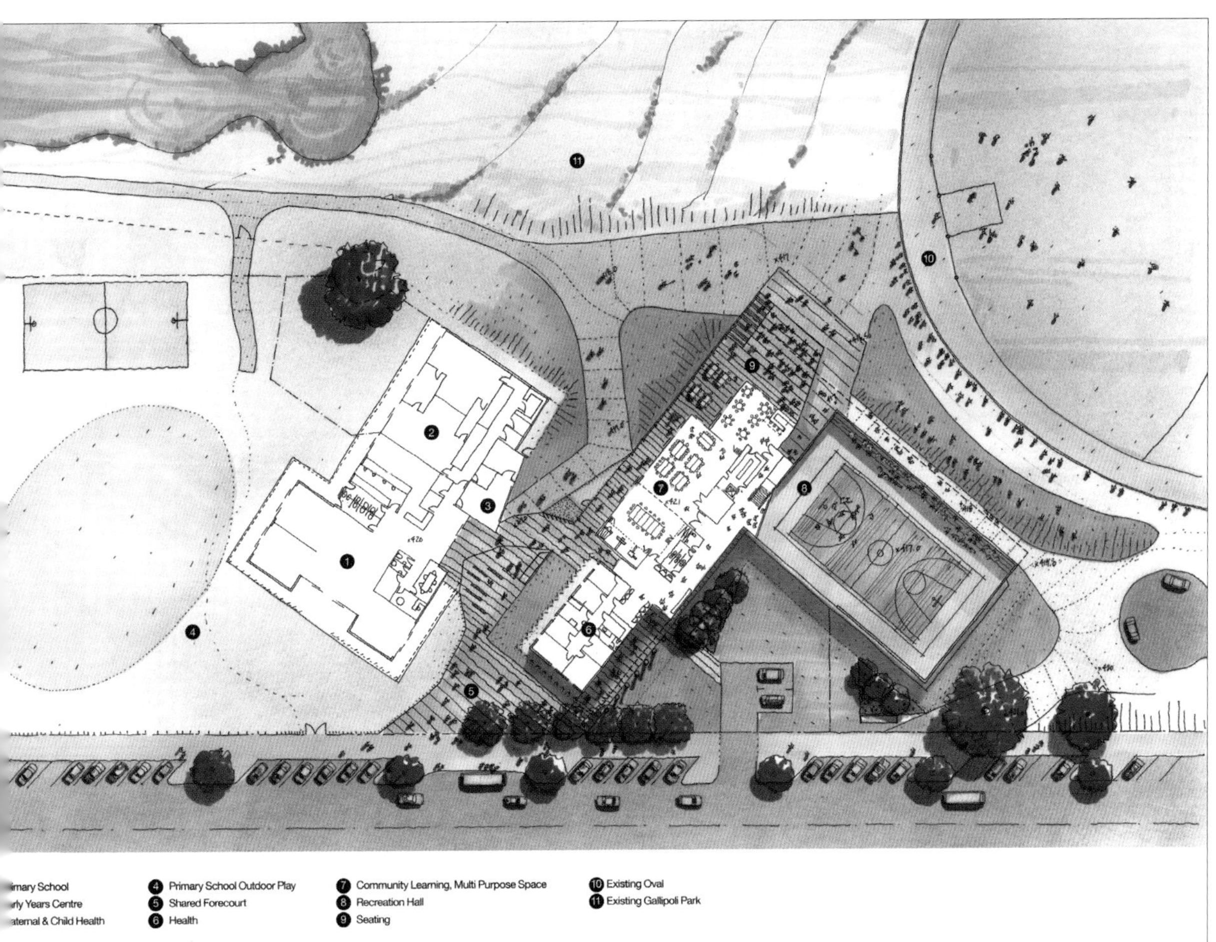

9.8 Marysville Town Plan and Community Hub Masterplan, Vic. 2009

delivery of basic services. The status of this public suburban infrastructure is, however, shifting. In part this is due to the reversal of formerly expansive visions for the provision of public space and its community ownership. In part it is due to rising land values and demands for denser housing and commercial developments, alongside radically different expectations of how public and private services should now be delivered. Councillors and other stakeholders might wish to take a 'long view' of local change, conserving specific buildings used by one group with the expectation that diminishing or expanding numbers in particular demographics (such as infants) will at some point return to 'normal'; the exigencies of land shortages, however, may make such conservation effectively impossible. Of the buildings investigated in this book, many have been demolished, many are in need of serious repair, while others have been gentrified through major renovations. But regardless of their physical state, many of the buildings are still not regarded with fondness, either because of their simple, lean, modern style or because of the socio-political 'statist' ideologies they are perceived to represent.

The ordinary buildings discussed in this book are often perceived as merely old or ugly. On this point, it is important to note that even the icons of modern architecture in the 20th century have garnered little public support for their heritage protection. There are international groups like DOCOMOMO, that are dedicated to the documentation and conservation of modern sites worldwide including in Australia, but they hold no power over planning decisions. For some historians and conservation practitioners the endeavour of conserving works of modernism is an anathema to heritage principles, with modern developments seen as the root cause of much destruction of the 'true' historical fabric of cities and town across the world, and thereby not worthy of protection now. For instance, influential and controversial postmodern architect Leon Krier has recently published a collection of his thoughts and drawings on architecture titled *The Architecture of Community* in which he makes a biting critique of the preservation of modern architecture, viewing it as antithetical to the renewal of liveable communities.[46] As the chapters in this book have reinforced, modernism and community are, however, completely bound together as cornerstone ideologies of the 20th century.

This study has attempted to draw historical and architectural attention to these often-ignored buildings in our local environs. There is no doubt that small public building types are poorly represented in local, state and national heritage registers, with attention only alerted when buildings are under threat. But there are very real dilemmas facing their successful conservation; around, for example, the material problems associated with post–World War II modern architecture in respect to the deterioration of concrete and steel, and the use of lightweight materials like fibre-cement. The challenges of maintaining open, expansive landscapes are particularly acute with the effects of a major drought in Australia, and longer term expectations of climate change. Current debates about the unsustainability of sprawling mid-century suburbs, appropriate densities, and infill design are all paramount in the face of depleting resources. Any adaptive re-use has to be mindful of dramatically changing social and political ideals about what is regarded as an appropriate 'civic contract' between citizens and governments and ensuing infrastructure management strategies – which increasingly favour the private rather than public sector.

Through their very ubiquity across Australian towns and suburbs, libraries, swimming pools, kindergartens, baby health centres and the like warrant more concerted historical documentation before they disappear. Despite an uncertain outlook, these small institutions and public places maintain their eloquence in shaping shared and individual memories and routines. They also embody the somewhat unexpected union of the high ideals of 20th-century modernist doctrine and mundane, 'make-do', pragmatism. As Henri Lefebvre says, the everyday and the modern meet in public modern places: 'they mark

9.9 Campaign poster, 'Save Coburg Olympic Pool', Vic. 2008

and mask, legitimate and counterbalance each other'. Recognition of their interconnectedness is crucial in understanding how modernism played out in the sphere of suburbia, and how, especially in Australia, it has profoundly affected the routines of everyday life. Perhaps it is indeed fitting that these places remain in the background of suburbia and are not commemorated in any overt or obvious sense.[47] These often ordinary, although sometimes extraordinary, small public sites should, however, be recognised as deeply complicit in the larger project of building modern Australia.

NOTES

Chapter 1 – Making the Modern Community

1 R Moore (dir.) *Beulah 1999: The Video*, National Film and Sound Archive, Canberra.
2 Caroline Butler-Bowden & Charles Pickett (2007) *Homes in the Sky: Apartment Living in Australia*, Miegunyah Press in assoc. with Historic Houses Trust, Melbourne.
3 For example, Robert Irving (ed.) (1985) *The History and Design of the Australian House*, Oxford University Press, Melbourne; Peter Cuffley (1989) *Australian Houses of the '20s & '30s*, Five Mile Press, Melbourne; Peter Cuffley (1993) *Australian Houses of the Forties and Fifties*, Five Mile Press, Melbourne; Renate Howe (ed.) (1988) *New Houses for Old: Fifty Years of Public Housing in Victoria, 1938–1988*, Ministry of Housing, Melbourne.
4 For example, Peter G Rowe (1991) *Making a Middle Landscape*, MIT Press, Cambridge, Mass.
5 Hugh Stretton (1970) *Ideas for Australian Cities*, Hugh Stretton, North Adelaide; Patrick Troy (ed.)(2000) *A History of European Housing in Australia*, Cambridge University Press, Melbourne.
6 Robin Boyd (1960) *The Australian Ugliness*, FW Cheshire, Melbourne; Sarah Ferber, Chris Healy & Chris McAuliffe (eds) (1994) *Beasts of Suburbia: Reinterpreting Cultures in Australian Suburbs*, Melbourne University Press.
7 Lewis Mumford (1961) *The City in History*, Penguin Books, Harmondsworth, UK, p. 563.
8 Graeme Davison (November 1995) 'Australia: The first suburban nation', *Journal of Urban History*, 22(1): 40–75.
9 Graeme Davison (1994) 'The past and future of the Australian suburb', in Louise C Johnson (ed.) *Suburban Dreaming: An Interdisciplinary Approach to Australian Cities*, Deakin University Press, Geelong, Vic., p. 120.
10 Adrian Forty (2000) *Words and Buildings: A Vocabulary of Modern Architecture*, Thames & Hudson, New York, p. 104.
11 Graham Day (2006) *Community and Everyday Life*, Routledge, London, pp. 5–6.
12 ibid., p. 21.
13 Raymond Plant (1974) *Community and Ideology: An Essay in Applied Social Philosophy*, Routledge & Kegan Paul, London & Boston, p. 38.
14 Plant, *Community and Ideology*, p. 39.
15 Day, *Community and Everyday Life*, p. 24.
16 Nikolas Rose (August 1993) 'Government, authority and expertise in advanced liberalism', *Economy and Society*, 22(3): 285.
17 ibid., p. 290.
18 Manuel Castells (1987) *The Information Age: Economy, Society and Culture*, vol. 2, 'The Power of Identity', Blackwell, Malden, Mass.; Eric Hobsbawm (1994) *Age of Extremes: The Short Twentieth Century 1914–1991*, Viking, New York, p. 428.
19 Nikolas Rose (August 1996) 'The death of the social? Refiguring the territory of government', *Economy and Society*, 25(3): 327.
20 Robert D Putnam (2000) *Bowling Alone: The Collapse and Revival of American Community*, Simon & Schuster, New York; David Halpern (2005) *Social Capital*, Polity Press, Cambridge, p. 29.
21 Productivity Commission of Australia (25 July 2003) *Social Capital: Reviewing the Concept and its Policy Implications*, viewed June 2009; <www.pc.gov.au/research/commissionresearch/socialcapital>.
22 See also Jody Hughes & Wendy Stone (2002) *Family Change and Community Life: Exploring the Links*, Australian Institute of Family Studies, Research Paper 32.
23 Christopher Wilk (2006) 'The healthy body culture', in Christopher Wilk (ed.) *Modernism: Designing a New World 1914–1939*, V&A Publications, London, p. 250.
24 Beatriz Colomina (June 1997) 'The medical body in modern architecture', *Daidalos*, 64: 61.
25 Andrew Shanken (2009) *194X: Architecture, Planning and Consumer Culture on the American Home Front*, University of Minnesota Press, Minneapolis, p. 68.
26 Frank Costello (April 1943) 'Town planning in post-war development', *Architecture*: 73.
27 'The City of Brisbane plan' (October–December 1945) *Architecture*, 34(4): 233.
28 ibid., p. 234.
29 Charles Whitaker (April 1943) 'How shall we provide good houses for all?', *Architecture*: 74.
30 Marta Gutman & Ning De Coninck-Smith (2008) *Designing Modern Childhoods: History, Space and the Material Culture of Children*, Rutgers University Press, New Brunswick, New Jersey, p. 2.
31 Harold Boas (July 1943) 'National planning and housing', *Architecture*: 119.

32 ibid.
33 Walter Bunning (1945) *Homes in the Sun: The Past, Present and Future of Australian Housing*, WJ Nesbit, Sydney, p. 80.
34 Paul Zucker (ed.) (1944) *New Architecture and City Planning*, Philosophical Library, New York, p. 565.
35 ibid., p. 369.
36 Andrew Saint (1983) *The Image of the Architect*, Yale University Press, New Haven, p. 97.
37 Cobden Parkes (1951) 'Artem promovemus una', *Architecture in Australia*, 31(3): 67.
38 ibid.
39 President of the RAIA, WT Haslam, addressed the AGM in Perth, April 1958, with the lecture 'Architecture and Modern Life', which appears in *Architecture in Australia* (July–September 1958): 89.
40 Parry said: 'Any action taken now, or the lack of it, will affect us vitally, both individually and collectively; and our children for centuries to come'. Mervyn Parry (September 1958) 'The Living City', transcript of lecture broadcast by the ABC, republished in *The Architect*, 2224: 11–17.
41 Suzanne Lawson & Brendan Gleeson (1997) 'Shifting urban governance in Australia', in Paul Smyth, Tim Reddel & Andrew Jones (eds) *Community and Local Governance in Australia*, UNSW Press, Sydney, p. 80.
42 Judy McNeill (1997) 'Local government in the Australian federal system', in Brian Dollery & Neil Marshall (eds) *Australian Local Government: Reform and Renewal*, Macmillan Education, South Melbourne, p. 19.
43 Margaret Bowman (1976) *Local Government in the Australian States: An Urban Paper*, Department of Environment, Housing and Community Development, Canberra, p. 19.
44 ibid., pp. 34–35.
45 See, for example, Nikolaus Pevsner (1976) *A History of Building Types*, Princeton University Press.

Chapter 2 – A Healthy Start: Buildings for Babies

1 Dr Main & Dr V Scantlebury (1926) 'Report to the Minister of Public Health on the welfare of women and children', in *Victorian Parliamentary Papers*, 2: 40–42.
2 'Tour of the Mallee', *Herald*, 12 October 1926, p. 8.
3 Lynette Finch (1998) 'Caring for colonial infants: Parenting on the frontiers,' *Australian Historical Studies*, 29(110): 110.
4 ibid., p. 121.
5 ibid., pp. 113–15.
6 Valerie Fildes, Lara Marks & Hilary Marland (eds) (1992) *Women and Children First: International Maternal and Infant Welfare, 1879–1945*, Routledge, London & New York.
7 Deborah Dwork (1987) *War is Good for Babies and Other Young Children: A History of the Infant and Child Welfare Movement in England 1898–1918*, Tavistock, London & New York, pp. 94–95.
8 Dwork discusses the development of the *Goutte de Lait* in the chapter 'From Goutte de Lait to Infant Milk Depot', in *War is Good for Babies*, pp. 93–123.
9 ibid., pp. 11–12.
10 ibid., pp. 114–15.
11 John F Sykes, quoted in Dwork, *War is Good for Babies*, p. 154. For information concerning the Health Societies, see Dwork, *War is Good for Babies*, pp. 143–54.
12 Margaret M Scott (August 1964) 'The world of the baby health centres in New South Wales', *Health in NSW*, 5(3): 8; Elizabeth J Mellor (1990) *Stepping Stones: The Development of Early Childhood Services in Australia*, Harcourt Brace Jovanovich, Sydney, pp. 100–01.
13 Scott, 'The world of the baby health centres', p. 8.
14 Mellor, *Stepping Stones*, pp. 104–05.
15 Children, Youth and Women's Health Service (SA), 'History', viewed 25 May 2010; <http://www.cyh.com>.
16 Mothers' and Babies' Health Association (SA), 'The first fifty years', September 1959, p. 12. 'Mothers' and Babies' Health Association papers (GA 351), held in the State Records of South Australia. The amount rose significantly over time: in 1934, it was £2500; in 1959, £66,000.
17 Heather Sheard (2007) *All the Little Children: The Story of Victoria's Baby Health Centres*, Municipal Association of Victoria, Melbourne, p. 12.
18 Mellor, *Stepping Stones*, p. 101.
19 Milton J Lewis (2003) *The People's Health: Public Health in Australia, 1788–1950*, vol. 1, Praeger, Westport, Conn., & London, p. 158.
20 ibid., p. 159.
21 Kerreen Reiger (1985) *The Disenchantment of the Home*, Oxford University Press, Melbourne, pp. 130–31.
22 Sheard, *All the Little Children*, p. 15.
23 ibid., p. 20.
24 Lewis, *The People's Health*, p. 160; Mellor, *Stepping Stones*, p. 102.
25 Wendy Selby (1996) 'Social evil or social good? Lotteries and state regulation in Australia and the United States', in Jan McMillen (ed.), *Gambling Cultures: Studies in History and Interpretation*, Routledge, London, p. 72.
26 Selby, 'Social evil or social good?', p. 73.

27 Department of Health and Human Services (Tas.), 'The history of the family, child and youth service in Tasmania', viewed 25 May 2010; <www.dhhs.tas.gov.au>.
28 Mellor, *Stepping Stones*, pp. 102–03.
29 Lewis, *The People's Health*, pp. 158, 160.
30 ibid., p. 160; Mellor, *Stepping Stones*, p. 104.
31 Mellor, *Stepping Stones*, p. 102.
32 Country Women's Association of New South Wales, 'About us', viewed 25 May 2010; <www.cwaofnsw.org.au/aboutUs/home.do;jsessionid=D1DD02E3881A267A9A1053C44F4307EE>.
33 Jennifer Jones (2010), 'Baby health centres and the colour bar in NSW country towns', in *Green Fields, Brown Fields, New Fields: Proceedings of the 10th Australasian Urban History, Planning History Conference*, University of Melbourne, p. 298.
34 Jones, 'Baby health centres and the colour bar in NSW country towns', p. 299.
35 ibid., pp. 301–02.
36 ibid., p. 307.
37 Deborah Tyler makes similar points about the kindergarten in the 1930s. See Deborah Tyler (1993) 'Making better children', in Denise Meredyth & Deborah Tyler (eds) *Child and Citizen: Genealogies of Schooling and Subjectivity*, Institute for Cultural Policy Studies, Faculty of Humanities, Griffith University, Nathan, Qld, pp. 42–43.
38 Janet McCalman (1984) *Struggletown: Portrait of an Australian Working-Class Community 1900–1965*, Penguin Books, Melbourne, pp. 208–09.
39 ibid., p. 209.
40 Judith Eathorne's work in mapping the position of baby health centres in Victoria in 1949 demonstrated the very strong correlation between their placement and that of railway stations. See Eathorne (1949) 'A brief survey of the development of baby health centres in Melbourne and the work of the travelling centres', BArch thesis, Faculty of Architecture, Building and Planning, University of Melbourne.
41 Commonwealth Department of Health, *The Infant Welfare Centre as a Community Service*, p. 12. Quoted by Rachel Ritson (1997) 'The birth of the baby clinic', *Transition*, 54(55): 45.
42 'Warm floors for health centre toddlers', *Herald* (Melbourne), 5 June 1949, as quoted in Eathorne (1949) 'A brief survey of the development of baby health centres in Melbourne and the work of the travelling centres', p. 12.
43 'Footscray has last word in baby health centre', *Sun* (Melbourne), 1 June 1949, as quoted in Eathorne (1949) 'A brief survey of the development of baby health centres in Melbourne and the work of the travelling centres', p. 12.
44 Letter from Shire Secretary, Shire of Dimboola, to Secretary, Department of Public Health, 3 July 1962, VPRS 7882/P/0001, Public Record Office of Victoria.
45 Letter from A Elizabeth Wilmot, Director of Maternal, Infant and Pre-School Welfare, to Shire Secretary, Shire of Dimboola, 13 July 1962, VPRS 7882/P/0001, Public Record Office of Victoria.
46 Department of Health (1944), *The Infant Welfare Centre as a Community Service*, Government Printer, Canberra, p. 17.
47 List of specifications from GV Stafford, Secretary General, Health Branch (Vic.), to the Shire Secretary, Shire of Dimboola, 3 March 1954, VPRS 7882/P/0001, Public Record Office of Victoria.
48 Victor H Wallace (1946) *Women and Children First: The Outline of a Population Policy for Australia*, Oxford University Press, Melbourne.
49 Kate Darian-Smith (2009) *On the Home Front: Melbourne in Wartime: 1939–1945*, 2nd edn, Melbourne University Press, p. 138.
50 ibid., p. 78.
51 Enid Lyons (1943) 'Women in peacetime', in Michael Cathcart & Kate Darian-Smith (eds) (2004) *Stirring Australian Speeches: The Definitive Collection from Botany to Bali*, Melbourne University Press, p. 201.
52 Sheard, *All the Little Children*, p. 77.
53 ibid., p. 79.
54 ibid., p. 78.

Chapter 3 – Early Learning: The Modern Kindergarten

1 'Miss Kent' (1916) quoted in Peggy Banff & Norma Ross (1998) *The Peppercorn Trail: The Story of the Creche and Kindergarten Association of Queensland and Its People 1907–1997*, Creche and Kindergarten Association of Queensland, Brisbane, p. 15.
2 Peter Spearritt (1979) 'Child care and kindergartens in Australia 1890–1975', in Peter Langford & Patricia Sebastian (eds), *Early Childhood Education and Care in Australia*, Australia International Press & Publications, Melbourne, p. 10.
3 ibid.
4 *The Kindergarten System*, Ward, Lock & Co., London. For an outline of Froebel's teaching philosophy, see Norman Brosterman (1997) *Inventing Kindergarten*, HN Abrams, New York.
5 *Advertiser*, 26 November 1906, p. 11.
6 Banff & Ross, *The Peppercorn Trail*, pp. 1–3.
7 ibid., pp. 12, 15.
8 Harriet Edquist (2008) *Pioneers of Modernism: The Arts and Crafts Movement in Australia*, Miegunyah Press, Melbourne, p. 228.
9 Kindergarten Association of Western Australia, ACC 2308A/41–46, Records 1911–1982, Battye Library, State Library of Western Australia.

10 Rosemary Kerr (1994) *A History of the Kindergarten Union of Western Australia 1911–1973*, Meeralinga Young Children's Foundation, West Perth, p. 31.
11 Theodate L Smith (1912) *The Montessori System in Theory and Practice*, Harper and Brothers, New York & London, p. 48.
12 Director's report for August & September 1923, Kindergarten Association of Western Australia, ACC 2308A/41–46, Battye Library, State Library of Western Australia.
13 ibid.
14 ibid.
15 *Argus*, 28 June 1930, p. 24.
16 *The Kindergarten Union of South Australia Through 75 Years 1905–1980* (1980) Kindergarten Union of South Australia, North Adelaide, p. 1; Kerr, *A History of the Kindergarten Union of Western Australia*, p. 42.
17 Banff & Ross, *The Peppercorn Trail*, p. 17.
18 *Argus*, 12 December 1927, p. 15.
19 *Movietone News* 16(21), National Film and Sound Archive, Melbourne.
20 Lyndsay Gardiner (1982) *The Free Kindergarten Union of Victoria, 1908–80*, ACER, Melbourne, p. 96.
21 Stefano de Martino & Alex Wall (1988) *Cities of Childhood: Italian Colonie of the 1930s*, Architectural Association, London. *The Colonia Elioterapica* was devoted to heliotherapy, the technique of the sun-cure for tuberculosis, an alternative to surgery and ameliorating malnutrition.
22 William Lescaze designed the modernist forms of the nursery school at the Oak Lane Country Day School, near Philadelphia, Penn. (1929). William Curry was principal of this school and was to become a major patron of Lescaze by commissioning him and architect Robert Hening for a series of uncompromising modernist school buildings at Dartington Hall, Devon, England (1931–38). See Kenneth Frampton & Silvia Kolbowski (eds) (1982) *William Lescaze*, Rizzoli International Publications, New York, pp. 26, 30–33, 60–61, 65–71.
23 Certificate for Ugly Men's Competition presented to WM Hughes, 1927, PICR11249 LOC OPD32, National Library of Australia.
24 JHL Cumpston & CM Heinig (1945) *Pre-School Centres in Australia: Building, Equipment and Programme*, Commonwealth Department of Health, Canberra, p. 89.
25 Elizabeth J Mellor (1996) 'Heinig, Mary Christine (1892–1979)', *Australian Dictionary of Biography*, vol. 14, Melbourne University Press, pp. 429–30. Prior to Heinig's involvement with the Commonwealth, her publications included *Play, The Child's Response to Life* (with Rose Alschuler, Boston, 1936) and *The Child in the Nursery School* (Melbourne, 1938).
26 Loma Rudduck (February 1966) 'The early history and establishment of the Lady Gowrie centres', *Australian Pre-School Quarterly*: 8–9. Melbourne-born and trained, JHL Cumpston, Australia's first director-general of the Australian Department of Health, had interests that ranged across schoolchildren's health, pulmonary disease among miners,studies in tuberculosis, diphtheria, quarantine, diet, housing and eugenics. In August 1920, at the Australasian Medical Congress in Brisbane, Cumpston spoke of himself as being among those 'who dream of leading this young nation of ours to a paradise of physical perfection'. In March 1921, he was appointed director-general of health and director of quarantine; he was also foundation chair (1927) of the Federal Health Council, which in 1937 was transformed into the NHMRC. See Michael Roe (1981) 'Cumpston, John Howard Lidgett (1880 –1954)', *Australian Dictionary of Biography*, vol. 8, Melbourne University Press, pp. 174–76.
27 Ada Mary a'Beckett (1872–1948), a biologist by training, was the first woman appointed to a lectureship by the University of Melbourne. She became involved with the Free Kindergarten Union at its inception in 1909 and was its president from 1920 to 1939.
28 Debbie Gahan (2007) 'Historical perspectives on kindergarten education in Queensland', in Jo Ailwood (ed.) *Early Childhood in Australia: Historical and Comparative Contexts*, Pearson SprintPrint, Sydney, pp. 9–10.
29 ibid., p. 10.
30 Cumpston & Heinig, *Pre-School Centres in Australia*, p. 87. Typical records included: social and developmental history forms, habit record – home-school (which detailed time in bed, family remarks, dinner and sleep habits), form of child's initial summary and subsequent case study meeting notes, and a report for schools that detailed a child's home conditions, physical, social and mental conditions, speech development and temperament.
31 ibid., pp. 5–6.
32 Lord Gowrie was Governor-General of Australia from 1936 until 1945.
33 Kindergarten Union of South Australia (15–16 September 1936) 'Report of Kindergarten Conference', p. 2. See also C Jean Bonython (February1966), *Australian Pre-School Quarterly*: pp. 5–6. The Australian Association for Pre-School ChildDevelopment changed its name to the Australian Pre-School Association in 1954.
34 Philip Goad (2007) 'Laboratories for the body and mind: The architecture of the Lady Gowrie centres', in S Loo & K Bartsch (eds) *Panorama to Paradise*, papers from the XXIVth Conference of the Society of Architectural Historians, Australia & New Zealand, 21–24 September, Adelaide, pp. 1–14.
35 Marcus Martin, in developing the typical plan of the Gowrie centres, was also responsible for giving Cumpston and Heinig advice on preschool facilities and was heavily involved in the design of their book, *Pre-School Centres in Australia* (1945). Under Martin's direction, Mrs JH Henderson made drawings of centre equipment and within his office; Allan Bogle (later to form the architectural firm of Bogle & Banfield) drew the floor plans of the six centres. See Cumpston & Heinig, *Pre-School Centres in Australia*, p. 219.

36 For example, in Melbourne, president of the centre was Mrs Essington Lewis (wife of Essington Lewis, chairman of BHP). In Sydney, Mrs Lloyd Jones, wife of businessman Charles Lloyd Jones, was a member of the house committee of the Sydney Lady Gowrie Centre. See *Argus*, 30 October 1940, p. 8. In Adelaide, Lady Jean Bonython was chairman of the Adelaide Lady Gowrie Centre Committee for more than twenty-five years.

37 The locations of the centres at the time of their opening were: Melbourne, 36 Newry Street, North Carlton; Sydney, Erskineville Park, Erskineville; Brisbane, 228 St Paul's Terrace, Fortitude Valley; Adelaide, 39a Dew Street, Thebarton; Perth, 248–250 Gloucester Street, Victoria Park East; and Hobart, McGregor Street, Battery Point.

38 Martin's involvement with the Yooralla Hospital School's Free Kindergarten appeared on his certificate of registration with the Royal Victorian Institute of Architects. It is presumed that Martin worked on this project as part of the short-lived partnership of A & K Henderson, Alsop and Martin (1921–24).
See Bryce Raworth (1986) *Marcus Martin: A Survey of His Life and Work*, Investigation Project, University of Melbourne, pp. 1, 3.

39 ibid., p. 3.

40 Two kindergartens completed by Marcus Martin & Tribe before1941 include the Coronation Free Kindergarten, Ascot Vale, Vic. (1940, destroyed) and Kildonan Home Kindergarten Cottage, Burwood, Vic. (1941).

41 Notable kindergarten and preschool work produced by Martin & Tribe in the immediate post-war years included the preschool centre, Broken Hill, NSW, for the Zinc Corporation (1946); and in Victoria, alterations, Collingwood Free Kindergarten, Keele Street, Collingwood (1946, destroyed); project, holiday home, Free Kindergarten Union, East Ringwood (1946); Ada Mary a'Beckett Free Kindergarten and Infant Welfare Centre, Port Melbourne (1947, destroyed); alterations, Boroondara Free Kindergarten, Anderson Street, North Richmond (1947, destroyed); Isobel Henderson Free Kindergarten, Fitzroy (1947); project, Hughesdale Free Kindergarten (1947); and playground redevelopment, Collingwood Crèche, Abbott Street (1949).

42 Horace J Tribe, FRAIA (November 1955) *Architecture and Arts*: 17.

43 *Argus*, 9 December 1939, p. 15.

44 *Architectural Review* (1948) 104: 31.

45 *Age*, 9 December 1939, p. 23.

46 Robin Boyd (1947) *Victorian Modern*, Victorian Architectural Students Society, Melbourne, p. 57.

47 ibid., p. 63.

48 See Matthew Conlon (2007) 'Re-Seeing modernist fragments: The Erskineville Housing Scheme, 1938', in Loo & Bartsch (eds) *Panorama to Paradise*, CD-ROM.

49 The 100 children were divided into classes and hence classroom sizes as follows:
Two-year-olds – 25 × 35 = 875 square feet; three-year-olds – 35 × 35 = 1225 square feet;
four-year-olds – 40 × 35 = 1400 square feet.

50 Cumpston & Heinig, *Pre-School Centres in Australia*, p. 14.

51 Isla Stamp (1975) *Young Children in Perspective: A Review of Thirty-Five Years of the Lady Gowrie Child Centres in Partnership with the Australian Pre-School Association*, Australian Pre-School Association, Canberra, p. 21.

52 Cumpston & Heinig, *Pre-School Centres in Australia*, p. ii.

53 Gladys E Pendred (December 1952) *An Analysis of the Work of the Lady Gowrie Child Centres from 1940 to 1952: Their Present Functions and Possible Future Development* (submitted to the Director-General of Health, Dr AJ Metcalfe), Australian Association for Pre-School Child Development, Canberra, p. 1.

54 Phyllis M Scott & Margaret Darbyshire (1972) *Early Education Programs and Aboriginal Families in Victoria*, Monash University, Melbourne, pp. 44–48.

55 See, for instance, Humphrey McQueen (2004) *Social Sketches of Australia 1888–2001*, University of Queensland Press, Brisbane, pp. 188–91; SeamusO'Hanlon (2005) 'Cities, suburbs and communities', in Martin Lyons & Penny Russell (eds) (2005) *Australia's History: Themes and Debates*, UNSW Press, Sydney, pp. 181–83; Jean Duruz (1994) 'Suburban houses revisited', in Kate Darian-Smith & Paula Hamilton (eds) (1994) *Memory and History in Twentieth-Century Australia*, Oxford University Press, Melbourne, pp.174–83.

56 The Olive Phillips Kindergarten in Bodley Street, Beaumaris, Vic., formed part of a co-located group of community buildings including the Beaumaris Bowls Club, Martin Street Tennis Club, 1st Beaumaris Sea Scouts and St Michael's Church, all adjacent to the Keys Street shopping centre. The Seabrook, Fildes and Hunt-designed kindergarten was replaced in 1975 by a new kindergarten designed by another local architect, David Godsell, who combined it with an infant welfare centre, virtually identical in form and materials.

57 *Outer Circle Mirror*, 18 July 1953, p. 5; 15 May 1956, p. 1; 23 October 1956, p. 3.

58 ibid., 15 May 1956, p. 1.

59 ibid., 6 March 1954, p. 3.

60 ibid., 19 February 1957, p. 1.

61 Ellie V Pullen (March 1985) 'The history of the first twelve years of the Ringwood Pre School Parents Club 1945–1957 later to be known as the Greenwood Park Kindergarten Parents Club', MS 12530, Box 3292/9 (a), p. 1, Manuscripts Collection, State Library of Victoria.

62 ibid., p. 3.

63 ibid., pp. 3, 8.

64 Ellie V Pullen (1985) 'Some of the links that formed a chain: Personal memoirs', MS12530, Box 3292/9 (a), p. 69, Manuscripts Collection, State Library of Victoria.

65 Pullen, 'The history of the first twelve years', p. 9.
66 Pullen, 'Some of the links', p. 71.
67 *Outer Circle Mirror*, 24 April 1956, p. 1; 26 February 1957, p. 1.
68 ibid., 30 October 1956, p. 1.
69 ibid., 24 April 1956, p. 3.
70 ibid., 30 October 1956, p. 1.
71 ibid., p. 3. See also *Eastern Suburbs Standard*, 2 December 1959, p. 1.
72 VPRS 7882/P/0001 unit 001181, Public Record Office of Victoria.
73 Caulfield & Krivanek, Graeme Butler, Francine Gilfedder & Associates, Ratio Consultants (May 1992) *City of Bendigo View Street Rosalind Park Study*, pp. 60–61.
74 *Cross-Section* 62 (December 1957).
75 *Cross-Section* 181 (November 1967).
76 See Philip Goad (1992) 'The modern house in Melbourne 1945–1975', PhD thesis, University of Melbourne, 6/49–6/55.
77 *Stock and Land*, 8 March 1961, p. 29.
78 Philip Goad, interview with James Earle, 31 March 2007.
79 Darlington Kindergarten Association Newsletter (May 1968).
80 See Paul Ritter (c. 1979) *Kids and Concrete: Six Successful Educreational Experiments with Sculpcrete*, PEER Institute, Kelmscott, WA, pp. 51–55.
81 See ibid., p. 55.
82 Paul Ritter (1964) *Planning for Man and Motor*, Pergamon Press, Oxford, p. 11.
83 See, for example, Paul Ritter (1966) *Educreation and Feedback: Education for Creation, Growth and Change*, Pergamon Press, Oxford.
84 See Ritter, *Kids and Concrete*, p.55.
85 Paul Ritter (1982) *Concrete Renaissance Through BuildingTechnology*, Down to Earth Bookshop Press, Perth, p. 59.
86 ibid., p. 61.
87 *Cross-Section* 29 (March 1955).
88 ibid., 65 (March 1958).
89 *Architecture in Australia* (June 1961): 76–78; *Cross-Section* 97 (November 1960).
90 *Cross-Section* 107 (September 1961).
91 ibid. (September 1962) 119. The St Ives kindergarten was the only example of its type featured in Robin Boyd (1963) *The New Architecture*, Longmans, Melbourne.
92 Kevin Borland's design philosophy with regard to the creation of educational spaces for children was heavily influenced by his commission and ongoing work at the progressive Preshil School, Kew, Vic. (1962–70) under its principal, Margaret Lyttle. See Doug Evans (ed.) (2006) *Kevin Borland: Architecture from the Heart*, RMIT Publishing, Melbourne. Evans relates the design of the Lady Forster Kindergarten to Borland's Preshil school hall (1962), while the Boroondara kindergarten has echoes of Roy Grounds' zig-zag walls at the contemporaneous National Gallery of Victoria (1968). See Evans, pp. 52–53.
93 *Cross-Section* 217 (February–March 1971).
94 GM Hibbins (1984) *A History of the City of Springvale*, Springvale City Council, Melbourne, p. 211.
95 Historical Society of Mooroopna (1989) *Mooroopna to 1988*, p. 83.
96 Anne Glover (1993) *The Early Childhood Service Needs of Aboriginal Communities in the Northern Country Areas of South Australia*, Children's Services Office, Department of Education, Employment and Training, North Adelaide, p. 3.
97 ibid.
98 ibid., p. 32.
99 Harry Van Moorst & Sue Graham (1995) *Kindergarten at the Crossroads: The Werribee Kindergarten Study*, Victoria University, Werribee, Vic., p. 29.
100 Harbour Family and Children's Centre, viewed 3 April 2010; <www.melbourneopenhouse.com.au/cms-docklands/the-harbour-family-and-childrens-centre.phps>.

Chapter 4 – Local Learning: The Municipal Library in Post-War Australia

1 *Argus*, 22 March 1926, p. 17.
2 AJ McIntyre & JJ McIntyre (1944) *Country Towns of Victoria: A Social Survey*, Melbourne University Press in assoc. with Oxford University Press, Melbourne, p. 165.
3 ibid., p. 161.
4 ibid., p. 164.
5 ibid., p. 166.
6 JDA Collier (1945) 'Library development in Tasmania', *Australian Quarterly* (September): 105–10.
7 David J Jones (2001) 'Public libraries: "Institutions of the highest educational value"', in Martyn Lyons & John Arnold (eds) *A History of the Book in Australia 1891–1945*, University of Queensland Press, Brisbane, p. 161.
8 John Balnaves (1966) *Australian Libraries*, FW Cheshire, Melbourne, p. 50.

9 Mary Matheson (1951) 'The Children's Library and Crafts Movement', *New Horizons in Education: The Journal of the New Education Fellowship*: 26.

10 Ralph Munn & Ernest Pitt (1935) *Australian Libraries: A Survey of Conditions and Suggestions for their Improvement*, Carnegie Corporation of New York/Australian Council for Education Research, Melbourne, p. 104.

11 GC Remington & John Metcalfe (July June? 1945) 'The Free Library Movement – 1935–1945', *Australian Quarterly* 17(2): 88.

12 Jones, 'Public libraries', p. 210.

13 Munn & Pitt, *Australian Libraries*, pp. 11–12.

14 Frank Tate, 'Introduction', in Munn & Pitt, *Australian Libraries*, p. 21.

15 Munn & Pitt, *Australian Libraries*, p. 23.

16 ibid., p. 103.

17 *Coventry Bookshelf* (January–February 1934), quoted in Munn & Pitt, *Australian Libraries*, p. 104.

18 Munn & Pitt, *Australian Libraries*, pp. 124–27.

19 *Free Public Libraries* (1937), Free Library Movement, Melbourne, p. 8.

20 Balnaves, *Australian Libraries*, p. 43.

21 Remington & Metcalfe, 'The Free Library Movement': 92.

22 *Canberra Times*, 10 May 1946, p. 2.

23 Riverina Regional Library Conference, 9–11 May 1947, Griffith, NSW.

24 *Canberra Times*, 13 October 1947, p. 2.

25 *Age*, 4 February 1948, p. 2.

26 Lionel R McColvin (1947) *Public Libraries in Australia: Present Conditions and Future Possibilities*, Melbourne University Press.

27 McColvin singled out for praise the following laymen: Frank Tate, Geoffrey Remington, Sir John Morris, Dr Irving Benson and Dr Grenfell Price. He also praised the Carnegie Corporation, the Library Group and the Australian Council for Educational Research. See McColvin, *Public Libraries in Australia*, p. 19.

28 *Age*, 4 February 1948, p. 2.

29 *Canberra Times*, 29 January 1947, p. 2.

30 David Nichols, interview with Cec Churm, 14 January 2008. All subsequent quotes from Mr Churm are from this interview.

31 *The Story of a Public Library* (1967), Bankstown Municipal Council, p. 6.

32 *Architecture* (October–December 1952): 126–27.

33 'A municipal library', *Architecture and Arts* (November 1954); 'Public library at Lindfield, NSW', *Architecture* (January–March 1955): 13.

34 Hawthorn City Library history, Hawthorn Library local history file; Graeme Butler (1983) *Hawthorn Commercial Area Conservation Study*, City of Hawthorn and the Australian Heritage Commission.

35 Now demolished. The Hawthorn Municipal Library was relocated to Glenferrie Road in 1969 and is now a branch of Boroondara Library.

36 The concept of an 'establishing' building was also exemplified in the case of Robert Warren's St Mark's Anglican National Memorial Library, Canberra (1955–59), which was the first building constructed as part of a series that would eventually comprise a college and church. See 'St Mark's Anglican National Memorial Library Canberra, ACT', *Architecture and Arts* (March 1959): 34–35.

37 'The Hamilton Art Gallery', *Architecture in Australia* (March 1963): 103–08.

38 'Library, Millmerran, Qld', see *Cross-Section* 95 (September 1960). The architect for the Millmerran building was the Brisbane firm of J Ure McNaught & GO Cowlishaw. Library, East Maitland, NSW, see *Cross-Section* 57 (July 1957). The architect for the East Maitland building was the Newcastle firm of Thelander & Deamer.

39 *Cross-Section*, 115 (May 1962). The architect for the Clarence building was the Hobart firm of Hartley, Wilson & Bolt.

40 'Kew proud of its libraries', *Outer Circle Mirror*, 28 August 1954, p. 1.

41 'A modern library for Bairnsdale', *Bairnsdale Advertiser*, 30 August 1951, p. 1.

42 Philip Goad, interview with James Birrell, 12 December 2007.

43 Grace Garlick, 'This is the story that I like to write …', *Sunday Courier Mail*, 1 September 1957.

44 Philip Goad, interview with Birrell. See also 'Impressive library faced with fancy plywood', *The Australian Timber Journal – Plywood Annual* (May 1958): 53; *Cross-Section*, 60 (October 1957).

45 *Observer*, 8 August 1957, p. 2.

46 ibid.

47 'Opening of Chermside Municipal Library', *Nundah Express*, 1 April 1958; *Cross-Section*, 68 (June 1958).

48 Philip Goad, interview with Birrell. Birrell was involved in the design of several swimming pools for Brisbane, including Centenary Pool, Toowong, Sandgate, Wynnum, Langlands Park and Corinda.

49 'Toowong library, Qld', *Architecture in Australia* (December 1961): 110–11. See also *Courier-Mail*, 4 October 1957, p. 17; *Cross-Section*, 82 (August 1959); 'Unusual design of Toowong Library', *Telegraph*, 24 March 1960; 'New Queensland Public Library with hexagon plan in exposed steelwork', *Building Materials* (May–June 1961): 67.

50 Philip Goad (1997) 'One of the lost tribe: James Birrell and that other tradition', in A Wilson & J Macarthur (eds) *Birrell: Work from the Office of James Birrell*, NMBW Publications, Melbourne, p. 19. In 1959, a Fuller-inspired geodesic dome was flown by helicopter from Brisbane to Surfers Paradise for the 9th RAIA Annual Convention. See *Cross-Section*, 80 (June 1959).

51 Mark Peel (1995) *Good Times Hard Times: The Past and Future in Elizabeth*, Melbourne University Press, p. 49.
52 City of Burnside Library and Information Service (2000) *History of Libraries in Burnside*.
53 Elizabeth Public Library (1957–62) *Annual Reports*, Elizabeth Local History Collection.
54 City of Burnside Library, *History of Libraries in Burnside*.
55 *Bankstown City Library: The Story of a Library for the People 1946–1983* (1983) Bankstown City Council, p. 5.
56 'Local library services' (1954) *Civic Development* 18: 5.
57 '1958 Sulman Award for library design', *Architecture Today* (July 1959): 8; Andrew Metcalf (1997) *Architecture in Transition: The Sulman Award, 1932–1996*, Historic Houses Trust of New South Wales, Sydney, p. 90.
58 'Kings Cross Library', *Architecture and Arts* (August 1959): 49.
59 Balnaves, *Australian Libraries*, pp. 45–46.
60 'Library, Dee Why', *Architecture in Australia* (August 1967): 601–06.
61 ibid.; *Cross-Section* 174 (April 1967); Norman Edwards (c. 1967) 'Library for the supermarket age', *Sydney Morning Herald* (undated clipping); *Woman's Day*, 23 January 1967; *Daily Telegraph*, 16 June 1967.
62 Jennifer Taylor (1990) *Australian Architecture Since 1960*, National Education Division, Royal Australian Institute of Architects, Red Hill, ACT, p. 48.
63 Colin Madigan (23 November 1991) Notes of talk given at the 25th Anniversary of Warringah Shire Library Service, Warringah. Courtesy of Colin Madigan.
64 Philip Goad, interview with Colin Madigan, 15 November 2008; see also Madigan notes.
65 Madigan notes.
66 ibid.
67 'Library for Warren Shire Council', *Architecture in Australia* (December 1969): 1025–27.
68 ibid.; *Cross-Section*, 205 (December 1969).
69 The firm also completed municipal libraries at Chatswood, Mona Vale and Mosman.
70 Taylor, *Australian Architecture Since 1960*, p. 100.
71 Ken Charlton (ed.) (2007) *The Contribution of Enrico Taglietti to Canberra's Architecture*, ACT Chapter, Royal Australian Institute of Architects, Canberra, p. 42; Cross-Section 212 (July 1970); 'Dickson District Library, Dickson Shopping Centre, ACT', *Architecture in Australia* (August 1970): 634–41.
72 Susan Conroy (April 1998) *Dickson Shopping Centre Refurbishment Project, Community Consultation and Profile Report.*
73 Charlton (ed.), *The Contribution of Enrico Taglietti*, pp. 57–58; *Construction Review*, (February 1974): 47(1): 7.
74 Discussion with Rose Nolan, librarian, St Kilda Library, 28 October 2009; Discussion with Gillian Garner, Garner Davis Architects, 29 January 2010.

Chapter 5 – Making Spaces for Recreation

1 Donald Horne (1971) *The Lucky Country*, Penguin Books, Melbourne, p. 37.
2 Ian Jobling (1991) 'Sport', in John Henningham (ed.) *Institutions in Australian Society*, Department of Journalism, University of Queensland, Brisbane, p. 228.
3 K Elford (1976) 'Sport in Australian society', in TD Jaques & GR Pavia (eds) *Sport in Australia: Selected Readings in Physical Activity*, McGraw-Hill, Sydney, p. 42.
4 Gary Wickham (1992) 'Sport, manners, persons, government, sport, Elias, Mauss, Foucault', *Cultural Studies*, 6(2): 221.
5 Eric Dunning & Norbert Elias (1986) *Quest for Excitement*, Blackwell, Oxford, p. 222.
6 JC Slaughter (1944) 'Planning – Its importance to civilisation', *Architecture*, 33(2): 34.
7 H Lefebvre (1991) *The Production of Space*, Blackwell, Oxford, p. 49.
8 *Argus*, 30 July 1932, p. 25. A new below-ground concrete swimming pool in nearby Brunswick was already being mooted as a favoured option.
9 EA Hepburn (1937) *The Health Bulletin*, Victoria, 5: 49–50.
10 See Ann Curthoys (2002) *Freedom Ride: A Freedom Rider Remembers*, Allen & Unwin, Sydney, pp. 115–70.
11 This is still the case today as with the 'No School, No Pool' government program. See Marie-Louise McDermott (2005) 'Changing visions of baths and bathers: Desegregating ocean baths in Wollongong, Kiama and Gerringong', *Sporting Traditions*, 22(1): 1–19.
12 *Canberra Community News*, 11 March 1927.
13 Manuka Pool, Griffith, entry to the Australian Capital Territory Heritage Register, 2004.
14 Heather Boyer's recollections of the pool in the 1960s. Cited in Anne Bolitho & Mary Hutchison (1992) *Stories of the Inner South: From a Day of Memories at the Manuka Pool*, The Arts Council of ACT, Canberra, p. 12.
15 EJE Landscape Architects Survey of Harbourside & Ocean Pools of the Sydney Metropolitan Region (2005) for the National Trust of New South Wales.
16 Historical Services Department (1996) *The Wonder Pool*, Stanton Library, North Sydney, p. 14.
17 HA Kingsbury (1945) *Brief Early History of Kalgoorlie and Information Concerning the Swimming Pool*, Kalgoorlie Town Council, Kalgoorlie, WA, p. 35.
18 Noeline Duncan (2001) *At the Deep End: A Century of Goldfields Swimming*, Kalgoorlie Swimming Club, WA, p. 5.
19 *Kalgoorlie Miner*, 22 January 1938; *Daily News*, Western Australia, 13 August 1938. Cited in Kelly Aris, Erickson & Taylor

Consultants and Goldfield Architects (2002) *Lord Forrest Olympic Pool: Heritage Assessment and Conservation Plan*, City of Kalgoorlie-Boulder, Kalgoorlie, WA, p. 16.

20 Kelly Aris, Erickson & Taylor Consultants and Goldfield Architects (2002) *Lord Forrest Olympic Pool: Heritage Assessment and Conservation Plan*, City of Kalgoorlie-Boulder, Kalgoorlie, WA, p. 53.

21 ibid., p. 9.

22 ibid., p. 11.

23 Lavinia Woods (1992) *Brisbane City Council Swimming Pools: The Next Twenty Years*, Brisbane City Council.

24 Dalby Swimming Pool Complex, entry to the Queensland Heritage Register, Place ID 602564, viewed January 2009; <www.epa.qld.gov.au>.

25 Catherine Reichert (2007) *The Footscray Pool*, Footscray Historical Society, Melbourne, pp. 6–13.

26 *Argus*, 23 February 1938, p. 4.

27 See, for example, HS Wootton to Town Clerk, Footscray, 1 July 1937, in AE Shepherd, 'Report on Public Swimming Baths', dated 23 October 1944, in VPRS8291/P0001/112; Ian McDonald, City Surveyor, City of Geelong, to AH Munro, City Engineer, Footscray, 28 January 1937, in VPRS8291/P0001/112, Public Record Office of Victoria.

28 DW Bonar, City Surveyor, to Town Clerk, Footscray, 16 December 1943, in VPRS8291/P0001/140, Public Record Office of Victoria.

29 Town Clerk, Richmond, to Town Clerk, Footscray, 21 December 1943, in VPRS8291/P0001/140, Public Record Office of Victoria.

30 *Argus*, 26 February 1935, p. 13.

31 Shepherd, 'Report on public swimming baths', p. 1.

32 ibid., p. 3.

33 *Argus*, 2 November 1932, p. 5.

34 ibid., 19 June 1928, p. 16.

35 *Parliamentary Debates*, Legislative Assembly, Victoria (1954) 245: 2218.

36 *Parliamentary Debates*, Legislative Assembly, Victoria (1956) 248: 3317; *Parliamentary Debates*, Legislative Assembly, Victoria (1955) 246: 25.

37 An exception was noted for the town of Derby where it had been decided that coastal waters presented unsuitable conditions.

38 *Hansard Parliamentary Records* (1960) 261: 387; *Hansard* (15 September 1959) 258: 189.

39 'Municipal swimming centre at Richmond, NSW' *Constructional Review* (1964) 37: 15.

40 Merle Field (1962) 'The history of the swimming facilities (baths and pools) of Western Australia', Honours thesis, University of Western Australia, p. 39.

41 *Hansard Parliamentary Records* (1958) 149: 2667.

42 Hannah Lewi (2008) 'Modern pools: The triumph of the artificial', in Ann Stephen, Philip Goad & Andrew McNamara (eds) *Modern Times: The Untold Story of Modernism in Australia*, Miegunyah Press, Melbourne, p. 83.

43 Andrew Whittaker (2006) 'From where to here?', conference presentation, Melbourne. See Ian McShane (June 2009) 'The past and the future of local swimming pools', *Journal of Australian Studies*, 33(2): 195–208.

44 Alex Roberts (July 2006) 'Pool politics: The emergence of a distinctive swimming pool culture in suburban Sydney, 1945–1972', Australian Historical Association, Biennial Conference, Canberra.

45 Panayotis Tournikiotis (2003) 'Rethinking the body: Sport and modern architecture', in Panayotis Tournikiotis (ed.) *The Body, Sport and Modern Architecture*, Future Publications, Athens, p. 33.

46 'Open air swimming pools', *Constructional Review* (October 1960): 20.

47 'Playland for swimmers', *Australian Architecture Today* (July 1960): 29–30.

48 'Folded plate concrete roof at Auburn Swimming Centre', *Constructional Review* (November 1959): 32.

49 The Centenary Pool in Brisbane was opened by the Governor of Queensland, Sir Henry Abel Smith, on 25 November 1959. This speech was reproduced in the pool's opening report: *Centenary Pool* (1959) Brisbane City Council.

50 Conrad Hamann (2006) 'Harold Holt Memorial Swimming Centre', in Doug Evans (ed.) *Kevin Borland: Architecture from the Heart*, RMIT Publishing, Melbourne, p. 167.

51 'Baths', *Architecture in Australia* (October 1969): 813–17.

52 Helen Stitt, interview with Daryl Jackson, 22 June 2009.

53 TD Jaques & GR Pavia (1976) 'The Australian government and sport', in Jaques & Pavia (eds) *Sport in Australia*, p. 154.

54 ibid., p. 155.

55 Nicholas Brown (1995) *Governing Prosperity: Social Change and Social Analysis in Australia in the 1950s*, Cambridge University Press, New York, p. 129.

56 Philip Perkins (1971) *Swimming Pools: A Treatise on the Planning, Layout, Design and Construction, Water Treatment and Other Services, Maintenance and Repairs*, Applied Science Publishers, London.

57 *Alternative Swimming Facilities* (1978) Report by Department of Youth Sport and Recreation, Melbourne.

58 ibid.

59 Helen Stitt, interview with Daryl Jackson, 22 June 2009.

60 Reichert, *The Footscray Pool*, p. 6.

61 For instance a local government survey conducted in 1972–73 ranked swimming clearly ahead of other organised

sporting activities in terms of participation rates.

62 DG Watkins et al. (1972–73) 'Recreation in Australia: An inquiry into the present patterns of participation in recreation: KEW', Commonwealth Department of the Environment. See also Sally Methven (1989) 'Recreation planning and the provision of swimming pools', PhD thesis, Department of Geography, University of Adelaide, p. 305.

Chapter 6 – Lawn Bowls: A Community Game

1 Robin Boyd (1967) *Artificial Australia*, The Boyer Lectures 1967, Australian Broadcasting Commission, Sydney, pp. 24–25.

2 Joan Lawrence & Catherine Warne (1995) *Balmain to Glebe: The Leichhardt Municipality*, Sydney.

3 The Fremantle Club, for instance, is the second oldest in Western Australia and opened in 1896.

4 Although two-thirds of Australians still opposed sports being held on Sundays in the late 1940s. Tony Ward (2009) 'Changing times 1960–75', *Soccer & Society*, 10(5): 648.

5 Leo Gamble (2003) *Mentone Through the Years*, Leo Gamble, Melbourne.

6 Brenda Llewellyn (1997) *A History of Earlwood Social and Bowling Club*, Earlwood & Bardwell Park RSL, NSW.

7 *Nambour Chronicle*, 9 June 1933.

8 Australia also came to dominate international bowling competitions that flourished in Commonwealth countries from the 1970s onwards, with an estimated half the world's bowlers said to be Australian. See also Anthony Sibillin (2008) 'New ball game', *Business Review Weekly* (18–24 September): 16.

9 Linda Heuser (January 2005) 'We're not too old to play sports: The career of women lawn bowlers', *Leisure Studies*, 24(1): 49.

10 Susan Reidy (2001) 'Something for everyone: How recreation and sport bowled into the Australian garden', in Georgina Whitehead (ed.) *Planting the Nation*, Australian Garden History Society, Melbourne, pp. 61–74.

11 Nan Hesse Dreher (1993) 'Public parks in urban Britain, 1870–1920: Creating a new public culture', PhD thesis, University of Pennsylvania, p. 117.

12 In contrast to England where wartime greatly affected the use of public parks, many amenities were given over to military training, the growing of food, or the controversial reclamation of children's playgrounds, and fees were charged to cover scarce maintenance labour. See Dreher, 'Public parks in urban Britain', p. 343.

13 Reidy, 'Something for everyone', p. 62; E Howard (1956) *Garden Cities of Tomorrow*, Faber and Faber, London, p. 84.

14 Christine Garnaut (2000) 'Towards metropolitan organisation: Town planning and the garden city idea', in Stephen Hamnett & Robert Freestone (eds) *The Australian Metropolis: A Planning History*, Allen & Unwin, Sydney, p. 54.

15 Peter Freeman (March 2005) Canberra Croquet Club Assessment Plan, Canberra Croquet Club, Yarralumla, ACT. Conservation Statement, Peter Freeman & Robert Boden.

16 Howard, *Garden Cities of Tomorrow*, p. 85.

17 Reidy, 'Something for everyone', p. 62.

18 John Bale (1994) *Landscapes of Modern Sport*, Leicester University Press, New York, p. 101.

19 Llewellyn, *A History of Earlwood Social and Bowling Club*, p. 8.

20 DG Bowd (1981) *Windsor Bowling Club, 50 Years Golden Anniversary, 1931–1981*, Windsor Bowling Club, Vic., p. 9.

21 Barbara Van Der Broek (May 1993) 'How to conserve parks of heritage significance', in *Urban Parks of Heritage Significance*, National Trust of Australia, Sydney, p. 8.

22 Many clubs assisted with, and took pride in, the maintenance of their gardened and bush surrounds, as in the case of the Mansfield Club.

23 Allan Shephard (1948) *The Story of Petersham 1793–1948*, The Council of the Municipality of Petersham, NSW, p. 137. Newspaper clippings from archive, Petersham Bowling Club.

24 Milo Dunphy (January–March 1956) *Architecture in Australia*: 34.

25 Peter Watson (1994) *55 Years: A History of Camden Bowling Club*, Camden Bowling Club, NSW, p. 10.

26 ibid., p. 23.

27 Helen Arrowsmith (ed.) (1988) *WALBA Inaugural History of Western Australian Clubs*, A Bicentennial Project, Perth.

28 John Briggs (2007) *Hawthorn Bowling Club Pavilion, 1 Wood Street, Hawthorn: Heritage Report.* For the City of Boroondara, Vic. p. 7.

29 Ward, 'Changing times 1960–75', p. 655.

30 'A Canterbury Women's Bowling Club Silver Jubilee', *Western Suburbs Courier*, 13 March 1953, p. 4.

31 Llewellyn, *A History of Earlwood Social and Bowling Club*, p. 27.

32 Graham Morton (1992) *Roll Back the Years: A Review of the History of Lawn Bowls and the Nambour Bowls Club*, Nambour, Qld, p. 79.

33 Robin Boyd (1960) *The Australian Ugliness*, FW Cheshire, Melbourne.

34 The Broome Bowling Club was rehoused in a decommissioned wireless station, constructed by the Postmaster General's Department in 1913. Heritage Council of Western Australia (1998) *The Broome Bowling Club Register of Heritage Places Assessment Documentation.*

35 Ward, 'Changing times 1960–75', p. 655; Heritage Council of Western Australia: Register of Heritage Places – Assessment Documentation, Coolgardie Bowling Pavilion, compiled 14 February 2003.

36 The Town Improvement Association wanted to lease part of the park for a bowling green in 1930 and by 1953 a clubhouse was built. The architect was TW Hodgson. See Bowd, *Windsor Bowling Club*, p. 9.
37 'Prahran Bowling Club, Leslie M Perrott & Partners' (March 1962) *Architecture in Australia*: 114.
38 See *Cross-Section* 72 (October 1958) & 101 (March 1961), *Cross-Section* Archive, Architecture Library, University of Melbourne.
39 'Latest extensions making history', *The Bankstown-Canterbury Torch*, 19 November 1980, Campsie Library Local History Archives, .
40 '50 years celebrated', *The Bankstown-Canterbury Torch*, 16 November 1983, Campsie Library Local History Archives.
41 'Club's closure – end of an era', *The Bankstown-Canterbury Torch*, 8 August 1984, Campsie Library Local History Archives.
42 Eric Kirk (1984) *Green Years: Maffra Bowls Club 1921–1983*, Maffra and District Historical Society, Maffra, Vic.
43 *Live and Prosper: A Record of Progress in Rochester and District* (1954) The Rochester Centenary Celebrations Committee, Rochester, Vic.
44 Arrowsmith (ed.) *WALBA Inaugural History*, p. 80.
45 Peter Morton (1989) *Fire Across the Desert*, Australian Government Publishing Service, Canberra, p. 249.
46 Helen Stitt (2004) 'A history of the Victorian Railway Institute', unpublished report, School of Historical Studies, Faculty of Arts, University of Melbourne, p. 13.
47 Bertram Hutchinson (1954) *Old People in a Modern Australian Community*, Melbourne University Press, p. 77.
48 EH Way (1977) *History of the Fitzroy Bowling Club*, Fitzroy Bowling Club, Melbourne, pp. 9, 16.
49 *Gosford City Bowling Club: 50 Years 1932–1982* (1983) Gosford City Bowling Club, NSW, p. 9.
50 'Blood, sweat and tears', *Canterbury-Bankstown Express*, 8 June 1994, Campsie Library Local History Archives.
51 Take as one example the Dalkeith Ladies Bowling Club, situated in one of Perth's wealthiest suburbs, unique in being one of only two women-only clubs that had complete autonomy and control over their development and finances. Greens were originally developed on land rented from the Nedlands Road Board, but by 1980 the Nedlands Council withdrew its subsidy of half the cost of the green's maintenance (at that time $6000) and the Ladies Club was amalgamated with the mixed Dalkeith and Nedlands clubs.
52 'Battle for bowlers: Women recall history', *Canterbury-Bankstown Express*, 25 June 1986, Campsie Library Local History Archives.
53 Robert D Putman (2000) *Bowling Alone: The Collapse and Revival of American Community*, Simon & Schuster, New York, p. 111.
54 'Battle for bowlers'.
55 Heuser, 'We're not too old to play sports', p. 55.
56 ibid., p. 58.
57 From anecdotal evidence and comments gathered through other studies and local newspapers.
58 Nicole Guihot, 'Lack of help bowls ladies', *Canterbury-Bankstown Express*, 29 June 1993, p. 1.
59 Heuser, 'We're not too old to play sports', p. 58.
60 ibid., p. 51.
61 Australian Sports Commission, viewed 25 November 2009; <www.ausport.gov.au/supporting/membergrowth/lawn_bowls>.
62 Media release by the Victorian Minister for Sport and Recreation, 21 January 2009, viewed 16 September 2009; <www.premier.vic.gov.au>.
63 Funding towards the maintenance of grassed greens through water cartage and recycling schemes, and in some cases the installation of synthetic turf. Some clubs, such as Seaford Bowls Club in Victoria, have taken their own action through club levies to develop recycling systems to avoid summer watering restrictions.
64 'No rain stops play', *The Sports Factor*, 19 March 2004, ABC Radio National.

Chapter 7 – The Community Can Do It! Planning for the New Civic Centre

1 Australian Broadcasting Commission (1945) *The Community Can Do It. Make a Plan*, The Commission, Sydney, p. 5.
2 F Heath (1941) *Report on the Future Swan Hill*, p. 10, Blyth and Josephine Johnson Papers, State Library of Victoria.
3 See N Brown (1995) *Governing Prosperity: Social Change and Social Analysis in Australia in the 1950s*, Cambridge University Press, Melbourne, for discussions of planning and understandings of community in the 1950s.
4 HC Coombs (4 December 1942) 'Seven million pairs of hands', transcript of a talk given on radio 3AR, Series SP300/1, Box 7, Australian Archives (NSW). Reproduced in Michael Cathcart & Kate Darian-Smith (eds) (2004) *Stirring Australian Speeches: The Definitive Collection from Botany to Bali*, Melbourne University Press, pp. 195–200.
5 See official histories of the government during wartime: P Hasluck (1952) *The Government and the People 1939–41*, Australian War Memorial, Canberra, and P Hasluck (1970) *The Government and the People, 1943–45*, Australian War

Memorial, Canberra.

6 K Darian-Smith (2009) *On the Home Front: Melbourne in Wartime 1939–1945,* 2nd edn, Melbourne University Press, Parkville, pp. 83–115.

7 *Argus*, 7 February 1941, p. 4.

8 E Gibson (1997) *Bag-Huts, Bombs and Bureaucrats: A History of the Impact of Town Planning and Compulsory Land Acquisition on the Town and People of Darwin 1937–50,* Historical Society of the Northern Territory, Darwin, p. 44.

9 H Burton (March 1943) 'Principles for post-war policy', *The Australian Quarterly*: 33.

10 *Argus*, 17 October 1944, p. 9; 28 October 1944, p. 6; *Australian Women's Weekly*, 27 March 1943, p. 18.

11 G Johns (December 1978) 'Building a suburb: The Peter Lalor Home Building Co-operative Society', *Melbourne State College Occasional Papers*, 1(2): 1–28.

12 Although as early as 1937 the Victorian Playgrounds Association was advocating a multi-service 'community centre' comprising a baby health centre, library, playground and sports ground, to be housed in the Malvern mansion Stonnington. *Argus*, 26 November 1937, p. 4.

13 [British] Ministry of Education (1945) *Community Centres*, His Majesty's Stationery Office, London, p. 27.

14 See the Department of Post-War Reconstruction, *Wartime Housing bulletins*, published between 1944 and 1945, and later collected in the volume *Australian Housing Bulletins 1–7* (1947) Department of Works & Housing, Melbourne. See also W Bunning (1945) *Homes in the Sun*, WJ Nesbit, Sydney, p. 82, note 146, for a list of relevant British Acts.

15 Seymour Shire Council and Ratepayers (nd) *Seymour: Your Town*, Vic., p. 3.

16 B Lowden (2010) *Mechanics' Institutes, Schools of Arts, Athenaeums, etc: An Australian Checklist*, 3rd edn, Lowden Publishing, Melbourne.

17 MA Dean (1983) *North Melbourne Free Library and Mechanics' Institute 1880–1956*, Melbourne City Libraries, North Melbourne, p. 3.

18 *Fifty Years History of the Town of Kensington and Norwood: July 1853 to July 1903* (1903) Webb & Son, p. 145.

19 Dean, *North Melbourne Free Library*, pp. 19–20.

20 AJ McIntyre & JJ McIntyre (1944) *Country Towns of Victoria*, Melbourne University Press in assoc. with Oxford University Press, Melbourne, pp. 192, 208.

21 *Kew Advertiser*, 12 May 1927, p. 1.

22 See 'Smith, Christopher (Chris) Arthur', *Architects of South Australia*, University of South Australia, Adelaide, viewed 29 March 2010; <www.architectsdatabase.unisa.edu.au/arch_full.asp?Arch_ID=39>.

23 KW Rathbone (2007) *From White Gum Flat to the Suburb of Rockdale*, publisher unknown, p. 46.

24 Helen Coulson (1950) *Horsham Centenary Souvenir Booklet: One Hundred Years of Progress*, Executive Council of Centenary Celebrations, Horsham, Vic., p. 31.

25 'Maitland town hall: Formal handing-over ceremony', *Maitland Watch*, 19 April 1940, p. 4.

26 See Elfrida Jensen (1969) *Barossan Foundations*, Nuriootpa War Memorial Community Centre, SA, chapter 14.

27 GV Portus (1944) 'The significance of Nuripoota to Australia', in *A Township Starts to Live: The Valley of Barossa, South Australia's New Community*, Common Cause, Adelaide, p. 31.

28 L Laybourne-Smith (1944) 'The Nuriootpa Community Centre: An architect's plans', in *A Township Starts to Live*, p. 35.

29 ibid., p. 33.

30 Australian Broadcasting Commission, *The Community Can Do It*, p. 70.

31 *The Shepparton Plan* (1946) Shepparton Borough Council and Shepparton *Advertiser*, Vic., p. 6.

32 ibid., p. 5.

33 ibid.

34 ibid., p. 24.

35 Australian Broadcasting Commission, *The Community Can Do It*, p. 30.

36 Community Centre Planning Committee (1944) *Community Centres*, National Fitness Council of New South Wales, Sydney, p. 1.

37 HH Smith (October 1947) 'An experiment in democratic town planning: The Springwood town plan', *Architecture*: 14–18.

38 ibid., p. 17.

39 ibid., p. 18.

40 KM Gordon (1943) *Community Centres*, LF Johnston, Canberra, p. 4.

41 ibid., p. 19.

42 R Windeyer (March 1945) 'Community centres', *Australian Quarterly* 17(1): 69.

43 L Hancox (September 1946) 'Why not community centres as war memorials?', *Argus Week-End Magazine*, p. 6.

44 K Inglis (2008) *Sacred Places: War Memorials in the Australian Landscape*, 3rd edn, Melbourne University Press.

45 'Living war memorial' (nd), *Examiner Press*, Launceston, Tas. CHS9 Community History Collection, Queen Victoria Museum and Art Gallery, Launceston.

46 *A Report of a Proposed Community Centre* (1944) City of Footscray, Melbourne, p. 5.

47 ibid., p. 6.

48 ibid., p. 10.

49 ibid., pp. 7, 10.

50 C Garnaut, I Iwanicki & R Freestone (2007) 'Modernism in the desert: The planning and design of Woomera Village 1947–1967', in *Panorama to Paradise: Proceedings of the XXIVth International Conference of the Society of Architectural Historians, Australia and New Zealand*, 21–24 September, Adelaide, pp. 1–16.

51 'Mayor's speech at opening of Shepparton's Civic Centre', MS page 3, 'Civic Centre Opening' folder, V/RS/020/01/05, Public Record Office of Victoria.

52 ibid.

53 See 'Fraser, James Reay (Jim)', *Australian Dictionary of Biography*, viewed 29 March 2010; <www.adb.online.anu.edu.au/biogs/A140714b.htm>.

54 ibid.

55 *Canberra Times*, 16 May 1950, p. 4.

56 ibid., 23 January 1950, p. 3.

57 Parents' and Citizens' Association of Beaumaris (1959) *Development in Beaumaris*, Melbourne.

58 R Ward (February 1959) 'To live in Brighton – 2059 AD', *Know Your City*, Southern Cross, Melbourne, p. 7.

59 R Block (April 1969) 'Office landscaping: A new concept in office planning', *Architecture in Australia*: 293–98.

60 Chief Officer Management Group (1983) *Appraisal of Camberwell Civic Centre: Overview Report*, City of Camberwell, Vic.

61 For instance, L Richards (1990) *Nobody's Home: Dreams and Realities in a New Suburb*, Oxford University Press, Melbourne.

62 E Dean, C Boland & A Jamrozik (July 1998) *Neighbourhood Houses in Tasmania: A Study in Community Development and Self-Help*, SWRC Reports and Proceedings, no. 74, Social Welfare Research Centre, UNSW, Sydney, p. 17.

63 Dean, Boland & Jamrozik, *Neighbourhood Houses in Tasmania*, p. 20. Western Australia was not to develop its neighbourhood house movement until the 1980s.

64 Melanie Oppenheimer (June 2008) 'Voluntary action, social welfare and the Australian Assistance Plan in the 1970s', *Australian Historical Studies*, 39(2): 167–82.

65 Dean, Boland & Jamrozik, *Neighbourhood Houses in Tasmania*, p. 21.

66 H Kimberley (1988) 'Consciousness and culture: A study of neighbourhood houses and learning centres in Victoria', PhD thesis, Graduate School of Education, La Trobe University, p. 16.

67 ibid., p. 18.

68 M Permezel (2001) 'The practice of citizenship: Place, identity and the politics of participation in neighbourhood houses', PhD thesis, Faculty of Architecture, Building and Planning, University of Melbourne, p. 106.

69 ibid., p. 102.

70 S Pickersgill (May/June 2002) 'Marion', *Architecture Australia*: 30–37.

71 *Hume Leader*, 2 March 2010, p. 5.

72 Australian Broadcasting Commission, *The Community Can Do It*, p. 42.

Chapter 8 – Commemorating and Enhancing the Everyday

1 Tom Bass (1955) 'Sculpture and architecture', *Architecture in Australia*, 44(2): 51.

2 KS Inglis (1998) *Sacred Places: War Memorials in the Australian Landscape*, Melbourne University Press, pp. 135–38; Register of War Memorials in New South Wales, viewed June 2008; <www.warmemorialsnsw.asn.au/>.

3 Inglis, *Sacred Places*, pp. 135–38.

4 George Taylor (12 June 1919) *The Building Journal*: 45–60.

5 Inglis, *Sacred Places*, p. 131.

6 Politicians also found this new mode of commemoration an attractive tax option. See Inglis, *Sacred Places*, p. 132.

7 Sally Symonds (1982) *Healesville: History in the Hills*, Pioneer Design Studio, Lilydale, Vic., pp. 96–97.

8 AG Turner (1936) *Swan Hill 1836–1936: The First Hundred Years*, Verona Press, Melbourne, p. 26.

9 Nicholas Brown (1995) *Governing Prosperity: Social Change and Social Analysis in Australia in the 1950s*, Cambridge University Press, p. 155.

10 Inglis, *Sacred Places*, p. 334.

11 M Ryan (ed.) (1979) *Lismore: The Story of a North Coast City*, Currawong Press, Sydney, p. 53.

12 Unnamed MS (1965) Launceston War Memorial Community Centre Association 20th Anniversary Cavalcade, Launceston War Memorial Community Centre Association archive, Launceston Community History Collection.

13 Peter Synan (1994) *City of Sale*, Sale, Vic., p. 223.

14 *The Miners Advocate*, 14 May 1949, p. 2.

15 Cynthia Hunter et al. (January 2003) *Newcastle Civic Centre and Cultural Precinct History Report*, Newcastle City Council, pp. 38–45. <www.ncc.nsw.gov.au/__data/assets/pdf_file/.../civichistory_pre1920.pdf>

16 Barry Maitland & David Stafford (1997) *Architecture Newcastle*, Royal Australian Institute of Architects, Newcastle, p. 24.

17 AE Hermann (2002) 'Floating and public baths', Developments of Rockhampton and District, Book 1, Central Queensland Family History Association, pp. 179–89.

18 Ian Maroske (1991) *Warracknabeal: A Municipal History 1861–1991*, Maryborough Printers, Vic., pp. 110–18.
19 Many other memorial pools can be found across New South Wales. For example, the Narrabri Memorial Pool (1958) included a clock tower erected in memory of the people of the Narrabri district who died in the Great War; Blacktown Memorial Swimming Pool; Tumut War Memorial Olympic Swimming Pool (1962); Moss Vale War Memorial Swimming Pool (1965); Port Macquarie War Memorial Swimming Baths and Braidwood War Memorial Swimming Pool both opened in 1966; Darlington Point War Memorial Swimming Pool (1971) and the Queanbeyan Memorial Swimming Pool, designed by Robert Warren (1960). Examples in other states include Rutherglen War Memorial Swimming Pool in Victoria; York Memorial Swimming Pool in Western Australia.
20 The pool memorial stone is dedicated as follows: 'To the sacred memory of fallen comrades who served with the Navy, Army, and Air Force during the memorial siege of Tobruk, Western Desert, Great War II, from April 9, 1941 to December 13, 1941. We shall remember them.'
21 John Patrick with Allom Lovell & Associates (2004) *Edinburgh Gardens, Brunswick Street North Fitzroy Conservation Management Plan*, City of Yarra, Melbourne, p. 48.
22 CEW Bean (1969) John Murtagh Macrossen lecture, Queensland University, Brisbane; Inglis, *Sacred Places*, p. 335.
23 'A medical centre war memorial for Melbourne', *Argus*, 28 October 1944, discussed the idea that an institute for sick and disabled children be designated a war memorial.
24 Rosemary Kerr (1994) *A History of the Kindergarten Union of Western Australia, 1911–1973*, Meerilinga Young Children's Foundation, Perth, p. 97.
25 Janice Newton, Karen Leadbeater Phillips & Paula Herlihy (1985) *Tracks to Trails: A History of Mt Evelyn*, Mt Evelyn History Group, University of Ballarat, Vic., p. 89.
26 *Argus*, 28 March 1945, p. 8.
27 Maroske, *Warracknabeal*, p. 143.
28 *Architecture* (January–March 1944): 10.
29 ibid., pp. 10–11.
30 See Brown, *Governing Prosperity*, p. 162.
31 See Margaret Garlake (1998) *New Art, New World: British Art in Postwar Society*, Yale University Press, New Haven & London.
32 Lewis Mumford, 'The death of the monument', in JL Martin, Ben Nicholson & Naum Gabo (eds) (1971 [1937]) *Circle International Survey of Constructive Art*, Faber and Faber, London, pp. 263–70.
33 Garlake, *New Art, New World*, p. 215.
34 ibid., p. 213.
35 ibid., p. 215.
36 Margaret Garlake (2003) 'Moore's ecclecticism: Difference, aesthetic identity and community in the architectural commissions 1938–58', in Jane Beckett & Fiona Russell (eds) *Henry Moore Critical Essays*, Ashgate, Aldershot, UK, p. 178.
37 Moore echoed Herbert Read in a speech to a UNESCO conference in 1946 when he stated that sculpture is above all a public art. See Herbert Read in Henry Moore (1966) *Henry Moore: Mother and Child*, New York American Library by arrangement with UNESCO. See also Herbert Read (1966) *Henry Moore: A Study of His Life and Work*, Praeger, New York, p. 7.
38 Garlake, 'Moore's ecclecticism', p. 179.
39 Tom Heath (September 1959) 'Public art and the developer', *Architecture in Australia*: 103.
40 *Architecture* (January 1950): ii.
41 Lenton Parr (May 1963) 'Sculpture in Australia since 1945', *Art and Architecture*: 21.
42 Transcript of interview between Margel Hinder and Esther Corellis (1972), held in Newcastle Regional Art Gallery.
43 Carol Aranovici (1944) 'Civic art', in Paul Zucker (ed.) *New Architecture and City Planning*, Philosophical Library, New York, p. 369. Civic art is defined as 'a synthesis of a wide range of the arts and art forms which embody the elements of creative communal living in harmony with the realities of practical functioning'. It was asserted for instance that the Victorian Sculptors Society annual show was testament to Melbourne sculptors and architects not merely paying lip-service to the complementary notion of the allied arts, but trying to make a real working liaison. See Ian Bow (November 1955) 'Art column', *Architecture and Arts*: 54.
44 Clem Meadmore (December 1962) 'Location of sculpture in the man-made environment', *Architecture in Australia*: 114–18.
45 Douglas Annand (April 1949) 'Mural painting', *Architecture*: 40.
46 Lenton Parr (July 1963) 'Sculpture in the urban environment', *Australian Planning Institute Journal*: 181–83.
47 Parr, 'Sculpture in Australia', p. 21.
48 David Saunders (September 1966) 'Sculptors, architects and the Centre Five Group', *Art and Australia*, 4(2): 129–35.
49 Peter Gelencser (September 1967) 'Architecture and sculpture', *The Architect* WA: 52–54.
50 'If he is to enrich the society in which he lives the artist must recognise as his patron and serve, not the rich individual, the uncommonly privileged, but the mass of his fellow-citizens, equally capable of providing patronage through their communal organisations, clubs, societies, local bodies, unions, city councils, business houses, and through our Government itself.' R Haughton James (April 1949), '2% for Australian murals?', *Architecture*: 53.
51 The encouragement of a renewed public art funded through government schemes, and managed through public

boards became implicated in new political ideals. For example, in 1956 the London County Council, advised by the Arts Council, embarked on a wider program to embellish its key properties with works of art. The results of this initiative further contributed to debates on public art and architecture. See Garlake, 'Moore's eclecticism', p. 216.

52 Sara Selwood (1996) *The Benefits of Public Art: The Polemics of Permanent Art in Public Places*, PSI Publishing, London, p. 31.

53 Lisanne Gibson (2001) *The Use of Art: Constructing Australian Identities*, University of Queensland Press, Brisbane, p. 49.

54 Hunter et al., *Newcastle Civic Centre*, p. 40.

55 Tom Bass (1996) *Totem Maker*, Australian Scholarly Publishing, Melbourne, p. xi.

56 ACT Heritage Register, Entry 1007, Ethos Statue.

57 Bass, *Totem Maker*, p. 68.

58 Beryl Henderson (ed.) (1988) *Monuments and Memorials*, Royal Australian Historical Society Register, Sydney, p. 5.

59 Alan Ingham, viewed February 2009; <http:/alaningham.com/index.php?option=com_frontpage&Itemid=28>.

60 Margo Hoeskstra & Genevieve Carson (2007) 'Totemic public sculpture', *Craft Arts International*, 70: 61–65.

61 Karen O'Connor (1989) *Our Babies: The State's Best Asset. A History of 75 Years of Baby Health Services in New South Wales*, NSW Health Department, Sydney, p. 75.

62 For a recent comprehensive study of Margaret Priest, see Philippa O'Brien (2009) *Margaret Priest: An Artist's Life*, Fremantle Arts Centre Press, WA, p. 97.

63 For a study of Kings Park memorials, see Hannah Lewi (2000) 'The commemorative anatomy of a park', in Jan Birksted (ed.), *Landscapes of Memory and Experience*, Spon Press, New York, pp. 9–30.

64 Bass, *Totem Maker*, p. 52; Moore, *Henry Moore*, p. 24.

65 Hughes, in contrast, championed Robert Klippel's sculpture of this period. Robert Hughes (May 1964) 'Robert Klippel', *Art and Australia*, 2(1): 18.

66 Graeme Sturgeon (1978) *The Development of Australian Sculpture 1788–1975*, Thames & Hudson, London, pp. 156–57.

67 Alan Powers (1996) 'A zebra at the Villa Savoye ...', in Neil Bingham (ed.) *The Modern House Revisited*, Twentieth Century Society, London, pp. 15–26. Other commentators have quite different formal interpretations and have explained this relationship between the universal figure and architecture as another technique in the endeavour to modernise the language of classicism.

68 Clem Meadmore (December 1962) 'Location of sculpture in the man-made environment', *Architecture in Australia*: 115.

69 Garlake, 'Moore's ecclecticism', p.178.

70 Harry Seidler (October 1940) 'Painting toward architecture', *Architecture*: 119–20.

71 This concept of play and *homo ludens* is a theme in Sarah Goldhagen & Rèjean Legault (2000) *Anxious Modernisms: Experimentation in Postwar Architectural Culture*, Canadian Centre for Architecture & MIT Press, Cambridge, Mass., p. 18. See also Johan Huizinga (1938) *Homo Ludens: A Study of the Play-Element in Culture*, Haarlem.

72 G Whitlam (1975) 'Leisure: A new perspective', in *Leisure – A New Perspective, Papers Presented at a National Seminar in Canberra*, Australian Government Publishing Service, Canberra, pp. 22–24.

73 Dirk Bolt, email correspondence with Philip Goad & Hannah Lewi, November 2009. In addition to the decorative concrete panels, the linear pavilion was to include balconies adorned with flower boxes and a restaurant on the upper deck to further add colour and animation. These elements were never built.

74 GE Kidder Smith (1949) *Sweden Builds*, Architectural Press, London, p. 225.

75 Kenneth McDonald (August–September 1958) 'Architecture and Arts presents 170 years of architecture in Australia 1788–1958', *Architecture and Arts*: 52.

76 'Apart from the large maintenance costs of any murals other than permanent mosaic, there is no evidence to suggest that anyone, here at any rate, can produce murals with a message on sport that would not date alarmingly and be repulsive to both sport lovers and those indifferent to physical prowess.' These comments were made in relation to the Melbourne Cricket Ground by Ian Bow (July 1956) 'Murals without message', *Architecture and Arts*: 31.

77 Tom Heath (March 1962) 'Three fountains – Sydney', *Architecture in Australia*: 124–25.

78 Luke Morgan (2008) 'Abstract fountains', in A Stephen, P Goad & A McNamara (eds) *Modern Times*, Miegunyah Press & Powerhouse, Melbourne & Sydney, p. 40.

79 Peter Laverty (January–March 1997) *Artemis*: 1. See also Morgan, 'Abstract fountains', p. 38.

80 Michael Hedger (1995) *Public Sculpture in Australia*, Craftsman House Press, Sydney, p. 96.

81 'Art in use' (July 1955) *Architecture Review*, 118(703): 78.

82 Milo Dunphy (April 1961) 'Playground sculpture', *Architecture in Australia*: 45.

83 The most striking evidence of this impact occurred at a nondescript outback primary school in Papunya, a settlement outside Alice Springs, in 1971. White art teacher Geoff Bardon initiated the painting of a mural of Aboriginal design on the external walls of the school, a project which was soon taken over by male elders. The resulting 'Honey Ant' mural, long since destroyed, is now recognised as the historic beginning of the Aboriginal acrylic painting movement, which went on to become a massive global success from the 1980s. See Paul Carter (2004) 'Introduction: The interpretation of dreams', in Geoffrey Bardon & James Bardon, *Papunya: A Place Made After the Story. The Beginnings of the Western Desert Painting Movement*, Miegunyah Press, Melbourne, pp. xiv–xx.

84 Sandy Kirby (1991) 'An historical perspective on the community arts movement', in Vivienne Binns (ed.) *Community Arts: History, Theory, Practice*, Pluto Press, Sydney, pp. 19–29.

85 Sandy Kirby (ed.) (1996) *Ian Burn: Art Critical, Political*, University of Western Sydney, p. 62.

86 For the US, see Eva Cockcroft, John Weber & James Cockcroft (1977) *Towards a People's Art: The Contemporary Mural Movement*, Dutton, New York, and David Greenberg, Kathryn Smith & Stuart Teacher (1977) *Megamurals and Supergraphics: Big Art*, Running Press, Philadelphia.

87 Information on Humphries and Monk and their mural projects mentioned in this section derives from <www.publicartsquad.com.au/Murals/body_murals.html>, viewed 7 January 2010; David Humphries & Rodney Monk (1982) *The Mural Manual: A Guide to Community Murals in Australia*, Arts Council of New South Wales, Division of Cultural Activities, NSW Premier's Department; and telephone conversations between David Humphries and Caroline Jordan, 6 January 2010; Geoff Hogg and Caroline Jordan, 7 January 2010.

88 Charles Merewether & Ann Stephen (eds) (1977) *The Great Divide 1977: An Ongoing Critique of Australian Culture Under Capitalism – Reviews of Oppositional Cultural Work and an Examination of Socialist Models*, privately published, Melbourne, pp. 85–88.

89 Discussion with Geoff Hogg and Suzy Pinchen by Caroline Jordan and Hannah Lewi, 5 December 2009.

Chapter 9 – Regenerating Communities: The 1970s and Beyond

1 Alan Stretton (1976) *The Furious Days: The Relief of Darwin*, Collins, Sydney, p. 196.

2 Report of the Darwin Reconstruction Commission (5 June 1975) *The Reconstruction of Darwin: A Report to the Minister for the Northern Territory in accordance with Section 9(2) of the* Darwin Reconstruction Act 1975, p. 8. A5915, 1861, 1975 Cabinet Records, National Archives of Australia, Canberra.

3 Bruce Juddery (1–7 March 1981) 'Study demolishes myths about Darwin disaster', *National Times*, pp. 20–21; Cities Commission (1975) *Planning Options for Future Darwin*, Australian Government Printing Service, Canberra, p. 14.

4 Barbara James, 'No man's land', in Bill Bunbury (1994) *Cyclone Tracy: Picking up the Pieces*, Fremantle Arts Centre Press, WA, p. 131.

5 Darwin Disaster Welfare Council (1976) *Final Report*, pp. 55–56.

6 On cultural commentary on the suburbs, see, for example, Sara Ferber, Chris Healy & Chris McAuliffe (eds) (1994) *Beasts of Suburbia: Reinterpreting Cultures in Australian Suburbs*, Melbourne University Press; and Graeme Davison, Tony Dingle & Seamus O'Hanlon (eds) (1995) *The Cream Brick Frontier: Histories of Australia Suburbia*, Monash University Publications in History, Melbourne.

7 Gough Whitlam (1985) *The Whitlam Government 1972–1975*, Penguin, Melbourne, pp. 182–83; quoted in Stuart Macintyre (2004) *A Concise History of Australia*, Cambridge University Press, pp. 235–36.

8 For instance, the Meerzicht Community Centre by Ton Alberts combined a community centre and services with 198 dwellings for the elderly; places and spaces between buildings were particularly accentuated to promote neighbourhood encounters and 'social traffic'. Martien de Vletter (2004) *The Critical Seventies: Architecture and Urban Planning in the Netherlands, 1968–1980*, NAI, Rotterdam, p. 54.

9 For discussions of the British Community Architecture movements, see Graham Towers (1995) *Buildings Democracy: Community Architecture in the Inner Cities*, UCL Press, London; and Nick Wates & Charles Knevitt (1987) *Community Architecture: How People Are Creating their Own Environment*, Penguin Books, London.

10 Prince Charles, fourth speech given to the building communities conference, 27 November 1986, in Charles Jencks (ed.) (1988) *Prince Charles and the Architects*, Academy Editions, London, pp. 45–46.

11 The influential study of looking at the 'street' is Robert Venturi, Denise Scott Brown & Steven Izenour, *Learning from Las Vegas: The Forgotten Symbolism of Architectural Form*, MIT Press, Cambridge, Mass.

12 'Soft Architecture' (April 1975) *Architecture in Australia*, student edn.

13 'Co-operative housing' (February 1971) *Architecture in Australia*, 61(1): 40–47; and 'The Hobart Co-op' (October 1973) *Architecture in Australia*, 62(5): 72.

14 RKH Johnson (December 1970) 'Suburbia in evolution: Community and privacy', *Architecture in Australia*, 59(6): 86. Serge Chermayeff & Christopher Alexander (1965) *Community and Privacy: Towards a New Architecture of Humanism*, Doubleday, Garden City, NY.

15 Jennifer Taylor (1990) *Australian Architecture Since 1960*, 2nd edn, National Education Division, Royal Australian Institute of Architects, Red Hill, ACT, p. 212.

16 'All Gough's children' (August/September 1977) *Architecture Australia*, 66(4): 67.

17 ibid., pp. 83–87.

18 Taylor, *Australian Architecture Since 1960*, p. 160.

19 ibid., pp. 160–62; and see *Architecture Australia* (1982) 71(3): 22–23.

20 Ian McDougall (January–February 2007) 'Radar Opinion: Why architecture matters 1', *Architecture Australia*, viewed 18 January 2010; <www.architecturemedia.com/aa/>.

21 Tim Harris (October 1997) 'Suburb with a past', *Age*. Port Melbourne Historical Society Garden City file.

22 Hassell Architects, viewed 18 May 2010; <www.hassell.com.au>; Melbourne Docklands, viewed 18 May 2010; <www.docklands.com.au>.

23 Lyn Richards (1990) *Nobody's Home: Dreams and Realities in a New Suburb*, Oxford University Press, Melbourne, p. 3.

24 ibid., p. 26.

25 ibid., p. 32.

26 Delfin (1999) *Mawson Lakes*, Delfin, Mawson Lakes, Vic., pp. 4–5.
27 Belinda Robson, *Building Lives, Building Community in Craigieburn and Roxburgh Park*, <www.mccaugheycentre.unimelb.edu.au/__data/assets/pdf_file/0007/156958/Building_Lives_Building_Community_Community_Report.pdf>, p. 9.
28 Hannah Lewi & David Nichols (August 2008) 'Caroline Springs', *Landscape*, 119: 46–48.
29 Delfin, *Mawson Lakes*, p. 4; 'New urbanites' (September 2003) *Urbano* 1: 4; Delfin (Autumn 2002) 'The 20 minute gourmet', *Living Options*: 10; Delfin (Autumn 2002) 'At home with the whole world', *Living Options*: 14.
30 Hamish Lyon (March–April 2010) 'DIY community', *Architecture Australia*: 35–37.
31 Shire of East Pilbara (November 2008) *Newman Tomorrow: Resourcing a Home for Generations.* <www.creatingcommunities.com.au/resources/NewmanTomorrow_excerpt.pdf>
32 ibid., p. 7.
33 Shire of Roebourne, Gegrafia in assoc. with CCS Strategic Management (January 2009) *Karratha 2020 Vision and Community Plan*, <www.roebourne.wa.gov.au/Assets/Documents/Karratha2020Report.pdf>, pp. 27–28.
34 Project Architect Brief (2009) *Karratha 2020 Vision and Community Plan*, p. 14.
35 Discussion between Hannah Lewi and Emma Williamson and Kieran Wong, CODA Architects, 29 November 2009.
36 Shire of East Pilbara, *Newman Tomorrow*, p. 16.
37 Martin Hook (June–July 2007) 'Community spirits', *Monument*, 79: 82–85.
38 Tom Griffiths (2009) '"An unnatural disaster"? Remembering and forgetting bushfire', *History Australia*, 6(2): 35.1–35.7, DOI: 10.2104/ha090035.
39 Neil Keene & Clementine Cuneo (8 January 2008) 'The people's pool – Closure defeated', *Daily Telegraph*, p. 11.
40 *Age*, 10 January 2007, p. 12.
41 *Sunday Age*, 27 December 2009, p. 8.
42 Ian McShane (November 2007) *Bringing in the Public: Arguments and Strategies for Renewing Community Infrastructure*, Building Communities Seminar Series, The Australian Centre, University of Melbourne, p. 8.
43 See, for example, Elizabeth Farrelly (20 December 2000) 'Let's clear the air over our city pools', *Sydney Morning Herald*, p. 12.
44 Richard Broome (1987) *Between Two Creeks*, Lothian Books, Melbourne, p. 38; 'Coburg could have new swim pool in two years' (13 November 1961) *Coburg Courier*, np; 'They call them the 1000 pound kids' (13 March 1962) *Coburg Courier*, np.
45 'Save Coburg Olympic Pool', viewed 6 March 2008; <www.savecoburgolympicpool.org/>. Discussion with Cate Hall, Kitty Owens, Janet Grigg and Hannah Lewi, 6 March 2008.
46 Leon Krier with Dhiru A Thadani & Peter J Hetzel (2009) *The Architecture of Community*, Island Press, Washington DC, p. 83.
47 Henri Lefebvre as cited by Mary McCleod (1997) 'Henri Lefebvre's critique of everyday life: An introduction', in Steven Harris & Deborah Berke (eds) *Architecture of the Everyday*, Princeton Architectural Press, New York, p. 19.

SELECT BIBLIOGRAPHY

Ailwood, Jo (ed.) (2007) *Early Childhood in Australia: Historical and Comparative Contexts*, Pearson SprintPrint, Sydney.

Arrowsmith, Helen (ed.) (1988) *WALBA Inaugural History of Western Australian Clubs*, A Bicentennial Project, Perth.

Australian Broadcasting Commission (1945) *The Community Can Do It. Make a Plan*, The Commission, Sydney.

Australian Housing Bulletins 1–7 (1947) Department of Works & Housing, Melbourne.

Bale, John (1994) *Landscapes of Modern Sport*, Leicester University Press, New York.

Balnaves, John (1966) *Australian Libraries*, FW Cheshire, Melbourne.

Banff, Peggy & Norma Ross (1998) *The Peppercorn Trail: The Story of the Creche and Kindergarten Association of Queensland and Its People 1907–1997*, Creche and Kindergarten Association of Queensland, Brisbane.

Bardon, Geoffrey & James Bardon (2004) *Papunya: A Place Made After the Story. The Beginnings of the Western Desert Painting Movement*, Miegunyah Press, Melbourne.

Bass, Tom (1996) *Totem Maker*, Australian Scholarly Publishing, Melbourne.

Beckett, Jane & Fiona Russell (eds) *Henry Moore Critical Essays*, Ashgate, Aldershot, UK.

Binns, Vivienne (ed.) (1991) *Community Arts: History, Theory, Practice*, Pluto Press, Sydney.

Birksted, Jan (ed.) (2000) *Landscapes of Memory and Experience*, Spon Press, New York.

Boas, Harold (July 1943) 'National planning and housing', *Architecture*, 32(3): 117–20.

Bowd, DG (1981) *Windsor Bowling Club, 50 Years Golden Anniversary, 1931–1981*, Windsor Bowling Club, NSW.

Bowman, Margaret (1976) *Local Government in the Australian States: An Urban Paper*, Department of Environment, Housing and Community Development, Canberra.

Boyd, Robin (1947) *Victorian Modern*, Victorian Architectural Students Society, Melbourne.

—— (1960) *The Australian Ugliness*, FW Cheshire, Melbourne.

—— (1963) *The New Architecture*, Longmans, Melbourne.

—— (1967) *Artificial Australia*, The Boyer Lectures 1967, Australian Broadcasting Commission, Sydney.

Broome, Richard (1987) *Between Two Creeks*, Lothian Books, Melbourne.

Brosterman, Norman (1997) *Inventing Kindergarten*, HN Abrams, New York.

Brown, Nicholas (1995) *Governing Prosperity: Social Change and Social Analysis in Australia in the 1950s*, Cambridge University Press, New York.

Bunbury, Bill (1994) *Cyclone Tracy: Picking up the Pieces*, Fremantle Arts Centre Press, WA.

Bunning, W (1945) *Homes in the Sun: The Past, Present and Future of Australian Housing*, WJ Nesbit, Sydney.

Burton, H (March 1943) 'Principles for post-war policy', *The Australian Quarterly*, 15(1): 33–42.

Butler-Bowden, Caroline & Charles Pickett (2007) *Homes in the Sky: Apartment Living in Australia*, Miegunyah Press in association with Historic Houses Trust, Melbourne.

Castells, Manuel (1987) *The Information Age: Economy, Society and Culture*, vol. 2, 'The Power of Identity', Blackwell, Malden, Mass.

Cathcart, Michael & Kate Darian-Smith (eds) (2004) *Stirring Australian Speeches: The Definitive Collection from Botany to Bali*, Melbourne University Press.

Charlton, Ken (ed.) (2007) *The Contribution of Enrico Taglietti to Canberra's Architecture*, ACT Chapter, Royal Australian Institute of Architects, Canberra.

Chermayeff, Serge & Christopher Alexander (1965) *Community and Privacy: Towards a New Architecture of Humanism*, Doubleday, Garden City, New York.

Cockcroft, Eva, John Weber & James Cockcroft (1977) *Towards a People's Art: The Contemporary Mural Movement*, Dutton, New York.

Collier, JDA (September 1945) 'Library development in Tasmania', *Australian Quarterly*, 17(3): 105–10.

Community Centre Planning Committee (1944) *Community Centres*, National Fitness Council of New South Wales, Sydney.

Costello, Frank (April 1943) 'Town planning in post-war development', *Architecture*, 32(2): 72–74.

Cuffley, Peter (1989) *Australian Houses of the '20s & '30s*, Five Mile Press, Melbourne.

—— (1993) *Australian Houses of the Forties and Fifties*, Five Mile Press, Melbourne.

Cumpston, JHL & CM Heinig (1945) *Pre-School Centres in Australia: Building, Equipment and Programme*, Commonwealth Department of Health, Canberra.

Curthoys, Ann (2002) *Freedom Ride: A Freedom Rider Remembers*, Allen & Unwin, Sydney.

Darian-Smith, Kate (2009) *On the Home Front: Melbourne in Wartime: 1939–1945*, 2nd edn, Melbourne University Press.

—— & Paula Hamilton (eds) (1994) *Memory and History in Twentieth-Century Australia*, Oxford University Press.

—— & J Willis (2007) 'A civic heart: Empowered citizenship and post-war public modernism', in S Loo & K Bartsch (eds) *Panorama to Paradise: Proceedings of the XXIVth International Conference of the Society of Architectural Historians, Australia and New Zealand*, 21–24 September, Adelaide, plus CD-ROM.

Davison, Graeme (November 1995) 'Australia: The first suburban nation', *Journal of Urban History*, 22(1): 40–75.

——, Tony Dingle & Seamus O'Hanlon (eds) (1995) *The Cream Brick Frontier: Histories of Australian Suburbia*, Monash University Publications in History, Melbourne.

Day, Graham (2006) *Community and Everyday Life*, Routledge, London.

Dean, E, C Boland & A Jamrozik (July 1998) *Neighbourhood Houses in Tasmania: A Study in Community Development and Self-Help*, SWRC Reports and Proceedings, no. 74, Social Welfare Research Centre, UNSW, Sydney.

de Martino, Stefano & Alex Wall (1988) *Cities of Childhood: Italian Colonie of the 1930s*, Architectural Association, London.

de Vletter, Martien (2004) *The Critical Seventies: Architecture and Urban Planning in the Netherlands, 1968–1980*, NAI, Rotterdam.

Dollery, Brian & Neil Marshall (eds) (1997) *Australian Local Government: Reform and Renewal*, Macmillan Education, South Melbourne.

Duncan, Noeline (2001) *At the Deep End: A Century of Goldfields Swimming, Kalgoorlie Swimming Club*, WA.

Dunning, Eric & Norbert Elias (1986) *Quest for Excitement*, Blackwell, Oxford & New York.

Dwork, Deborah (1987) *War is Good for Babies and Other Young Children: A History of the Infant and Child Welfare Movement in England 1898–1918*, Tavistock, London & New York.

Eathorne, Judy (1949) 'A brief survey of the development of baby health centres in Melbourne and the work of the travelling centres', BArch thesis, Faculty of Architecture, Building and Planning, University of Melbourne.

Edquist, Harriet (2008) *Pioneers of Modernism: The Arts and Crafts Movement in Australia*, Miegunyah Press, Melbourne.

Evans, Doug (ed.) (2006) *Kevin Borland: Architecture from the Heart*, RMIT Publishing, Melbourne.

Ferber, Sara, Chris Healy & Chris McAuliffe (eds) (1994) *Beasts of Suburbia: Reinterpreting Cultures in Australian Suburbs*, Melbourne University Press.

Fildes, Valerie, Lara Marks & Hilary Marland (eds) (1992) *Women and Children First: International Maternal and Infant Welfare, 1879–1945*, Routledge, London & New York.

Finch, Lynette (1998) 'Caring for colonial infants: Parenting on the frontiers', *Australian Historical Studies*, 29(110): 109–27.

Forty, Adrian (2000) *Words and Buildings: A Vocabulary of Modern Architecture*, Thames & Hudson, New York.

Frampton, Kenneth & Silvia Kolbowski (eds) (1982) *William Lescaze*, Rizzoli International, New York.

Gardiner, Lyndsay (1982) *The Free Kindergarten Union of Victoria, 1908–80*, Australian Council for Educational Research, Melbourne.

Garlake, Margaret (1998) *New Art, New World: British Art in Postwar Society*, Yale University Press, New Haven & London.

Garnaut, C, I Iwanicki & R Freestone (2007) 'Modernism in the desert: The planning and design of Woomera Village 1947–1967', in S Loo and K Bartsch (eds) *Panorama to Paradise: Proceedings of the XXIVth International Conference of the Society of Architectural Historians, Australia and New Zealand*, 21–24 September, Adelaide.

Gibson, E (1997) *Bag-Huts, Bombs and Bureaucrats: A History of the Impact of Town Planning and Compulsory Land Acquisition on the Town and People of Darwin 1937–50*, Historical Society of the Northern Territory, Darwin.

Gibson, Lisanne (2001) *The Use of Art: Constructing Australian Identities*, University of Queensland Press, Brisbane.

Glover, Anne (1993) *The Early Childhood Service Needs of Aboriginal Communities in the Northern Country Areas of South Australia*, Children's Services Office, Department of Education, Employment and Training, North Adelaide.

Goad, Philip (1997) 'One of the lost tribe: James Birrell and that other tradition', in A Wilson & J Macarthur (eds) *Birrell: Work from the Office of James Birrell*, NMBW Publications, Melbourne.

—— (2007) 'Laboratories for the body and mind: The architecture of the Lady Gowrie centres', in S Loo & K Bartsch (eds) *Panorama to Paradise: Proceedings of the XXIVth International Conference of the Society of Architectural Historians, Australia and New Zealand*, 21–24 September, Adelaide, plus CD-ROM.

Goldhagen, Sarah & Réjean Legault (2000) *Anxious Modernisms: Experimentation in Postwar Architectural Culture*, Canadian Centre for Architecture & MIT Press, Cambridge, Mass.

Gordon, KM (1943) *Community Centres*, LF Johnston, Canberra.

Greenberg, David, Kathryn Smith & Stuart Teacher (1977) *Megamurals and Supergraphics: Big Art*, Running Press, Philadelphia.

Griffiths, Tom (2009) '"An unnatural disaster"? Remembering and forgetting bushfire', *History Australia*, 6(2): 35.1–35.7, DOI: 10.2104/ha090035.

Gutman, Marta & Ning De Coninck-Smith (2008) *Designing Modern Childhoods: History, Space and the Material Culture of Children*, Rutgers University Press, New Brunswick, NJ.

Halpern, David (2005) *Social Capital*, Polity Press, Cambridge.

Hamnett, Stephen & Robert Freestone (eds) (2000) *The Australian Metropolis: A Planning History*, Allen & Unwin, Sydney.

Harris, Steven & Deborah Berke (eds) (1997) *Architecture of the Everyday*, Princeton Architectural Press, New York.

Hasluck, P (1952) *The Government and the People, 1939–41*, Australian War Memorial, Canberra.

—— (1970) *The Government and the People, 1943–45*, Australian War Memorial, Canberra.

Henderson, Beryl (ed.) (1988) *Monuments and Memorials*, Royal Australian Historical Society Register, Sydney.
Henningham, John (ed.) (1991) *Institutions in Australian Society*, Department of Journalism, University of Queensland, Brisbane.
Hibbins, GM (1984) *A History of the City of Springvale*, Springvale City Council, Melbourne.
Hobsbawm, Eric (1994) *Age of Extremes: The Short Twentieth Century 1914–1991*, Viking, New York.
Howard, E (1956) *Garden Cities of Tomorrow*, Faber and Faber, London.
Howe, Renate (ed.) (1988) *New Houses for Old: Fifty Years of Public Housing in Victoria, 1938–1988*, Ministry of Housing, Melbourne.
Hughes, Jody & Wendy Stone (2002) *Family Change and Community Life: Exploring the Links*, Australian Institute of Family Studies, Research Paper 32.
Huizinga, Johan (1938) *Homo Ludens: A Study of the Play-Element in Culture*, Haarlem.
Humphries, David & Rodney Monk (1982) *The Mural Manual: A Guide to Community Murals in Australia*, Arts Council of New South Wales, Division of Cultural Activities, New South Wales Premier's Department.
Hutchinson, Bertram (1954) *Old People in a Modern Australian Community*, Melbourne University Press.
Inglis, KS (1998) *Sacred Places: War Memorials in the Australian Landscape*, Melbourne University Press.
—— (2008) *Sacred Places: War Memorials in the Australian Landscape*, 3rd edn, Melbourne University Press.
Irving, Robert (ed.) (1985) *The History and Design of the Australian House*, Oxford University Press, Melbourne.
Jaques, TD & GR Pavia (eds) (1976) *Sport in Australia: Selected Readings in Physical Activity*, McGraw-Hill, Sydney.
Jencks, Charles (ed.) (1988) *Prince Charles and the Architects*, Academy Editions, London.
Jensen, Elfrida (1969) *Barossan Foundations*, Nuriootpa War Memorial Community Centre, Nuriootpa, SA.
Johns, Gary (December 1978) 'Building a suburb: The Peter Lalor Home Building Co-operative Society', *Melbourne State College Occasional Papers*, 1(2): 1–28.
Johnson, Louise C (ed.) (1994) *Suburban Dreaming: An Interdisciplinary Approach to Australian Cities*, Deakin University Press, Geelong, Vic.
Johnson, RKH (December 1970) 'Suburbia in evolution: Community and privacy', *Architecture in Australia*, 59(6): 86.
Jones, Jennifer (2010) 'Baby health centres and the colour bar in New South Wales country towns', in *Green Fields, Brown Fields, New Fields: Proceedings of the 10th Australasian Urban History, Planning History Conference*, University of Melbourne.
Kerr, Rosemary (1994) *A History of the Kindergarten Union of Western Australia 1911–1973*, Meeralinga Young Children's Foundation, West Perth.
Kidder Smith, GE (1949) *Sweden Builds*, Architectural Press, London.
Kimberley, H (1988) 'Consciousness and culture: A study of neighbourhood houses and learning centres in Victoria', PhD thesis, Graduate School of Education, La Trobe University.
The Kindergarten System (nd), Ward, Lock and Co., London.
Kirby, Sandy (ed.) (1996) *Ian Burn: Art Critical, Political*, University of Western Sydney.
Kirk, Eric (1984) *Green Years: Maffra Bowls Club 1921–1983*, Maffra and District Historical Society, Maffra, Vic.
Krier, Leon, with Dhiru A Thadani & Peter J Hetzel (2009) *The Architecture of Community*, Island Press, Washington DC.
Langford, Peter & Patricia Sebastian (eds) (1979) *Early Childhood Education and Care in Australia*, Australia International Press & Publications, Melbourne.
Lawrence, Joan & Catherine Warne (1995) *Balmain to Glebe: The Leichhardt Municipality*, Sydney.
Lefebvre, H (1991) *The Production of Space*, Blackwell, Oxford.
Lewi, Hannah & David Nichols (August 2008) Caroline Springs, *Landscape*, 119: 46–48.
Lewis, Milton J (2003) *The People's Health: Public Health in Australia, 1788–1950*, vol. 1, Praeger, Westport, Conn. & London.
Live and Prosper: A Record of Progress in Rochester and District (1954) The Rochester Centenary Celebrations Committee, Rochester, Vic..
Llewellyn, Brenda (1997) *A History of Earlwood Social and Bowling Club*, Earlwood and Bardwell Park RSL, Bardwell, NSW.
Lowden, B (2010) *Mechanics' Institutes, Schools of Arts, Athenaeums, etc: An Australian Checklist*, 3rd edn, Lowden Publishing, Melbourne.
Lyon, Hamish (March–April 2010) 'DIY community', *Architecture Australia*: 35–37.
Lyons, Martin & Penny Russell (eds) (2005) *Australia's History: Themes and Debates*, UNSW Press, Sydney.
Lyons, Martyn & John Arnold (eds) (2001) *A History of the Book in Australia 1891–1945*, University of Queensland Press, Brisbane.
McCalman, Janet (1984) *Struggletown: Portrait of an Australian Working-Class Community 1900–1965*, Penguin Books, Melbourne.
McColvin, Lionel R (1947) *Public Libraries in Australia: Present Conditions and Future Possibilities*, Melbourne University Press.
McDermott, Marie-Louise (2005) 'Changing visions of baths and bathers: Desegregating ocean baths in Wollongong, Kiama and Gerringong', *Sporting Traditions*, 22(1): 1–19.
McIntyre, AJ & JJ McIntyre (1944) *Country Towns of Victoria: A Social Survey*, Melbourne University Press in association with Oxford University Press, Melbourne.
Macintyre, Stuart (2004) *A Concise History of Australia*, Cambridge University Press.
McMillen, Jan (ed.) (1996) *Gambling Cultures: Studies in History and Interpretation*, Routledge, London.

McQueen, Humphrey (2004) *Social Sketches of Australia 1888–2001*, University of Queensland Press, Brisbane.
Maroske, Ian (1991) *Warracknabeal: A Municipal History 1861–1991*, Maryborough Printers, Vic.
Martin, JL, Ben Nicholson & Naum Gabo (eds) (1971 [1937]) *Circle: International Survey of Constructive Art*, Faber & Faber, London.
Mellor, Elizabeth J (1990) *Stepping Stones: The Development of Early Childhood Services in Australia*, Harcourt Brace Jovanovich, Sydney.
Meredyth, Denise & Deborah Tyler (eds) (1993) *Child and Citizen: Genealogies of Schooling and Subjectivity*, Institute for Cultural Policy Studies, Faculty of Humanities, Griffith University, Nathan, Qld.
Merewether, Charles & Ann Stephen (eds) (1977) *The Great Divide 1977: An Ongoing Critique of Australian Culture Under Capitalism – Reviews of Oppositional Cultural Work and an Examination of Socialist Models*, privately published, Melbourne.
Methven, Sally (1989) 'Recreation planning and the provision of swimming pools', PhD thesis, Department of Geography, University of Adelaide.
Moore, Henry (1966) *Henry Moore: Mother and Child*, New York American Library by arrangement with UNESCO.
Morton, Graham (1992) *Roll Back the Years: A Review of the History of Lawn Bowls and the Nambour Bowls Club*, Nambour, Qld.
Morton, Peter (1989) *Fire Across the Desert*, Australian Government Publishing Service, Canberra.
Mumford, Lewis (1961) *The City in History*, Penguin Books, Harmondsworth, UK.
Munn, Ralph & Ernest Pitt (1935) *Australian Libraries: A Survey of Conditions and Suggestions for their Improvement*, Carnegie Corporation of New York/Australian Council for Education Research, Melbourne.
Newton, Janice, Karen Leadbeater Phillips & Paula Herlihy (1985) *Tracks to Trails: A History of Mt Evelyn*, Mt Evelyn History Group, University of Ballarat, Vic.
O'Brien, Philippa (2009) *Margaret Priest: An Artist's Life*, Fremantle Arts Centre Press, WA.
Oppenheimer, Melanie (June 2008) 'Voluntary action, social welfare and the Australian Assistance Plan in the 1970s', *Australian Historical Studies*, 39(2): 167–82.
Peel, Mark (1995) *Good Times Hard Times: The Past and Future in Elizabeth*, Melbourne University Press.
Permezel, M (2001) 'The practice of citizenship: Place, identity and the politics of participation in neighbourhood houses', PhD thesis, Faculty of Architecture, Building and Planning, University of Melbourne.
Pevsner, Nikolaus (1976) *A History of Building Types*, Princeton University Press.
Plant, Raymond (1974) *Community and Ideology: An Essay in Applied Social Philosophy*, Routledge & Kegan Paul, London & Boston.
Portus, GV (1944) *A Township Starts to Live: The Valley of Barossa, South Australia's New Community*, Common Cause, Adelaide.
Putnam, Robert D (2000) *Bowling Alone: The Collapse and Revival of American Community*, Simon & Schuster, New York.
Rathbone, KW (2007) *From White Gum Flat to the Suburb of Rockdale*, publisher unknown.
Read, Herbert (1966) *Henry Moore: A Study of His Life and Work*, Praeger, New York.
Reichert, Catherine (2007) *The Footscray Pool*, Footscray Historical Society, Melbourne.
Reiger, Kerreen (1985) *The Disenchantment of the Home*, Oxford University Press, Melbourne.
Remington, GC & John Metcalfe (July 1945) 'The Free Library Movement – 1935–1945', *Australian Quarterly*, 17(2): 87–97.
Richards, Lyn (1990) *Nobody's Home: Dreams and Realities in a New Suburb*, Oxford University Press, Melbourne.
Ritson, Rachel (1997) 'The birth of the baby clinic', *Transition*, 54(55): 42–53.
Ritter, Paul (1964) *Planning for Man and Motor*, Pergamon Press, Oxford.
—— (1966) *Educreation and Feedback: Education for Creation, Growth and Change*, Pergamon Press, Oxford.
—— (c. 1979) *Kids and Concrete: Six Successful Educreational Experiments with Sculpcrete*, PEER Institute, Kelmscott, WA.
—— (1982) *Concrete Renaissance Through Building Technology*, Down to Earth Bookshop Press, Perth.
Rose, Nikolas (August 1993) 'Government, authority and expertise in advanced liberalism', *Economy and Society*, 22(3): 283–99.
—— (August 1996) 'The death of the social? Refiguring the territory of government', *Economy and Society*, 25(3): 327–56.
Rowe, Peter G (1991) *Making a Middle Landscape*, MIT Press, Cambridge, Mass.
Ryan, M (ed.) (1979) *Lismore: The Story of a North Coast City*, Currawong Press, Sydney.
Saint, Andrew (1983) *The Image of the Architect*, Yale University Press, New Haven.
Scott, Margaret M (August 1964) 'The world of the baby health centres in New South Wales', *Health in New South Wales*, 5(3).
Scott, Phyllis M & Margaret Darbyshire (1972) *Early Education Programs and Aboriginal Families in Victoria*, Monash University, Melbourne.
Selwood, Sara (1996) *The Benefits of Public Art: The Polemics of Permanent Art in Public Places*, PSI Publishing, London.
Seymour Shire Council & Ratepayers (nd) *Seymour: Your Town*, Seymour, Vic.
Shanken, Andrew (2009) *194X: Architecture, Planning and Consumer Culture on the American Home Front*, University of Minnesota Press, Minneapolis.
Sheard, Heather (2007) *All the Little Children: The Story of Victoria's Baby Health Centres*, Municipal Association of Victoria, Melbourne.

Shire of East Pilbara (November 2008) *Newman Tomorrow: Resourcing a Home for Generations*, WA.

Shire of Roebourne, Geografia in association with CCS Strategic Management (January 2009) *Karratha 2020 Vision and Community Plan*, WA.

Slaughter, JC (1944) 'Planning: Its importance to civilisation', *Architecture*, 33(2).

Smith, HH (October 1947) 'An experiment in democratic town planning – The Springwood Town Plan', *Architecture*, 35(3): 14–18.

Smith, Theodate L (1912) *The Montessori System in Theory and Practice*, Harper and Brothers, New York & London.

Smyth, Paul, Tim Reddel & Andrew Jones (eds) (1997) *Community and Local Governance in Australia*, UNSW Press, Sydney.

'Soft Architecture' (April 1975) *Architecture in Australia*, student edn, Australian Institute of Architects.

Stamp, Isla (1975) *Young Children in Perspective: A Review of Thirty-Five Years of the Lady Gowrie Child Centres in Partnership with the Australian Pre-School Association*, Australian Pre-School Association, Canberra.

Stephen, Ann, Philip Goad & Andrew McNamara (eds) (2008) *Modern Times: The Untold Story of Modernism in Australia*, Miegunyah Press in association with Powerhouse Publishing, Melbourne & Sydney.

Stretton, Alan (1976) *The Furious Days: The Relief of Darwin*, Collins, Sydney.

Stretton, Hugh (1970) *Ideas for Australian Cities*, Hugh Stretton, North Adelaide.

Sturgeon, Graeme (1978) *The Development of Australian Sculpture 1788–1975*, Thames & Hudson, London.

Symonds, Sally (1982) *Healesville: History in the Hills*, Pioneer Design Studio, Melbourne.

Synan, Peter (1994) *City of Sale*, Sale, Vic.

Taylor, Jennifer (1990) *Australian Architecture Since 1960*, 2nd edn, National Education Division, Royal Australian Institute of Architects, Red Hill, ACT.

Tournikiotis, Panayotis (ed.) (2003) *The Body, Sport and Modern Architecture*, Future Publications, Athens.

Towers, Graham (1995) *Buildings Democracy: Community Architecture in the Inner Cities*, UCL Press, London.

Troy, Patrick (ed.) (2000) *A History of European Housing in Australia*, Cambridge University Press, Melbourne.

Turner, AG (1936) *Swan Hill 1836–1936: The First Hundred Years*, Verona Press, Melbourne.

Van Moorst, Harry & Sue Graham (1995) *Kindergarten at the Crossroads: The Werribee Kindergarten Study*, Victoria University, Werribee, Vic.

Venturi, Robert, Denise Scott Brown & Steven Izenour, *Learning from Las Vegas: The Forgotten Symbolism of Architectural Form*, MIT Press, Cambridge, Mass.

Wates, Nick & Charles Knevitt (1987) *Community Architecture: How People are Creating Their Own Environment*, Penguin Books, London.

Watson, Peter (1994) *55 Years: A History of Camden Bowling Club*, Camden Bowling Club, NSW.

Way, EH (1977) *History of the Fitzroy Bowling Clubs*, Fitzroy Bowling Club, Melbourne.

Whitaker, Charles (April 1943) 'How shall we provide good houses for all?', *Architecture*, 32(2): 74–78.

Whitehead, Georgina (ed.) (2001) *Planting the Nation*, Australian Garden History Society, Melbourne.

Wickham, Gary (1992) 'Sport, manners, persons, government: Sport, Elias, Mauss, Foucault', *Cultural Studies*, 6(2): 219–31.

Wilk, Christopher (ed.) (2006) *Modernism: Designing a New World 1914–1939*, V&A Publications, London.

Windeyer, R (March 1945) 'Community centres', *Australian Quarterly*: 62–71.

Woods, Lavinia (1992) *Brisbane City Council Swimming Pools: The Next Twenty Years*, Brisbane City Council.

Zucker, Paul (ed.) (1944) *New Architecture and City Planning*, Philosophical Library, New York.

PHOTO CREDITS

Chapter 1 – Making the Modern Community

1.1 Cover of community booklet, *Balwyn – Deepdene Community*, Vic. 1949. Appendix to undergraduate thesis, FR Russell (1949) 'Community centres', University of Melbourne

1.2 'Suburbia Forever' – gelatin silver photograph (1970) National Gallery of Australia, NGA 89.876. Photographer: Wesley Stacey. Courtesy of Wesley Stacey

1.3 Springwood Town Plan, Harold H Smith, NSW, 1947. From *Architecture Journal* (October 1947)

1.4 Paddling pool and children in boat at a Lady Gowrie Child Centre playground, unknown location. Battye Library of Western Australia, BA1215/26

1.5 Child on tricycle at John Byrne Court public housing, Glebe, NSW 1973. Glebe Photographic Essay on the study of a community. Photographers: Geoff Beeche, Caleb Carter, Leon Gregory, David Hewison, Sue Heweston and Steve LaPlant. Sydney Reference Collection, SRC14422, City of Sydney Archives

1.6 Subiaco Civic Centre and Theatre Complex in Rankin Gardens, Subiaco, WA (first stage built 1957). Architects: FGB Hawkins and D Sands with Peter Parkinson. Photographer: Michal Lewi

1.7 Woomera Swimming Pool and Bowling Green, SA. Private Collection, Andrew Saniga

Chapter 2 – A Healthy Start: Buildings for Babies

2.1a Child Welfare Centre, Kensington, Vic. c. 1927. Architect unknown. Photographer: Julie Willis

2.1b Baby Health Centre, Oakleigh, Vic. 1928. Architect unknown. Photographer: Judy Eathorne. Judy Eathorne (1949) 'A brief survey of the development of baby health centres in Melbourne and the work of the travelling centres', BArch thesis, Faculty of Architecture, Building and Planning, University of Melbourne

2.1c Baby Health Centre, Concord, NSW 1943. Architect unknown. Photographer unknown. State Library of New South Wales

2.1d Maternal and Child Health Centre, Black Rock, Vic. 1939. Architect unknown. Photographer: Julie Willis

2.1e Baby Health Centre, Lakemba, NSW 1947. Architect: Davey & Brindley. Photographer: Helen Stitt

2.1f 'Front Elevation and Ground Floor Plan – Baby Health Centre and Rest Rooms'. Department of Health pamphlet, *The Infant Welfare Centre as a Community Service* (1944) Canberra, p. 23

2.2 *The Baby Health Centres: What They Are and What They Do* (1929) Division of Maternal and Baby Welfare, Office of the Director-General of Public Health, Sydney

2.3 Analysis of requirements for Infant and Child Welfare Centre. Annual report to the Director of the Department of Health, Vic. 1944–45 State Library of Victoria

2.4 Baby Health Centre, Campsie, NSW 1956. Photographer unknown. State Library of New South Wales

2.5 Plan and view of the Baby Health Centre, Footscray, Vic. 1949. Architect: J Plottell. Plan source: Judy Eathorne (1949) 'A brief survey of the development of baby health centres in Melbourne and the work of the travelling centres', BArch thesis, Faculty of Architecture, Building and Planning, University of Melbourne. Photograph source: Department of Health, Vic. (c. 1954) *Child Care: A Manual for the Guidance of All Caring for Infants and Young Children from 0–6 Years*

2.6 Baby Health Centre, Auburn, NSW c. 1940s. Photographer unknown. State Library of New South Wales

2.7 Prams parked at the Baby Health Centre, Concord, NSW 1943. Photographer unknown. State Library of New South Wales

2.8 Health chart, Glen Waverley Infant Welfare Centre, Vic. 1967. Courtesy of Helen Stitt

2.9 Baby Health Centre, Brighton-le-Sands, NSW 1956. Photographer: David Nichols

2.10 Baby Health Centre, East Brunswick, Vic. c. 1940. Photographer: Julie Willis

2.11 Mobile baby clinic van, Qld 1968. Photographer unknown. Brisbane City Council

2.12 Jean Coates Memorial Baby Health Centre, Mascot, NSW 1946. Photographer unknown. NSW Government Printer series, Health Department, State Library of New South Wales

Chapter 3 – Early Learning: The Modern Kindergarten

3.1a Bowden Free Kindergarten, SA 1928. Photographer: Richard E Collett, State Library of South Australia
3.1b Kindergarten, Casterton, Vic. 1954. Architect: James Earle. Photographer unknown. Courtesy of James Earle
3.1c Bendigo Kindergarten, New Creche and Day Minding Centre, Rosalind Park, Vic. 1957. Architect: Eggleston, McDonald and Secomb. Photographer: Cliff Bottomley. National Archives of Australia
3.1d Kindergarten, Rose Park, SA 1958. Architect: The office of Philip R Claridge; Design architect: Brian Claridge. Photographer unknown. *Cross-Section* Archive, Architecture Library, University of Melbourne
3.1e Kindergarten, Whale Beach, NSW 1958. Architect: Peter Muller. Photographer: Thomas Trudeau
3.1f Darlington Kindergarten, WA 1969. Architect: Ken Waldron. Photographer: Mia Schoen
3.2 Paddington Kindergarten, Qld 1915. Architect: Hall and Dods. Photographer unknown. John Oxley Library, State Library of Queensland
3.3 JHL Cumpston & CM Heinig's (1945) *Pre-School Centres in Australia* was published by the Commonwealth Department of Health and became a primer for post-war kindergarten design across Australia. Courtesy of Philip Goad
3.4 Plan, Lady Gowrie Child Centre, Carlton, Vic. 1939–40. Architect: Marcus Martin. From Cumpston & Heinig (1945) *Pre-School Centres in Australia*
3.5 Folding doors from the three-year-old nursery open onto outdoor learning and play spaces at the Lady Gowrie Child Centre, Carlton, Vic. 1939–40. Architect: Marcus Martin. From Cumpston & Heinig (1945) *Pre-School Centres in Australia*
3.6 Children asleep in the three-year-old nursery, Lady Gowrie Child Centre, Thebarton, SA 1940. Architect: F Kenneth Milne in association with RV Boehm and LC Dawkins. From Cumpston & Heinig (1945) *Pre-School Centres in Australia*
3.7 The sunny interior of the Robert Cochrane Kindergarten, Auburn, Vic. 1951. Architect: Horace Tribe. Architecture Library, University of Melbourne
3.8 Jack and Jill Kindergarten, Beaumaris, Vic. 1958. Architect unknown. Photographer: Julie Willis
3.9 Glass Street Kindergarten, Kew, Vic. 1956. Designer (engineer): Roland Chipperfield. Photographer: Helen Stitt
3.10 The polygonal form and plan of Rockingham Park Kindergarten, WA 1969. Architect: Paul Ritter, Ralph Hibble and the Planned Environment and Education Research (PEER) Institute. From Paul Ritter (c. 1979) *Kids and Concrete: Six Successful Educational Experiments with Sculpcrete*, PEER Institute, Kelmscott, WA
3.11 Located away from the street, the kindergarten and clinic's outdoor play space adjoined council-owned parkland at Erindale, SA 1960. Architect: Brian Claridge. Photographer: Ingerson Arnold. *Cross-Section* Archive, Architecture Library, University of Melbourne
3.12 Set among native eucalypts and designed like a large-scale, contemporary, rural 'home' – St Ives Kindergarten, NSW 1961–62. Architect: Collard, Clarke and Jackson. Photographer: David Moore. *Cross-Section* Archive, Architecture Library, University of Melbourne
3.13 The Harbour Family and Children's Centre, Melbourne Docklands, Vic. 2009. Building Architects: DesignInc and Williams Boag Architects in collaboration. Play space design: HASSELL and Children's Landscapes Australia in collaboration. Clients: City of Melbourne, VicUrban, Bovis Lend Lease. Photographer: Andrew Lloyd

Chapter 4 – Local Learning: The Municipal Library in Post-War Australia

4.1a Carnegie Library, Hobart, Tas. 1904–06. Architect: Alan Cameron Walker and Douglas Salier. Photographer unknown. Archives of Tasmania
4.1b Annerley Library, Qld 1957. Architect: James Birrell. Photographer unknown. Brisbane City Council
4.1c Opening of the Merredin Public Library, WA 1960. Photographer unknown. State Library of Western Australia
4.1d Library at Community Place, Greenacre, NSW 1961. Architect: D England. Photographer: Helen Stitt
4.1e Mt Isa Public Library, Qld 1974. Architect: Lund Hutton Newell and Pauson. Photographer unknown. State Library of Queensland
4.1f Toorak–South Yarra Library, South Yarra, Vic. 1973. Architect: Yuncken Freeman. Photographer: Wolfgang Sievers. National Library of Australia
4.2 Hawthorn Library, Vic. 1926; new facade 1938. Architect: Marsh and Michaelson. Photographer unknown. State Library of Victoria
4.3 Interior, Chermside Library, Qld 1957–58. Architect: James Birrell. Photographer unknown.
4.4 Interior, Toowong Library, Qld 1959. Architect: James Birrell. Photographer unknown. Brisbane City Council
4.5 Program for the opening of Warringah Shire Library, Dee Why, NSW 1966. Architect: Edwards Madigan Torzillo & Partners. *Cross-Section* Archive, Architecture Library, University of Melbourne
4.6 Plan and section, Warringah Shire Library, Dee Why, NSW 1966. Architect: Edwards Madigan Torzillo & Partners. From Harry Sowden (1968) *Towards an Australian Architecture*, Ure Smith, Sydney
4.7 Interior view, Warringah Shire Library, Dee Why, NSW 1966. Architect: Edwards Madigan Torzillo & Partners. Photographer: Harry Sowden. From Harry Sowden (1968) *Towards an Australian Architecture*
4.8 Plan, Warren Shire Library, Warren, NSW 1966. Architect: Edwards Madigan Torzillo & Partners. *Cross-Section* Archive, Architecture Library, University of Melbourne

4.9 Northam Town Council Offices and Library, WA 1971–74. Architect: Iwan Iwanoff. Photographer: Michal Lewi
4.10 Interior, Toorak–South Yarra Library, South Yarra, Vic. 1973. Architect: Yuncken Freeman. Photographer: Wolfgang Sievers. National Library of Australia
4.11 Dickson District Library, ACT 1969. Architect: Enrico Taglietti. Photographer unknown. *Cross-Section* Archive, Architecture Library, University of Melbourne
4.12 Concept sketch for St Kilda Library, Vic. 1972–73. Architect: Enrico Taglietti. *St Kilda Today*, August 1971

Chapter 5 – Making Spaces for Recreation

5.1a City of Brisbane Corporation Baths, Spring Hill, Qld c. 1910. Photographer unknown. John Oxley Library, State Library of Queensland
5.1b Swimming Pool, Enfield, NSW 1933. Architect: Rudder and Grout. Photographer: Ted Hood. Hood Collection, State Library of New South Wales
5.1c 'People given work during the Depression to build the Parkes [NSW] Swimming Pool'. Photographer: Mr A Burgess. 'At Work and Play – Images of Rural Life in NSW 1880–1940' Collection, State Library of New South Wales
5.1d Dalby Swimming Pool, Qld 1936. Photographer unknown. Supplied by Department of Environment and Resource Management, Qld
5.1e Coloured postcard of Albury Olympic Pool, NSW (postcard c. 1957). Photographer unknown. 'Beautiful Views in Colour of Albury NSW', State Library of Victoria
5.1f Toowong Swimming Pool, Brisbane, Qld 1959. Architect: James Birrell. Photographer unknown. Brisbane City Council
5.2 Promotional brochure (printed 1937), Richmond City Baths, Vic. Private collection
5.3 Sketch plan for Canberra Swimming Baths, Manuka, ACT 1930. National Archives of Australia
5.4 Lord Forrest Olympic Swimming Pool, Kalgoorlie, WA, opened in 1938. Architect: WG Bennett. Photographer: Robert McKeich. State Library of Western Australia
5.5 Drawing of Brunswick City Baths, Vic. c. 1979. Artist unknown. Moreland City Libraries
5.6 Swimming pool signage, clockwise from top left:
> Conditions of entry sign, Byron Bay War Memorial Swimming Pool, NSW. Photographer: Caroline Jordan
> Promotional poster, February 1909, for Fitzroy Municipal Baths, Vic. Courtesy of Fitzroy Library Local History Photograph Collection
> 'The Great Pool Party' poster, c. 1980, Harold Holt Memorial Swimming Centre, Malvern, Vic. Stonnington Local History Collection
> Plaque, Lismore Memorial Baths, NSW. Photographer: Caroline Jordan
> Conditions of entry sign, Monkton Aquatic Centre, Armidale, NSW. Photographer: Caroline Jordan
5.7 Canberra Olympic Pool, ACT 1955. Architect: Canberra Branch of the Department of Works. Photographer unknown. Australian Capital Territory Heritage Library
5.8 Centenary Swimming Pool, Spring Hill, Qld 1957–59. Architect: James Birrell. Photographer unknown. Courtesy of James Birrell
5.9 Harold Holt Memorial Swimming Centre, Malvern, Vic. 1969. Architect: Kevin Borland & Daryl Jackson. Photographer: David Moore. Courtesy of Doug Evans
5.10 L-shaped pool at the Collingwood Swimming Pool, Vic. 1970. Architect: Daryl Jackson. Photographer: John Gollings. Courtesy of John Gollings
5.11 Berridale Baby Pool, NSW (image 1998). Photographer: Denise Ferris. 'Country Life in the Snowy Mountains Region' Collection, National Library of Australia. Courtesy of Denise Kerns

Chapter 6 – Lawn Bowls: A Community Game

6.1a Adelaide Bowling Club, SA c. 1900. Architect unknown. Mortlock Pictorial Collection, State Library of South Australia
6.1b Hawthorn Bowling Club, Vic. 1938. Architect unknown. Photographer: Helen Stitt
6.1c Maitland Memorial Park Bowling Club, SA. Architect unknown. Photographer: David Nichols
6.1d Nambour Bowling Club, Qld (image 1967). Architect unknown. Photographer unknown. Sunshine Coast Libraries
6.1e Prahran Bowling Club, Vic. 1961. Architect: Leslie M Perrott & Partners. Photographer: Mark Strizic. State Library of Victoria
6.1f Design for Bowling and Recreation Club, Peakhurst, NSW 1958. Architect: Loder & Dunphy. *Cross-Section* Archive 72 (October 1958), Architecture Library, University of Melbourne
6.2 *The Perth Bowling Club 1894–1944*, cover of the jubilee souvenir history
6.3 Fastidiously maintained greens at the East Fremantle Bowling Club, WA. Architect unknown. Photographer: Hannah Lewi
6.4 Hamilton Bowling Club and Park, NSW (image 1930). Architect unknown. Photographer unknown. Mort Collection, Newcastle Region Library
6.5 Bowling club signage (clockwise from top left):
> South Coogee Bowling Club, NSW
> Alice Springs Bowling Club, NT

> Belfield Bowling & Recreational Club, NSW

> Alice Springs Bowling Club, NT

> Hurlstone Park Bowling Club, NSW

> Maroubra Bowling Club, NSW. Photographer: Helen Stitt

6.6 Bowling club interiors (clockwise from top left):

> Hawthorn Bowling Club, Vic. 1938. Photographer: Helen Stitt

> Alphington Bowling Club, Vic. Photographer: Hannah Lewi

> Clovelly Bowling Club, NSW 1951. Photographer: Helen Stitt

> Earlwood Bowling Club, NSW (image May 1957). Photographer: Ken Renshaw. 'Sydney People, Places and Events 1953–1987', Australian Photographic Agency Collection, State Library of New South Wales

> Mildura Bowling Club dining room, Vic. (image c. 1950). Photographer unknown. State Library of Victoria

6.7 Yandina Ladies Bowling Club opening, Qld May 1956. Photographer unknown. Sunshine Coast Libraries

6.8 Bowling club entrance gates (clockwise from top left):

> Alphington Bowling Club, Vic. Photographer: Hannah Lewi

> Campsie South Bowling Club, NSW. Photographer: Helen Stitt

> Henley Bowling Club, Adelaide, SA. Photographer: David Nichols

> Murrayville Memorial Bowling Club, Vic. Photographer: David Nichols

> Ardrossan Bowling Club, SA 1962. Photographer: David Nichols

> Hampton Bowling Club, Vic. Photographer: David Nichols

6.9 Canberra South Bowling Club, ACT 1959. Architect: Harry Seidler & Colin Griffiths. Photographer: Max Dupain Studio. Courtesy of Harry Seidler & Associates

6.10 City of Prahran Bowling Club newsletter, *Cop This*, Vic. 1967. Stonnington Local History Collection

6.11 New Lambton Bowling Club, NSW. Photographer unknown. State Library of New South Wales

6.12 Southport Ladies' Bowls Club, 70th anniversary celebration, Qld 1999. Photographer unknown. Gold Coast City Council

6.13 The green at Clovelly Bowling Club, NSW 1951. Photographer: Hannah Lewi

Chapter 7 – The Community Can Do It! Planning for the New Civic Centre

7.1a and b Social infrastructure was considered central to the modern community. From Shepparton Borough Council (1946) *Shepparton: Today and Tomorrow*, Shepparton Borough Council & *Shepparton Advertiser*, Vic., p. 12

7.2 'Modern town-planning applied to Darwin', 1945. From (1945) *Salt: Authorized education journal of Australian Army and Air Force*, pp. 1–4. Courtesy University of Melbourne Special Collections

7.3 The Peter Lalor Home Building Co-operative Society 'Materials Stockade'. From G Johns (December 1978) 'Building a suburb: The Peter Lalor Home Building Co-operative Society', *Melbourne State College Occasional Papers*, 1(2): 1–28

7.4 Robert Arthur Gardner (1945) *Community Centres*, Opportunity Club for Boys and Girls, Melbourne. Illustrator unknown. National Library of Australia

7.5 'Township of Seymour, Civic Centre, Aerial View', Vic. 1947. Architect: Frank Heath. MS 13214, Blyth and Josephine Johnson Papers, State Library of Victoria

7.6 Plan for Nuriootpa, SA c. 1940s. Architect: Louis Laybourne-Smith. From *A Township Starts to Live: The Valley of Barossa, South Australia's New Community* (1944) Common Cause, Adelaide

7.7 'Proposed Civic Centre'. Shepparton Borough Council (1946), *Shepparton: Today and Tomorrow*, Shepparton Borough Council & *Shepparton Advertiser*, p. 7. State Library of Victoria

7.8 Australian Broadcasting Commission (1945) *The Community Can Do It. Make a Plan*, The Commission, Sydney. Illustrator unknown

7.9 'Main Entrance to War Memorial Town Hall' and 'Another View of the Crazy-Pavement Court', Cottesloe, WA. From *Cottesloe War Memorial Town Hall and Civic Centre* (1950) Elswood Press, Mosman Park, WA. Photographer unknown. State Library of Victoria

7.10 'Living War Memorials', *Examiner Press*, Launceston, c. 1950s. QVMAG Community History Centre, Launceston, Tasmania

7.11 Plans and section, 'First Stage Development Beaumaris Community Centre'. From Parents' and Citizens' Association of Beaumaris (1959) *Development in Beaumaris*, Melbourne. State Library of Victoria

7.12 Civic Centre, Brighton, Vic. 1960–62. Architect: Oakley & Parkes. Photographer: Peter Wille. State Library of Victoria

7.13 Marion Cultural Centre, SA 2001. Architect: Ashton Raggatt McDougall & Phillips Pilkington. Photographer: John Gollings. Courtesy of John Gollings

Chapter 8 – Commemorating and Enhancing the Everyday

8.1a Interior of the new Memorial Hall, Sea Lake, Vic. 1924. Photographer unknown. Ron Foster Collection, Sea Lake

8.1b Soldiers Memorial School of Arts, Wyalong, NSW 1928. Photographer: Caroline Jordan

8.1c 'Proposed Services Memorial – Club Rooms and Shrine'. From Shepparton Borough Council (1946) *Shepparton: Today and Tomorrow*, Shepparton Borough Council and *Shepparton Advertiser*. State Library of Victoria
8.1d Memorial Baths, Lismore, NSW 1928. Architect: FJ Board. Photographer: Caroline Jordan
8.1e Memorial Pool, Gunnedah, NSW 1959. Photographer: Caroline Jordan.
8.1f War memorial and memorial gates in front of Alphington Bowling Club, Vic. c 1950s. Photographer: Hannah Lewi
8.2 Memorial Hall, Healesville, Vic., Armistice Day, 1939. Photographer unknown. Healesville Historical Society Collection
8.3 'The War Memorial Community Centre, Launceston, Tasmania' 1953. Illustrator unknown. QVMAG Community History Centre, Launceston, Tas
8.4a Bas reliefs of Aboriginal life, bronze doors, eastern entrance of the Public Library of New South Wales, Sydney, 1940–42. Sculptor: Daphne Mayo. Photographer: Frank Hurley. National Library of Australia
8.4b *Two Piece Reclining Figure No. 9*, outside the Australian National Library, ACT 1969. Sculptor: Henry Moore. Photographer: Michal Lewi
8.4c Maquette for sculpture at public gardens in flats, Melbourne, Vic. c. 1950s. Sculptor: Anne Marie Graham. Artist's collection
8.4d Baby Health Centre, NSW c. 1960s (image dated June 1964). NSW Government Printer series, Health Department. State Library of New South Wales
8.4e James Cook Memorial Fountain, Civic Park, Newcastle, NSW 1961–66. Sculptor: Margel Hinder. Photographer: Bernadette Geraghty
8.4f Community art mural on Broadmeadows Neighbourhood House, Vic. 1985. Private Archive: Geoff Hogg and Suzy Pinchen
8.5 *Figure Group*, Newcastle War Memorial Cultural Centre, NSW 1957. Sculptor: Lyndon Dadswell. Photographer: Ronald John Morrison. Newcastle Regional Library
8.6 *Ethos*, Civic Square, Canberra, ACT 1959–61. Sculptor: Tom Bass. Photographer: Michal Lewi
8.7 *Mother and Child*, Baby Health Centre, Campsie, NSW 1956. Architect: Davey & Brindley. Sculptor: F Lumb. From *Architecture in Australia* (January–March 1956) 45(1): 10
8.8 Pioneer Women's Memorial Fountain, Kings Park, Perth, WA 1968. Sculptor: Margaret Priest. Photographer: Michal Lewi
8.9 Bathing pavilion, Lower Sandy Bay, Tas. 1962. Architect: Dirk Bolt of Hartley, Wilson & Bolt. Photographer: Frank Bolt. Dirk Bolt Archive 091104.4, Scotland
8.10 Glass mosaic frieze, Beaurepaire Swimming Pool, University of Melbourne, Parkville, Vic. c. 1957. Artist: Leonard French. Photographer: Michal Lewi
8.11 Turana Youth Training Centre mural, Brunswick, Vic. 1979–81. Artists: Geoff Hogg and the Turana mural team. Courtesy of Geoff Hogg
8.12 *Bondi the Beautiful*, community mural, courtyard of Bondi Pavilion, NSW 1980. Artists, directed by David Humphries & Rodney Monk – Public Art Squad. Photographer: Oliver Strew. © Public Art Squad
8.13 *Children of the Billabong*, community muralist training project, Casuarina Swimming Pool, Darwin, NT 1984. Artists, directed by David Humphries & Rodney Monk – Public Art Squad. Photographer: Rodney Monk. © Public Art Squad
8.14 (clockwise from top)
> Mural, *Koor Koorliny Bilya*, John Williamson 2000 on wall of Moora Council Chambers and Library building, WA
> Andor Mészáros' c. 1959 statue of William Shakespeare outside the 1955 Ballarat Civic Hall
> Mural en route to the Bombala pool from Monaro Highway
> Statuettes of Australian and American cartoon characters at Bombala and District War Memorial Swimming Pool (1968). Photographer: David Nichols

Chapter 9 – Regenerating Communities: The 1970s and Beyond

9.1 *Undulant*, installed at the Logan Community Health Centre, Qld 2005. Architect: Alice Hampson & Sebastian Di Mauro. Photographer: David Sandison
9.2 Cover of 'Soft Architecture', a special student-edited issue of *Architecture Australia*, April 1975
9.3 Community Health Centre, Brunswick, Vic. 1985–90. Architect: Ashton, Raggatt, McDougall. Photographer: John Gollings. Courtesy of John Gollings
9.4 Tom Price Community Centre, under construction, WA, November 1966. Photographer: Aerial Surveys Australia. Battye Library of Western Australia, 268492PD. Courtesy of Aerial Surveys Australia
9.5 Bulgarra Community Centre Design Proposal, WA 2010. Architect: CODA Architects. Courtesy of Kieran Wong and Emma Williamson, CODA
9.6 Walmajarri Community Centre, Djugerari Community, Great Sandy Desert, WA 2006. Architect: Iredale Pedersen Hook. Photographer: Shannon McGrath
9.7 Marysville sports pavilion, Gallipoli Oval, Vic. 2007, which did not survive the fires of 2009. Photographer: Hannah Lewi
9.8 Marysville Town Plan and Community Hub Masterplan, Vic. 2009. Architect: NH Architecture. Courtesy of NH Architecture
9.9 Campaign poster, 'Save Coburg Olympic Pool', Vic. 2008. Artist: Janet Grigg. Courtesy of Save the Coburg Pool Campaign Group

Chapter openers

2 A Healthy Start: Buildings for Babies (page 24)

Row 1

Left Merlynston Baby Health Centre, Vic. c. 1940s. Photographer: Julie Willis

Middle Newcastle Child Health Centre, NSW 1967. Photographer unknown. State Library of New South Wales

Right Maternal and Welfare Home, Rockhampton, Qld c. 1923. Photographer unknown. John Oxley Library, State Library of Queensland

Row 2

Left East Kew Baby Health Centre, Vic. 1925. Photographer: Helen Stitt

Middle Baby Health Centre, Bexley NSW 1945. Photographer unknown. State Library of New South Wales

Right Baby Health Centre, North Richmond, Vic. 1930. Photographer: Judy Eathorne. From Judy Eathorne (1949) 'A brief survey of the development of baby health centres in Melbourne and the work of the travelling centres', BArch thesis, Faculty of Architecture, Building and Planning, University of Melbourne

Row 3

Left Country Women's Association Baby Health Centre, Casino, NSW 1950. Photographer: Caroline Jordan

Middle Infant Health Centre, Nedlands, WA 1937. Photographer: Hannah Lewi

Right Infant Health Centre, Bentley, WA c. 1965. Photographer: David Nichols

Row 4

Left Baby Health Centre, Earlwood, NSW 1952. Architect: Davey & Brindley. Photographer: Helen Stitt

Middle Baby Health Centre, Glebe, NSW c. 1950. Photographer: David Nichols

Right Baby Health Centre, Concord, NSW 1943. Photographer: David Nichols

Row 5

Left Truby King Baby Health Centre, Coburg, Vic. 1926. Architect: RMcC Dawson. Photographer: Hannah Lewi

Middle Baby Health Centre, Willoughby, NSW 1938. Architect: Eric Nicholls. Photographer: David Nichols

Right Infant Welfare Centre, Brunswick West, Vic. 1932. Architect unknown. Photographer: Julie Willis

3 Early Learning: The Modern Kindergarten (page 52)

Row 1

Left Lucy Morice Free Kindergarten, North Adelaide, SA c. 1940. Mortlock Pictorial Collection, State Library of South Australia

Middle Kindergarten, Paraburdoo, WA 1974. Photographer: Wolfgang Sievers. National Library of Australia

Right Kindergarten, Snowy Mountains Hydro-Electric Scheme, NSW c. 1960. Photographer: W Pedersen. National Archives of Australia

Row 2

Left Albuera Street Infant School, Hobart, Tas. c. 1940. Archives Office of Tasmania, State Library of Tasmania

Middle Kindergarten, Rushcutters Bay, NSW 1953. City of Sydney Archives

Right Central Kindergarten, Warrnambool, Vic. c. 1960. Photographer unknown. Corangamite Regional Library Corporation

Row 3

Left Kindergarten, Darwin, NT 1951. Photographer: J Fitzpatrick. National Archives of Australia

Middle Woolloongabba Kindergarten, Qld 1911. Photographer unknown. John Oxley Library, State Library of Queensland

Right Kindergarten, North Cottesloe, WA 1974. Photographer: Fritz Kos. State Library of Western Australia

Row 4

Left Kindergarten, Bannister Garden, Griffith, ACT 1950. Photographer: David Nichols

Middle Junee RSL Memorial Preschool, NSW c. 1930s–40s. Photographer: David Nichols

Right Kindergarten, North Broken Hill, NSW. Photographer: Wolfgang Sievers. National Library of Australia

Row 5

Left Kindergarten, Manly, NSW c. 1960. Architect: Edwards, Madigan, Torzillo & Briggs. Photographer: Max Dupain. *Cross-Section* Archive, Architecture Library, University of Melbourne

Middle Wilston-Grange Kindergarten, Brisbane, Qld c. 1960. Brisbane City Council

Right Lady Gowrie Child Centre, Erskineville, NSW 1940. Photographer: David Nichols

4 Local Learning: The Municipal Library in Post-War Australia (page 84)

Row 1

Left Hellyer Regional Library, Burnie, Tas. 1970. Photographer unknown. State Library of Tasmania

Middle Subiaco City Library, WA 1971. Photographer: Fritz Kos. State Library of Western Australia

Right Gordonvale Library, Qld c. 1958. Architect: Barnes and Oribin. *Cross-Section* Archive, Architecture Library, University of Melbourne. Courtesy of Mulgrave Shire Library, Image 6644-1

Row 2

Left Wallsend Branch Library, NSW 1948. Photographer unknown. Newcastle Morning Herald Collection, Newcastle Region Library

Middle Mayfield Public Library, NSW 1953. Photographer unknown. Hood Collection Part I : 'Sydney Streets, Buildings, People, Activities and Events, c. 1925–1955', State Library of New South Wales

Right Newcastle City Branch Library, NSW 1976. Photographer unknown. Newcastle Region Library

Row 3

Left Carmila Library, Broadsound Shire, Qld c. 1960. Photographer unknown. State Library of Queensland

Middle Darwin Public Library, Daly Street, NT 1951. Photographer unknown. Northern Territory Library

Right Dajarra Public Library, Cloncurry Shire, Qld c. 1970. Photographer unknown. State Library of Queensland

Row 4

Left Murgon Library, Qld 1938. Photographer unknown. John Oxley Library, State Library of Queensland

Middle Nundah Library, Qld 1968. Photographer unknown. Brisbane City Council

Right Winton Library and Shire Hall, Qld c. 1962. Photographer unknown. State Library of Queensland

Row 5

Left Clarence War Memorial Library, Bellerive, Tas. 1960. Architect: D Hartley Wilson and Bolt. *Cross-Section* Archive, Architecture Library, University of Melbourne

Middle Malvern City Library, Vic. 1959. Architect: Stewart Handasyde. Photographer: Ritter-Jeppesen Studios Pty Ltd. *Cross-Section* Archive, Architecture Library, University of Melbourne

Right Opening of Elizabeth North Library, SA 1960. Photographer unknown. City of Playford Local and Family History Service

5 Making Spaces for Recreation (page 112)

Row 1

Left Richmond Baths, Vic. 1897 (photo c. 1915). Richmond Library Local History Photograph Collection

Middle Scarborough Ocean Baths, NSW 1926. Photographer: David Nichols

Right Andrew ('Boy') Charlton Pool, previously known as the Domain Baths or Municipal Baths, Sydney, NSW (image c. 1970). Photographer unknown. City of Sydney Archives

Row 2

Left Bega Swimming Pool, NSW. Photographer: Brendan Bell. National Library of Australia

Middle Lord Forrest Olympic Swimming Pool, Kalgoorlie, WA 1938. Architect: WG Bennett. Photographer: Government Photographer, WA. State Library of Western Australia

Right Cloncurry Pool, Qld. Photographer: Gordon Undy. National Library of Australia

Row 3

Left Sir Dallas Brooks, Governor of Victoria, opening the Middle Brighton Baths (Vic.) in Brighton's centenary year 1959. Photographer unknown. Bayside Library Service

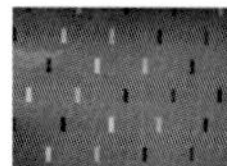

Middle Exterior wall tiles, Auburn Municipal Swimming Centre, NSW 1960. Architect: Frank R Hines. Photographer: Helen Stitt

Right Auburn Municipal Swimming Centre, NSW 1960. Architect: Frank R Hines. Photographer: Helen Stitt

Row 4

Left Tamworth Olympic Pool, NSW. Photographer: Caroline Jordan

Middle Swimming Pool, Manuka, ACT 1931. Architect: E Henderson. Photographer: Hannah Lewi

Right Kellerberrin Pool, WA. Photographer: David Nichols

Row 5

Left Dubbo Olympic Pool, NSW 1935. Photographer unknown. 'At Work and Play: Images of Rural Life in NSW 1880–1940' Collection, State Library of New South Wales

Middle The slide entry at Narrandera Swimming Pool, NSW. Photographer: David Nichols

Right Lambton Olympic Pool, NSW 1965. Photographer: DL Hilder. Newcastle Region Library

6 Lawn Bowls: A Community Game (page 140)

Row 1

Left Helicopter being used to install lights around greens, Charlestown Bowling Club, Lake Macquarie, NSW (photo 1977). Photographer unknown. Newcastle Region Library

Middle Maroubra Bowling Club, NSW. Photographer: Helen Stitt

Right Cloncurry Bowling Club, Qld. Photographer: Gordon Undy. National Library of Australia

Row 2

Left Albert Park Bowling Green, St Vincent Gardens, Vic. (postcard c. 1908). Photographer unknown. Shirley Jones Collection of Victorian Postcards, State Library of Victoria

Middle 'The Bowling Green, Bundaberg', Qld (hand-coloured photograph, c. 1914). Photographer: W Blaikie, *Souvenir of Bundaberg*, published by W Blaikie, Bundaberg, c. 1914, John Oxley Library, State Library of Queensland

Right Biggenden Bowling Club, Qld (photo c. 1925). Photographer unknown. John Oxley Library, State Library of Queensland

Row 3

Left Birregurra Bowling Club, Vic. 1968. Photographer: Julie Willis

Middle Clovelly Bowling Club, NSW 1951. Photographer: Helen Stitt

Right New Norfolk Bowling Club, Tas. Photographer: Mike Key. National Library of Australia

Row 4

Left Belmont Bowling Club, NSW (photo 1957). Photographer unknown. Hood Collection Part I: 'Sydney Streets, Buildings, People, Activities and Events, c. 1925–1955', State Library of New South Wales

Middle ICI ANZ Lawn Bowls, NSW (photo 1967). Photographer: Jack Hickson. Australian Photographic Agency (APA). Collection: 'Sydney People, Places and Events, 1953–1987', State Library of New South Wales

Right Alice Springs Bowling Club, NT. Photographer: Helen Stitt

Row 5

Left Kalgoorlie Bowling Club, WA. Photographer: Aaron Bunch. National Library of Australia

Middle Donald Bowling Club, Vic. Photographer: David Nichols

Right North Perth Bowling Club, WA. Photographer: Hannah Lewi

7 The Community Can Do It! Planning for the New Civic Centre (page 168)

Images for this chapter are derived and redrawn from the following original images:

Robert Arthur Gardner (1945) *Community Centres*, Opportunity Club for Boys and Girls, Melbourne.
Illustrator unknown. National Library of Australia

Plan for Nuriootpa, SA c. 1940s. Architect: Louis Laybourne-Smith
From *A Township Starts To Live: The Valley of Barossa, South Australia's New Community* (1944) Common Cause, Adelaide

Plans and section, First Stage Development Beaumaris Community Centre
Parents' and Citizens' Association of Beaumaris (1959) *Development in Beaumaris*
State Library of Victoria

Buchan Laird & Buchan for Housing Commission, Vic.
'East Geelong Area'
Courtesy of David Nichols

Stephenson & Turner
'Dunlop Village Beaumaris Site Plan' (June 1945)

'The Future City' Plan
From Shepparton Borough Council (1946) *Shepparton: Today and Tomorrow*, Shepparton Borough Council
& *Shepparton Advertiser*, p. 26
State Library of Victoria

8 Commemorating and Enhancing the Everyday (page 200)

Row 1

Left Mural, Flinders and Far North Community Health Service, Port Augusta, SA. Artist unknown. Photographer: Helen Stitt

Middle Play Sculpture, Commonwealth Park children's pool, Parkes, ACT 1967–70. Sculptor: David Tolley. From National Capital Development Commission (1981, [1980]) *Works of Art in Canberra*, 2nd edn, NCDC, Canberra, p. 55

Right Soldiers and Sailors Memorial Literary Institute, West Wyalong, NSW 1928. Photographer: Caroline Jordan

Row 2

Left War Memorial Olympic Pool, Casino, NSW 1952. Photographer: Caroline Jordan

Middle *Sculptured Form*, aluminium sculpture situated in the town plaza, Woden, ACT 1970. Sculptor: Margel Hinder. Photographer: Hannah Lewi

Right *Lintel Sculpture*, copper lintel sculpture above the entrance to the National Library of Australia, Canberra, ACT 1968. Sculptor: Tom Bass. Photographer: Hannah Lewi

Row 3

Left The Canberra Times Fountain, intersection of City Walk and Ainslie Avenue, Civic, ACT 1979. Sculptor: Robert Woodward. Photographer: Hannah Lewi

Middle *Botany* (tribute to Sir Joseph Banks), Bankstown Town Hall, NSW 1964. Sculptor: Lyndon Dadswell. Photographer: Helen Stitt

Right War Memorial Literary Institute, Gilgandra, NSW 1923. Photographer: Caroline Jordan

Row 4

Left Heraghty Park Olympic Pool, Parkes, NSW. Photographer: Caroline Jordan

Middle *Symmetry of Sport*, Trophy Hall mural, Beaurepaire Swimming Pool, University of Melbourne, Parkville, Vic. c. 1957. Artist: Leonard French. Photographer: Helen Stitt

Right Public sculpture, Canberra, ACT. Sculptor: Norma Redpath. Photographer: Michal Lewi

Row 5

Left Wardell & District War Memorial Hall, NSW 1925 (new front 1953). Photographer: Caroline Jordan

Middle War Memorial Swimming Pool, Redcliffe, Qld. Photographer: Elizabeth Bennett

Right Plaque, Memorial Pool, Gunnedah, NSW 1959. Photographer: Caroline Jordan

ACKNOWLEDGMENTS

Alphington Bowls Club; Ashton Raggatt McDougall; Elizabeth Bennett; James Birrell; Kirsten Broderick, Rockdale City Library; Kelly Butler; Nanette Carter; Cec Churm; CODA Architects; Julie Collins; Siobhan Dee, National Film and Sound Archive; Sebastian Di Mauro; Jim Earle; Denise Ferris; Robert Freestone; Christine Garnaut; Don Gazzard; Bernadette Geraghty; John Gollings; Alice Hampson; Harry Seidler & Associates (HAS); HASSELL; Keiran Hodgkinson; Geoff Hogg; Iredale Pedersen Hook; David Humphries; Bryn Jones and Alma Mitchell, Healesville Historical Society; Launceston LINC; Michal Lewi; Cameron Logan; Sue McClarron; Chris McConville; the staff at Newcastle City Library; NH Architects; Carla Pascoe; Suzy Pinchen; Keir Reeves; Jamie Ritchie, Playford History Service; the Save the Coburg Pool campaigners; Natica Schmeder; Sarah Schmitt, National Library of Australia; Ross Smith, Queen Victoria Museum and Art Gallery, Launceston; Wesley Stacey; Mark Strizic; Thomas Trudeau; David Tuck, Stonnington History Centre; Jeff Turnbull; University of Melbourne Publication Committee; Deborah Van der Plaat; Nick Vlahogiannis; Marion Watts, St Arnaud Library; Damien Williams.

This project was generously sponsored by publication grants from the Australian Academy of the Humanities and the University of Melbourne, and supported by the Faculty of Architecture, Building and Planning and the Australian Centre, School of Historical Studies in the Faculty of Arts.

INDEX

Note: Page numbers in *italics* refer to photographs.